A Hosting:

Interviews with Irish Writers

1991–2026

A Hosting:
Interviews with Irish Writers
1991–2026

Martin Doyle

THE LILLIPUT PRESS
DUBLIN

First published 2026 by
THE LILLIPUT PRESS

62–63 Sitric Road,
Arbour Hill,
Dublin 7,
Ireland
www.lilliputpress.ie

10 9 8 7 6 5 4 3 2 1

The interviews included in this book were mainly undertaken for *The Irish Post* and for *The Irish Times* and reproduced here with their kind permission.

A CIP record for this title is available from The British Library.

Paperback ISBN 978-1-84351-975-1
eBook ISBN 978-1-80762-001-1

Lilliput gratefully acknowledges the financial support of the Arts Council / An Chomhairle Ealaíon.

Set in 11pt on 16 pt Adobe Garamond Pro by Compuscript
Printed and bound in Ireland by Sprint Print

To my father, John,
and my children,
Isobel, Ruairi and Martha

CONTENTS

INTRODUCTION

It has been an immense privilege over the past thirty-five years to have had the opportunity to interview many of my favourite Irish writers. The transcription may be a chore and writing it up is often a challenge but the reading is always rewarding, the research enlightening and the encounter enjoyable, whether it be Pat McCabe in a pub on the Kilburn High Road in 1992 or Sebastian Barry at his old rectory in west Wicklow in 2025.

If, as Wordsworth wrote, the child is father to the man, then as the son of the teenager who was inspired and shaped by writers such as Frank O'Connor, Jennifer Johnston, Joan Lingard, Brian Moore and Bernard MacLaverty, it was a particular thrill to meet and interview the latter two.

Writers are remarkably forthcoming about their art, influences and passion for literature, their writing practice and their struggles, and how their own lives colour their work. Pain, loss and alienation often lie at the root of the narrative impulse. It is the interviewer's job to probe and the interviewee's right to keep some things private, but I often came away with not just a deeper appreciation of the work but with a greater admiration for the person who had created it.

This gathering is a career retrospective so is not intended to be canonical or comprehensive – there are many more writers I would like to have included – but I believe it fairly represents the best of contemporary Irish writing. As Books Editor of *The Irish Times*, I polled sixty writers, critics, academics and booksellers last year to produce a list of the top hundred Irish works of fiction of the twenty-first century so far. The authors of twenty-two of the top twenty-five titles are interviewed in this book.

I worked as a journalist in London from 1990 to 2006, including nine years at *The Irish Post*, so many of those interviews were written for it while on the staff or as freelance. I am grateful to its owner, Elgin Loane, for permission to reproduce them here. I have been on the staff of *The Irish Times* since 2007 and have worked on its books pages since 2013. I thank my editor, Ruadhán Mac Cormaic, for permitting me to republish my work here. Several of the later interviews were written up during a residency at the Centre Culturel Irlandais in Paris. My thanks to its director Nora Hickey M'Sichili and her team.

These interviews are longer and more in depth, looking beyond the author's latest book to survey their work as a whole, but even the shorter ones contain much to ponder. A book would be dull if every sentence and chapter were of uniform length.

Similarly, there is no unifying theme or trend to identify or assert. One of the reasons for the remarkable success of contemporary Irish literature is its diversity of theme and approach.

Sebastian Barry is happy to declare: 'Lyric language is my lexicon.' Kevin Barry is rightly celebrated for the wild lyricism of his prose. John Banville and Anne Enright are also great stylists, superb at a sentence level.

'Southern writers tend to gild the lily a bit,' Pat McCabe says, whereas Border and Northern writers such as Eugene McCabe favour 'a very flinty kind of dialogue rather than this baroque speech'. Conor O'Callaghan, another Border writer, was a poet before he became a novelist: 'Any twit can write a lyrical sentence. A novel is a feat of imaginative engineering.'

Belfast author Wendy Erskine says: 'What some people think of as fine writing is very misguided. It's like the Dolly Parton thing, "it takes a lot of work to look this cheap". My dialogue is edited over and over to get it just right.'

Yet Eoin McNamee from Kilkeel, County Down, is regarded as one of our finest stylists. And the critic Robert Gottlieb has tracked Sebastian Barry's evolution as a writer from the poet and dramatist he began as, forsaking prose that 'occasionally goes all purple'. Bernard MacLaverty's combination of lavishness and restraint was hailed by one critic as 'the ultimate Northern Irish prose style, all Catholic curlicues and Calvinistic sparseness'.

It is striking how many more women than men interviewed here declare James Joyce an influence – Mary Costello, Anne Enright, Eimear McBride, Sally Rooney.

The resurrection of the Catholic novel, or at least the persistence of writers' engagement with faith and a spiritual dimension, is striking. It is not orthodox, and is often combined with severe criticism of the Church, but it is abundantly present in the works of Sally Rooney, Deirdre Madden, Donal Ryan, Emma

Donoghue, Frank McGuinness, Brian Moore and (although not included here) Niamh Mulvey's *The Amendments*.

So, if you are open to nuance rather than dogma, read on. I hope it inspires you to seek out the work of the writers interviewed here, even if you have already read them once.

'At the end of [*Doctor Copernicus*] is written DC,' John Banville told me. 'It could be Doctor Copernicus but I meant it as da capo, start again. People imagine when they have read a book, they have read the book. No, start again. You would never listen to a piece of music and think: *oh, I now know that.*'

Claire Keegan said: 'I don't think you've read anything properly, understood it, until you've read it twice, and closely. I think the tail of the dog feeds back into the jaws.'

Happy (re)reading.

JOHN BANVILLE

27 September 2025, The Irish Times

Like a gondolier on the Canale Grande, John Banville seems right at home in Venice, the setting for his new novel, although, like his odious protagonist, Evelyn Dolman, he has a love–hate relationship with La Serenissima, 'that pestilential city squatting in the mudflats of its befouled lagoon'.

'I hate the place,' the author, ever the provocateur, says. He visits every year because he is on the jury of the Nonino literary prize in Friuli and drops by to renew hostilities. 'It smells, it's crawled over by tourists like an anthill and Venetians are impossibly avaricious. I was walking down one of those alleyways with a friend at twilight and a rat ran across and sank down a drain but left its big, pink, naked tail out. We both said: Venice!

'Of course, it's charming. I understand the beauty and uniqueness of the place, it's an extraordinary city, like nowhere else in the world, and I've had some wonderful times there but I find it a very sinister place.' He had an eerie experience in a Venetian club only to discover that Giordano Bruno, a philosopher burned at the stake in Rome for heresy and who features in his fiction, had sheltered there for months.

'Venice has this darkness that the Dublin of my imagination from the 1950s had,' which inspired the Quirke & Stafford series under his pen name Benjamin Black. 'I do love it. I have a great fondness for the grotesque. I love grotesque conjunctions. I love talking to people who hate me and being really nice to them.'

Deception and mask-wearing are at the dark heart of *Venetian Vespers* – 'Oscar Wilde said, "Give a man a mask and he'll tell you the truth"' – which is published next week, just over two months ahead of his eightieth birthday, but it feels so wickedly entertaining that the author must have had fun writing it too. 'I wouldn't keep doing it if there weren't rewards,' he says. 'It's hard work, but anything easy is not worth doing. I enjoyed doing this book, though.'

It is 1899 and Dolman, an arrogant English hack, is honeymooning with his bride, Laura Rensselaer, estranged daughter of an American millionaire. Exhausted by travel, feverish, an impotently mute monoglot abroad, he falls in with twins he meets in a bar on his first night, the louche Freddie, who claims to have been at school with him, and the enchanting Cesca. After a shocking incident, his world turns upside down.

It's a ripping yarn filled with dark desire, melodrama and suspense, blackguards and women wronged, suspicious deaths and chance encounters, scheming and mystery, an arch entertainment elevated by a master stylist's elegant prose – gondolas are described as sinister craft, 'rearing and plunging their haughty, gilded prows, like so many glossy-flanked racehorses crowding at the starting-rope'.

Venetian Vespers takes its name from Monteverdi's composition that is playing in St Mark's when Dolman is accosted there by a prostitute. 'It's a beautiful piece of music, but that's a very eerie place. It doesn't look like anything in the Western world, it's a Byzantine cathedral. The floors are uneven. I don't see it as Christian, I see it as a pagan temple, it scares me.' Was he ever accosted? 'In St Mark's Basilica? Are you joking? Happy thought.'

The book has an erotic charge, a sense of obsession. 'I remember obsession, years ago. I have always wanted to write a ghost story. I have always wanted to write an erotic novel, and in this I almost get there. It's a bit of both.

'I wanted to write an erotic novel because I think *Story of O* by Pauline Réage is a masterly book. Certainly when you read it a second time you realize it's not about sex at all, it's about power. O, the woman who is being abused, she is the one with power. That fascinated me. And this is in a way a book about power. Dolman thinks he has power, but he is at the mercy of these people.'

This fascination is present too in Banville's *Time Pieces: A Dublin Memoir*, where he recalls the girls of his youth and the prostitutes who plied their trade near his home – 'oh, well-named Mount Street'. Likewise, his soft spot for a canal, Dublin's though, not Venice's – 'that stretch of placid water, rustling reeds and dark-umber towpath from Baggot Street down to Lower Mount Street is the loveliest aquascape I know of, trumping even that other Canale Grande, the one with the warbling gondoliers'.

Venice, though, is a city rich in cultural resonances. *Vespers* 'is very much influenced by Thomas Mann's *Death in Venice* and *Don't Look Now*, which I saw again recently. It's a masterpiece. [Daphne du Maurier's] story is not terribly good, but Nicholas Roeg's film is wonderful, the way he uses colour.' When he first saw it, the film was about twenty-five minutes shorter, courtesy of the Irish censor, but Banville thought it was better without the sex scenes. 'I never believe actors doing sex, and Julie Christie looks like a boy.'

The epigraph is from *The Turn of the Screw* by Henry James, whose *The Aspern Papers* is also set in Venice. Is this novel then an homage?

'Oh, I never do homages to anyone except myself,' he chuckles. Surely Mrs Osmond, though, is his bow to Henry James. He concedes the point. 'Doing a sequel to *The Portrait of a Lady* would be like a jackal feeding on the body of a lion but, what the hell. I must have thought I needed a new direction.'

He wrote it while living on campus in Chicago. 'There wasn't even a bar. I did nothing but write. It was like an out-of-body experience. I would lean back and look at my hand moving. I felt I could go for a cup of coffee and come back and have another page written. I would use words that I didn't know the meaning of [a common sensation for his many readers, I suspect] – the *ebullient* cauldron. I didn't know ebullient meant boiling, until I looked it up. Where did that come from?'

Perhaps from another language, I suggest, but he admits only to 'a bit of German, some French and a smattering of English'. His versions of Kleist plays, he says, were really reworkings of existing translations. 'The glory of English is that it is such an impure, ambiguous language. One of my characters is called Cleave, which can mean its complete opposite. I love that.'

Banville's fiction is peppered with dictionary words, such as *contemnor*, which the humble reader must look up. What does it mean again, I ask? 'I can't remember,' he says. However, 'I found a wonderful word the other day, a new one on me, *invaginate*. It doesn't mean what you think it means, it simply means to form a sheath.' Where did he find it, dare I ask? 'In the dictionary.' He leafs through them? 'Of course, the dictionary is one of the great inventions of humankind.'

'I set out to be a lord of language who in time would be placed among the immortals,' Dolman declares. Is he channelling Banville? 'Well yes, but then there is a second half of it, too, where he becomes a hack.' Is that him too? 'Of course, part of me is. I love writing reviews. When you've written it, it's gone, whereas a book is like a reserved sin, one you have to go to a bishop to get absolution for.

'Perfection is an idea. Humans are imperfect, so every work of art is a failure. [John] McGahern used to say: there's verse and there's prose and then there's poetry, and poetry can happen in either and it happens more often in prose.'

His novels are often spin-offs from the original idea, he has said, satellites sent into orbit while the mother ship is jettisoned.

'You never write the book that you think you'll write, inevitably it changes along the way,' he says. 'When I was in my twenties it would take me three to five years to write a book. By the time I finished it I was a different person to the one who started it, and even still to some extent that is true, although I am now an ancient of days. *Doctor Copernicus* [about the Polish scientist] started out as a novel about the Norman invasion of Ireland. *The Newton Letter* came closest to achieving what I set out to achieve but it's only about eighty pages. All novels should be about eighty pages. Why people expect them to be about 240 pages I don't know.' *Vespers* is 316 pages.

Banville started out writing short stories but wouldn't be able to write one now.

'I need the breadth of a novel. It starts out like a doddle, but then six months later I am wading through mud up to my armpits, ready to cut my throat. I have to finish this damn thing and it can take years, and when I finish it I think it's just another damn book. Iris Murdoch was once asked why she wrote so many books. She said, you always hope the next one will exonerate me for the ones that went before. That's how I feel as well.'

I wonder if the stakes were lower with this one, akin to one of what Graham Greene called his entertainments. 'His novels are far funnier than his entertainments, unintentionally so,' Banville responds, waspishly. 'He treated me very badly with that GPA prize back in '89, he tried to take it away from me. Tony Ryan very generously gave two prizes.' He created an unflattering caricature based on Greene in *The Untouchable* (1997). 'I had my revenge.' Was he still alive? 'No, he was dead, unfortunately.'

As well as signalling the Jamesian connection to Venice, the epigraph captures his protagonist Evelyn Dolman's predicament. 'He doesn't know what he is doing, he thinks he knows everything but he's a complete idiot.' An innocent abroad, except he is far from innocent. 'He is a despicable little twerp who deserves everything he gets. He's called Dolman, you know [i.e. doll man] and he has an androgynous first name.

'A book-editor friend likened Dolman to Victor Maskell in *The Untouchable* and said, you're really good at conjuring horrible men. I said, why wouldn't I be?' The implication being, he is horrible too? 'I think all human beings are horrible,' Banville says.

Dolman is a dupe but also behaves abominably. Did Banville feel he had to tread carefully writing certain scenes? 'If I were to tread carefully, I would be lying,' he replies. '*Granta* published an extract from *The Untouchable*. In the first paragraph, Victor Maskell is almost run down by a bus, which he says was being "driven by a grinning blackamoor". The proofs had been changed. I said, "the point is you cannot censor me". They would try it now with all this wokeist nonsense. Thank God it's coming to an end. In *The Untouchable*, there is anti-Semitism throughout. I'm a philosemite, I still defend the Israelis. I was shaped by the death camps. My view of the savagery of human beings was formed by my childhood memories of what was coming out of Germany. I once tripped on blue twine that was used to bind bundles of *The Irish Times*. Six people helped me up. I remember thinking in different circumstances these same people would be pushing me into a cattle truck.

'I think all right-thinking people have a dark view of human beings, we are not a very nice species. All this stuff about Gaza, which is terrible, of course, but nobody gave a damn when Assad was killing 350,000 of his own people, no one cared about Rwanda. It's nascent anti-Semitism. Someone sent me a statement. I wrote back saying I will not sign this, there is no mention of Hamas. Of course, they gave Netanyahu and his horrible gang the excuse to commit atrocities. But they started it.'

The conflict did not start on 7 October 2023, I say, but the author diverts to an amusing anecdote about the Jewish literary editor David Marcus. 'When he was a little boy in Cork in 1945 or '46 there was a knock at the door one Easter. A huge priest was standing there, who said: "I'm here for the dues."'

Banville spent many years as a subeditor on *The Irish Press* and *The Irish Times*. This had no bearing on his writing, he says, except perhaps a certain economy of language. Working night shifts did mean, however, that he wrote in the morning and afternoon. 'I've always been a creature of the night. Tim Pat Coogan [a former editor of the *Press*] hated subs, he defined us as "people who change other people's words and go home in the dark". I loved subbing.'

He also enjoyed being literary editor of *The Irish Times*. 'I loved that job, ten marvellous years. My iron rule was, when you send out a book for review, when the review comes in, you have to accept it. I'm sure there were writers who were annoyed [by a bad review]. But literature, art, book reviewing, these are areas of truth. In a world that has given up the notion of truth having any value, this is going to be one area that will help us through. You can't make untruthful art. If you do, it is not art, it's kitsch. An artist may be a total liar in life like myself, but when you sit down to write I can't lie. When I was doing *Copernicus*, halfway through I realized historians will shout at me about this. A friend said: "don't be mesmerized by fact, fact is not truth, what you are doing is truth".'

He was desperate to win the Booker Prize in 1989 when he was shortlisted for *The Book of Evidence*, not for the validation but because if he had won, he could have left journalism to write full-time.

'I didn't realize the Booker only lasts for a year and then you're a nobody again. If you were to regard the prize as some judgement of your work, you'd be in trouble. As Roddy Doyle said when he won, "if it had been five different judges someone else would have won" and it's true, it's a lottery. I came across a wonderful saying by Philip Larkin the other day: "I don't think I write particularly well, just better than everyone else."' He chuckles. Would he go so far? 'Of course. God, I'll get into such trouble for this. But I have lots of friends with a sense of humour. Everything I write is second- or third-rate, by my standards, but my standards are impossibly high.'

He doesn't get edited, he says, then corrects himself. 'The crime books get edited because I fall asleep now and then. One editor said to me, do you realize you've actually demoted Strafford from one book to the next?'

He recalls finishing *The Lock-Up* in Annaghmakerrig writing retreat on a Friday night but felt it was a bit banal. He suddenly realized another character could be the killer so on Saturday morning he wrote another 3,000 words, a new ending. 'That's the essence of that kind of writing, it has to be spontaneous.'

He was in a self-catering chalet so avoided the evening meals with fellow writers. Hell is other writers, I suggest, paraphrasing Sartre, and he laughs but later lists several writer friends.

'McGahern told me, the only reason we get on is we are so unalike. He was wonderful company. In the old days my wife and I used to visit him in the house above the lake. We used to drink so much, laugh so much, he was one of the best storytellers.'

I wonder if he agrees that *The Book of Evidence* is his best work. 'I can't be asked to judge my own work because I bring all the baggage of the years of writing, all the mistakes, all the failures, compromises, so I can't read them with an innocent eye.'

I quote that wonderful lapidary line from *The Sea*, which seems to capture a recurring theme in his work: 'The past beats inside me like a second heart,' and he says: 'It's strange, everyone remembers that line. I didn't think it was special but everyone remembers it. There are lots of others.

'In *The Infinities*, there is a line where the god Hermes speaks, complaining that the gods are being coerced by humans: "Fine gods we are that we must muster to a mortal must." When I wrote it, I thought: my poor translators.

'There are few things more pleasurable than writing a well-made sentence. That's a great privilege. Our greatest invention as a species is the sentence. This is what made us civilized. And I've spent my life working with this marvellous invention. What a privileged life. I know I write beautiful sentences, but they are to other people, not to me. It would be fatal if I loved my own work.'

Did he take satisfaction in seeing Dolman's arrogance, typical of a certain Englishman abroad, crushed? 'No, I am one of those rare creatures, I have no trace of nationalism. I like Ireland because of the climate and the sense of humour. We are so adept at mocking ourselves, even at our most serious we don't take ourselves seriously, I love that.'

He is disappointed that some don't recognize the humour in his work. 'The good readers do.' The connoisseurs? 'No, I don't want connoisseurs. My wife was in M&S and a woman at the checkout saw the credit card and asked if she was related to me. "Tell him *The Sea* is the most beautiful thing I've ever read." That to me is worth 500 rave reviews, they are the people I write for, not fellow writers, academics, critics or book reviewers. I write for the woman at the checkout in M&S. A huge number get it, many don't, but if you appealed to everyone you would be a mere bestselling author.'

Unlike Dolman, Banville appreciates classical music and seeks to emulate it in his prose. 'It's paramount. I've always had huge admiration for Nabokov's prose but I read an interview where he said he was tone deaf. I thought, that's what it is, there is no music in his prose, it's all pictorial, visual.

'I regard music as a kind of magic, it's extraordinary that these little black marks on a white page turn into this storm of sound. I listen to music all the time, Bach, Beethoven, Benjamin Britten. I don't like pop music. My partner Patricia Quinn plays the viol.' He speaks his work aloud when he is revising. 'I used to have this strange Oxbridge-accented voice I would hear myself reading a sentence in. I said to myself, *where did that come from? Copernicus* is music from start to finish. At the end of it is written DC. It could be Doctor Copernicus but I meant it as da capo, start again. People imagine when they have read a book, they have read the book. No, start again. You would never listen to a piece of music and think, *oh, I now know that.*'

There is a sense of playfulness at times in *Vespers*, highlighting the artifice of storytelling. 'Art is transcendent play,' he agrees. 'I'm playing. At least three times a week I'll look up from my desk and say, "I'm supposed to be a grown-up human being. What am I doing, telling these stories?"'

Like a playpen, I suggest. 'I'll steal that,' he says. 'T.S. Eliot says inexperienced writers borrow; experienced writers steal. It's stolen.'

He is halfway through another Quirke crime caper, while his autobiography, *Out of True*, is progressing slowly. Will it be a tell-all or a tell-some? 'It's a novel,' he laughs. 'I could never keep a diary. I have no interest in myself as a person to write about. I love my life, the people around me. It will be full of banalities. Life is banal; that is part of its glory.'

He used to write eight hours a day but now, on the cusp of his ninth decade, he can't do more than three. 'The writing life requires physical strength. When I started, houses didn't have central heating. Your legs would be frozen. But I write twenty-four hours a day, even when I am dreaming.' A novel, he has said, is a vehicle to convey the weight and power of a dream. *Vespers* begins and ends with an image from Dolman's dream that turns out to be a premonition.

Banville allies himself with Beckett and Kafka over Joyce. 'I'm not a Joycean. I regard the world as a very strange place. I've been alienated since I reached the age of reason, I'll die alienated but there is a wonderful quote from the astronaut Jim Lovell: "People often say, 'I hope to go to heaven when I die. In reality, you go to heaven when you're born.'" Earth is beautiful, it's terrible too but my God, look at clouds, we ignore them only because we are used to them. I was on a flight to Oslo, flying above the fjords, but there were clouds above the plane reflected in the fjords, pure magic.'

Banville was born in Wexford in 1945. A former literary editor of The Irish Times, *he won the Booker Prize for* The Sea *(1985) and was shortlisted for* The Book of Evidence *(1989), which won the Guinness Peat Aviation Prize. The latter was part of a trilogy with* Ghosts *(1993) and* Athena *(1995).* Doctor Copernicus *(1976),* Kepler *(1981) and* The Newton Letter *(1982) formed the Revolutions trilogy.* Eclipse *(2000),* Shroud *(2002) and* Ancient Light *(2012) make up the Cleave trilogy. As Benjamin Black, he wrote the bestselling* Quirke *crime series.*

KEVIN BARRY

1 June 2024, The Irish Times

Kevin Barry is in an Airbnb in Valencia, in Spain, when we meet over Zoom – he's in a T-shirt, I'm in a fleece – reacquainting himself with the sun after an endless Connacht winter, preparing himself for the hamster wheel of publicity that will accompany the publication of his cracking new Cork-accented western.

He is constitutionally incapable of delivering a dull sentence.

'They're clawing their eyes out of their heads to get out of the country,' he says of Knock airport's exodus. 'It's been fuckin' desperate, with cold winds like you're on the steppes.' He and his partner, Olivia Smith, spent January and February in California, researching his next book, but the eight weeks since they've been back have featured only two good days. 'I call it brown season. Everything is just mud-coloured and shite.'

Little wonder, perhaps – what with our misfortunate climate on top of the constraints of colonialism and Catholicism – that we have long been an emigrant nation, which offers our writers an irresistibly rich global canvas.

Barry's new novel is set in the United States, and the next one might be, too, or possibly early-1990s London. 'I'm always threatening the London-Irish novel. I was there as a 21-year-old. Also, the Irish newspaper office novel. I always have a couple competing to see which is going to be the next one. I just see where I can get a bit of flow going. I like to have one started as one is coming out.'

Barry, at fifty-four, is an old hand, one of the finest, most influential Irish writers. His debut story collection, *There Are Little Kingdoms*, from 2007, won the Rooney Prize. *Dark Lies the Island*, from 2012, and *That Old Country Music*, from 2020, both won the Edge Hill Short Story Prize. *Beer Trip to Llandudno* won the *Sunday Times* short-story award. His first novel, *City of Bohane*, won the International Dublin Literary Award in 2013; *Beatlebone* won the Goldsmiths Prize in 2015; and *Night Boat to Tangier* was longlisted for the 2019 Booker Prize.

He was a 29-year-old greenhorn, however, when he first conceived of the Irish western that twenty-five years later has become *The Heart in Winter*, whose darkly lyrical world of doomed lovers, emigrant Irish, eccentric villains and dissolute excess make it a novel Shane MacGowan might have given his two front teeth to write.

'This is a long, bitter story,' he says, with the good humour that a happy ending allows. 'I've made a living since the age of nineteen as a freelance writer of one stripe or another. It's a source of pride.' Barry had left college in Limerick for a job on a local paper, but it folded within a year. 'I was freelancing in Cork in the 1990s, writing for the *Examiner*, doing shifts for *The Echo*, sending features to Patsey Murphy on the *Irish Times Magazine*. People don't believe me, but I got £250 a week for a 450-word column in the *Examiner*. I used to call the Crosbies' – the *Examiner*'s former owners – 'my Medicis. But I decided in a kind of sniffy way I was better than all this: it was time to write the novel. I'd been making half-arsed attempts at fiction, bits of stories written at four in the morning after coming home from a nightclub.'

Barry decided he needed three or four months to focus properly, so he wrote a rake of features, bought a caravan for £400, 'a real Father Ted job', parked it on the beach in Allihies, in west Cork, laid out his notebooks and pens and … 'I had fuckin' nothing. The bits of stories had been sex and drugs and nightclubs. I was twenty-nine. I had nothing to write fiction about.'

So he started exploring the Caha Mountains and their abandoned copper mines. He knew a bit about the miners emigrating to Butte, Montana, and slowly realized, 'There's a western in this, and it's a western I can write because all the accents will be County Cork. I know what these fuckers sound like.' He researched in University College Cork's Boole Library. Butte was booming in the 1890s, as electrification required copper from its mines. Soon there were 30,000 people there, one-third of whom were from Cork. As *The Heart in Winter* puts it, 'There were by now ten thousand Hibernian to the town and they had the place fucking destroyed.'

'Soaked in an ambience of death from the cradle, they believed themselves generally to be on the way out, and sooner rather than later, and thus could be inclined to put aside the niceties of the living realm. Terrible people, born of a terrible nation.'

They had the usual MO for new Irish, says Barry. The first thing they did was open thirty-eight pubs. Then they took over the police and the political apparatus. 'I thought, *Jesus, this is a great world for me, I'll have to go.*' So he lit out for Butte, flying to Seattle, then spending eighteen hours in a Greyhound bus. 'With age you become a little more reserved. At that age I wasn't. I was literally stopping people in the street, saying, "I'm writing a novel. What have you got for me?" They were incredibly kind, the loveliest people, still very proud of their Irish heritage.'

Librarians brought out boxes of letters sent back to Beara from Butte in the 1890s, townsfolk brought him drinking – winding up many a night in the Irish Times pub in the town – and he was introduced to the Yank Harrington, born in 1903 to parents from Castletownbere, who played a mean fiddle and was the subject of an Irishman's Diary piece Barry wrote for *The Irish Times* in 2000. But that was all he wrote.

'I had all this great material and texture, I came back weighted down with notebooks, but I had no chops: I didn't know how to write a novel. I didn't publish a book till I was thirty-seven. I thought I must have been an awful fuckin' waster, but looking back, because I kept a work diary, it was quite poignant: I wrote 120,000 words of fiction that year. It's in the house under a bed, this manuscript. I can't bring myself to look at it. Awful stuff. I thought I needed to do the whole story: the mines, the political system, the police, the bars, Cecil B. DeMille set pieces. After eight or nine months I abandoned ship. I couldn't control the material. Looking back, the fundamental thing was, I had no strong characters.'

When the TV series *Deadwood* came out, in 2006, it struck him that this was how to do the Butte novel – the exact kind of profane language that West Cork miners would have been using in 1891. *City of Bohane*, set in a futuristic city that was a cross between Cork, Limerick and Deadwood, was influenced by that abandoned novel, 'my own version of that Sin City. It's very much a Western in its own way, one character in a white suit, another in a black suit.' He revisited it recently for a college class and found it very much a first novel in its structural engineering, but with vitality and a freshness in the language. He could sense his own excitement at hitting a note with it. Working-class Cork and Limerick voices were creeping into Irish literature for the first time.

Late in the pandemic, in October 2021, a dreary time for many, he had started and quickly abandoned a novel about a stoner detective in early-1990s Amsterdam, as he didn't know enough about that world. Social restrictions had him walking in the woods of the Bricklieve Mountains, which reminded him of a typical western locale.

'I thought, *Butte, Montana, maybe now is the time*. It has to be runaway lovers: they need to get out of Butte. He's called Tom; she's called Polly.' He spent a week writing Tom's story first, the stations-of-the-cross pub crawl that opens the book. 'Not coincidentally, he's the same age I was when I went to Butte. There's a lot of autofiction in the description of this dissolute 29-year-old, a yoke with vague literary ambitions.' The following Monday morning he started on Polly. Twenty minutes in, he thought, *I have a book*. 'I just had her voice. It was ready. Writing fiction is a strange, esoteric business. I would hate ever to use a phrase like "the trick of it", but the trick of it is to find out what the right story is for the desk at a particular time in your life.

'The next ten months were the happiest experience I've had in my writing life. It just kind of ran down the road for me. The western is very forgiving in terms of momentum and plot. People are always just getting up on horses and lighting out; there's movement, and they're going to be meeting people. It was a joy to write it, and on a personal level it was like repaying a debt to my younger self. I was saying to myself, *you weren't such an eejit. This is actually a really good idea*. I just didn't have the knack for it at the time.' He salvaged one line from the original 120,000 words as a nod to his younger self. 'She got fuck knots in her hair.'

Some write with the eye, Barry has said, but he writes with the ear. Everything comes through speech. He reads his work aloud as he writes to make sure the tone is right. And he spins a yarn and turns a phrase like few others. He recalls ordering a cheeseburger at the M&M diner in Butte, which opened in 1890. 'I said to the waitress, "I heard this place has never closed." She said, "It's been a long shift."'

Lesser writers' coined words seem corny and counterfeit. Barry's neologisms feel, by comparison, like freshly laundered dirty money. There is an earthiness to his word-making, but is he conscious of the risks? 'Absolutely. I read it aloud a lot with pen in hand as I go along. It has to feel right; can you hear it? They didn't speak in Dakota like they do in Deadwood. David Milch uses an Elizabethan register, incredibly profane, in no way accurate, but it feels right.'

I wondered why Barry avoided depicting the shoot-out scene in his novel. Was it too much of a cliché? 'It was subconscious at first but then very definitely a decision to keep violence off-screen, because the book is above all a love story. I thought bringing the gore and the violence on-screen would break the romantic spell of the book.'

Similarly, there is the suggestion that Tom and Polly are escaping problematic pasts, but this is not explored. '*Tangier* kept going forward, then drifting into the past. With this one I wanted, in honour of the genre, to keep the forward momentum, lighting out to whatever was coming down the line.'

How did he access the intense first flush of young love?

'My way into the character was: Tom is twenty-nine, he's come from Castletownbere, what's he like? I was thinking, *what was I like?* That's the easiest way. I got it: he was poisoned with literary ambition. It's an exalted state to find yourself in, and it's also a catastrophe. I came up with the perfect tagline for the novel, and we didn't use it in the end, because it gives too much of the story away: "He wanted to die for love; he just hadn't met the right girl yet." What made the story work for me is when Polly came into it, the way lovers bring each other into definition. She is incredibly sure of who she is; he doesn't know who he is, and he's trying on different accents and demeanours.'

Barry cheerfully admitted to *The New Yorker* magazine that doomed romantics are his stock in trade – 'He drew a thumb along the line of her cheekbone and the horse leaned in as though a sideman or confrere. The hooktip of her nose was cold and blue as a berry and he kissed it ... The edge of the forest here felt fated in the way of a final place and this thrilled her to an unholy degree and when she looked up to his eyes again there was a deathloving shine to hers.'

The year 1891 is very interesting, he says – every main street suddenly had a photographic studio. 'For the first time ordinary people were thinking, *how do I look?* Polly and Tom get more and more into how they present themselves.' This self-mythologizing reminds me of Bonnie and Clyde. 'I think Cormac McCarthy said once, books are made out of books; there is no mystery to it. They are also made out of films and music. The strongest influences on this I listed in that *New Yorker* interview, films like *Days of Heaven* and *Badlands*, Terrence Malick films from the 1970s; *McCabe & Mrs Miller*. *Deadwood* was a huge influence.

'Then books, you go to the best to see how it's been done before. Charles Portis's *True Grit*, which I have to say stands up. You can't write a western now without paying at least a vague homage to Cormac McCarthy, because he is the writer who kept the genre alive. He had such genius; he saw there were still possibilities with this hoary old form. I read *All the Pretty Horses*. Fuck, he knows a lot about horses. I thought, well, maybe if my character knows nothing about horses and is totally winging it, I'll be able to get away with it. In terms of historical fiction, I go back in a devotional, almost religious way to Hilary Mantel, how she makes it seem so fresh and contemporary – there is never a sense of research on the page, she wears it so lightly.'

Setting is a strong factor in all his works. 'I do go quite method, or at least I set myself up as a location scout. I go to the places. *Night Boat to Tangier*, I was in the ferry port in Algeciras, writing my Cork gangster dialogue on site, drinking cafés con leche. It all went a bit nuts with *Beatlebone*. It's about John Lennon going to an island, primal-screaming. I went a bit far, out on a rock in Clew Bay, screaming. I felt great after it.

'I gave a bit of myself away in the book, which I [normally] never do. I want the books to be very intimate experiences for the reader and them to know absolutely nothing about me at the end of it. That's the ambition, and it's important to keep myself back.'

Barry broke the fourth wall by interrupting the narrative to explore his own motivation for writing the novel and why he identified with Lennon. He has no regrets, though. 'No, because it saved the book, I thought, writing the chapter about the reason for writing the novel, a kindred spirit who loses a parent early. It needed an emotional heart. Without that it was just a kind of caper with John and his driver Cornelius in the far extremities of Connacht. It was the most difficult of the novels, the baggiest and the loosest and also in a way my favourite, *because* it was difficult.'

In his preface to Anthony Cronin's biography of Flann O'Brien, however, Barry contends that 'a writer's style is a direct projection of the personality, in fact of the soul, if such a thing can be said to exist. As that style is channelled directly from the subconscious, it contains base and original truths, and it all comes out on the page. A writer cannot hide from himself or herself on the page, most especially in the writing of prose fiction.'

He develops that idea. 'You can lie in an essay; you can't in fiction. You always give yourself away. It all comes out despite your best efforts. That's part of the game of it: how much can I keep back? Two things for me about fiction: first, learning to exert control on the page takes a lot of work and effort, before becoming the puppet master; and then what's really interesting is, now can I lose control? Can I let it go wherever it wants to? I'm not sure if it ever got there. I definitely tried to with *Beatlebone* and *Bohane*, let it go nuts and see what happens. I've been a stricter ringmaster with *Tangier* and *The Heart in Winter*. And they're technically better novels. I do find, weirdly, at the age of fifty-four, that I'm only getting going with the novels. I've always been a slow starter. I learned to cycle at the age of fourteen, I learned to swim when I was twenty-nine, and now I'm an avid swimmer and cyclist. Only fools rush in.

'I know now how to get under the hood of a novel, that blend of wildness and control. I go back to someone like Dermot Healy. *A Goat's Song* is a crazy book but such extraordinary skill; we need to keep talking about him. Living in Sligo gives his work an extra dimension.'

I ask what else his work has in common. 'The four novels to date and the vague ones I'm just starting revving the engines for are all engaged with genres to some degree. *Night Boat to Tangier* has elements of noir. *Beatlebone* is the most derided of all the genres: it's fan fiction. *City of Bohane* is a mad mix of dystopia and western gang-war novel. I'm mangling some quote, but I'm just looking for a bridge to get my soldiers across.'

Barry is coming into his own as a novelist, but the short stories with which he made his name are drying up. 'They come seldom enough now, one or two a year max.' *Finistère*, in *The New Yorker* recently, is his first published since *Pure Winter*, in *The Irish Times* in December 2021. 'I remember when I was putting that first collection together for Declan Meade at *The Stinging Fly*. I had five or six, and he said, "We'll probably need another six." I said, "Give me two months."' He laughs. 'As a relatively young man I could knock one out in a week. I hit a really good seam.

'Short stories are very different for me. I write them much more quickly, obviously, but they come across you like a shadow, and you have to write them when it's there.' Short stories alone would bore him now, he says – he likes writing screenplays, playscripts. Every novel has been optioned, and the screenplays are a significant part of his income. *Dark Lies the Island* has been filmed, and *Tangier* and *Bohane* are both at very advanced stages. 'I enjoy the sociability of it, the Zooms; it gets me out of the shed. It's why I like the three to four weeks in July I spend on *Winter Papers*, line-editing, a great holiday from myself, not having to think about my own pages for a month.'

Winter Papers, the cloth-bound annual arts anthology he edits with Olivia will mark its tenth edition this year. The pair were admiring the artisan bookmaking in a comic shop in Montreal called Drawn & Quarterly and he thought of the designer John Foley, from his Cork days, and the idea took off. 'It's become a lovely part of the year, a natural rhythm and a social life, living in rural Sligo. Without getting into the backslapping thing about Irish literature, you get the sense of a lot of people working in an extremely serious, committed way. I like that we get people from different crafts to talk to each other about how they do it. We are also opening up the archive this year online, keeping those pieces alive.'

Richard Harris once said that every Limerick man is at heart an old ham, and Barry has become famous for his live readings. 'I love doing live readings. I just did the audiobook. I remember saying to myself, *Now don't go to town on the Cornish accents*. What did I do? I went to complete fuckin' town. My Yorkshire is good; the Cornish is a hate crime. I sold rakes of the *Tangier* audiobook. Most audiobooks are awful – trained actors. I'm not leaving them out of my hands, hammy as they are.'

Barry was born in 1969 in Limerick. He is the author of three collections of short stories: There Are Little Kingdoms *(2007),* Dark Lies the Island *(2012) and* That Old Country Music *(2020). He is also the author of four novels:* City of Bohane *(2012),* Beatlebone *(2015),* Night Boat to Tangier *(2019) and* The Heart in Winter *(2024), which was shortlisted for the Walter Scott Prize.*

SEBASTIAN BARRY

5 September 2026, The Irish Times

If the divided loyalties and complex identities of his forebears gave Sebastian Barry the key subject and the essential structure for his career as a writer, witnessing while a student at Trinity College the loyalist bombing of Dublin in May 1974, which killed twenty-seven people, was the catalyst.

The description of the aftermath of the South Leinster Street bombing in his latest novel, *Old God's Time* (2024), is so vivid, it feels like lived experience. The shrapnel scars are still visible on Trinity's perimeter wall and the images are still vivid more than fifty years on in the writer's mind.

The UVF bombing of Parnell Street minutes earlier is also at the heart of his play *The Pride of Parnell Street* (2011).

'I was a very ignorant, sheltered, middle-class Irish student,' Barry says. 'My first instinct was to leave the country and be done with it completely because I couldn't understand why anyone on the island would want to incinerate shoppers going home. It was also an enormous, high-speed education in what people were suffering in the North of Ireland, that mysterious country that we could never really get our heads around.

'If you're a sensitive or even vulnerable person coming out of Lincoln Gate and there is this enormous noise … My first innocent thought was that a butcher's shop had been blown up because there were literally steaming cuts of meat, then I saw people kneeling to these and whispering, a moment of humanity and inhumanity.'

As soon as he graduated, he left for Paris, Greece and Switzerland, but then set up home for seven years in North Great George's Street with Ali, who is now his wife, which gave him a deep identification with the people of the inner city and an understanding of the history that had befallen them.

'It created an ineradicable sense of home. Living there made it important to me that I was born between the canals. That's where the little fire was lit for feeling I could possibly, truthfully be from here. That inexplicable murderousness in Dublin that day both cancelled my passport but was the beginning of a truer sort of documentation, all written with blood and in the heart.'

We are talking in the old Church of Ireland rectory in West Wicklow, which he and Ali have restored and where they raised their family. It's an obvious metaphor for his writing, which has sought to make Ireland a warmer house for those who do not conform to the Catholic, nationalist tradition that created a narrow notion of Irishness.

He recalls reading Joseph O'Neill's great 9/11 novel *Netherland*, whose enormous explosion triggered memories of the Dublin bombing, 'everything blackened and ruined. The book is like a forensic reconstruction after a plane crash and he somehow makes it again that you could fly it. That's what I feel I was doing for decades, trying to find all the bits and put them back together..'

He has also built a towering reputation, twice winning both Costa Book of the Year and the Walter Scott Prize for historical fiction. *The Secret Scripture* has been called 'an alternative history of Ireland', a description that could sum up his life's work, and he has been praised as 'an unrivalled chronicler of lost lives'. 'So much Irish history is about othering people – we belong, you don't – that to create a sense of communion for someone who has no gift for it, it's compensatory in a way.' 'Ireland has a tangled wool basket of history and indeed contemporary life,' he has said, 'and we try to unpack the knots.'

Robert Gottlieb, reviewing all his novels to date in a stellar *New York Review of Books* essay, wrote that Barry should 'be widely read and reviewed … he ought to be a laureate for fiction everywhere', a reference to his then-role as Laureate for Irish Fiction. 'Barry's novels give us lives, not plots – that is their power … His family's past is his material, not his subject.' He recognizes Barry's early tendency to poetic excess, prose that 'occasionally goes all purple' and 'an unabashed delight in metaphor' but traces his evolution from the poet and dramatist he began as.

Barry sent Gottlieb *Old God's Time* and he replied, referencing Toni Morrison's *Beloved*, which he had edited. 'I'm that passport-less, tentative individual that I've always been yet he is bringing to my efforts this graceful majesty. When he died recently I felt as if I had lost a brother, father, angel.' He had a similar friendship with Harold Pinter, who wrote him a beautiful letter praising *The Secret Scripture* and *A Long, Long Way*. 'I thought it was from my father as they used the same black ink. I opened it with concern as he only ever wanted to put a razor slash inside me.'

He didn't in fact read Gottlieb's article but Colm Tóibín had briefed him of its content and import. 'Colm's two months older than me so he's my big brother.'

But telling tales has come at a high price for Barry. Like Tóibín, Barry was a friend and long-term patient of the psychiatrist Ivor Browne. Whereas Tóibín's father had died young, Barry's father, Francis, an architect, poet and a womanizer, was very much alive but they were hopelessly estranged, as Barry was from his mother, the actor Joan O'Hara, and maternal grandfather Jack. His childhood, and that of his siblings, was a troubled one. His parents were 'selfish, not very nurturing, narcissistic', he says. Their Monkstown home sold for €1.75 million in 2017, but material privilege was matched by emotional poverty.

When I suggest that his family is the structure around which he has built his work, he corrects me that Ali and his children and dogs are his family. His books and plays deal with his previous family. Is his happy home a riposte to how he was raised? 'It's a miracle,' he says. 'You might be surprised to hear this but I was awful good-looking once. I think Ali noticed I was in need of the sort of rescue she could supply, she had the skills from her own childhood. She is a very good doctoring presence to me. I'm probably one of those GPs who should be struck off; nevertheless, I try to reciprocate. I think in a more primitive psychiatric atmosphere I would have been sectioned, descended into a depression so deep, I wouldn't have got out. At a certain point you have to dispense with the aural history and write *The Odyssey*, that's really all I've been doing for fifty years.'

He once expressed surprise that John McGahern had written a memoir, effectively decoding his fiction. Might he follow suit?

'I was trying manfully – not my strong point,' he asides wryly, 'to think about, with these nine books, these supposed strands, the Dunnes and the McNultys. What unites them is the marriage of my parents, which I did manfully try to touch on in my most recent book, *Old God's Time*.' A German critic shocked him by deciphering that in it he effectively had his father shot.

But when he attempted in 2024 to write a memoir, 'the whole idea of traipsing through the whole thing again, which one has done endlessly in therapy, there was absolutely no engine for it. Maybe I'm just not at the right door. Essentially every book is truthfully a found object, it's already there. The joy of it is having the patience and absence and discipline and freedom and time to uncover it, recover it from whatever silence it sits in.'

When he hit upon the opening line for his award-winning novel *Days Without End* – 'The method of laying out a corpse in Missouri sure took the proverbial cake' – 'once I had that right, somehow I could tilt that sentence and see the rest of the book, like a range of sentences stretching out for 300 pages'.

I can't help noticing a pile of books with a Native American theme on the table beside us. Having already written a sequel, *A Thousand Moons*, is he planning a third? Somewhat to his surprise, there is. 'I am working on a book [*The Newer World*, September 2026] about Tennyson Bouguereau, who is the freed man in those two books.'

Like Tóibín, Barry could not read or write till he was seven or eight and is still a slow reader so research is laborious. It must be buried deeply 'so that anything that rises up in your manuscript, it's as if it's from your own experience. It is tuppenny-ha'penny, using tin instead of silver, things banged together but it always intrigues me that it can still make a serviceable object, anything made out of human birdsong.'

Barry reviewed Brian Moore's *Black Robe* positively in *The Irish Times*. I wonder if his fellow author's Native American novel somehow planted a seed for his own novels in that field. 'That stayed with me, that book, even though Brian Moore is being forgotten. What a tremendous thing to do. I can sit here with you seeing that book as if it were in some ways my own. What really affected me is the way the native characters were translated, all cursing roundly. He had noticed another thing outside himself and in an act of tremendous empathetic access had tried to inhabit it, become it, show his findings. He had gone so far in his imagination; in a different generation, all emphasis would have been on the Jesuit priest but he had gone further.'

Closer to home, he was inspired to write about gay friendship in *Days Without End* after his son Toby came out. With Toby's blessing, he also wrote a letter to *The Irish Times* to back a Yes vote in the marriage equality referendum.

As a bohemian Irish boy, who felt he didn't belong, Barry had identified with Jewishness. He aspired to be the next Bob Dylan and grew his hair down to his waist, which may have got him the part of Tonto in a Trinity play, 'a part with no lines, interestingly enough. I had a huge desire to give lines to Tonto.'

He was staying in another old rectory in Kerry in 1974 when he visited a neolithic fort, which inspired the line of poetry: 'They huddle in the walls where the creepways end.' That one good line told him he could be Sebastian, not Bob. 'In that moment I had identified as a writer. Not a choice; it found me.'

The Barrys had moved to London for work and Sebastian had returned with a London accent, which he had to shed swiftly lest his Dalkey schoolmates murder him. 'This is why I felt a strong identification with Ali, who is a Dublin Presbyterian. I was odd and presented as odd to other children. I never felt that anything I was could be included in a sense of Irishness. I think a lot of people felt they didn't have enough of the adjectives describing Irishness to qualify. Certainly Dublin Protestants were told they didn't really belong. I have spent fifty years trying to include some adjectives into the mix. I now feel profoundly Irish but I fought for it.'

He insists it is not enough for Ireland to accommodate outliers or newcomers but to appreciate and welcome them.

Barry wrote a laureate lecture called 'The Fog of Family' about his parents but it was too honest so he rewrote it to be more palatable if less true. 'A lot of people loved my mother professionally. I got a lot of letters when she died. It felt churlish to say "yes but ..." She was an interesting, extravagant person, probably bipolar. It was difficult to be a child of such a person. If she were here now, she could actually manage this conversation, she was so fearless. My father much less so. For the last thirty to forty years of his life, I was the enemy because I had spoken certain truths and that was unforgiveable. He followed his appetites to an extreme degree. Womanizing was the least of it. It was destroying my mother. She needed to live with certain myths intact. Any truth-telling was as unwelcome for her as it was for him. They were difficult people. And we are sundered people.'

Even in death, there was pain. He did not attend his father's funeral and was away for his mother's. Scattering her ashes on Knocknarea, he fell and cracked two ribs. He loves his siblings but his sister Siuban lives far away in France and he hasn't seen his brother Guy since 2007, and doesn't know where he is. 'His memories are too painful to be near fellow survivors. In the classic Abbey play we would reach a scene where people apologize to each other, but no.'

In a creative sense, he very much followed in his parents' footsteps; in terms of character, he rejected them.

His mother and grandfather brought him up on a well of family stories but 'wells get spoiled'. He shared a bedroom in Monkstown with his grandfather Jack, who inspired *The Temporary Gentleman.* Wasn't that odd? 'No, it was a great benefit because it was freezing. He told me stories about his war years. He needed to think of himself as pretty magnificent.' He was a recovering alcoholic and his wife had died of alcoholism. She inspired Barry's play *Our Lady of Sligo*. 'He was as near as I could get to a person I was close to. He introduced me to his parents. I never saw it as material, I was just a little boy, grateful for companionship. He wasn't loving or demonstrative but he spent time with me. We did have a falling-out over me writing stories, he hated that because I described his parents' house as poverty-stricken, not a truth he wanted propagated. I never had the wisdom to make peace with him. I was too young and stubborn and stupid. Conflict and mutual hurt are a given in human affairs. Our job is to find a little path of common ground. There was no reconciliation possible with my parents as they weren't looking for reconciliation. For them I was utterly in the wrong.'

Barry has been a lifelong full-time writer, a rare breed, 'not so much an occupation as a preoccupation'. In his early years, 'I was probably depressed, certainly hypochondriacal, neurotic, but I did notice if you got up in the morning and had a story by the evening it was an extreme form of compensatory happiness, the feeling of making something.'

Donal McCann's performance in the title role of Barry's theatrical masterpiece *The Steward of Christendom* made it the finest production I have ever seen. Its success in first London, then Dublin and off Broadway enabled the Barrys to buy their first home.

There is a fine self-portrait by McCann on Barry's wall, with a map of Australia on his forehead like a cross-section of his brain, drawn while touring *Steward* down under. They had a unique bond. *The Steward*'s phenomenal success was 'a bit defining'. It led some to mistake him for the new Friel or even primarily as a playwright. 'As Thomas Kinsella said, there is no mantle and it does not fall.' He was writing *The Whereabouts of Eneas McNulty* at the same time, his first mature novel.

'I didn't give up on the theatre but something happened, which was that Donal died. One of the reasons I came to the earth was to meet Donal. It was a perfect conjunction, an actor in two years of sobriety, a play he thought somehow I had thieved out of his brain. He made a total identification with it;

I made a total identification with him. He was the great actor of my childhood. He could be absolutely terrifying but never to me. He showed me the greatest level of mercy, he treated me like a god. He was so pleased when it [the play] made a lot of money, we were able to buy the house in Greystones. Before, when we were rehearsing he was giving me a pound or two for McDonald's. He was so proud because he knew he had caused it. Ali made him smoked mackerel, I can still see him sitting there, he was not given to happiness, looking like the most contented man in Ireland. Mostly it's forgotten because fewer and fewer are around who saw it, but for me it's the sine qua non of my existence because it calved everything else. It's not that I stopped writing plays but, although I loved Jim Culleton, when Donal died part of me died and I had to resurrect myself as a novelist.'

McCann's death, together with a crisis in Guy's life, triggered a breakdown. Barry had previously suffered one after the Dublin bombing and again in Paris in 1981. 'The cure for it was running. I'm so glad people talk about these things now because in 1999 when I was utterly unable to function and so anxious my agent told me not to say it to anyone because you might be considered disabled. But all the excitement of the novels was yet to come, it wasn't disabling in any way, so that's my message to people when they are suffering.

'Ivor Browne, who was my friend but also substitute father, after my breakdown after *Steward*, said, "Your trouble is having climbed the mountain you have to go back to supply camp and start again".'

By chance, his home is not far from Kiltegan and Baltinglass, places associated with Thomas Dunne from *The Steward* and his daughter Annie Dunne, from the novel of that name. A 'noble' builder called Christy Moran helped him restore it and Barry rewarded him by naming a character in *A Long, Long Way* and *On Blueberry Hill* after him. There is a carpenter's pencil on his writing desk, a sturdy tool, whose lead looks unbreakable. Two of his poodles come bounding in, not the fluffy toy variety but muscular standard poodles, as big as Labradors. Originally they were hunting dogs, duck hounds. Similarly, you sense there is body armour beneath Barry's velvet jacket.

Barry's work is adorned with saving graces, life's small joys and mercies. His friend Viv Roche made a seaweed sculpture of his line from *The Secret Scripture* – 'The world is indeed beautiful.' Barry spontaneously finishes the sentence: 'And if we were another creature than man we might be continuously happy in it.'

No mean stylist himself, he reveres Eoin McNamee as 'probably the best prose stylist of his generation, just as Roy Foster is the best non-fiction prose stylist.' Of his own style, he has said: 'Lyric language is my lexicon.'

'At the end of *Annie Dunne,* she says "although we are like the spider in his web, nevertheless something of us ever after will remain". The thing is, Martin, it won't because nobody cares about two old ladies, so I wrote *Annie Dunne* to make that true.'

He doesn't see his family saga as a national project. 'You'd have to be some mighty healer to heal history, wouldn't you?'

He likes to notice and salvage lost words like 'sockdologer', from the mid-1900s, which means a lucky punch at the end of boxing match.

Tom Kettle, the 'old policeman with a buckled heart', reminded me of Thomas Dunne. 'I didn't think of that until very recently,' he says, 'it is almost a carbon copy.' Kettle is named after the poet whose line gave *The Secret Scripture* its title. The real-life Kettle, an Irish patriot who died a British soldier in the First World War, with his conflicted allegiances and tragic fate, could be a Barry character. 'He was the best talker of his generation. Here we are back to tectonic pressure. When put under that pressure, he wrote this poem there is nothing to match, "To My Daughter Betty". "Know that we fools …"'

A Long Long Way was almost titled 'The Secret Scripture' but Barry felt it was a bit grandiose for Willie Dunne, so he kept it, 'then it just seemed quite natural for a novel about a lady putting stuff under floorboards'.

'The quote for *Whereabouts* is "he who is not written into the book of life shall be cast into the lake of fire". I have had that anxiety. Roseanne says, if you don't have anecdotes associated with your name then you are destined to be just a cipher in a family Bible.

'It's a reluctance on my part to allow Aunt Annie to pass away with nothing. I've thought about them every day. There is something in them of almost infinite value, the person no one will give credit to. I'm interested in writing them into the book of life. That is not high-art ambition, more an anxiety that they not be lost.

'Once you get to the point of waiting for Roseanne or Tom Kettle or Annie or Winona, then you've got to get yourself out of the picture. It's not a conversation; *they* are going to talk. I have to be their amanuensis. Any movement, even a physical movement, can move the conversation from where it is heading. I haven't written the work, I have heard it, singing in my genes and in my blood. My grandfather would put a hubcap in the garden for the birds to draw them. You have to sit as still as you can or they will fly out of the garden.'

It's part of the art of the interview too, to know when to shut up, to sit back and listen.

'The unprompted things that arise naturally in the mind are not the same as things prompted by questions. It's the private mind, not the prompted mind. To reach into the private mind of someone who never technically existed is so outrageous, it's worth doing. You're going back to the 1850s to find a private mind. What could be more elusive? I fished for salmon in the Moy for fifty years. If you see a salmon the fisherman says you might as well go home because then you won't catch one. Don't for a minute think I am not immensely proud that I was granted time to stand under dripping leaves and know how to stand.'

Barry told me before that he had visited Joseph Conrad's grave and that Axel Heyst, protagonist of Conrad's novel *Victory*, was his favourite character.

'He was living a fictional version of the life I thought I was living when I read the book. At the end, having suffered attacks, he set the house on fire and the two are burning on the bed. In that unreconstituted age when I was trying to put everything back into place, you did feel you were in a burning environment. Also, what I noticed about Conrad and Thomas Hardy is you only had to read three lines and you knew who was writing. I thought it was in me to write with a recognizable signature like Conrad, whereas the tradition at the time was a different sort of absence, language unadorned, impersonal, neutral. I was never interested in that. I loved archaic language. The reason I can exult in the broken language of *Days Without End* is I can see it as archaic language worth retrieving. It is an undertaking towards music. If writing hadn't been invented I'd have to put it out on the air, memorize it. I don't feel like a writer, I feel like a rememberer of things that never happened.'

Barry is not afraid to visit dark places with his work. *On Blueberry Hill* is set in Mountjoy Jail and he staged it there. 'Talk about going home. Every day I walked up along the Royal Canal, I had a great curiosity about the people in Mountjoy. I thought, *why have we put these people in there as a society?* Is that the best answer when people are living on the clippings of tin?

'Next day they said to their teacher, "it's obvious Sebastian was in here". That is such an accolade to your instincts, to the very unlikely outcome of your ignorance. I have wondered what it's like, and I have wondered what it's like to be a young Lakota woman. The next stage of my wonderment is to try to imagine what it is. The feeling of communion was so lovely.'

Again, as laureate, he visited the Central Mental Hospital in Dundrum.

'I can never forget the feeling of discomfort and foreboding walking up that avenue. It's where they put you by reason of insanity. If you wanted to find a room of ostensibly lost people who were living with the radiance of an Aquinas, that was the place. It was the grateful realization that these cancelled people were of greater value as citizens than myself.

'Under great pressure, seemingly discounted people are Homer, in the tectonic pressure of their lives they are the greatest poets who ever lived, the tickertape that comes out of their mouths is of the highest import. I think it has been worth doing for fifty years.

'It would be hard to underestimate the incoherence of my life. When I wake up, I have to talk to myself for half an hour to put myself in a place that doesn't feel uncomfortable, panicky. If I am anything I am that, the dispeller of the enemy, the black dog. Although, of course, I own and love three black poodles.'

Barry was born in Dublin in 1955. A novelist, playwright and poet, he has twice won the Costa Book of the Year Award, for The Secret Scripture *(2008) and* Days Without End *(2016). He has also won the Walter Scott Prize for Historical Fiction twice, for* Days Without End *and* On Canaan's Side *(2011).* The Secret Scripture *won the James Tait Black Memorial Prize and was shortlisted for the Booker Prize, as was* A Long, Long Way *(2005). The latter was Dublin's One City One Book choice in 2007. His play* The Steward of Christendom *(1995) won the Christopher Ewart-Biggs Memorial Prize. He was Laureate for Irish Fiction 2018–2021.*

COLIN BATEMAN

13 July 1996, The Irish Post

'I was upstairs with a girl I shouldn't have been upstairs with when my wife whispered in my ear, 'You have 24 hours to move out.' – *Divorcing Jack*. 'Miller was twenty-eight when his father died, too old to be considered an orphan in anyone's eyes but his own.' – *Cycle of Violence*. 'Peace had settled over the city like the skin on a rancid custard. Everybody wanted it, just not in that form. The forecast remained for rain, with widespread terrorism.' – *Of Wee Sweetie Mice and Men*.

Colin Bateman has an ex-journalist's belief in the effectiveness of an attention-grabbing introduction. Throw in a stand-up comic's flair for the one-liner and you've got a combustible combination. With remarkable economy, he sets the scene and simultaneously sets out his stall as a comic thriller writer of wit and pace.

The critics haven't been backwards in coming forward with the compliments either, usually in the form of unlikely connections. 'The 39 Steps rewritten for the '90s by Roddy Doyle' (*Time Out*). 'The Day of the Jackal out of the Marx Brothers' (*Sunday Press*). 'Will do for Belfast and South Armagh what Bram Stoker did for Transylvania' (*RTÉ Guide*).

But Bateman is also a word-of-mouth success, a cult author. Once discovered, you want to tell your friends about him: 'Look what I've found.'

Northern Ireland's Troubles and sectarianism have brought out the worst in a lot of people. But along with the senseless violence and the overdeveloped sense of history is a sassy sense of humour more closely related to the slap on the back of the head than the tickle under the arm. This is the rich vein that Bateman dips into with such relish.

Divorcing Jack introduced us to Dan Starkey, a Belfast journalist who likes his whiskey like his marriage, on the rocks. His drinking, a hangover from student days, leads him off the straight and narrow and he becomes enmeshed in an unlikely and yet believable tale of intrigue and low politics. Forget Russia. The North is a riddle wrapped in an enigma on your doorstep.

Bateman's second novel, *Cycle of Violence*, features another journalist, Miller, sent by his editor from the Big Smoke to small-town Crossmaheart to replace another reporter who has disappeared – to no one's great surprise, since Crossmaheart is a notoriously fatal place to ask questions. Of course, Miller not only asks questions, he also gets drunk and starts stepping out with his presumed deceased predecessor's girlfriend. His 'investigations' lead him to a Protestant pub where he gets so drunk he fails to stand for the Queen at the end of the night. Cue pool cues. Intoxicated again on Catholic premises, he approaches the bar. 'Fuck the Pope,' he slurs. The landlord asks him to repeat himself and reason reasserts itself. 'Vodka and Coke.'

The terrifically prolific Bateman has just brought out his third book in two years, *Of Wee Sweetie Mice and Men*. Dan Starkey is back on the case, but Bateman has begun to flex his imaginative muscles, and the action soon shifts from the mean streets and green fields of Norn Iron to New York and Cape Cod.

Starkey has been hired to write a book on Fat Boy McMaster, a hopeless heavyweight with more paunch than punch, whose manager has wangled him a St Patrick's Day fight in the Big Apple with Mike Tyson. Of course, no sooner do Sharkey and the Great White Dope set foot in Manhattan than Fat Boy blunders through a press conference and manages to insult the city's Black population. Murder and mayhem ensue 'from Belfast to the Bowery, from the sweat of the gym to the salt spray of a less than peaceful whale-watching cruise'.

Starkey, meanwhile, is trying to pick up the pieces of his broken marriage. But he might as well be wearing boxing gloves and suffering from concussion for all the success he has.

Bateman was born in 1962 in Newtownards, County Down, and lives in nearby Bangor, an affluent Protestant town where the divide is between the have-yachts and the have-nots. He joined the local paper, the *County Down Spectator*, straight from school. 'I started writing at seventeen about punk rock and Bangor. That's almost a contradiction in terms. We are all very nice and polite down in Bangor.' (In fact, Bangor rates a mention in Stiff Little Fingers' punk classic 'Alternative Ulster' but let's not quibble.)

Bateman's first article was on the hypocrisy of local shops banning the Sex Pistols' *Never Mind the Bollocks* album, only to sneak it back onto the shelves a few weeks later. He hadn't written the name out in full, in deference to the imagined sensibilities of his editor, a middle-aged Sunday school teacher, but she insisted on it. 'That encouraged me to be a bit more adventurous. It led directly to the style of journalism I wrote.' A fictitious, satirical gossip column resulted. 'Because the column was so successful, people were always telling me to write a book, so I did.'

He thought of the title first, then wrote a couple of chapters. 'I painted myself into corners and then I had to work out how to get out again, which seems to have gone down well because people who are reading it tend to end up in corners as well.'

Bateman's journalism, meanwhile, was earning him recognition. He covered the good works of a local charity in Uganda. 'It was an eye-opener being out there because you tend to think of poor Northern Ireland with all its troubles. But those were real troubles. What we have is Disneyland in comparison.'

He won a three-month scholarship to Oxford University. 'It was supposed to be three months' research on Uganda to write a big paper, but I'd never been to university so I managed to squeeze in three years of socializing, spent a lot of money and got very, very drunk. It was supposed to be a big bridge-building exercise, making connections to do you the rest of your life. But I think I blew up more bridges than the Germans during the war. But it was fun.'

Bateman didn't foresee Starkey becoming a serial character. 'I liked the character, but I had no ambitions for my writing. You have an idea sometimes that some of the lines are funny. Occasionally you have a laugh at the typewriter. But most of the time you don't know if the humour works. I didn't think *Divorcing Jack* was any good. Certainly, the initial response wasn't good. It took a year to get it published. I persisted because I'd spent so long writing it and because my wife had read it and thought it was brilliant. It was my wife who told me to send it to HarperCollins. A lot of it's down to luck. There must be a lot of good books in the slush pile that never get published. Luck is the one constant in my writing career.'

Indeed, HarperCollins have since stopped accepting unsolicited manuscripts, a case surely of shutting the stable door after a potential Grand National winner has wandered in off the street.

Bateman pulls no punches when it comes to the bigots and the paramilitaries that have made Northern Ireland such a grand wee province. But he doesn't live in fear of the tap on the shoulder or the muzzle in the kneecap.

'I don't live in an area where I'm likely to encounter people who would be involved. People reading the books might think I have this in-depth knowledge of how the IRA and UVF work, but I don't. I make it up. Anyone who lives in Northern Ireland knows as much about it as me.'

You wonder what keeps Bateman banged up in Bangor. He has a good time at his Belfast characters' expense as they flounder abroad in New York, opening their mouth only to put their foot in it. Of course he's having a go at political correctness. But isn't he also revealing the narrowness of the province, where a Black face is a novelty? He is understandably disenchanted with metropolitan London and its TV folk, who want to analyse everything and have him explain the background of his characters. But wouldn't he be more at home in a more multicultural society? 'I travel,' he says, 'but without speaking, apart from ordering Diet Pepsi in a hundred languages. I'm more of an observer than a communicator. I communicate through the books. My beady eye rules over all.'

What does he make of Northern Ireland? 'It's difficult to say. I'm not a great thinker about what goes into the books. I don't think about politics consciously and I don't think about religion. I don't care if there's a united Ireland. It comes out in the characters automatically though, so maybe that's subconscious.'

But is it a nice wee province peopled by decent skins or …?

'Oh, we're all perfectly decent. We just like to murder people once in a while. I think it's a tiny minority. We've seen, in places like Bosnia, mass psychotic behaviour. I suppose in Northern Ireland we should be pleased that it is confined to only a very small percentage of the population. There is no general support for "let's go out and kill some Catholics or Protestants". I feel there should be a new series of leaders emerging who are a bit more sensible.'

Bateman sees himself as a commercial writer producing hard-boiled work that doesn't need an Arts Council grant to survive. He is certainly terrifically prolific. A *Divorcing Jack* screenplay is already written for the BBC. Another screenplay, *Bring Me the Head of Oliver Plunkett*, a fast-paced funny caper movie about the theft of Oliver Plunkett's head from Drogheda Cathedral, is written and ready to go. His next novel, *Empire State*, involves the taking hostage of the American president in the Empire State Building. And then comes the third Dan Starkey novel, *Turbulent Priests*. 'It's set on Rathlin Island when religious mania breaks out. I always wanted to do Dan Starkey every other book. It means I can play around between books.'

His career as a fiction writer has already forced him to cull his column as his jokes had a new home, and soon he plans to give up journalism completely. Isn't he afraid of losing daily contact with people? 'I'll miss the interaction and the one-liners. I can interact with my one-year-old son, but you don't get too many good lines from him.'

Bateman was born in Newtownards, County Down in 1962. The first of ten novels to feature Dan Starkey, his debut Divorcing Jack *(1994) won a Betty Trask Award and was adapted into a 1998 film starring David Thewlis.* Cycle of Violence *(1995), one of nine stand-alone novels, was made into a film,* Crossmaheart. *He has also written two novels based on his BBC television series* Murphy's Law, *several screenplays and a series of books for children.*

RONAN BENNETT

20 January 2024, The Irish Times

Eighteen years after the publication of his previous novel *Zugzwang*, Ronan Bennett returns with *Jaq: A* Top Boy *Story*. As literary hiatuses go, it's a long one, but, as the book's subtitle suggests, he has not been idle.

Jaq is a novelization of the fifth and final series of his acclaimed crime drama, which aired last September, the programme revived by Netflix in 2019 with the support of the rapper Drake after Channel 4 dropped the show despite two successful series in 2011 and 2013.

Set in a predominantly Black housing estate in the inner London borough of Hackney, where Bennett has lived for more than twenty years, the show revolves around the violent activities of a drug gang but always makes room for other issues such as discrimination, deprivation, gentrification and the threat of deportation, as well as the characters' complex personal lives. Jasmine Jobson was twice nominated for a Bafta for her powerful portrayal of Jaq, a ruthless yet ultimately caring drug dealer whose gender and sexuality made her, in her creator's words, 'an outsider in a world of outsiders'.

But why wait until the final series of his hit TV series to turn it into a novel? And why focus on Jaq rather than on the main characters, the gang leaders Dushane and Sully? Did *Top Boy*'s ending free him somehow?

'Very much,' says Bennett, who is speaking from the Spanish city of Cádiz, where he has a second home – one of the perks of a hugely successful writing career.

'I held on to the novelization rights right from the start, which indicates I had in mind for a long time to do something in fiction based on *Top Boy*. I was excited about the character of Jaq, interested to explore that world from the point of view of a young woman, gay, in the inner circle but not quite.'

He has no time for those who say writers should stick to their own experiences, 'as if being one thing precludes you from writing about another'.

'It is reductive and dismaying for a writer to be told you can't write this because it is not your experience, that I can only write about the experience of a straight man growing up in my generation in Belfast. It would be the end of art.

'Obviously, I'm not from that world. To treat that world and the people in it with respect, you have to listen carefully, not trample over their world and impose your sensibilities. Try to immerse yourself in that world, find out what's said, felt, believed, what dreams exist.

'How do you do it? It's listening when they are talking to you directly but also when they are talking to other people. It's not hard. It's what journalists and writers do all the time, find someone who knows things, knows the history. When I hear people say it's thoroughly researched, no one should expect brownie points for doing the basics. But once we're up and running, any writer has to feel completely free to write what they want.'

Witnessing a young boy dealing near his local supermarket piqued Bennett's interest in the subject, but he needed the help of a respected local man, Gerry Jackson, his personal trainer, to vouch for him and introduce him to people who gave him the insights he needed to create the fictional world of the Summerhouse estate. Jackson became a script consultant for the series.

But there are parallels between Bennett's experience of the police as a Belfast republican and that of Black youths in London. One character in *Jaq* describes the Metropolitan Police as 'just like another London gang'.

At the premiere of a previous season of *Top Boy*, he said he was inspired by a notorious photograph of a 'No Blacks, No Dogs, No Irish' sign in an English boarding-house window and by Phil Lynott's 'More Blacks, More Dogs, More Irish' T-shirt.

'I came from a community that was demonized, discriminated against,' he said. 'When I came to London the Black, brown community was equally treated with suspicion.

'*Jaq* was written during and after the controversies that have engulfed the Met in the last couple of years to do with sexual violence, corruption. If you've lived a bit you'll have a perspective on the Met, know it had a very troubled history – the corruption of Scotland Yard and the flying squad.'

The author had his own run-ins with the Met, of which more anon.

There has always been a strong Irish aspect to *Top Boy*, with Lisa Dwan, Barry Keoghan and Brian Gleeson playing significant roles. Sully's real name is Gerard Sullivan, hinting at his part-Irish heritage. 'I would like to have explored that. When you get ten hours you think you'd be able to go off on tangents, but the world we created was so dense and rich there just was not the time to explore everything.'

Mandy is a community activist whose social conscience was formed in prison. She tries to interest Jaq in the writings of Bernadette Devlin as well as Black heroes such as Angela Y. Davis and persuades her to join a demonstration against the planned deportation of her friend Kieran.

'I wanted it not to be just about gangs and guns. I wanted that other side. The scene in the final season and the book of stopping the removal of Kieran was based on a real event that took place in Glasgow in 2021. That was a rare win for community activism against the establishment.'

Bennett's return to fiction would be unremarkable except that he has written two stand-out contemporary Irish novels. *The Catastrophist*, from 1998, a love story gone sour set against the backdrop of Patrice Lumumba's Congolese independence movement, was shortlisted for the Whitbread Prize and drew comparisons to Graham Greene. *Havoc, in Its Third Year*, from 2004, about a good man's struggle to do the right thing in seventeenth-century Puritan England, won the Irish Novel of the Year award and bears comparison to Hilary Mantel's *Wolf Hall* trilogy.

In the same way that Joseph O'Connor sees *Star of the Sea* as the real start of his career as a mature writer, Bennett acknowledges that his first two novels, *The Second Prison*, from 1991, and *Overthrown by Strangers*, from a year later, while full of promise, were apprentice works. 'For sure. I didn't really know what I was doing with the first two books. Some debut novels are amazing. I wasn't in that category; I had to learn. The first two were written quickly – six months each – but it wasn't so much the time spent writing; it was the time spent thinking.'

Zugzwang, from 2006, was another historical thriller; set in St Petersburg in 1914, it tackled chess, psychoanalysis and anti-Semitism. But Bennett's growing success as a screenwriter meant his fiction was sidelined.

'There have been a couple of failed attempts. Honestly, there are enough mediocre novels in the world for me to add to that list. I wasn't satisfied with what I was writing. It is a depressing truth that most artistic endeavour is mediocre. It's painful because you want to produce something special. If I suspect what I'm writing isn't special then I can't proceed.'

I first interviewed Bennett in 1993 when the BBC screened *Love Lies Bleeding*, a prescient Troubles drama starring Mark Rylance as a released IRA prisoner struggling to navigate a post-ceasefire landscape, and again the following year when Channel 4 screened *A Man You Don't Meet Every Day*, a London-Irish drama set to a Pogues soundtrack. His first feature film, *A Further Gesture* (1997), starring Brendan Gleeson and Stephen Rea, also had a Troubles theme. David Trimble tried to have his 2001 series *Rebel Heart*, a major BBC drama about the Irish War of Independence loosely based on Ernie O'Malley's life, banned.

But Bennett's career has gone from strength to strength, and his range has expanded. His TV series include *Fields of Gold* (2002), written with the then-*Guardian* editor, Alan Rusbridger, about GM crops; *Hidden* (2011), a thriller starring Philip Glenister; and *Gunpowder* (2017), with Kit Harrington as Robert Catesby, who with Guy Fawkes conspired to blow up the British parliament. Feature films include *Face* (1997), a superb heist movie starring Robert Carlyle; the prison-break comedy *Lucky Break* (2001); *The Hamburg Cell* (2004), about the 9/11 bombers; and *Public Enemies* (2009), starring Johnny Depp as the bank robber John Dillinger.

His multimillion-euro remake of *The Day of the Jackal* as a series for Sky, starring Eddie Redmayne and directed by the Armagh-born film-maker Brian Kirk, is due out at the end of the year. Like *Top Boy*, it has a strong Irish element, Bennett says.

His current project could not be more topical. 'Before the events of 7 October I'd already started work on a script about Palestine. I wanted to do a drama showing the story from the Palestinian side. I've found whatever tiny thing you do, anyone who shows any interest or solidarity, they say thank you, because Palestinians feel so abandoned.'

The solo art of novel writing is a blessed break from screenwriting by committee, he says.

'Writing the novel after fifteen years of screenplays was unbelievably pleasant and stress-free. My publisher Jamie Byng completely believed in it. I wasn't sure *Top Boy*'s hardcore fans would be interested in a novel, and people who didn't know *Top Boy*, why would they read it? It took him probably two to three years to convince me that I was wrong and he was right. Time will tell, but I'm glad he persuaded me.

'These days with big-budget screenplays, executives now crawl all over the scripts. Everyone has an opinion. As one of my agents put it, this is the only business in which people with no accomplishments can tell people with lots of accomplishments what to do. I get far more notes now than I did when I started thirty years ago. Having lots of people giving their opinions on something is not a recipe for success.'

Bennett turned sixty-eight this week but looks at least a decade younger, although with his post-pandemic beard he looks more grizzled than chiselled these days. 'I am grateful to be grey-bearded and grey-haired. Honestly, just to be here still when so many of those we love are not. I say, give me those birthdays,' he says.

His wife, Georgina Henry, then-deputy editor of *The Guardian*, died of cancer ten years ago next month, in February 2014, three months after my wife, Nikki, died. We had kept in touch over the years, so we met up the next time I was back in London, to reflect on our shared experience. Some of the most powerful passages in *Jaq*, and in *Top Boy* generally, are reflections on grief and loss.

'Losing someone is like being in a car crash,' Sully tells a bereaved Jaq. 'You survive but you walk away with a limp. You're gonna have that limp for the rest of your life.'

I recognize the sentiment, but Bennett tells me they are in fact my own words. Writers, even in mourning, are magpies. 'That's what writers do: everything goes into the mix. Obviously, the grief passages in *Jaq* come directly from Georgina's death.'

'Ask me what time it is. I don't know. Ask me what day it is. I don't know. Ask me what year it is. I don't know. I don't know if it's day or night. I don't know if the sky is blue. I don't know what colour the leaves on the trees are. I don't know left from right. I don't know up from down. I don't know anything. I'm numb.'

He recalls reading a grief memoir in which the author says not ten minutes go by that they don't think about their lost love but people don't believe them. 'Ten years on, it's pretty close to ten minutes,' he says. 'It is a bit like being hit over the head with a hammer, but you know you need to become unconcussed for the sake of your children.'

His son, Finn, is an actor who stars alongside Jodie Foster in *True Detective: Night Country*. His daughter, Molly, has just graduated from Trinity College Dublin. It delighted him that she studied in Ireland, but 'it was entirely her decision. I'm not a helicopter parent. I've just tried to be present and calm and thoughtful or kind. Their mother was more than half Irish, though in person she couldn't be more English. Obviously I'm very keen for them to explore that side of their heritage. Molly was a bit shocked by the attitude of some students in the South to Northerners, not seeing them as Irish; she just thought of the Irish as one people.

'There was a wonderful Irish ambassador in London, Bobby McDonagh, who used to do these embassy parties, and someone from the South called me a plastic Paddy. It was shocking and hurtful, but it's part of a larger phenomenon that saddens every Northerner.'

The conflict in the North has shaped Bennett's life, even though he left Belfast in the mid-1970s and has never moved back. He has worked on a film script that covers the period from the Battle of the Bogside to Bloody Sunday and said recently that he felt the time might be right to tell the story of the Troubles in a novel, but I wonder whether he has considered writing a memoir, given his own remarkable life.

'I would have to convince myself that it wasn't an exercise in narcissism, that it would have some value for a potential reader,' he says. 'At the minute I'm not sure what that would be.'

He co-authored *Stolen Years: Before and After Guildford*, the 1990 memoir of Paul Hill, one of the Guildford Four wrongly convicted of the Guildford and Woolwich bombings. Bennett himself was wrongly convicted of the 1974 murder of an RUC inspector, William Elliott, during an Official IRA bank robbery in Belfast. He was cleared in 1975 after a formative year in Long Kesh, during which the prison was burned down by republican inmates, which he recounted in 'Fire and Rain', a BBC radio documentary from 1994. His status as a former convict cuts little ice back home. 'I do get teased back in Belfast. "Ronan, you were hardly in long enough to have a shower, a shave, a shite and a smoke." Typical Belfast humour.'

He moved to England, mixing in radical, anarchist circles. In 1978 police raided his London flat and found a copy of *The Anarchist Cookbook*, wigs, false moustaches, balaclavas and false documents. He was charged with 'conspiring to commit crimes unknown against persons unknown in places unknown', then spent twenty months on remand before successfully conducting his own defence at the Old Bailey, sitting in T-shirt and jeans alongside the barristers Michael Mansfield, Helena Kennedy and Geoffrey Robertson, who were representing other defendants in the case. This fed into his debut novel, *The Second Prison*, from 1991.

He graduated with a first in history from King's College London, where he met Georgina, of Irish Protestant background, born in Aden to a future colonel in the British army. He was awarded a PhD on crime and law enforcement in seventeenth-century England, which would inform *Havoc, in its Third Year*; that same year he was hired by Jeremy Corbyn, the future leader of the British Labour Party, as a parliamentary researcher focusing on the Guildford Four case before MPs voted to rescind his security pass.

He is disappointed at the way the world has gone in recent years but not disillusioned, he insists. The Israeli onslaught on Gaza particularly appals him. 'Some international solidarity at government level would be useful here. I'm not the only Irish person to criticize an Irish man in the White House [Joe Biden] for a lack of solidarity. What he has failed to understand from the history of his own people about colonialism. These are dark times, no question.'

The British Labour Party's treatment of Corbyn, his old boss, disgusts him, reminding him of Chris Mullin's novel *A Very British Coup*.

'Had Jeremy and John [McDonnell] won, there would have been real change and that is why the establishment in the Labour Party as well as outside rallied against him, as they knew he was an existential threat. What the party did to Jeremy is unforgivable.'

When we spoke in 1994, he described the British position post-ceasefire as 'the beginning of the long goodbye'. Have things moved more glacially than he expected?

'Honestly, I don't think I expected to see a united Ireland before I was seventy. Decolonization is a process; it's not going to happen instantly. I'm a supporter of a united Ireland, and it has to be done with consent. I can see increasing signs for hope there. People from the Protestant tradition are looking increasingly North—South rather than east—west, but there's a long way to go. It won't be easy. But the sooner the conversation starts in earnest in the South among the political leadership the better, because they are just kicking the can down the road otherwise.'

Bennett, born in Belfast in 1956, lives in London and Cádiz. He is the author of six novels but is best known as a screenwriter (The Day of the Jackal, Top Boy, MobLand, Public Enemies). *His debut novel* The Second Prison *(1991) was shortlisted for the 1991* Irish Times/*Aer Lingus Prize.* Overthrown by Strangers *(1992) was followed by* The Catastrophist *(1998), shortlisted for the Whitbread Novel Award.* Havoc, in Its Third Year *(2004) won the Irish Novel of the Year award.* Zugzwang *(2006) was first published serially in the* Observer. Jaq *(2025) was based on a character from his TV series* Top Boy. *He co-wrote, with Paul Hill,* Stolen Years: Before and After Guildford *(1990).*

MAEVE BINCHY

June 2008, Saga Magazine

When Maeve Binchy turned sixty the author, whose bestsellers reflect her positive outlook, did something that seemed totally out of character – she gave up.

She had written her last novel, she announced, though it wasn't storylines she was running out of but stamina. She had just returned from a nine-city US tour, exhausted and lame, yet conscious that wherever she went, Stephen King had been the week before, because in publishing promotion is almost as important as prose.

'I thought, *I'm too tired for this, I've breathing difficulties, I can't do it anymore*,' she recalls, 'but they won't allow me to continue writing and not do the publicity. It would be unfair to take their money and not try to help them sell the book. It was a pity because I liked meeting people, I'm not shy.'

So Maeve, a well-brought-up barrister's daughter, was doing the honourable thing by falling on her pen. Of course, her publishers persuaded her that her failing health exempted her from touring.

In her sixty-ninth year, ever the improver, she has just published *The Maeve Binchy Writers' Club*, a self-help guide for budding authors, and her fifteenth novel, *Heart and Soul*, is due out in October.

The author has just been sent the blurb for the book in her US publisher's catalogue and wants it changed. 'The emphasis is wrong as it sounds like a loser's book: "Clara is a cardiologist who is pushed into a small siding to run a heart clinic and how she assuages her disappointment." In fact it is a terribly cheerful book about telling people how to live with heart disease, that's what her clinic is about, they come in sometimes despairing and leave light-hearted. She recognizes the work she's doing there is as important as anything she might have done in an operating theatre.'

Maeve also has a film adaptation out this month, *How About You?*, starring Vanessa Redgrave, Imelda Staunton, Brenda Fricker and Joss Ackland as four bad-tempered grouches in an old people's hotel. 'It's lovely, very touching,' she says. 'Brenda and Imelda play these dysfunctional sisters, Joss is a retired drunken judge, and Vanessa Redgrave is a retired chorus girl. She is seventy in real life but still has a gorgeous face.'

The writers' guide is based on a lecture series she gave to an adult education college in Dublin. 'They got a marvellous badge at the end, which says "I went all the way with Maeve,"' she laughs. 'Adult education is great, it gives people a second chance. That's one of the things I like about America, people never think they're past it, they start studying at sixty.'

Maeve has discovered through her fiction this truth about herself, that she is more of a moralist than she thought. In her novels, the good tend to get rewarded, but only those who help themselves.

Happiness has to be earned, she believes, and good fortune should be repaid with generosity. So to offset the indulgence of dining out on oysters, Binchy will stop off en route to drop off some books at Oxfam. It is not Catholic guilt, for she is not a believer, but that of a scampi socialist, who has done so well out of life that she feels obliged to throw some of her catch back into the sea.

'I've had such a good deal,' she says. 'I didn't expect that I would fall in love and be happily married or that I'd stay so friendly with my brother and sisters. I thought my life would be a series of fancying the wrong men, that, like a heat-seeking missile entering a room, I would find myself drawn to the one most likely to do the maximum destruction. I didn't think that when I wrote books they'd be a success. I never thought anybody but Irish people would be interested in them, yet I have thirty-eight foreign publishers.' Today, three of her fourteen novels are in the top four places on Eason's list of all-time bestsellers.

Maeve lives happily ever after in her native Dalkey, one of Dublin's most delightful seaside suburbs, with her husband of thirty years, Gordon Snell. Her novel *Light A Penny Candle* broke the record for a publishing deal for a first novel, fetching £52,000. Her publisher told her to sit down before he broke the news. He was so thrilled Maeve had to ask whether he or she got the money. 'I'm very much afraid,' he said, 'that you do.'

So she paid off the mortgage on the idyllic cottage whose repayments she had been struggling to meet. When Oprah picked *Tara Road* for her book club in 1999, her fame and fortune multiplied.

She might live in Polly Villa, next door to Anna Villa, but she is no Pollyanna, writing feel-good fiction with Hollywood endings. In fact, Hollywood had to rewrite *Circle of Friends* to give it a happy ending. (She subscribes to the Elmore Leonard philosophy: 'My book, their film.')

'I think I write about quite serious things,' she says. 'People say, sort of patting you on the head, oh that's a Maeve Binchy novel, there'll be no sex and it'll all turn out all right. But there's plenty of sex, just not described move by move. In so many modern novels every twenty pages the clothes have to be peeled off and the plunging and thrusting have to begin.

'But things that are the result of sex, like betrayals, separations, bringing up children on your own, jealousy, envy, restlessness, all of these are in my books. I don't think I am a Pollyanna. I try to face everything. There's abortions, divorce, murder. I don't live in cloud cuckoo land.'

In her personal life, however, she is an optimist, a positive thinker. Her cup is not half-empty, or even half-full, it runneth over.

'Perhaps,' she says, 'there *is* too much of the Pollyanna about me, that I am so good-tempered, for I am after all a fat, lame, breathless, ex-school teacher with no children – because I would have liked children – whose parents died young, with no future because I don't believe in angels.

'You'd think I could be quite unhappy in many ways but I have been very lucky. I think I was dealt a good hand. I have happy genes.'

Maeve began to lose her faith while living on a kibbutz in Israel in 1963.

'I lost my faith in Jerusalem, of all awful places to lose it. I was in the room of the Last Supper and I said to a soldier with his rifle trained on no man's land, "was that really the place of the Last Supper?" He said, "yes". I said, "but it's just a cave". He removed his eye from his target for a moment and said, "what did you expect, a Renaissance table set for thirteen?" I said to him, "so none of it's true, then, the angels and the shepherds?" The soldier said, "I don't know, lady."

'There must be something, though. We can't believe it all ends in the grave. A very nice thing happened to me when my father died very suddenly. About 40 per cent of people say the wrong thing, 49 per cent say sort of the right thing and one person says something that makes a difference for ever. This person said, "a marvellous spirit like that can't be just extinguished because they are dead. He'll be alive as long as you remember him." That was a help.'

One of Maeve's sisters died recently. 'It was terribly hard. It felt so unfair, my sister was a psychiatrist and she was so good at helping people with troubled marriages. A lot of friends told me she had treated them, and I never knew. That cheered me up. But I can't look at my wedding movie now, it's such a memento mori, so many people in it have died.'

Not believing in an afterlife where the poor and downtrodden will inherit the earth makes her more charitable, she says.

'I think if you don't believe in an afterlife you'll be a bit nicer because you can't think it'll all be sorted out in the end. If you don't believe in the Sermon on the Mount, blessed are the meek because they will see God, if you think, cursed are all these people, then you try and do something about it. You don't pass the buck to God. So I am more generous. I saved for a blender to make soups, we put a pound aside each week, then we saw an ad in the paper for cancer patients who couldn't eat anything solid so needed a blender. I was so shocked I took mine to a cancer charity shop still in its packaging.'

She doesn't dwell on her own health. '"How are you?" is a greeting, not a question,' she says. She is no longer fit for long flights but is not one for self-pity. 'I don't want to go on because it's so boring and people write in telling you either to pray to Padre Pio or to have open-heart surgery, and I have plenty of good people telling me what's wrong with my heart.

'I've had several friends die recently, it annoys me very much, just as we're all getting sensible. We've got it all worked out, we've become mellow and nice to each other, but our bodies are letting us down. If I ran the world we'd get a bit more athletic and filled with energy as we got older. Eighty is the new sixty. It's only our bodies have got old.'

Maeve's career in journalism began when her father sent one of her letters describing her foreign travels to *The Irish Times*, who published it. She became its women's editor but never burned her bra or joined in the excitement of importing contraceptives from Belfast by train for fear of mortifying her widowed father.

She and Gordon, a broadcaster, decided they wanted to leave something more permanent behind, so she took up fiction and he became a children's author.

Her love letters were not so successful, however. When she was sixteen she used to write every fortnight to Marlon Brando, advising him to leave that awful Movita for her, only to get a note back thanking her for her loyalty to his fan club.

'Eventually my friend put me straight,' says Maeve, 'that if he did come to Ireland I would have to take him to Dalkey. That silenced me because Dalkey was so dreary in those days. Of course, now if the poor man was alive and in Ireland he'd *live* in Dalkey.'

He would be neighbours with Chris de Burgh, Bono, The Edge, Lisa Stansfield and Neil Jordan. 'My visitors can't believe it. They think there must be some kind of salon here. There may be but I'm not invited,' says Maeve.

But growing up, she says, her friends used to feel sorry for her living there. 'Dalkey was the absolute boondocks. I used to pray that my father, who was a barrister, would become a judge so that we could live on Baggot Street.

'I often wish my parents could have lived, not to see my huge, embarrassing, vulgar success – that wouldn't have been what they would have loved so much – but to see their children still living in Dalkey and Killiney, happily married and successful in their jobs.'

Today, she wouldn't swap her home for anywhere. The books have paid for an architect to create a light-filled space upstairs where the couple write, and a flat behind so they can have friends to stay without having them for breakfast. 'This was our idea of a house to grow old in. Americans have a very horrible expression, "is this your final home?" But it is our final home. When we can't manage the stairs we can put a lift in.'

They are also building a room for books. She buys up her remainders at 10c each, 'the Americans print so many', so that she can sign them and send them off for charity events. 'Years ago I wrote *Maeve's Diary*, an absolute disaster, nobody bought it. Fred Hanna hates me telling this story as he says he spends most of his life making me a fortune, paying for that Mercedes outside the front door, but he had ordered thousands of these books and only sold five, so he filled his window with the books priced 5p. I was mortified. I asked my sister Joan to buy them up. She went in and asked for a hundred. They went off to fetch boxes of them from downstairs but she said, "no, I want the ones in the window".'

Her journalism background is a great help as a writer, she believes, because a blank page holds no terrors. 'Columns do not appear in the papers saying the muse didn't attack Maeve today. The discipline helps. I will start a new book on the 1st of June, I will sit here and I will do ten pages a day and I won't leave till that is done.

'My new book is really about the new Ireland, it's about a Polish girl's attempts to fit in to society here. There's quite a few more – I hope not token – immigrants.' She was startled when she first saw the Polish-language section in the *Evening Herald* but now even her books are imported in Polish for the community here and she insists on going to Polish restaurants, when she is invited out, in the name of research.

Maeve prefers writing short stories to novels – several of her novels are interconnecting stories, and the new one is no different.

'I'm calling it a novel because it begins at the start of the year and finishes at the end of the year. My books are like a bar of Toblerone. If you write ten connected stories like *Evening Class* or *The Copper Beech*, it can peak like a Toblerone and then come down again. If you're writing a novel, it's much slower, you get up to a plateau and you mustn't lose the momentum, it's longer and there are more dangers of tedium.'

Maeve claims in her writer's guide that what drove her on to get up at 5 am three days a week to write was the dream of a glamorous launch party, which in the end she paid for herself with one-fifth of her advance. But she admits that her inspiration was Edna O'Brien, who, 'even though she lived a much more glamorous and exciting life than I did, was writing about ordinary things we could all recognize.

'I was quite successful in *The Irish Times* writing about ordinary things. Without analysing too deeply, my best pieces were things that exposed people's innocence and vulnerability and hope. The most successful piece I ever wrote was about etiquette in hotels, whether it was acceptable to make the bed or not. I said when I was nineteen I didn't know, and was afraid if I made it they would think I was a poor servant class of person who wasn't worthy to stay here and if I didn't they'd think I was a slut, so I just folded it back neatly. I got hundreds of letters.'

Maeve was once on a 'desperately literary, poncey and poseurish' show in France, *Apostrophes*, discussing the heart. She was to speak on platonic love, on account of her description of female friendship in *Light a Penny Candle*. She had all her words ready, '*une amitié pure, sensible*' when suddenly the host said to her, with twenty-one million people watching, 'what, madam, is your philosophy of life?' 'Your best friend wouldn't ask you that,' says Maeve. 'My publisher is wringing his hands, panic-stricken in case I say something wrong. I said in French, "you're only dealt one hand and you've got to play it as well as possible while you're here". I was afraid of catching anybody's eye in case they said "pass the sick bag", but the host nodded and said, *"oui, c'est juste"*.'

Binchy was born in Dalkey in 1939 and died in 2012, aged seventy-three. A former Irish Times *journalist, she wrote thirteen bestselling novels. Her play* Deeply Regretted By *won a Jacob's Award. After two short-story collections,* Central Line *(1978) and* Victoria Line *(1980),* Light a Penny Candle *(1982) sold for the largest sum ever paid for a first novel. She received the British Book Award for Lifetime Achievement (1999), the Irish PEN Award (2007) and a lifetime achievement award from the Irish Book Awards (2010).* Scarlet Feather *(2000) won the WH Smith Book Award for Fiction.* A Week in Winter *(2012) won the Irish Popular Fiction Book Award. Film adaptations included* Circle of Friends, Tara Road *and* How About You?

JOHN BOYNE

6 September 2008, The Irish Post

After Auschwitz, Theodor Adorno once claimed, writing poetry was barbaric. The German philosopher subsequently admitted, however, that 'perennial suffering has as much a right to expression as a tortured man has to scream'.

The Holocaust is the backdrop for Irish author John Boyne's phenomenally successful fifth novel, *The Boy in the Striped Pyjamas*, which like Mark Haddon's *The Curious Incident of the Dog in the Night-Time* was first published as a book for children before becoming a crossover success. The film version starring David Thewlis and Sheila Hancock is out this month.

Boyne's novel is the story of nine-year-old Bruno, who lives in Berlin. His sister is 'A Hopeless Case' and his father's office is 'Out of Bounds at All Times and No Exceptions' because his father works for The Fury, who has promoted him to run a place called Out-With.

Bruno wants to know how far from Berlin Out-With is, is it more than a mile away? A child with no conception of time or distance is unlikely to appreciate the full enormity of the Holocaust, yet his innocent child's-eye view is a powerful device to open the reader's eyes anew to the horrors of the past. Sibling squabbles and misunderstood adult conversations are centre stage while the horrors that Bruno fails to comprehend lurk beyond the page.

Bruno, bored to tears in Out-With, wanders off and befriends a boy called Shmuel who wears striped pyjamas and lives on the other side of a big, long fence. When his father eventually gives in to his mother and tells Bruno Out-With is no place for children, Bruno innocently replies that there are hundreds of children there, just on the other side of the fence.

Boyne dislikes his work being described as a Holocaust novel, finding it reductive, but acknowledges the influence of other books with a Holocaust theme, starting with Ian Serraillier's *The Silver Sword*, about Polish children fleeing the Nazis, and William Styron's *Sophie's Choice*.

'What bothers me is people say do we need another book about the Holocaust in a way that they don't say do we need another film set in New York? People tend to say they've seen *Schindler's List* and that's enough. But of course, that's not enough. The reason there are so many books written is because the books keep asking different questions.

'If you are reading a book set during the Holocaust, you're not just reading about the Holocaust. *Sophie's Choice* addresses issues of madness, sexuality, friendship, jealousy.'

Without realizing it, Boyne had been researching the background to this novel for almost fifteen years, ever since he read Primo Levi's *The Periodic Table* when he was a teenager.

'When the idea for this book came to me, it started with the image of the two boys at the fence talking to each other but I knew what I could justify changing and what I could leave exactly as is. I moved the commandant's house outside the fence, I de-electrified the fence. I didn't change the ending of the book, which was the true ending for most people who experienced those times. It's a novel at the end of the day. I tell schoolchildren, it's not to teach you about the Holocaust, it's a story that gets you interested in educating yourself about the subject.'

Boyne wasn't taught about the Holocaust at school in Ireland. 'I think there was still an issue about the role of the Catholic Church in the Holocaust. It would be ludicrous to blame the Catholic Church for the Holocaust but it would be fair to say there were moments when they could have alleviated things. Now they do study the subject.'

Boyne does not believe Ireland is or was particularly anti-Semitic, but there is a famous quotation in Joyce's *Ulysses* where a character boasts that Ireland was the only country never to have persecuted the Jews, because it never let them in.

Three decades later, Irish diplomat Charles Bewley persuaded de Valera to deny a desperate European Jewry refuge in neutral Ireland.

Boyne did not set out to write a children's book but after a couple of chapters he realized that the tone he was writing in matched the viewpoint of a nine-year-old and so he set out to maintain that consistency of tone.

'I did write a children's novel and that's who I wanted the audience to be. As time has gone on I didn't see any reason why adults wouldn't come to it as well. I deliberately put in layers that Bruno wasn't understanding but adults and older children would see, such as the relationship between his mother and Lieutenant Kotler. But a year and a half down the line I'm completely disinterested in the distinction.'

All of Boyne's novels are historical but it is not deliberate, he says. 'I love doing research, finding out little anecdotes that work really well in the story. Obviously, you can explore contemporary themes even in books set in the past. A lot of books set in the present are very shallow. But look at *I Claudius*, *Rites of Passage* or *Earthly Powers*, which are historical but are as relevant to today as to those times. It's really just a setting.

'The first novel was a conscious decision to change the kind of novel I was writing in my early twenties, which was all me, me, me as every young writer is. So I just removed myself from the story.'

His next book, *Bligh and I*, is told by the cabin boy on the *Bounty*. 'In my novel Captain Bligh is the good guy and Fletcher Christian the bad guy, which in fact is more historically accurate. I loved those movies but the more I read the more I realized everything we were told in those movies was completely wrong. The ship had the best disciplinary record in naval history. Why is Bligh portrayed as a monster when in fact he wasn't?'

The author is very conscious that he is part of the last generation to have the chance to speak to Holocaust survivors. 'Writers who follow me in twenty years' time and write about the Holocaust won't have that experience. I think that is the best thing that has happened to me, it's quite a privilege.'

Did the sensitivity of the subject matter add to the burden of getting it right? 'I've held my breath but I have never received criticism from a Holocaust survivor, so I'm not worried if younger people say, isn't Bruno too naive? or something. If every survivor I met had said they found it inappropriate or insulting or insensitive that would have been quite difficult.'

Boyne is concerned that Irish children are no longer brought up to care about the rest of the world.

'There's a line in the children's edition that says fences like this exist all over the world; we hope we never have to encounter such a fence. We knew about fences like that in South Africa. I go into schools and kids have no idea about what is going on in the world and no interest. They are only interested in *Heat*, *Big Brother* and becoming celebrities.

'My contribution was to visit at least a hundred schools in the last year and every hour that I spend hope they will put down *Heat* and pick up *The Irish Times*. I just hope kids will open their minds a bit to what is going on in the world and do something about it.'

One of the most controversial fences in the world today is that being built by Israel to protect it from suicide attacks but which encroaches on and divides Palestinian territory. Boyne shies away from the subject.

'Honestly, I don't feel entirely qualified to answer this. Perhaps my words would be given more merit than they are due because I am not a student of Middle Eastern politics. I prefer to stick to what I know.'

Boyne flew to Hungary this summer to see his book being made into a film. 'It was surreal. I felt very strange the morning I walked into the square in Budapest, which was all decorated with Nazi memorabilia, and soldiers, it was like stepping back in time. I thought, *what if there are elderly people who wander into the square and don't know this is happening*? I don't want them to have a heart attack. The iconography is very scary. I found myself walking away from Nazi officers.

'When I saw the whole family interacting, I felt quite proud. That's something I created. But the characters belong to the actors and the set to the director. As a writer you're on your own but suddenly I felt part of something, like being in a band rather than a solo singer.'

Asked for his view on the validity of Adorno's line on art and Auschwitz, Boyne recalls a recent book tour with Marcus Zusak, author of *The Book Thief*, which explores similar subject matter.

'As the week went on we both came to the realization that what we wanted to bring out in our books were moments of beauty, moments of joy. Of course it is a tragic story, a terrible situation but as pieces of literature there are moments of beauty in there. I like to think that this uplifting moment of friendship when the two boys hold hands defeats the hatred and prejudice around them. So to get back to your question, I suppose I disagree, you can aim for [poetry] anyway.'

Boyne was born in Dublin in 1971. His YA novel The Boy in the Striped Pyjamas *(2006) has sold more than eleven million copies and was made into a film. As well as five other YA novels, he has written eighteen novels for adults. His latest,*

The Elements *(2025), made up of his four novellas,* Water, Earth, Fire *and* Air, *won France's Prix du Roman FNAC.* A History of Loneliness *(2013),* The Heart's Invisible Furies *(2017) and* A Ladder to the Sky *(2018) were shortlisted for Irish Novel of the Year and the latter won Kerry Group Irish Novel of the Year Award. He has won four Irish Book Awards, the Hennessy Literary Hall of Fame Award, and many international literary prizes.*

ANNA BURNS

14 March 2026, The Irish Times

It is seven years since Anna Burns won the Booker Prize for *Milkman* but she has not been idle since then. She has been in pain.

After we greet each other in Belfast's Grand Central Hotel, before she sits down she places a wooden board on her seat, which relieves the discomfort of nerve damage caused by surgery that went wrong in July 2014, delaying *Milkman*'s completion for two years. She is hopeful that a specialist will be able to help her and has just begun a series of operations.

For a writer whose method requires sitting completely still at her desk, calmly waiting for the voices of her characters to make themselves heard, this incapacitation must be excruciating.

'When I got damaged in surgery, nothing else mattered, but I've always kind of lived like that, in survival mode. I don't write as well now, only for about half the amount of time. It interferes, it builds up.'

She doesn't like taking regular painkillers so she manages the pain through physiotherapy and her own techniques. In the meantime, she has just finished a 5,000-word essay, which in part addresses how she feels about this medical calamity. 'It's quite an angry piece but writing the essay did not compound the emotional experience of having been damaged in surgery. This can happen sometimes with me and writing, in that the distress about something gets worse rather than eased if I try to write about it. I'm glad to have got it out of me. It's helped me, brought me to something I needed.'

Anna Burns's 2001 debut novel, *No Bones*, about a young girl growing up during the Troubles, was shortlisted for the Orange Prize, now the Women's Prize for Fiction, and universally praised. Well, almost. Writer and former Sinn

Féin figure Danny Morrison attacked it as a 'misanthropic portrayal of the nationalist people of [Ardoyne]' and worried that 'a Southern Irish or English audience would read this novel believing the fictional context to be a faithful representation of reality, even if the story is completely blown by its surrealist affectations'. How would she respond? 'I don't have any comment to make on Danny Morrison's dismissal of *No Bones*,' Burns says.

Little Constructions followed in 2007, the story of a chaotic clan of violent criminals and damaged children. Just as characters in *Milkman* don't have first names but are identified only as Middle Sister or Maybe Boyfriend, the ones in *Little Constructions* have very similar names that blur their individuality, such as Jetty, Janine, Joshuatine, Janet, Jennifer. Was that intentional? Even if not, what effect does she think it has?

'The similar names was intentional only insofar as I recognized early on in the writing that these J names were coming out and seemed to persist in being there,' she replies. 'I kept them but didn't plan them in advance. *Little Constructions* is an abuse story; abuse re-enacted almost exactly and passed down through generations. So I suppose the names tumbling into each other reflect, even if only in a small, spontaneous way, a sense of repetition and compulsion.

'The title came from a conversation with a friend, who was talking about a pilot who referred to making constant little adjustments when flying planes. I said, "Oh, just like life" but I misremembered "little adjustments" as "little constructions". I knew right away that that was going to be the title for my book.'

It makes me think of her writing method, a bit like a jigsaw, various little constructions assembled into a novel. 'Yes, I liked it for that, that's how I work. You kind of know when you've got the business, playing around with things, moving it about, then it takes off somewhere else and you follow the energy.'

Next came a self-published novella, *Mostly Hero* (2014), 'the hilarious, hell-raising descendant of Quentin Tarantino and the Brothers Grimm'. But in *Milkman* (2018) she produced a modern masterpiece, which won the Booker Prize, the Orwell Prize for Political Fiction and the International Dublin Literary Award and topped an *Irish Times* poll in 2025 of sixty authors and critics to be voted the best Irish fiction of the twenty-first century so far.

Milkman is set in an unnamed city that is recognizably the author's native Belfast. The eighteen-year-old narrator, 'middle sister', lives in an enclave under the coercive control of a militant faction opposed to the repressive, discriminatory state, its groupthink-prone inhabitants doubly besieged and surveilled. The eponymous Milkman, a much older, predatory paramilitary, stalks her. To stay independent and true to herself, she takes refuge in nineteenth-century literature, reading as she walks to navigate this claustrophobic environment whose inhabitants are trapped by history, poverty and paranoia. Burns's feisty, feminist narrative is circuitous rather than linear, its repetitiveness reflecting her characters' entrapment, but it is surprisingly, surpassingly funny, with sly, often absurdist humour.

'It manages that alchemy that Irish books are so good at,' Anne Enright wrote, 'of turning our difficulties and our shames into some strange kind of glory.'

'At the novel's narrative heart,' wrote Declan Long, 'is the extreme, exhausting absurdity – the routine horror and maddening comedy – of everyday reality in this society of incessant, micro-political pressure and unrelenting sectarian suspicion … a work of disconcerting literary invention: estranging and exciting in its audacious transformation of vernacular conventions.'

Having grown up in Ardoyne in north Belfast, where one-quarter of the victims in the thirty-year conflict known as the Troubles were killed, it seems likely that she must have witnessed terrible things but she has never spoken of it, perhaps never been asked.

'I did see people getting killed,' she says. 'My father and a neighbour were shot. He survived but the neighbour didn't, God love her. That turned up to my surprise [in her fiction].' Colette Meek, a 47-year-old mother of four, was killed by a stray bullet outside her home on 17 August 1980, during an IRA assault on an RUC patrol.

'Another time, someone [Trevor McKibben, a nineteen-year-old IRA man] had been shot dead by soldiers and I was mitching school. My friend Sean McBride asked if I was going to the chapel. I said no, I don't do that, I never went to the chapel with the coffins. I was going on home and had got to the top of the street and a bomb went off. Loyalists had put a bomb in one of the wreaths and my friend was killed.' Sean was eighteen when he was murdered in the 1977 attack, alongside nineteen-year-old Sean Campbell.

'A few months before, another friend of ours was shot, John Savage. I was just turned fifteen and he was seventeen, he was lovely. Soldiers told the car to stop. John was hanging out of the car, said don't shoot, we're not armed. He was a mad boy but he was seventeen, his hormones were all over the place. My sister said there is a clip on YouTube of a soldier boasting about shooting John. I want to watch it but can't do it yet because I know how angry I'll get. That was a terrible death, I've written about that.' In 2025 the British ministry of defence reached an out-of-court settlement with John Savage's family over the killing by paratroopers of the unarmed teenager in December 1976.

Burns works through this trauma, both in fiction and non-fiction. Sometimes it's a means of getting them out of her system. She has spoken about clearing a space for fiction by writing cathartic non-fiction, which she keeps for a while as evidence that she has got it out before throwing it away in regular clear-outs. But on other occasions, fiction emerges that is based on real events, working its way out in a different guise, such as the shooting of her father and Colette Meek.

Burns grew up in a part of Belfast known as the Murder Triangle, bounded by Antrim Road, Crumlin Road and Cliftonville Road, the latter also known as Murder Mile. 'My brother says he first heard names like Fenian and Taig from a neighbour on the other side of our back yard. It was another reason to leave.'

When Catholics were burned out of their homes at the start of the Troubles in August 1969, Burns and her family were evacuated to Finner army camp in County Donegal for three months. 'I remember the spaciousness of it. I was afraid of the sheep, worried I wouldn't be able to climb the stiles in case the sheep chased me. There was loads of food; we didn't grow up with that. We got into Belfast and Derry gangs. I think we thought they were Protestants. We cried our eyes out when we had to go to school, then there were Free State children so we bonded against this new threat. The nuns were friendly. I still have a wee booklet one of [them] gave me.'

Burns was one of seven siblings and lived most of the time across the road from her parents in her aunt's house. 'I had that nice peacefulness but also the rowdiness, I liked having both. Me and my sister would play school, with the teachers shouting, and play with dolls, beating them up. One day the neighbours, these old ladies, came – they were really nice – asking us not to make so much noise.'

Burns disliked school, but was later inspired at night school by Pat McCann, who taught her English. She was also working night shifts as a copytaker for newspapers.

She moved to London in 1987 to study for a Russian degree. She loved the literature but was drinking a lot (night shifts on Fleet Street didn't help) and realized that her real purpose in leaving Belfast was to get sober, so she quit drinking and studying and started writing.

'I didn't go to AA,' Burns says, 'as I was frightened of "13th stepping", getting hit on. You go to a meeting and you're a mess, someone else there is also a mess but wants to take you under their wing. I sensed I wouldn't be safe there so a friend took me to Adult Children of Alcoholics. They want to go deeper. I found this helpful for understanding myself and my own motives for drinking. My understanding is AA want you to get sober, they don't look into why you were drinking.'

Why was she drinking?

'Because of the Troubles and it was the culture, Belfast was a very boozy place, and I started young. I can remember asking adults to get me drink and they'd do it. You could go to a bar with an empty bottle and say this is for my da and they'd fill it up.'

She started going to writing classes in London. 'I started doing these exercises for the class but nothing wanted to finish. I didn't mind as I wasn't looking to be published.' Charles Palliser spoke of writers who plan and plot, and others who don't know what's coming at the end of a sentence. He advised those like Burns in the latter group to look at everything they had written and they would see where it was pulling them, even if they didn't know when they were writing it. She went home and laid everything out on the table and it started to crystallize. She realized she had a recurring character and there was a lot about the North of Ireland. 'I started focusing, the other stuff faded away. It told me I was writing a book set in Northern Ireland and so I started writing things that ended up as *No Bones*.'

Her method is to be peaceful, quiet, present at her desk, waiting for voices to manifest themselves. What is her understanding of where those voices come from? Is it essentially her subconscious, similar to a dream?

'I never think about it,' she says, 'it doesn't matter to me. To start analysing it, you might lose it. I don't mind if people think I'm crazy.' In the early days, she would go to sleep with a Dictaphone and a notebook by her pillow. She might wake up with just one word, but it would have meaning for her, or a better version of a sentence she had already written.

'I commit to turning up, I put in the hours whether things come or not. I go for a walk and then it might suddenly shift.' I wonder if there is a parallel to her work as a copytaker, but no.

'I would see a character, then two characters taking. I would listen in on their conversation. At some point my thinking head comes in. It's not all dictation though it's lovely when it happens. Two stories in *No Bones* were like that, I thought, *this is great, I'm getting it all for nothing.*

'Sometimes I have the sensation of taking down a huge chunk of writing that comes to me quickly and effortlessly. It's a wonderful experience but it's rare. Certainly, I'm in flow when it's happening. I do, though, also feel in flow at other times when I don't have that sensation – it's just a slower flow.'

Her first agent struck a great deal for *No Bones* but there was a personality clash so on the back of its success she negotiated her own deal for *Little Constructions*. She spent years working on another book but then the characters from *Milkman* took over. She had run out of money by this stage so did a lot of house-sits as it had become harder to rent, having to prove you had income for a year, and two months' rent up front. *Milkman* was started in London, then along the south coast, between Brighton and Eastbourne.

She and her family had drifted apart but after the Booker Prize there was a reconciliation and she moved home, staying first with a sister near Belfast and now in the beautiful Antrim coastal village of Cushendun. But there was also a push factor.

'England is getting more and more authoritarian. I thought if I don't go I might not get out, I don't feel safe here. I wanted to get back to my family, my sisters in particular.'

Two key influences as writers are Alice Miller and Jeffrey Masson, specialists on the effect of inter-generational trauma on families and individuals. I sense that there is a personal story here but she is reluctant to expand on it as it is not just her story to tell.

'But even just take the Troubles, the conditioning of what is supposed to be normal. When I was living in England, I thought, *it's not bloody normal.* I knew cerebrally it was crazy, but I felt everyone is traumatized over there and they're all being ignored.

'When I came back one thing I noticed is people are talking more about their experience, I find that's really healthy. No one ever did when I was growing up, you just got on with it.

'I remember coming over to Milltown [cemetery] to look for friends' graves and it was shocking walking up some of the paths. Oh my God, I know this person or I remember that happening. And then things on gravestones like

"Murdered by the British army". I thought, *this is truly shocking*, and they were so young. My sister was the same, we had to stop. My God, this is horrific, and we never noticed how shocking this was. It was really so sad.'

I ask her which other Troubles fiction impressed her and she singles out Eoin McNamee. 'At a sentence level, *The Bureau* is very emotional, it brings up the sadness and the waste. I loved *The Blue Tango*, the first one of his I read. Someone told me about *Resurrection Man*, about the Shankill Butchers. That book was amazing. Some of my mother's friends were killed by the Butchers, two of my brothers' friends. I remember people who were chased. I told Eoin I sent him a fan mail and I'm so glad he didn't get it because it was so gushing and mad.'

Burns has described the language in *Milkman* as a mix of Belfast dialect and archaisms. Might this be because the characters are stuck in the past – Elizabethan English for a sixteenth-century quarrel?

'I do like that interpretation,' she says, 'but again, as with the J names, I really don't know. It came out that way and it felt right. I'm not the kind of writer who plans out my books in advance. Instead, I wait for my characters to come and to reveal to me what the story is about and to show me how things work in their world. I discover it as I'm getting it.

'In the initial stages it seems I don't have much control in the matter. I wait and try to be still and to sense for energy and for clues. I don't attempt to interpret or classify or tidy up anything to make it make sense to me as I'm getting it, especially if I'm being taken off on a path I could not have anticipated – which often happens.'

I wonder if Middle Sister's circumlocution is a defence mechanism, when to be straightforward is to give oneself away. 'Yes, I think the narrator's circumlocution is an unconsciously learned defence,' the author says, 'and I come across this in real life – and not just in the North. It seems to link with a sense of instinctive wariness about declaring oneself, or worse, of having oneself declared, in potentially frightening or threatening circumstances.

'In *Milkman*, as in my upbringing, it was unsafe to be straightforward about anything. I think the characters' preference for nameless anonymity reflects this. So does the language restrictions and the use of rumour and their obsessive hypervigilance to protect what's really important to them.'

As well as Miller and Masson, Burns has been influenced by all sorts of people and places and things. 'Some people don't really like that answer. They seem to think it's a cop-out from admitting that one has influences at all and from pinpointing who or what they are. Well, I know not to be influenced by anything would make for a dearth of a life and I do not aspire to that.

'But I don't really know all my influences in writing or living. I think so much comes up from the unconscious and the subconscious and weaves itself in and out and through my writing life, also through all other bits of my life as well. This is why I was attracted to Miller and Masson, who wrote on the unconscious and on re-enactment behaviour and on human psychological states. In my early thirties I read the works of both these writers before I had any idea I would also become a writer. The Northern Irish Troubles, of course, was also an influence.

'As for inspirational writers on writing, I would name Julia Cameron who wrote *The Artist's Way*. This is a book about discovering one's own creativity and dealing with all sorts of obstacles to unfolding that creativity. Other great influencers on writing, in my opinion, are Natalie Goldberg, Dorothea Brande and Brenda Ueland. I particularly like their idea of following your instinct when you write and not worrying about it having to make sense in the early stages. Just commit and turn up and let whatever wants to come, come. This works well for me as I can't really write any other way.'

Does she, like Middle Sister, prefer nineteenth-century fiction to modern fiction? 'I used almost exclusively to prefer nineteenth-century fiction when I was younger, in my teenage years mainly. That changed in my twenties with *The Master and Margarita* by Mikhail Bulgakov and *The Third Policeman* by Flann O'Brien. They seemed to open the twentieth-century literature door for me in an invitational, exciting way. I think, though, I still feel more at home in the older stuff.'

Burns was born in Belfast in 1962. Her third novel, Milkman *(2018), won the Booker Prize, the Orwell Prize for Political Fiction, the International Dublin Literary Award, the National Book Critics Circle Award for Fiction and the Christopher Ewart-Biggs Memorial Prize, and was shortlisted for the Women's Prize for Fiction. Her debut novel,* No Bones *(2001), won the Royal Society of Literature's Winifred Holtby Memorial Prize for the best regional novel and was shortlisted for the Orange Prize. Her other works are the novel* Little Constructions *(2007) and the novella* Mostly Hero *(2014).*

JAN CARSON

4 April 2026, The Irish Times

For a writer who likes to put the magic back into realism and find new ways to tell stories about the North of Ireland, discovering a politician's visionary or madcap scheme to drain Lough Neagh and create another county was manna from heaven.

The inspiration for *Few and Far Between*, Jan Carson's fourth novel, was an early Christmas present. 'It has a really good genesis story,' she says. 'I was on a residency in France and it was a bit dire. I was writing a novel that just refused to write itself. Three months into it and getting nowhere, I had emailed my agent saying I think you need to just drop me. I'm never going to write another book. And she said, give yourself a break. It's Christmas.'

Then on Christmas Eve, a friend sent her an email with the subject header: 'this sounds like a story you would write'. 'You get a lot of those,' she says drily. But this one was an article about Terence O'Neill's 1958 drainage plan and Carson thought: 'you know what, this is actually something that I would want to write. So, I opened a bottle of nice French red and googled what would happen if you drained Lough Neagh.'

She found that the Victorians had partially drained the lough to create farmland and then discovered topographical maps showing elevated areas just under the surface which would become visible if the waterline dropped.

'I could see this archipelago [a group of islands, which she shortened to the Ark, symbolic and easier to pronounce] and began to think about who would be living there. In the late '60s, as you're starting to move into conflict, perhaps it would be a space where people sought sanctuary. That just felt like the plot of a novel.'

Populating her Ark took several months, 'people who felt unsafe or persecuted in what they call mainland Northern Ireland: people in mixed marriages, gay couples, Sandra, who's a trans woman, anyone who was challenging notions of diversity.'

She needed a narrator. A voracious reader, she had just discovered Barbara Pym, who had worked at the African Institute and whose novels are peppered with anthropologists, who she often uses as an outward gaze in small-minded communities, people who have seen other places. 'There's a lot of extended metaphors in this novel. Growing up in the North in the '80s, there were almost no people moving here, challenging how we did things, that maybe our way of life wasn't the only way.'

So, the anthropologist R.J. Connolly was born, who would lead the Ark, only he proved to be a bit of a monster, complicating the narrative. With such a deeply flawed father, his children Marion and Robert John might be 'safe from bombs and guns. But there are so many other ways to destroy a child.' His family wilts in his shadow, stagnating like the lough. 'Absenting herself is how [Ursula, his wife] copes.' Marion 'scrolls and scrolls until her thumb feels bruised. She does not post or comment. Marion prefers to lurk.' On the sports pitch, 'it's unclear whether [Robert John's] a player or a spectator. As in football, so in life.'

Few and Far Between follows *The Fire Starters* and *The Raptures* to create a significant sequence of works exploring not just Northern society but family and community dynamics.

'I wouldn't see them as a natural trilogy,' Carson says, 'but different perspectives on the same story. They're set in different periods but there are overlaps. With *The Fire Starters*, the focus is on politics and its impact on community. In *The Raptures*, the religious aspect is front and centre, interrogating that evangelical Protestant thing. *Few and Far Between* is more about how we've dealt with trauma in the North. There are lots of images of things being submerged and hidden and not dealt with, not all overtly related to the Troubles. Robert John is feeling a lot of trauma from his relationship with his father. There's a temptation to separate things out and say, these are normal traumas and there's this trauma related to the conflict, but I see it as much messier. A lot of our notions of masculinity, around how women are treated and violence against women, and mental health: they're all tied up into what happened.'

Brought up on Bible stories, magical realism came naturally to Carson, and life in the North, where swings were locked up on the Sabbath and people were made to disappear, was often stranger than fiction.

'Something that I've been interested in for a long time is what I call writing at the end of the possible, where facts are so bizarre and outlandish that they almost feel like fiction. And so there's a blurring in this novel. A lot of early readers are asking which bits are true and which are made up.' I ask if the publicity shot of the bucket men lining up to empty the lough is factual. 'No, I made that up, so I like that you're asking because I wanted to blur that line.'

The various islands host different communities. Church Flat is inhabited by the Almost-Dead, a Bardo-like liminal space for the dying. 'This being the North, with its award-winning rates of heart disease, it's mostly heart attack victims who loiter on Church.' The suicidal go to Tom's Hard: 'More people [5,000] have now died by suicide in Northern Ireland post-Good Friday than during the entire duration of the Troubles, which claimed 3,600 lives.' 'I've had a couple of people who are not from the North ask if those statistics are real? Again, an example of something that's factual that feels made up or exaggerated.'

Middle Flat is home to women in a coma, victims of Sleeping or Resignation Syndrome. 'This novel deliberately blurs the line between fact and fiction. The sleepers have been so impacted by trauma they've gone into this comatose state but that's a real condition.'

'Buried things are starting to reappear' on Eglish, where things are dumped. 'As the peace descends, the trauma will surface. So many people have been done in by the last 30 years.' 'You can look at the island that swallows things and put that in a box of fantasy and process it in a way that you use for metaphors, whereas how do you process the draining of the lough? A lot of what happens in the North feels like it occurs at the end of the possible. We have slightly laxer laws about owning big cats so there's someone in Ballymena that's got tigers in their garage.'

Why is the North so misogynistic? 'I think misogyny often happens behind closed doors. Particularly during the conflict, there was an isolation where people could get away with awful things because there was a distraction. Northern Ireland was such an isolated goldfish bowl geographically.'

Robert John is unlovable but Carson softened his portrayal. 'If Robert John had been given an opportunity to experience other cultures, he could have been an intellectual but we were brought up with a fear of anyone different. That's a subsidiary issue of the conflict. This inherent fear that you take through life because we were brought up in segregated schools and housing estates. When you don't know somebody, you start to fear them and there's not a big jump from that to hating someone. Initially Robert John had a much nastier end because I saw him as not very nice but I rewrote him a lot because he's as much a victim as he is a misogynist. He's inherited opinions without the opportunity to challenge them.'

As a reader, Carson graduated from Enid Blyton and Nancy Drew, 'nice safe narratives where you do good things and right will out', to subtler texts such as *The Catcher in the Rye*. 'I always remember discussing *To Kill a Mockingbird* in school within the context of Northern Ireland, how awful it was to be prejudiced against people just because they were different, and then one of the girls saying, I have to get down to the bus station because we've got a fight with the ones from the Catholic school. So, I don't think a book can change anyone, but a lifetime's exposure to books can – critical thinking in nuanced thought and empathy, a window into other people's perspective. If young people are brought up with that, it forms citizens capable of thinking beyond their own experience and making informed decisions, having kindness and empathy and all that good stuff.'

Books that felt like light-bulb moments for her include Sam Hanna Bell's *December Bride*, 'a beautiful book about my community but also really radical; Ian Cochrane's *F is for Ferg*, about rural, working-class Protestants. *Milkman* is huge. What Anna [Burns] got away with in structure and voice felt really freeing. It's okay to be playful, to not always be realist and write in a linear way. And the vernacular is so important for me.'

Writing the books is one thing; engaging readers is another.

'It's the withering disinterest that is really hard. Some of that is peculiarly Protestant. If *Derry Girls* had been Presbyterian Wives, I don't know that we would have been as quick to laugh at ourselves, maybe because there has been so much satire and lambasting of that brand of Protestant culture that they're always on the defensive. It comes from past hurt.'

How do you attract the people who need to read your work most?

'I'm making myself culpable. I'm not writing from a distance. I'm writing things that are very close to me, that I was part of. I'm highlighting the stuff that's beautiful and worth celebrating as well as the stuff that needs to be critiqued. People love seeing places and experiences that they know referenced, like the caravan park in *The Last Resort*. That stuff is important.'

Carson delights in dialect, language that lilts and soars. 'Houl yer wheest, plootering, foundered'; 'The Big Flat weans were wee dotes'; an ice cream is given 'a slabbery lick'.

'I spend a lot of time writing in coffee shops in Ballymena, so I've got the ear open. There are strange ways of arranging a sentence and peppered with odd little bits of Ulster Scots. Those words are so rich, I want to reflect that, to honour where I come from and to put the foot down saying, we don't all have to sound the same. I took *The Raptures* back to my primary school and did some writing workshops and the kiddos wrote short stories full of wee Ulster Scotisms. A child put her hand up and said, please, miss, what's a better way to say that? Which is heartbreaking because I had the Ballymena knocked out of me with elocution lessons. It was cool to hold up the book and say, people speak like you in here.'

Having got Northern accents on to the BBC, the next step, she says, is to ensure narratives are not reduced to Belfast and Derry but include Banbridge and Ballymena, our respective home towns.

In her novel, consigning a gun to the lough bed marks 'the end of one way of being. The beginning of whatever will come next.' But progress is slow. 'The Peace they're currently living with isn't the all-encompassing peace they were promised in '98...there is still a deep divide running through the heart of the place.' The snag list is long: peace walls, unintegrated schools, violent murals, mass emigration and suicide. 'Still, turning a country's no small feat. It's not the kind of casual flip that's going to happen overnight.'

Carson says: 'I would position myself as a critical friend. I don't think it's doing anybody justice as a writer to ignore some of the glaring holes, particularly structural things. A lot of great work has been done with integration and tolerance but I find it endlessly frustrating that 91 per cent of schools aren't integrated. Nearly all my characters have become accustomed to disappointment: my life's mediocre, but it could be a lot worse. The lough is a stagnant place, not just the algae, but everything else.'

She grew up fourteen miles from the lough. Her family had picnics where the novel's barbecue scene is set. 'One of the last walks I took with my Dad before he died was along the lough shore.' And yet the lough is unloved, almost unknown. 'The algae outbreak has not been the point of consternation that it should have been. If the north coast all went green or the Giant's Causeway started to fall apart, there would be popular outrage but Lough Neagh is a weirdly inaccessible area of actual beauty. People aren't invested in it in the same way they are in the Mournes.'

Very little has been written about it. She cites Polly Devlin's work; Alexander Irvine's *My Lady of the Chimney Corner*; Ciaran Carson's *Fishing for Amber*; and Seamus Heaney's *Lough Neagh* cycle. 'It is the biggest freshwater lake in the UK and Ireland. Imagine if nobody has written about Windermere or Loch Ness. Maybe we need a monster.'

She worked with a sensitivity reader, Josephine Chick, to ensure her portrayal of Sandra, was accurate. 'There was originally a desire to tone down some of the awful things that R.J. and Robert John said about Sandra and Josephine said no, those are things people say to me and say about me all the time, so they need to stay in. I had the privilege of meeting a few older trans people and their narratives are quite absent. Sandra probably wouldn't call herself trans. She left Coleraine in the late '60s before there was a terminology so her understanding of herself is quite pure: I don't have a label on me, I am me, this is who I am.'

Sandra is a painter, who seeks to capture in her work 'Not how it was. More, how I wish it'd been.' Is that Carson's writing project too? 'Absolutely. It's very insightful to pick that up. I'm working on a novel about Ballymena and really trying to hold on to the realism of what having grown up there was like, but also to weave in what I wish it had been like, holding those two things in tension.'

Carson acknowledges 'this book like every other book I've ever written is mostly formed in conversations' and she lists twenty-nine writer friends. 'You sit down with a fellow writer and try to work out a kink or an issue. I sat outside a cafe in Paris with Karl Geary for three hours and we worked out how to end Robert John's section. More frequently for me, it's the validation of being part of a group of ideas people, all thinking and coming at stuff from different perspectives. It gives you permission to do your own thing.

'Sometimes it's having your peers throw up stuff that just sparks things in your head. I facilitate Stinging Fly workshops with emerging writers. Sheila Armstrong came and spoke about her practice of building up emotional intensity in the story and how the emotional arc is just as important as the plot arc, which really opened up something for me. What is unique about Ireland is we have all those people at our fingertips. If you're a writer in some other place, you might be isolated or people might be snobby and not want to help, but there's a million people I can pick up the phone and ask.

'There is a book festival pretty much every week, so we're all circulating and having these chats together. When you're outside Ireland, somebody says something like, do you know Anne Enright? You know everybody! We've all been stuck in some B&B with each other. You've had a few too many and had a great conversation and we all know each other's work inside out as well.'

It's funny that Carson mentions the genesis of the book because the epigraph is from Genesis. The Bible influences her language but more importantly her narrative structure.

'I am getting more comfortable saying I often write parables. I think that's a deeply untrendy, unsexy thing to say because the current trend is for writing books without an agenda. I hope there's still a story that you want to read and characters you want to follow, but I think it's okay to want your fiction to say something.'

Carson is a serious writer but a funny one too. The barbecue sausages slathered in red sauce and wrapped in a slice of pan loaf are a 'poor man's hot dogs'. Laconically, the narrator observes of another O'Neill wheeze, a festival celebrating fifty years of Partition as the Troubles took off: 'Unsurprisingly enough, Ulster '71 was not the catalyst for a Troubles-era tourism boom.'

'I have a chronic inability to be entirely serious for too long. A lot of the humour comes from the awkwardness of Robert John and Marion. My two favourite sections are when Marion goes to Dunnes to buy a bra and then when Robert John goes to the cinema and is trying to pretend that he wants to see an art-house film, but really wants to see *Gone in Sixty Seconds*, the lies that they're telling themselves about who they are.'

O'Neill was not always amusing. 'It is frightfully hard to explain to Protestants,' Carson quotes him saying in 1969, 'that if you give Roman Catholics a good job and a good house, they will live like Protestants because they will see neighbours with cars and television sets; they will refuse to have eighteen children. But if a Roman Catholic is jobless, and lives in the most ghastly hovel, he will rear eighteen children on National Assistance.'

Such patrician prejudice from a putatively progressive Protestant politician is a suitable epitaph for the old Stormont regime if not the statelet itself.

Carson has four more books on the go. She is incredibly productive given that she always seems to be touring. She writes two hours a day in a café. 'That's 1000 words for me, and then within three months you've got a first draft. I can't write imaginative stuff when I'm on the road but I can edit. I've been lucky.

I've had at least one residency a year for the last three so that gives you a longer chunk of time to get maybe 60,000 words down. I didn't come up through a writing program. I've never done a single class in writing, not a single workshop. I couldn't think of anything more heinous, even though I teach them. I wrote my first novel in the Coffee Island in the middle of the Tower Centre in Ballymena between shifts. So, my practice has always been: it's noisy; it's busy; I've got forty-five minutes; what can I get done?'

'If you do a PhD in creative writing and you've got three years of uninterrupted time to write a novel, it can ruin you. That's why a lot are struggling with the second book, because their practice is shaped around this thing that doesn't exist in the real world.'

How has her writing evolved? 'It's not as shit as it used to be. I was lazy in my early books. I didn't want to do twenty-five drafts, so I let things slip. By editing students' work, I've learned to be a better editor of my own. *Few and Far Between* went to nearly thirty drafts, some with an editor and some with me just going no, it's not quite right, I need to haul this apart and do it again. Editing is not a punishment; it can be a creative part of the process.'

Jan Carson was born in Ballymena, County Antrim, in 1980 and lives in Belfast. She is the author of four novels: Malcolm Orange Disappears *(2014);* The Fire Starters *(2019), which won the EU Prize for Literature for Ireland;* The Raptures *(2022), shortlisted for the An Post Irish Novel of the Year, the Dalkey Book Prize and the Kerry Group Irish Novel of the Year Prize; and* Few and Far Between *(2026). Her short story collections are* Children's Children *(2016) and* Quickly While They Still Have Horses *(2024). She has been shortlisted for the Sean O'Faolain Short Story Prize, the BBC National Short Story Prize and Irish Short Story of the Year Award and won the Harper's Bazaar Short Story Prize.*

PHILIP CASEY

17 December 1994, The Irish Post

One of the finest fictional debuts of the year comes from the pen of Philip Casey, an established poet who although born in London was brought up in Wexford and now lives in Dublin.

The Fabulists, set largely in contemporary Dublin, tells of the relationship between a couple in their thirties, both chastened by broken marriages. Swept together by chance – Dublin city centre is no place to be if you don't want to bump into someone – they are held together by the stories they tell one another, made-up stories to be sure but made up from the fragments of their lives and given an extra spin or shine.

What comes across is a sense that life is hard, be it lived in a damp, one-bedroomed flat in the city or on a remote farm in the country. But also that it holds the possibility of joy, be it found in the heady possibility of a love affair or in the steadier relationship between parent and child.

Mungo has to live with the crippling knowledge that he almost burned his family to death by drunkenly dropping a lit cigarette in his children's bedroom, an event that destroyed his marriage. Tess has left her husband but must continue to move in his orbit to be near their child. Mungo and Tess's relationship is dictated as much by the demands of their families as by desire. One of the most striking features of the novel is not so much the sex scenes that seemed to transfix most reviewers but the tender portrayal of the relationship between parent and child.

'Thank you very much,' says the author. No, he does not himself have children. 'I do have a great liking for children, partly because of my time in hospital as a child. Also, I know from simple observance that children are of paramount importance to people, really dictate the way their lives go in terms of personal relationships.'

The main theme of the book, however, one whose significance is reflected in the title, is the way the characters oil the wheels of their relationship by telling stories to reveal themselves obliquely. A romance can mean both a love story and the telling of extravagant lies. Casey here unites the two.

'This is a kind of play on the old spoofing idea,' Casey says. 'The characters are very hurt in themselves. People in that situation are very reluctant to reveal the truth about themselves. Sometimes they are so overwhelmed that they don't really see the truth. It's also tapping into the Irish storytelling tradition.

'Part of the book is a story about telling a story. You see that the characters get their stories from incidents in their own lives, embellish them and put them in different settings.'

The 1950s London setting for Casey's next novel [*The Water Star*] is very autobiographical. The working title, 'Citizen Road', the name of a street in Hornsey, appears on his birth certificate. 'The whole era does haunt me to a great extent. I had a curious experience when launching the book in the Green Ink bookshop in Archway. I was driven up the Holloway Road and I kept seeing scenes from my childhood, including the Royal Northern Hospital where all my physical troubles began back in 1953. By the time I got to Green Ink I was shaking. When I told my parents this, my mother told me I used to get on the Underground at Tufnell Park on my own at three or four years of age and go and play on bomb sites at Archway. So I was literally going back to launch my book forty years later on the bombsite where I used to play.'

Casey had cancer as a child and has lived with the consequences of the treatment he has received ever since – he is an amputee. Obviously his whole life has been affected by this but has it thrown a shadow over his writing? 'I can't really give an honest answer. It doesn't really affect me in my everyday life except if I want to go into town I need crutches. In what is hopefully the next novel to be published, the child does die in the hospital where all my trouble started. There is something to be resolved there.'

Although he spent a long time in hospital as a child, don't go searching for the influence of Dickens or Twain in his writing. In the rural Ireland of his day, comics were his staple reading diet. 'I was always a storyteller. I told my brother stories from an early age. Whether it was in the blood or from the introversion that comes from illness, I don't know. '

Eoin McNamee's thoughtful review of *The Fabulists* highlighted 'the power of the imagination to transform and to heal'. Casey enlarges on the spiritual side of storytelling.

'I've been trying to write a poem along those lines. Nothing cohered and there was no chance of healing or ease. I hope this isn't too grandiose. I'm going to say it anyway. I'm beginning to think that the coherence of a story that sets the facts of one's life in order in some symbolic way – symbols can be quite powerful as well – does have a healing effect psychologically.'

Casey *was born in London in 1950 to Irish parents, moving as a child to Gorey, County Wexford. He died in Dublin in 2018. A member of Aosdána, he published three novels –* The Fabulists *(1995),* The Water Star *(1999) and* The Fisher Child *(2001) – and four poetry collections:* Those Distant Summers *(1980),* After Thunder *(1985),* The Year of the Knife *(1995) and* Dialogue in Fading Light *(2006).*

MICHAEL COLLINS

19 June 2010, The Irish Post

First, a declaration of interest. I came to Michael Collins's ninth book, *Midnight in a Perfect Life*, with a pre-conceived idea, namely that on the strength of his previous eight he is one of the finest living Irish writers.

Yet despite his work winning several awards and being shortlisted for both the Man Booker Prize and International Dublin Literary Award, he is relatively unknown, and when I recommend him to people, their instinctive reaction is, 'you don't mean …?' as you watch them try to reimagine the War of Independence hero as a plotter of fiction, not revolution.

The author, according to family lore, is a relative of the patriot, though more distant he realizes now, than he imagined when growing up in County Limerick, where he was born in 1964. 'If someone said to me who is my model,' says Collins, 'it is him, a hardcore political figure who took people down, murdered, was politically expedient, but also an absolute pragmatist, who negotiated what he could get, who decided you do things in stages.'

Collins left for the USA on an athletics scholarship to the University of Notre Dame. He never went home, completing a PhD in Chicago, where he narrowly survived a brutal mugging in which he was stabbed repeatedly with what he recalls as 'a Crocodile Dundee-type' knife.

Unable to afford a move away from the borders of the ghetto where he lived, he started running again. A few months after being stabbed he ran the Chicago Marathon and, on pure adrenaline, finished in 28th place. Collins still runs. Boy, does he run. In 2006 his Fire and Ice Challenge saw him run marathons in both the Sahara and at the North Pole in the space of six weeks. This year, he hopes to represent Ireland again in the world 100km championships in Gibraltar.

A short career as a Microsoft engineer in Seattle followed his studies, before the success of his third novel, *The Keepers of Truth*, written longhand after hours at work 'like a Neanderthal aboard a space ship', secured him an American publisher and a couple of movie deals, encouraging him to pursue his true vocation, writing politically-motivated thrillers, sugaring his sociological philosophising with suspense, about the economically devastated rust belt of America, the workers and their families churned up and spat out by Reaganomics, the American dream turned sour.

'It seemed the dismantling of America and the death of industrialization was for each American a personal guilt trip and not an occasion for workers to band together in unions to try and preserve their jobs …' he muses on his website. 'The notion of taking responsibility for your own economic and spiritual salvation was the single most important thing I learned about how America works.'

The US edition of his brilliant last novel, *The Secret Life of E Robert Pendleton*, was renamed *Death of a Writer* and his new book, *Midnight in a Perfect Life*, could easily share that title, for it is the story of Karl, facing 'the frailty of forty', a troubled author forlornly chasing literary immortality with his dubious opus while in truth he is failing even to make ends meet as a hack and a ghost writer. Meanwhile, his wife wants biological immortality in the form of a child. Karl, whose father killed himself after apparently murdering his mistress, reflects: 'trying to get pregnant seemed to me about as absurd as trying to get polio'.

Karl, who has already secretly remortgaged their home to pay for his mother's nursing home costs, now juggles credit card applications to pay for Lori's fertility treatment, while his writing leads him down dangerous alleys, first a magazine assignment with the beautiful Marina, a mysterious Russian performance artist, and then a challenge from Fennimore, the crime writer he ghosts for, to find him the perfect real-life victim, implying that his next work could be a snuff novel (another echo of Collins's last work).

The subject matter is dark, but the writing glitters memorably and, if the plotting sometimes feels underdone, this book of ideas is thought-provoking like few others, tackling modern notions of sexuality, IVF as a scam on career women in their forties, the culture of easy credit, and the place of fiction in the free world.

'There is no more sombre enemy of good art than the pram in the hall,' wrote the critic Cyril Connolly, so how does Collins combine writing with being a father, not to mention the long-distance running?

'It has its challenges,' he admits. 'I have four children under the age of eight and one had a brain cyst. The priority has to go towards the children. With kids the intense concentration that you need for art is obviously compromised, I don't mind that. I used to write from 11 at night to 4 am, now it's compressed to 1 am or 2 am.'

He has always combined writing with a full-time job, making notes during the day, writing them up at night. 'I've understood that the mania of what you're trying to express can draw you away from human contact. When you live within your mind, when your mind is your office, that can become overbearing and lead to insanity.'

Today he teaches at a community college in the small town where he lives thirty miles away from Notre Dame. This is the territory where his books are set, 'which look at the devastation of poverty, the dignity of the individuals who are oppressed by economic circumstances. In terms of writing political novels about disenfranchised groups of people this is a kind of haunt for me.'

The way Collins describes an upmarket apartment in the language not of an estate agent but an existentialist philosopher reminds me of Eoin McNamee, another author of big ideas and dark deeds.

'He is around the same age as me, there's a strain of writers who are not so much plot-oriented as politically oriented or philosophically oriented. Plot is a secondary concern,' says Collins, referencing the grinding poverty of 1970s Limerick, which formed his social consciousness and conscience, the era, he says, of Boomtown Rats singing 'I Don't Like Mondays', not love songs.

Karl is a dark character but Collins defends him against critics' charges that he is racist or misogynistic. 'I feel sad for him but he's honest about the male preening, women aggressively in the workplace, the economic joke of credit applications, private enterprise raping people, he recognizes the endgame for society, he is a soothsayer, a marginalized figure, maddened. He lives in the greatest democracy in the world where you can say anything but no one wants to listen.

'I constantly react against modernism in terms of taking away your psychological dignity; you can't say what you want to say because everything is politically incorrect, it's a minefield to speak your mind. In physical terms, America is a country of obese people and cars.'

In a Western world gone mentally lazy and physically flabby, Collins bucks the trend, running like mad, thinking like crazy. 'Going for a run, doing something physical, with the endorphins, if there are issues on your mind, it percolates, things crystallize. I go for a run for twenty miles and this is when I really think.

'For me as an artist it has always been about truth. Early on I landed on the title *The Keepers of Truth*, and this book is about uncovering truth. Lori looks like she's pregnant but she's wearing a pregnancy belly.' In Limerick, he says, fathers he knew in one sphere by day were involved in the IRA at night.

He has been accused of being a highbrow writer 'slumming' it as a crime writer, another casual insult to a genre that often beats the literary genre at its own game. How true is he to his true self as a writer? Collins admits that when no one would publish *Emerald Underground* in America, despite its success in Europe, he decided he wouldn't let economic reality stop him writing so 'to gain a readership, to gain the eye of an editor who thinks it might sell, I consciously decided to do a dismemberment novel, a philosophical novel where you throw in the crime element of a murder … but the essential nature of closure where things are solved didn't settle with me.'

He describes as anathema the idea of introducing a cop figure who would clear everything up, just as he didn't want to write a novel that an eighth-grader could understand, because there is no neat or happy ending, he believes, in a world and economy that is falling apart in an expanding universe. Closure is a nineteenth-century conceit, he says, and that is why he is annoyed that the title he gave his novel was changed.

'I understand I'm going to get hammered, so you need a title to condition people to see what you're trying to do with the book. The original title, 'Of Uncertain Significance', was a harrowing term I first heard from doctors in describing my daughter's brain cyst. The doctors could not determine if it was the underlying cause or not.

'In writing the novel, in reviewing my time at Microsoft and the general aimlessness of modernity and the decentralized nature of information, I think the prevailing theme for the book firmly settled on the idea of life as Of Uncertain Significance.

'I think a novel has to have an underlying philosophical intent. I personally adhere to the prevailing view of the universe as described by modern mathematics that there is no essential closure or certainty in the universe. This sense of chaos or entropy has been firmly established for decades in the mathematical realm and forms the basis of how the universe is perceived and studied.

'What is disheartening for me as a writer, and what I think is a pitfall of our craft, is how confined we are intellectually and structurally by our ordinary audience, where there is limited tolerance for intellectual deviation from the time-honoured tradition of narrative as having a beginning, middle and end. The standard by which popular fiction is judged falls on notions of "completeness" and "satisfaction", towards the comfort of the "known and easily understood".

'If I could say *Midnight* is politically prophetic, it would be in anticipating and railing against the financial madness of the last decade, which is now under post-mortem as if it can be fixed or really understood. My question is, who didn't know it was a scam all along?

'Much of modern fiction is a last refuge for fools. I try to push against the crushing ordinariness of this fiction, and at least challenge convention. Alas, with a few more damning reviews, I might be silenced … but I'll go down swinging.'

Collins was born in Limerick in 1964 and now lives in the United States. His novel The Keepers of Truth *(2000) was shortlisted for the Booker Prize and the International Dublin Literary Award and won the Kerry Group Irish Novel of the Year Award. Other significant novels include* The Resurrectionists *(2002),* Lost Souls *(2003) and* The Secret Life of E. Robert Pendleton *(2007). He has also published two short-story collections,* The Meat Eaters *(1992) and* The Feminists Go Swimming *(1996).*

MARY COSTELLO

2 March 2024, The Irish Times

There is a particular poignancy to Mary Costello dedicating her fourth book and second short-story collection to her late father Thomas, twenty years after his death.

A recurring theme in *Barcelona*, from the titular opening story to the closing one, 'The Killing Line', is humankind's treatment of animals and how this subject can be divisive in relationships. The author, a vegetarian with a lifelong concern for animal rights, is, like the troubled protagonist Oliver in 'The Killing Line', the child of a beef farmer.

'I had the character Oliver in my mind for a long time,' Costello says. 'I know the territory of his life, what he wrestles with, the love of a father. I know we have to mediate opposites. I wouldn't write if I didn't have to. I write whatever consumes me. If I'm upset by something it will eventually germinate. Some image or story will prompt it.

'The animal issue has probably tormented me for thirty years and I grew up on a farm. I had a very good, loving father who was a very progressive farmer, very good about animal welfare.' Because society as a whole chooses to exploit animals, she does not assign blame to any one group, farmers or industry, 'but the animal issue is, I suppose, a question of mercy for the weak. Milan Kundera said humanity's real moral test is our attitude to those who are at our mercy and he counted animals in that number. Man is the only being that kills for sport. Every other hunts for food.'

The strong have always crushed the weak, she says. 'Look at what's happening in Gaza. It's hard sometimes not to despair.' So her dedication is a deliberate statement, she agrees, a recognition of a loving bond that is deeper than even a fundamental disagreement.

'Yes,' she says. 'I had a very loving relationship with my father and I probably tormented him for many years, arguing. He would have been concerned for me because I had a few years of great despair over animal suffering because I saw it everywhere. I had to pull back from that isolation and pain. As with Gaza, it's terribly hard, but one has to mediate it somehow and plough on.'

Costello, like her writing, is quietly impressive. The Stinging Fly published *The China Factory* in 2012 and it was nominated for the Guardian First Book Award and an Irish Book Award. Reviewing this debut collection, I wrote: 'it's clear Costello is the real deal, capable of turning clay into porcelain'. Her first novel, *Academy Street* (2014), about an Irish woman carving out a life in New York, won both Irish Novel and Irish Book of the Year Awards and was shortlisted for a Costa award. I loved her second, *The River Capture* (2018), a Joycean homage meditating on art, nature and the life of the mind, which was shortlisted for three Irish novel prizes.

Yet she was a reluctant writer. Despite having two stories published in *Hennessy New Irish Writing* in her early twenties, she found the compulsion to write burdensome. She became a primary schoolteacher and writing slipped to the margins but when her marriage broke up in her thirties she began to devote more time to it. When her first book was published, she quit teaching. She quit the Dublin suburbs too after twenty-five years and lives a very quiet life, married to a writer, about forty minutes from where she grew up in rural Galway.

'I wasn't right when I wasn't writing, I wasn't right either when I was but it was less wrong,' she says. 'I did feel it was a burden. I felt it like a disturbance in my life, I didn't know what to do with it, but a story would kind of push up. I would write it and purge it and six months later another would push up.

'I found something gnawing at me, an impulse, an urge to put my finger on something, to know what to think. Joan Didion said: "I write to know my own mind." She was studying Carl Jung around the same time and likens the urge to write to his 'impulse towards consciousness'. Similarly, Tess in *Academy Street* 'doesn't find enough sustenance in ordinary life, she finds it in poetry, in Mass, choral music'. A character in *The China Factory*'s final story also channels Costello: 'All my life, music and books have been the refuge of my mind, the means of striving towards something pure and absolute and sublime.'

'Barcelona' is the collection's oldest story, commissioned by Kevin Barry for a Faber anthology he edited. 'This is ten years' work,' she says of the book. 'It takes me five or six months to complete a story. Getting the voice right is really important, the right tone, mood, then very precise, exact language. I like writing that's honest, no tricks or pyrotechnics. A friend was at a John McGahern workshop. Someone said: "I've used the word illuminate twice in this story. Is that too much?" McGahern said: "Once is too much."'

'I love the fine anatomy of a perfectly constructed sentence,' says the protagonist of 'My Little Pyromaniac', a copy-editor, who takes revenge on an ex-lover who she sees abusing the family pet. 'I suppose when I first started writing it was the Americans I turned to,' says Costello. 'John Cheever, Richard Ford, Flannery O'Connor, Ellen Gilchrist. Alice Munro was like finding home, very exacting language. It was that crisp voice – Frank O'Connor's famous lonely voice – clarity, simplicity. I like long stories that unfold unexpectedly.' Ian McEwan's short stories blew her away, then she discovered Mary Lavin, McGahern, Edna O'Brien.

'My style would be spare and honest. Annie Ernaux said one of the most important things is to record historical data honestly as it happens. I want no marks of labour on the writing, I don't want the interference of the writer's hand on the page, nothing contrived or ornamental. I like stories that are not flashy but slow burners, that have a slight sense of menace or unease, disquiet below the surface.'

'Barcelona' was inspired by a trip to the Catalan capital, 'a beautiful city but I was assaulted by sensory stimuli, birds and animals locked up in cages, the big markets, with trays of tongues and hanging hams'. A woman's memory of a former lover, an antivivisectionist who died tragically, is triggered by watching her new partner eating quail. Other troubling memories surface, spoiling the city break, reminiscent of Joyce's masterpiece 'The Dead'.

'Deus Absconditus', first published in *The Irish Times* in 2014, also features a foreign city. Its protagonist Martin, who appeared in a story from her first collection, visits his scientist son in Paris and is troubled to learn he is to work for a US government lab, recalling an incident of animal cruelty from his childhood and fearing what his child might be capable of.

Martin reflects: 'Travel heightens the senses, makes small, easily forgotten details more acute, significant, imperishable.' The same could be said for fiction. Costello's stories are studded with sharp observations and elegant descriptions, which she records in notebooks, a habit James Salter describes as 'gathering ammo', and which deliver for her readers what Anne Enright calls 'an accumulation of tiny pleasures'. 'If I don't write it down, I might not remember it. A notebook is a very practical, mundane thing.'

'With travel there is a sense of wariness, watchfulness,' says Costello. 'Everything is coming at you, I think it was James Salter who said travel is essential, rejuvenating.' The story, which turns on the terror of what scientists might unleash, ends on a rhapsodic note capturing the majesty of the universe, a sublime moment inspired by the author's imagination taking flight as she drives west on the M6 beyond Loughrea.

'Those moments usually happen in rewrites,' the author says. 'Sometimes my characters have glimpses of the sublime. I am very interested in science, astronomy. I don't know much about astrophysics but I love the thought there is a unifying force, an interconnectedness between everything.

'I want my characters to be rattled by something and come to some small insight. A lot of life happens in your head. A lot of my characters have inner lives that are full of turmoil, they keep secrets, there is shame, they are dealing with moral paradoxes, dilemmas. How do we live with and love people who have harmed us? The issue of forgiveness and compassion, mediating opposites. Conflict and tension are where the growth is. Frances in 'The Choc-Ice Woman' has to deal with a husband who has deceived her and damaged her.

'A lot of stories deal with man's treatment of each other and our fellow species. A lot take place in small, confined spaces, which are gold to a writer – in a car, in a room, in the suburbs. They get a bad rap but I always think about teeming lives behind front doors. Ordinary people have deep lives. Joyce said of *Dubliners* he used the ordinary bread of life. What happens behind the brow is what interests me.' The most confined space of all perhaps.

Costello is unafraid to elide the distinction between author and protagonist. In 'At the Gate', her character observes that she and J.M. Coetzee's creation Elizabeth Costello share the same surname.

'Coetzee is probably the living writer that I admire most and who has influenced me most, the integrity of the writing and the man. He deals with substantial issues: life, death, suffering, the lives of animals, our treatment of each other. He wrestles and suffers, I think. We went to see him in Listowel and my boyfriend at the time was unimpressed. That was the germ of the story. Coetzee himself says all writing is autobiographical. [*The River Capture*'s protagonist] Luke O'Brien's thoughts, which he lets out in his dark night of the soul, are my thoughts. I was letting rip. McGahern too said he reimagines and reinvents, has to write life at a slant, paraphrasing Emily Dickinson.'

It has been suggested that Coetzee's Costello, an Australian animal rights campaigner of Irish ancestry, is his fictional alter ego. Hers too? 'A fictional mother,' she replies. 'Coetzee does women really well. He writes her with such empathy I can feel her decades of pain. With this character, there's no escape from the self, no shirking of awkward truths.' The same might be said of Mary Costello's fiction.

In 'The Killing Line', Oliver lectures on Franz Kafka's *In the Penal Colony*, in which a harrow is transformed into an execution device, its needles inscribing the condemned man's crimes ever deeper in an eventually lethal tattoo. Such barbarism is mirrored in Costello's story's eponymous abattoir killing line, which Oliver visits as a boy.

'One of the tasks of the writer is to imagine the unimaginable, it's about facing it, not looking away.' Similarly in 'The Choc-Ice Woman', first published in *The New Yorker*, the embalming process is described in gruesome detail. 'That came about very organically,' she says. 'If I'm in the mind of the character, it's very up close and intimate. In Frances's case, her brother is going to be embalmed, so she has googled it.' Costello is no stranger to search engines. 'I do like to face things. It is somewhat brutal and unpleasant but I don't like to turn a blind eye.'

Frances discovered long ago from the top seat of a bus that her husband was cheating on her. 'In the space of five minutes and five yards her whole life began to slide sideways.' This epitomizes what a lot of Costello's stories try to capture, the turning point of a life.

It feels ironic that our interview takes place on Valentine's Day. Romance is dead or dying in many of these stories. No space is more confined perhaps than that surrounding an unhappy couple. 'A lot of McGahern stories are about men and women,' she says of a writer wrongly pigeonholed as pastoral. 'In the same way, my stories are not dealing with the everyday but the hidden lives of women and men, what is unsaid, those tensions and misunderstandings.'

Mary Costello was born in Galway and lives in Dublin. A former teacher, she writes full-time. She has written two short-story collections, The China Factory *(2012), nominated for the* Guardian *First Book Award, and* Barcelona *(2024).* Academy Street *(2014), her first novel, won the Irish Novel of the Year award and the Irish Book of the Year and was shortlisted for the International Dublin Literary Award, the Costa First Novel Prize and the EU Prize for Literature. Her other novels are* The River Capture *(2019) and* A Beautiful Loan *(2026).*

PATRICIA CRAIG

18 July 1992, The Irish Post

'For all the disagreeable images associated with Northern Ireland – bigotry, aggressiveness, a backward-looking mentality, and so on – we find in the literature of the last 200-odd years continuous acknowledgment of its fascination and its virtues, including the virtue of egalitarianism, which has always interposed itself between competing prejudices.'

With these introductory words, Patricia Craig, the London-based, Belfast-born literary critic, sets out her stall for *The Rattle of the North: An Anthology of Ulster Prose* (Blackstaff Press, 1992), which celebrates the distinctiveness and distinction of Northern prose over the past 200 years.

Craig is now a well-established book reviewer and anthologist, despite having attended art school rather than going on to study English. She admits that art school was a mistake as her first and abiding love was books ever since she bought her first in Belfast's Smithfield market at the age of six.

'I was born and brought up in Belfast for the first twenty years of my life and then came to London as an arts student and somehow got into writing sort of sideways,' she says. 'I taught in a girls' school for a year and hated it, so I had to do anything to get out of that. I wrote an article on Virginia Woolf that was published by the *Observer*, which was wonderful. Of course, then they never asked me to do anything else, at least not at that time anyway.

'I then wrote a study of girls' fiction called *You're a Brick, Angela!* (Gollancz, 1976) in collaboration with Mary Cadogan. After that people started asking me to review, so I started writing for the *Times Literary Supplement*. I then wrote a biography of Elizabeth Bowen in the Penguin Lives of Modern Women series, and went on to do various anthologies, most recently the *Oxford Book of English Detective Stories* (1990) and the *Penguin Book of British Comic Stories* (1992).'

The Rattle of the North, whose title was inspired by Belfast poet W. R. Rodgers, is a substantial 443 pages, but when one considers the scope of the project, it is obviously a remarkable feat of research and selection.

'Yes, it meant absolutely masses of research,' agrees the editor. 'I mean, I started with an advantage. Most of the subjects I knew something about, so I knew where to look, but even so for the anthology that I'm working on now, I expect to have at least twice as much material as I need. I suppose it took about a year to put together, but I had to be very strict with myself in the end. Hundreds of things had to be left out. One or two people do have two essays in the book, like Seamus Heaney, but this is simply because they couldn't be left out. The subjects were so interesting.'

Craig makes clear in her introduction the criteria she employed to make her selection. Extracts had to be able to stand up on their own, which excluded the work of Brian Friel and Bernard MacLaverty, whose short stories she felt had to be taken as a whole.

'In assembling this anthology, I have tried to confine myself to those pieces of prose literature, both fiction and nonfiction, which express a peculiar and very vivid Northern Irishness. Among the qualities I have looked for are resonance, illumination, high-powered analysis, vigorous recollection, or re-creation.'

The anthology is divided into sections, beginning with a series of historical pieces from Eamonn McCann, A.T.Q. Stewart and Marianne Elliott, whose purpose Craig states as being 'to set the scene for much of what follows'. Other sections deal with autobiographical writing, fiction and critical pieces given over to discipline, such as architecture, nature studies, sociology and linguistics.

Such writing is by no means dry, however, and some of the most pertinent and persuasive pieces come from surprising sources, such as James Stevens Curl's masterly essay on the Londonderry Plantation. A black humour peculiar to the North is a feature of this anthology, represented by such as William Carleton, Clogher Valley peasant and nineteenth-century novelist. Craig relates one comic incident.

'There is a marvellous set piece in his novel, *Valentine McClutchy* (1857), in which a Protestant convert, Darby, comes face to face with his Catholic counterpart, Bob. Gradually, a subtle shift in positions occurs as the two men revert to their original faiths. It isn't long before they come to blows, with support from co-religionists of both persuasions. However, as it happens, "the Catholics, ignorant of the turn which the controversy had taken, supported Bob and Protestantism, while the Protestants, owing to a similar mistake, fought like devils for Darby and the Pope".'

It has been said that Southern writers tend to gild the lily whereas Northerners are more given to a sharper, more astringent style. 'I think that's true, and it's a quality of Northern writing that I particularly like,' Craig says. 'I do think you get this astringency and this rather biting wit, and slight elements of bitterness in some cases, but there's always an element of humour, I hope.'

Craig is indebted to Michael Longley, who, as literature editor of the Arts Council in Belfast, first suggested the anthology; to the writer Robert Johnstone; and to Belfast's Linen Hall Library, 'an invaluable source – I haunt the place'; but most of all to the late poet John Hewitt, her hero and mentor.

'John Hewitt stood for all that's good about Northern Ireland, the egalitarian drive at its most extreme. For Protestant integrity, protestant ideally with a small p, in its most cogent form, you should turn to John Hewitt, who never felt his Planter ancestry excluded him from the deepest affiliation with Northern Ireland or, for that matter, Ireland.'

An interesting dialectic is established in the book between Hewitt, the returned émigré, and Louis MacNeice, fellow poet and Ulsterman but unreconciled exile.

'With MacNeice, though, it was always a case of '*odi atque amo*' [I hate and I love], as he put it himself, of being repulsed by the place and drawn to it at the same time. This, indeed, is a rational attitude. Northern Ireland has much to repudiate and much to cherish. John Hewitt and Louis MacNeice represent two opposing attitudes to Northern Ireland. Hewitt really immersed himself in the place, whereas MacNeice couldn't wait to get out of it, though the piece in the book by him shows, I think, that when he came back he realized it wasn't as bad as he remembered.'

In compiling the anthology, Craig was determined to present Ulster warts and all, but through enlightened eyes and gifted prose. She is refreshingly unabashed in declaring that 'I would hope as well that an anti-sectarian stance is implicit throughout this anthology in so far as it posits a good deal of common ground shared by the two communities.

'This is a very important point. Everyone who thinks about Northern Ireland thinks about bigotry, but it is so much more complicated than that. Alongside that there has always been this drive towards tolerance, towards understanding your neighbour, this egalitarian impulse.'

Although subtitled *An Anthology of Ulster Prose*, *The Rattle of the North* omits writers from Monaghan and Cavan, but includes Donegal, thus respecting neither political nor provincial boundary. 'This is purely a personal thing. I had to use the word "Ulster" in the title and that does carry a certain political connotation. Some people don't like that term, but I then qualify that it's not in fact the nine counties, it's seven. Donegal for me is part of the North, whereas the other two for some reason aren't. I know people do think that Patrick Kavanagh is a Northern writer. I can't see him in that light. He associated himself so much with Dublin, living there for most of his life.'

As Craig herself admits, people who are aware of Northern literature tend to think of poetry rather than prose. Did she have trouble keeping verse from invading her work?

'Yes, I did. Well, I smuggled a few poems into the introduction. I would like to do an anthology of poetry as well, but one of the points of the book was to demonstrate that a lot of good prose had also been written in Northern Ireland.'

In fact, the wily poets inveigled their way into the collection anyway, with Heaney, Ciaran Carson, MacNeice and Hewitt appearing as comfortable with prose as with poetry. Craig's personal favourite in the collection is Carson's compelling piece, 'Question Time'.

In the light of the controversy over Field Day's neglect of Irish women's writing in its anthology, is Craig concerned about the shortage of women in her book?

'There is a shortage of women. I'm not sure why. I could have put more women in, but I wasn't doing the anthology to make a feminist point. I wanted good writing and I didn't really care where it came from. My complaint about the Field Day anthology was more along the lines that they had no women editors. They had thirty-three editors and not one woman among them.'

Craig is happily ensconced in Blackheath, one of London's pleasanter suburbs, with her husband, the Welsh painter Geoffrey Morgan, and her work as a reviewer ties her somewhat to the capital. Ireland exerts a definite pull, however.

'You don't absolutely have to be London-based but it does help. It is also necessary to be in touch with publishers in connection with the other anthologies I am working on. Also, I quite like it over here. I suppose I've just got used to it. I must say, though, I'd hate not to go back to Northern Ireland. I have to get back at least three times a year.'

Patricia Craig returned to Belfast in 1999, where she still lives. Her books include the anthologies You're a Brick, Angela!*;* The Girls' Story 1839–1985 *(1976);* The Lady Investigates: Women Detectives and Spies in Fiction *(1986)*; The Penguin Book of British Comic Stories *(1992);* The Oxford Book of Modern Women's Stories *(1994);* The Oxford Book of Ireland *(1998);* Twelve Irish Ghost Stories *(1998);* Brian Moore: A Biography (2002)*; and the memoirs* Asking for Trouble *(2008);* A Twisted Root – Ancestral Entanglements in Ireland (2012)*; and* Bookworm: A Memoir of Childhood Reading *(2015).*

MARTINA DEVLIN

25 August 2007, The Irish Post

Given the subject of her previous book, it is somehow appropriate that Martina Devlin's new novel, *Ship of Dreams*, begins on a *Titanic* lifeboat.

For she is a survivor too. *The Hollow Heart*, 'the true story of how one woman's desire to have a baby almost destroyed her life', sets out for the first time in the first person the traumatic effect on a woman of infertility, IVF treatment and coping with the failure to conceive.

It is a painfully personal account of the author's journey from bewilderment at being diagnosed as infertile, the emotional and physical rollercoaster of IVF treatment, and finally the slow realization that not only has her hope of being a mother been destroyed but also her marriage.

However, there is an uplifting end to the story. Devlin also recounts how she learnt to channel her thwarted desire to procreate into becoming a budding author, and she passes on her philosophy of life which comes across not as glib and superficial but as hard-won and insightful.

Devlin met her husband in London where she was a reporter. A native of Omagh, County Tyrone, she wanted to move back to Dublin to start her married life and start a family with her husband, a fellow expatriate.

She was blissfully happy, but also blissfully ignorant of her infertility.

She jokes how, as a mature student at Trinity, she was the only student who wanted to get pregnant. But slowly it dawned on her that there was a problem. Despite thermometers, four-poster beds in country house hotels, miraculous medals, medicinal herbs and a sex life subjugated to conception, it just wasn't happening.

When she learns that her fallopian tubes are damaged, she feels betrayed by her body, contemptuous of it. 'I felt profoundly, intrinsically, forlornly defective.'

She almost bleeds to death after a ruptured ectopic pregnancy and comes to the painful realization that only a miscarriage, not marriage or a mortgage, makes her feel for the first time like an adult. This is fully-grown suffering.

'Up until that I had a very smooth ride,' Devlin says. 'Suddenly you realize you're not in the driving seat. I realized how fragile life is. We take our good luck for granted. I always assumed I would be able to have children.'

The couple decided to sacrifice all their disposable income to IVF treatment, but if this put a strain on things it was nothing to the effect of Devlin's desire to have a baby, which turned into an obsession. As after each IVF session she lost her embryos, which she calls her maybe babies, her obsession grew and her relationship with her husband slowly withered.

'In my heart I rejected him as an inadequate substitute,' she recalls. 'I did not want his arms around me. I wanted my own around a baby.'

Looking back, she is struck by the lack of counselling available for couples undergoing IVF. She describes how her husband felt unnerved, bewildered and excluded as she turned into a 'hormonal harpy', who needed to be petted and consoled but failed to understand he had his own sorrow.

'We didn't realize love alone was the prize and anything else was a dividend.'

Today, she says, clinics still need to do more to educate couples about the side effects.

'You're put into a fake menopause with one barrage of drugs, then you're put on another barrage of drugs and your ovaries are stimulated. You feel like a battery hen, you produce 10–14 eggs instead of one, your emotions are all over the place, euphoric or tearful at the drop of a hat. I think counselling would have helped my husband.

'It would have helped me too, I thought I just was coping badly, I wasn't strong enough. I'd already learnt my body was defective, now I thought everything else about me is defective as well.'

Coming out the other side, her marriage over, already seriously depressed, Devlin suffers a near-fatal car accident, breaking her sternum and detaching a retina. She becomes addicted to sleeping pills but recovers to look back and understand that her former self may have been happier and brighter but also weaker, with no concept of adversity.

Knowing pain helps you value joy, she says. 'It's not what an indifferent fate lobs your way that matters, but how you respond to it … Failing doesn't make you a failure. It makes you someone who cared enough to try … Love the life you have, not the life you think you should have.'

These are pearls of wisdom, mother of pearl.

In her seven years with PA, Devlin's was always the first hand to come up when the assignment was to interview an author.

'I always fancied interviewing writers,' she says. 'I wanted to ask them how they wrote. My favourite was interviewing Anthony Burgess in the Savoy. He would always take all the leftover cakes and biscuits. He would call over his wife, the Contessa, and she filled her handbag.'

Her oddest encounter, however, was in Parkhurst prison with Reggie Kray, who was promoting a book on Cockney rhyming slang.

'He lifted me up and kissed me on the mouth. I was so taken aback I never asked a single difficult question. I was in a state of catatonic shock for the rest of the interview. He started writing to me. I lived on his patch in Bethnal Green. You'd know there was something unusual about the person writing, very spidery, random use of upper and lower case. My features editor encouraged me to write back and develop a good relationship but I didn't. I brought his letter to a handwriting expert as part of another assignment. When she got to it, she dropped it as if it burned her hand, she said to me "this person is pathological".'

While Devlin's book is a powerful and valuable insight into a subject that affects many people, it also presumably intrudes on her ex-husband's own grief and, although he is not named, infringes his privacy.

'I suppose I'm an ex-husband's worst nightmare really,' Devlin admits. 'I would just say in my defence that I tried to be much harder on myself than on my husband. It was my own behaviour I was trying to study and criticize. I invaded my own privacy a lot more than I invaded his. At some stage as a writer, you've got to set that to one side, you're never going to please everybody.

'But what persuaded me to write the book in the first place was I knew there was a group of people out there, disenfranchised and isolated by the fact that they were infertile. Nobody had ever spoken about it, I thought it was time someone stepped up to the plate and said this happened to me, it does make a wasteland of your life but there is light at the end of the tunnel.

'Anyone I ever heard about who had IVF had been successful. I was very struck by the fact that they were the rare ones, the success rate is something like one in five. You're not aware how slim the chances are and that the drugs you take will make a whirligig of your life. I and my husband weren't prepared for the kind of person I turned into.'

Was writing *The Hollow Heart* a catharsis or was there a price to be paid, revisiting pain?

'I never found it cathartic, I found it very painful, for to write authentically you had to go back to that time and place and person you were. It brought a lot of grief back. Technically it was the easiest book to write, the plot was already laid out, but emotionally it was the hardest, because I had to take a long, cold look at myself and see a lot of flaws.

'I'm more interested in historical writing now. It's very difficult for women writers to set books in contemporary times and not be packaged as chick lit. I don't think the content of my books is chick lit but you would think so from the covers, which signal mass market because it leads to higher sales.'

Having put herself under the microscope in *The Hollow Heart*, Devlin takes out a historical telescope for *Ship of Dreams*, unearthing and reimagining the true story of an ancestor who went down with the *Titanic*.

'*Ship of Dreams* is inspired by my family history. It opens on a *Titanic* lifeboat and it follows the fortunes of six survivors. My great-grandmother's brother eloped with a woman. They ran away on the *Titanic*. He went down with it but she survived, landed in New York and had his baby five months later. I was just fascinated by that, all these Irish emigrants thinking their ship had come in, but two-thirds of them never made it. It's nearly a hundred years on, it happened in 1912, but we're still transfixed by the *Titanic* story.

'This was the machine age and man thought he had mastered everything including the elements and the sea, and the iceberg showed him clearly that he hadn't. Then there's the whole idea of multimillionaires and penniless emigrants going down together. It seemed to be the last hurrah of empire, the idea that English people acted in a particular way as an example to the rest of the world, these ideas of women and children first, the captain exhorting his crew to be British.

'I weave real and fictional characters together. I don't know why they eloped. They signed on as husband and wife but they would have had to as they were sharing a cabin. He had four sisters in Chicago and they paid for his passage. The people you can ask are now long dead. I have spoken to some relatives in America but they don't know about the Irish side.

'In some ways it's a paradigm of modern life. We still think we've conquered the elements but very clearly the elements are fighting back with global warming. In some ways the aftermath of the *Titanic* reminds me of the aftermath of 9/11, the same shock and disbelief.'

Martina Devlin's twelve books include the memoir The Hollow Heart *(2005) and the novels* Edith *(2022), about the writer Edith Somerville;* About Sisterland *(2015);* The House Where It Happened *(2014); and* Ship of Dreams *(2007). Her latest is* Charlotte: A Novel *(2024) about Charlotte Brontë. She won a Hennessy Literary Award for her first short story in 1996 and has won or been shortlisted for several literary awards including the Royal Society of Literature's VS Pritchett Prize. She writes a weekly column for the* Irish Independent *and has been named National Newspapers of Ireland columnist of the year. She holds a PhD in literary practice from Trinity College Dublin, where she was awarded the Pyle Bursary for her research. She was born in Omagh and lives in Dublin.*

EMMA DONOGHUE

11 April 2026, The Irish Times

If you read Emma Donoghue's latest novel, *The Paris Express* (2025), inspired by the Montparnasse rail crash in 1895, followed by *Haven* (2022), based on the founding of a monastery on Skellig Michael in the seventh century, then her debut novel, *Stir-Fry* (1994), a coming-out story set in the Dublin of her youth, it is striking how dated the latter feels, while the others have a timeless quality.

Donoghue, a strikingly cheerful, good-humoured interviewee, agrees that *Stir-Fry* feels as if it is set in another world. 'It's as if Ireland changed so fast that the geological layers are compressed,' she says. *Stir-Fry*'s student protagonist is so innocent and so closeted, she is almost in Narnia. She has no inkling that her flatmates are gay or herself for that matter. 'It's funny, contemporary fiction dates much faster. One reviewer thought *Stir-Fry* was set in the 1960s. Of course, that was Ireland in the '90s.'

She is chatting via Zoom from London, Ontario, where she set up home with her Canadian partner who she met while studying in Cambridge University.

'There is not such a gap between the two countries now,' she says. 'I could live fine in Ireland but in 1990, that was a good time to go. It lifted the crushing weight of being the only gay in the village, not that I was ever in a village.'

Stir-Fry was autobiographical insofar that it dealt with a student coming out but whereas she was a suburban Dubliner crossing the road to UCD, her protagonist was a country girl in the Edna O'Brien tradition, giving the story more of a shape by adding cultural tension in the 'stranger who comes to town' mould. Her second novel, *Hood*, was more autobiographical, based on her convent school, Muckross Park. 'Like many writers, I needed to start with my own life material.'

Donoghue was fourteen when she realized both that she was gay and that she wanted to be a writer. 'Like many teenage writers, love was my great theme. Falling in love with a girl at fourteen promoted a huge tsunami of poetry. So it felt as if there was a libidinal impulse in the writing and also a drive towards empathy and understanding people who weren't myself.' It gave her a passionate, secret subject to write about. 'But equally being a writer helped me come out. I'd sold two books to Penguin. I didn't want my mother to read about them in a book review in *The Irish Times*. That gave me a deadline to come out.'

Donoghue's parents were 'pretty liberal for Irish Catholics with eight children'. Her father, the critic and UCD academic Denis Donoghue, confronted her about it when she was nineteen, telling her not to stop going to Mass and fretting that she might not get her first. 'He feared that lesbianism was going to be so distracting, so potent. I assured him I would still get my first-class honours, which I did.' Her mother had already guessed when Emma was sixteen but never spoke to her or her husband about it. 'We had one of those classic Irish silences for five years, so she had got used to the idea. She said something lovely like, "you'll have to blaze your own trail but you're good at that." No matter how many fans you have, if your family have rejected you there's no healing that wound.'

Donoghue believes that being gay taught her that bonds between human beings come in all forms and made her interested in the outsider, the scapegoat, freaks, the enslaved. 'I'm fascinated by the underdog. I grew up very normal and approved of and yet I had this secret side that I thought everyone would consider foul. Every one of us can be the nice normal person and the monster.'

'For every opportunity that I missed because of someone's homophobia, I'm sure I've been given others because of the novelty factor.' She was on *The Late Late Show* twice in the early '90s, talking about her work. 'It did feel like instant fame.' Its paternalistic host Gay Byrne feared she might regret it later. 'I assured him I wouldn't suffer.

'I remember some Irish journalist ringing up and asking what do Irish lesbians think about this and I thought, *I'm living in England, am I the only one you could find?* Luckily there was a lesbian on *Big Brother* who was quickly more famous than me and I thought, *what a relief to pass the torch.*'

Moving to Cambridge and then to Canada gave her psychological freedom. 'It felt like a more aerated culture, things were looser, part of a colourful palette.'

She was determined, though, not to be defined by her sexuality. 'Every writer struggles with how much to represent their home community, whether that be class, ethnicity or disability, anything that marks you. About a third of my books has a same-sex story line but I feel very relaxed about it.'

Donoghue, a novelist, screenwriter, playwright and literary historian, is one of Ireland's most versatile writers, always ready to try something new and to switch effortlessly between genres.

'I know that I enjoy the work enough that I will always come back to it, so I'm happy to be distracted to buy a pair of flip-flops while researching something. Similarly,' she says laughing, 'if I am working on the novel and suddenly get an idea for a short story, a little adulterous weekend with the short story will just refresh me for the marital commitment of the novel.

'My process is quite light-hearted and promiscuous and open to whatever happens. If I'm on holiday and suddenly get an idea for something I start taking notes, whereas for some writers I think books come one at a time and perhaps painfully and very intensely, so they have to give it their all. My parents had eight children so that's my mindset, a busy household with people coming and going. Projects are like that. I don't want to get smug and repetitious, it's good to experiment.'

She has just finished a screenplay based on Helen Macdonald's *H Is for Hawk*. 'I don't know why they asked me. I'm not known for my knowledge of the bird kingdom. I thought it could be impossible to adapt for it's a multi-genre non-fiction book but it was so beautifully written, I love that kind of task. I work quite fast. Also with film writing you don't know which one is going to make it, so it is good to intersperse it with other things.'

Her first musical, *The Wind Coming over the Sea*, about an Irish family emigrating to Canada in Famine times, premiered in 2025. 'The theme is oddly timely. There are such waves of hostility to emigration, it feels political to do a show about an immigrant who is a vulnerable, needy outsider but is also bringing all this energy, drive and hard work to the country.'

She is conscious of being part of a long tradition of Irish emigration to Canada, including the Belfast writer Brian Moore. 'I was very aware of ancestors, comfortable moving first to England then to Canada, conscious of a long tradition in both places. I could go to the pub and hear Irish music, feel connected. It softens the sting of emigration.

'I've been familiar with [Moore] since I was a teenager. I was at a party here in the '90s and some academic said to me, "you'll suffer from the Brian Moore problem". "What's that?" I asked. I thought he was a very honourable ancestor. He said, "your reputation will be fatally divided between several literary traditions. You won't be 100 per cent Irish or Canadian." I decided I wouldn't worry about my literary reputation, that's not something writers should be trying to shape themselves. We should just work on our projects and, if people like them, reputation will accrue.'

Such labelling is retrograde, anyway, she thinks. 'So many of us live hybrid, complex lives. I loved Gethan Dick's novel *Water in the Desert, Fire in the Night*. She is Irish but lives in France. It struck me as so unbounded by the conventions of Irish fiction. What sense does it make to say to her: pick a side?'

Donoghue shows me her treadmill desk, where she exercises while researching a topic or dealing with emails. 'It is perfect for that, whereas if I want to write a brand-new scene, I do like to sit down. A lot of our day is not absolutely raw creation.'

Her computer screen is balanced to an ergonomic height on the *Field Day Anthology of Irish Literature* – the corrected version featuring volumes 4 and 5 to include women writers. Donoghue contributed a lesbian section.

She credits Ailbhe Smyth with opening her eyes to the absence of women from the UCD English syllabus, bar Jane Austen, Emily Brontë and Emily Dickinson. But didn't her father set the curriculum? 'He was a gentle patriarch; we just so enjoyed talking about books,' she says. 'We had more in common than we had differences. He may only have written about canonical women authors but he did take them very seriously. He was so proud that I was a writer. He sent me a lovely postcard after each book. He gave me ideas for stories, told me "Ruskin had a terrible wedding night when he couldn't consummate his marriage – you should look at that."'

The Paris Express features a sympathetically drawn anarchist would-be suicide bomber. Was it influenced by Ireland's home-grown revolutionaries?

'It was part of the mix but I was just as interested in the idea of the suicide bomber, a vulnerable person, rather than a cold-blooded killer, that wouldn't interest me. My dad was Northern and retained a certain sympathy for the 32-county ideal but he was repelled by violence. My family was typical of

Southern Catholics. I grew up thinking of the IRA as that mad shower north of the Border who were kneecapping people in our names.'

The Paris Express reminded me of Robert Harris. 'Oh, I am honoured, I've never been compared to him but I have all his books, I love him. Isn't he marvellous at wearing his historical knowledge lightly, no sense of "let me share what I know" with the readers, just relaxed enough to share tiny details?

'I remember being struck by literary writers such as Julian Barnes and Margaret Atwood turning to historical fiction, who didn't seem to be weighed down by genre conventions. They were liberating as role models.'

She did find *The Paris Express*'s big cast of characters a challenge. Some characters after a few scenes weren't earning their keep so she had to go back and cut them out of every scene. It required a lot of darning. 'Yet to write about a train is to commit yourself to a large group. It's not a car, it's mass transit. I needed that sweep of society. I can almost picture readers walking away, "oh no, another character", or medieval monks, or vomit or smallpox pustules. That's always a key moment where I re-commit to the book. Those readers weren't going to like it anyway so there is no point pursuing them or watering it down to suit them.'

She is fearless at this stage. There is no subject she wouldn't touch, however oddly she might approach them. They would be like exotic holidays for her to tackle. There are limits, though. One of her future novels is set during a war 'but there will be no battle scenes, Martin'. She had to consult friends for the card-game scenes in *Frog Music* and anything to do with alcohol as she is teetotal. Her next novel, *Blaze* (2027), is set in the near future, 'a first for me, apart from a novella. Again, I feel like a newbie.'

Haven is possibly my favourite of her works. Like Edna O'Brien and Brian Moore, whose novella *Catholics* similarly deals with a wayward offshoot of the Church on a remote Irish island, she has moved from the personal to the political.

'Writing books set in the past is often sneered at as escape into convention but actually no, it's the broader picture, historically and politically, bigger subjects. I don't know why anyone would stay limited to the era they are living in any more than the place they are living in. If you can write about Japan, why can't you write about the seventh century?'

There is something darkly funny, an ecological parable, about these ancient monks worshipping God on an island so barren they are reduced to cooking puffins on a fire fuelled by burning puffins, a 'perfectly hideous' historical fact she found scouring records from seventeenth-century Newfoundland.

Haven's dictatorial leader refuses to trade with the mainland. Is he partly inspired by de Valera? 'Not consciously, but unconsciously it's all in there. Having grown up in Ireland and felt this culture is too small and having made my escape, I would have a natural nervousness about the island's isolationism and above all cultural purity. It's a very feminist book. Gender comes up all the time. The leader thinks that by leaving women behind he can leave all bad stuff behind. That false notion of purity gives me the willies.'

I am struck by the unlikely resurrection of the Catholic novel, from Sally Rooney's *Intermezzo* to Niamh Mulvey's *The Amendments*.

'It's very interesting. In both *Haven* and *The Wonder*, I had to go deep into my Catholic heritage and wanted to avoid kneejerk judgmentalism because in both cases, whether mid-nineteenth century or seventh century, I found a lot to treasure as well. Just as early Christians divided God up into Father, Son and Holy Spirit, I tried to divide up Christianity. I gave the more hateful aspects to Art, the practical, sturdy bits to Cormac [named after Cormac Kinsella, the book's publicist] and made the young monk the St Francis of Assisi at one with nature. You can't read St Patrick's Breastplate and not be moved by it.'

When I turn to her most successful novel, *Room*, inspired by the notorious Joseph Fritzl case, she congratulates me for getting an hour into the interview without mentioning it. Why does she think it was so successful?

'I think it would have worked even if it was not based on a real case. I was lucky enough to happen on a storyline that has an archetypal quality. Many people feel their lives are too small, they are imprisoned in some sense and want to escape to a bigger life. The highly specific and weird storyline of Ma in the locked shed does remind people of their own childhoods or bad marriages or other times their lives felt limited. People in China and Iran have written it is clearly a political allegory.

'Some people were surprised I included the second half. They thought it would just be an escape story, but the second half is crucial, all those moments when Jack is missing Room, he prefers a smaller world. A lot of people have those feelings when they leave their old country – the nostalgia of the emigrant, confused feelings about the bad part of the past.'

'*The Pull of the Stars* got its most passionate readers from doctors and nurses. *Room* has a much greater range. All I can claim credit for is I knew the child's perspective would be fresh. Kidnapped women had been written about before. The defamiliarization device also made it bearable. Jack is not unhappy, he doesn't feel he is in a nightmare because of his mother's love.

'When I was writing *Room*, I thought a lot about child narrators such as Roddy Doyle's *Paddy Clarke Ha Ha Ha*, a novel I not only loved but also noticed because he won the Booker with it, but also L.P. Hartley's *The Go-Between* and *Spies* by Michael Frayn, the painful ironies of what a child knows, especially about sex, which makes no sense to kids.

'The reason I hit on the storyline is I had two small children. That sensitized me to the psychological bond between mother and child, the perfect convergence of motherhood and the storyline.'

So the pram, or double buggy, in the hall was a help, not a hindrance. 'Motherhood also made me write more thoroughly, because I had less time.'

Her son and daughter turn up in all her books. 'They find it quite amusing how they morph in different books. Both kids have a very hearty appetite. In *The Wonder*, I remember thinking if this was 1850s Ireland and if you were rewarded for not eating, how might all this intelligence and wit be funnelled into a weird form of mysticism? They end up inspiring characters who are not very like them but have something of their energy. Finn picked up *Haven*. "Am I the weird, gangly monk who's climbing up the cliffs?" "Yes, you are."'

Donoghue is slightly embarrassed to admit what a cold-blooded Apollonian planner she is. 'Pantsers [who make it up as they go along] get all the limelight, this myth of writing as an inspired fever dream, like taking drugs and going into the Outback, a vision quest. Writing may have elements of vision and mystery, like "how did that idea drop in my lap?" but the doing of it, especially a full-length novel, requires a lot of planning and organization.

'I bristle a bit that it sounds uncool, but writing requires a lot of moving the pieces around. Planning is very liberating because if you have a half-hour free, the Scrivener creative-writing programme is a lot of boxes within boxes, so you can work on one little scene, as opposed to waiting to be completely in the zone. I want to be able to snatch time as it arises, so I have it all on my computer. I can see how it might help moving scenes from a longer to a shorter chapter.'

Her English degree and PhD help, 'quite apart from the chats with Dad on Dún Laoghaire pier'.

Did the success of *Room* free or pressurize her?

'I was lucky to get published when life was really cheap, living in a housing co-op in Cambridge. I didn't have a mortgage and kids; I have not felt the pressure of earning to constrain my art. What *Room* did was give me many more readers, not so much the money but more people will take a punt on reading my books. I did think it could be like a gun to my head but it was such a one-off, a freaky story line, that I couldn't churn out a series like that. I will never, ever write a sequel to that book. It doesn't require one. Let the success of this book just be a rising tide of confidence but I don't have to be on the bestseller list every time.'

She loves adapting her work, collaborating with Lenny Abrahamson on a screenplay or Cosa Bisset on a stage production, embracing the way the story naturally needs to change. 'I'm not focused on protecting or retaining my story, just enjoying what becomes of it in a different form.'

Screenplays, she has observed, are a much more modern format than the novel yet much more rigid. The novel has no rules.

'This all has to do with the gluteal muscle,' she says. 'If it's a time-based artform like a play or a film, people are sitting down. [I think instinctively of the Sean O'Casey trilogy at the Abbey, whose seats make Ryanair's feel like armchairs.] With novels, people can take their own time.'

Donoghue was born in Dublin in 1969. She is best known for Room *(2010), which won the Irish Book Award and was shortlisted for the Booker Prize. Her screenplay for the film adaptation won her an Oscar nomination. Her debut novel,* Stir-Fry *(1994), was a finalist for the Lambda Literary Award.* Hood *(1995) won what is now the Stonewall Book Award for Literature.* The Sealed Letter *(2010) was joint winner of the Lambda Literary Award for Lesbian Fiction.* The Wonder *(2016) was made into a film starring Florence Pugh in 2022.* Haven *(2022) was shortlisted for the International Dublin Literary Award.*

RODDY DOYLE

17 July 1993, The Irish Post

Roddy Doyle, asked what kind of a teacher he was, replies: 'I ruled in a way, by entertainment.' The author writes in a similar vein, winning him a different sort of captive audience.

Doyle is a master storyteller, whether it's the rise and fall of a Dublin soul band, the ups and downs of teenage pregnancy or the strains on family and friendship caused by the breadwinner's unemployment.

Hollywood and the BBC haven't been slow to appreciate Doyle's flair for strong storylines, loveable characters and authentic, funny dialogue.

Alan Parker made *The Commitments* into an internationally successful film and Stephen Frears repeated that success with the BBC screenplay of *The Snapper*. Plans are already underway to produce *The Van* in Dublin and Doyle has just written a four-hour-long serial, *Family*, for the BBC to be filmed later this year. *Family* was written at the same time as his new novel, *Paddy Clarke Ha Ha Ha*, which is the story told in the first person of ten-year-old Paddy Clarke, who breathlessly recounts his many experiences, the harshest of which is his witnessing, without fully understanding, the gradual break-up of his parents' marriage.

'I often write two things at the same time,' explains Doyle, 'because I think the ideas bounce off each other. *Paddy Clarke* is sort of a tender book. It's really quite warm. It's funny though it's sad at the same time. There is warmth in *Family* from some of the characters, but basically it's a quite dark and grim story.'

Paddy Clarke is full of the mischief of childhood. The shoe lost in mud, the Grand National races over neighbours' fences, the bullying of little brothers, all innocent of irony.

'The trite enough reason,' according to Doyle, why his new novel is set in 1968, 'is because of the short little chapter where Paddy and his father are watching the European Cup Final, and George Best scores. It worried me for a while because he's ten and I was ten in 1968. So people might presume it's my story, but not to the extent of leaving it out because I think it's important to have that moment of tenderness between him and his father.'

George Best is also involved in an incident, which marks the end of the age of innocence for Paddy Clarke. His father has given him a football annual with an introduction from George Best, complete with facsimile signature, which Paddy thinks is real.

'George Best had great handwriting. It slanted to the right. It was long and the holes were narrow. There was a dead straight line under the name joining the G and the B all the way to the T at the end and a bit further. It finished with swerve, like a diagram of a shot going past a wall.'

Disillusionment is not long in coming, however. 'A year after that, I knew it wasn't George Best's real autograph at all; it was only printing and my da was a liar.'

Paddy Clarke may be set in Barrytown, the same invented Northside Dublin suburb of his first three novels. But it represents a major change and challenge met for the author. For the first time, there's a narrator and the book is set in a different era.

'One of the things I'm very happy with about *Paddy Clarke* is that it's different to the others. I had great difficulty writing *The Snapper*, having written the first one, because I didn't know if I could write another one and I felt the same after *The Van*. It came quite easily – I wrote it in a year – but I wondered was I stuck in a rut, a nice rut. Now, I have more confidence that I can do a lot of different things. Having said that, I don't know what the next one will be about.

'I suppose one of the successes of the book is the capturing of a ten-year-old's mind. If you tell the story, there's nothing to it, but the words are chosen in such a way that hopefully it seems a ten-year-old is creating them and not a 35-year-old.'

The insights into a child's mind, the capturing of a child's patterns of thought and speech and the conjuring up of an Ireland of the recent past with a troubled outside world looming like a scary cartoon combine to suggest a parallel with Patrick McCabe's marvellous but much darker *The Butcher Boy*.

'The power of that book,' Doyle agrees, 'is in the words and the way the character drives those words so I suppose there is a similarity there in the language.'

Becoming a father fascinated Doyle to the extent that he gave up his teaching job as his enthusiasm was diverted to his own two children. It also opened a door in his mind back into his own childhood.

'I was spurred on by the birth of my first son, Rory. I started thinking about my childhood in a way that I hadn't before. It was like the gates opened and I went back six years that I didn't think I would be capable of.'

Memory is not truth, however, just as total recall alone does not make for literature.

'I'm told that I have an amazing memory. If my parents are consulting about what happened when, they generally ask me. But it's imagination as much as anything else. I do recall running through a field and a pheasant flying up, and that's in *Paddy Clarke*. I take the memories all right, but I twist them.

'I listed off very early on the names of TV programmes and a lot of them brought back memories. I do remember one Saturday being in trouble and the punishment was that I wasn't allowed to watch *The Man from U.N.C.L.E* and if I'd been given the choice between having my leg sawn off or not being allowed to watch *The Man from U.N.C.L.E* I'd have taken the leg any day.'

Did becoming a father inspire in Doyle some sort of long view of himself as part of the human chain?

'Two things happened immediately. I began thinking back a lot further than I ever had. But on the other hand, I began to be very aware of my own mortality. I'm an atheist, so I don't have any problems with that. But suddenly, within a couple of days of Rory being born, I began to feel very vulnerable, not on my own behalf but on behalf of the people I'd be leaving behind.

'As against that, the joy of watching him grow is fascinating and it's bound to come into my writing somewhere along the line. But I haven't actually thought of parenthood as a writing possibility. I'm not going to be doing Paula Yates manuals on how to rear your children,' he laughs.

Will he guide his children in what they read, as Paddy's father does in the book when they visit the library?

'I read this book by child psychologist Bruno Bettelheim, *Recollections and Reflections* [an influence on Jim Sheridan when writing his screenplay *Into the West* coincidentally] and he said: let your kids follow their nose and back them up. So if you bring them to the museum and they get nothing out of it, accept defeat. My parents were very supportive when I got wildly interested in soccer. That's what I tried to do as well, not try to mould my kids into little versions of myself.'

One of the most striking things about *Paddy Clarke* is the amount of Irish language in it, complete with annotated translation into English.

'I felt it was important that I had it, but that I include people who wouldn't understand it. There's nothing more irritating, I find, than picking up a Penguin Classic and being confronted with a bit of French you don't understand.'

Doyle, however, is in two minds about the language itself. 'Like a lot of people, I'd be torn between wanting it to be retained. It's part of us. But I do resent having to do an oral Irish exam to be a teacher of English and geography. That sort of thing isn't doing the language any favours.'

Does Doyle also bear in mind his foreign audience when he is writing in English?

'I think it's important that I write what I think is true,' he responds. 'I have a very good publisher in that never once have they suggested that I take out, for example, a reference to the 1916 Rising because who's going to understand that outside Ireland? I think they recognize they are solidly located in a part of Ireland. If there is a universal appeal it's because one, people are curious about it and two, the stories themselves are about universal subjects – marital breakdown, pregnancy, that type of thing. I would never dilute what I do for a market. I don't think in those terms.'

Doyle's first abortive attempt at a novel was a satirical effort entitled *Your Granny's a Hunger Striker*. Might the dire state of Irish politics not tempt him towards another effort?

'I don't know, perhaps. There's a lot of anger in me. I just don't express it that often and I wouldn't want it to be sustained anger either because on another level I'm very content. I don't like the way Irish politics operates. I think it's even constructed to celebrate the parish pump. You can't help but think there's an inner circle that has divided the country among themselves.

'There is a lot that isn't admirable. But at the same time as a place to live and as a place for rearing children, I would much rather live in Ireland than anywhere else.'

Doyle was born in Dublin in 1958. He won the Booker Prize for Paddy Clarke Ha Ha Ha *(1993) and chaired the 2025 Booker Prize jury. His first three novels,* The Commitments *(1987),* The Snapper *(1990) and* The Van *(1991) were later published together* as The Barrytown trilogy *and all three were made into films,* The Commitments *screenplay winning him a Bafta.* The Guts *(2013) won Irish Novel of the Year. His TV series* Family *(1994) led to the* trilogy The Woman Who Walked into Doors *(1996);* Paula Spencer *(2006); and* The Women Behind the Door *(2024). He has also written three short-story collections, books for children, plays and non-fiction. He co-founded the creative-writing centre Fighting Words in Dublin in 2009.*

PAUL DURCAN

29 May 1993, The Irish Post

For all his mild demeanour, Paul Durcan is a turbulent poet. Provocative titles such as 'Archbishop of Kerry to Have Abortion', a style whose accessibility and repetitions have drawn the fire of critics, together with an unrivalled reputation as a reader of his work, have given him a profile unusually public for a poet.

Durcan writes with authority yet intimacy of his loves, his family and friends, and of many an odd encounter with strange strangers along the way. While some of his poems are irredeemably prosaic, others undeniably work wonderfully as verse, moving with their meaning and uplifting with their rhythm.

Endsville, his first collection, was published in 1967, and this year sees the publication of *A Snail in My Prime*, his *New and Selected Poems*. So does this mark the beginning of the end or the closing of a chapter?

'I'd say it is all right, although I didn't realize that when I set out doing it. It's two books in one, a new book, and also a selection of thirty years' work. Thirty years seems like a reasonable period of time, even possibly a lifetime. It's a load off my shoulders.'

Durcan agrees that the poems he has chosen are simply his favourites, but 'they have to balance one another', he qualifies. 'To keep it simple, they are poems that I felt worked.'

The collection is prefaced by the following quotation by Francis Bacon, the late Irish-born painter, much admired by Durcan and celebrated in a couple of his poems: 'I would like my pictures to look as if a human being had passed between them like a snail, leaving a trail of the human presence and memory traces of past events as the snail leaves its slime.'

I pointed out that this, together with his work's title, suggests he is an admirer rather than a creator of art.

'That would indeed be very fair to say. Some of the poems at the end of the book are to do with being a creature who writes, but I think we are all members of the audience. What I'm most interested in in the end is reading or looking at pictures or going to the cinema or listening to music.'

Is he then specifically an admirer of the arts rather than the wider beauty of the world? 'Well, art is part of life. I don't for a moment see it as divorced from everyday life at all.'

Bacon is by no means the only artistic or public figure to appear in Durcan's poetry. In his thirteen new poems alone appear Mary Robinson, Francis Stuart, Seamus Heaney, Donal McCann, Samuel Beckett and two of Durcan's own daughters for good measure.

Was this a deliberate common thread in his new work? And, in any case, what is the significance of naming familiar names?

'Nothing at the beginning is deliberate. It is one of the things Francis Bacon was always talking about, the accidental aspect of art, the accident of life, chance. I didn't know when I started on this particular collection that I would end up with this particular collection of poems or that title. That's just how it worked out.

'Anyone who is interested in reading or music, it's as natural to attempt to write about that as anything else.'

In one of his poems, Durcan speaks of having 'to prepare my soul for tonight's public recital'. What store does he set by the reading of his work, this poet who, according to his peer Derek Mahon, with a microphone for a lute, can, like Orpheus, charm the birds from the trees?

'The saying of poetry is what poetry is, so I don't think of the two things as separate. They go together. It's a form of music. Every time you read, you never know if the house of cards is going to collapse or whether you'll get over Becher's Brook. Perhaps that's a better way of looking at it. These riders have ridden over the course God knows how many times but they never know if this is going to be the day.'

An off day can be down to 'the venue, the audience, yourself, the day that's in it, someone moving about at the back. You can lose your concentration, play badly, forget a note.'

Durcan reaches again for a musical analogy to counter a suggested contrast between the solitary nature of writing and the public aspect of reading poetry. 'Although you are making this distinction, which is absolutely true, if you listen to a concert pianist or uilleann piper, whether they are in a large hall or a small kitchen, if they are going to really try and listen, they have to be, in a certain sense, very alone.'

Durcan has his disciples and his detractors. For some of the latter, he is not a poet at all. How does the poet cope with such diverse responses? Is each appreciation a boost, every disapproval a small hurt?

'When you are walking along the streets and you meet a complete stranger for whom something you've written, they have a particular feeling about it, that's really what it's all about. When that happens, as long as you balance it with some kind of humility, that means an awful lot to you. A guy once asked my name rhetorically. He obviously recognized me. I admitted to being myself and he said: "*The Berlin Wall Café*?" And I said "yes". And he looked me straight in the eye and said: "fucking dreadful book". But these things happen.'

Durcan swears by two slogans, Never Conform, which speaks for itself, and Provincials to the Wall, which perhaps requires a little elucidation, coming as it does from a poet proud of his Mayo roots.

'That is open to misinterpretation. I am thinking very much of something Patrick Kavanagh said. Years and years ago he made a very clear distinction between what he called the parish and the province. He said all great civilizations are based on the parish. Provincial is something else. It is subservient. It looks to the capital for all its values. So up the parish!'

Speaking of the style, subject matter and development of his work, Durcan admits to the storytelling tag that for some is a laurel, for others a stick.

'There's that, but there's also the music, different tones and shades and humours. I try to write about a very wide range of things. That has been deliberate. Some people write the one kind of thing, and that's fine too.

'I think the essence of art is to change all the time. But someone remarked that these last poems were quite like the first poems. And now that's been said, I can see that after going out and along I've circled back. But there's nothing unusual in that, in that way. To me, it's the end of the road.'

Has he then completed the circle? 'Well, no. That has a finality to it. Even those spirals at Newgrange, they're not finished, but almost perhaps I feel a sense of relief that this is out, and I'll go on writing.'

As a kind of postscript to this interview, Durcan spoke of having spent several years after leaving school in London, that England had been good to him and that the IRA were now, not only for English people but also for many Irish, more associated with grief than grievance.

'Like many Irish people, I feel helplessly angry with what the IRA do because London was a home to me when I had nowhere else to go. It gave me work, work which I wouldn't have got back in Ireland. I worked in the London Planetarium, where my official job title was Stellar Manipulator – I was the guy who flung the stars up on the ceiling – and here I was married and here my children were born. This country has been home to thousands and thousands of Irish people.'

Durcan has no confidence, however, that what Seamus Heaney described in his play *The Cure of Troy* as 'a great sea change' has taken place, even post-Warrington [an IRA bomb that killed two children in the Cheshire town] in the Irish Republic.

'I don't. So much has happened before. There's a poem in this book, 'In Memory of Those Murdered in the Dublin Massacre, May 1974'. And I noticed when I read the poem here or back in Ireland, people don't remember. They've forgotten.'

Paul Durcan was born in Dublin in 1944 and died there in 2025. He was a founding member of Aosdána in 1981 and Ireland Professor of Poetry from 2004 to 2007. One of the most popular poets of his generation, renowned for his highly engaging readings, he won the Patrick Kavanagh Poetry Award for his debut, O Westport in the Light of Asia Minor *(1975), the Cholmondeley Award and the Whitbread Award for* Daddy, Daddy *(1990). His collections include* The Berlin Wall Café *(1985) and* A Snail in my Prime *(1993),* Going Home to Russia *(1987),* Greetings to Our Friends in Brazil *(1999) and* Praise in Which I Live and Move and Have My Being *(2012).*

ANNE ENRIGHT

25 October 2025, The Irish Times

'I'm in a bit of a lull,' Anne Enright says, when I ask her what she's working on. 'You wait for a catch, a snag to your interest. The wonderful Annie Dillard has a story about an Inuit woman, who has a baby to feed and no fish so she slices tiny bits of her own thigh as bait. "This is what a writer does," she says. That's Annie Dillard, though, not me.'

The New Yorker has since published her short story 'The Bridge Stood Fast,' and Jonathan Cape a brilliant career retrospective of her non-fiction, *Attention*, reflecting on her life, writers and art, Ireland and the world, so she has not been idle but taking stock.

'I'm in a lull because of the world, probably also because my parents are both gone and the family home. I'm trying to recalibrate after a long decade of elder care for me and my siblings.' Her mother, Cora, died in November 2023, her father, Donal, in June 2016, a few months before Donald Trump was first elected US president.

'I lost a wonderful man from my life while the world gained a terrible one,' she wrote in an essay in *No Authority* (2019), a collection of her writings as the inaugural Laureate of Irish Fiction, in which she addressed, among other things, misogyny and male privilege. 'I knew many good men and very few bad ones. Was this male goodness also illusory? What, I wondered, came between these individual, well-intentioned men and the wider enactment of equality?'

She reprises the subject in fictional form in her *New Yorker* story. 'Even though the story is set in the 1980s, you want to feel it is saying something relevant to now. The world is so different, you want to meet that change in some way. The story is very strongly based on me going down to Clare with my dad, picking blackberries and mushrooms. I wanted to capture that fantastic thing of having your dad all to yourself when you were eleven. Any girl who is stuck on their da, I had access to that easily.'

In the story, the father suddenly has to leave and a darker masculinity takes centre stage. It asks the question, if men are more or less good, how did we get saddled with such a damaged patriarchy? There is also an undercurrent of Ireland's urban–rural divide.

While Enright once found *New Yorker* fiction editors 'almost anti-voice', wanting to turn colourful sentences beige, she has always admired its editing as 'a lesson in clarity, foregrounding things the reader needs to know', one she passes on to her students at UCD where she is professor of creative writing. 'Don't be hiding things under your jumper. There's something you're not telling.'

Enright has enjoyed consistent critical success since her debut short-story collection *The Portable Virgin* (1991) won the Rooney Prize for Irish Literature. Winning the Booker Prize with *The Gathering* (2005) made her name internationally. 'It was fantastic timing, it very much did its job for me.' She didn't think she had written a Booker winner. 'I was rearing small kids and locked away for a few hours a day in Bray. I was hauling it out of my guts and thought no one is going to like this.'

The late *Irish Times* literary critic Eileen Battersby was unimpressed. 'I realized that the people who didn't like you weren't going to like you because you won the Booker; they were going to dislike you more.'

In my view, she has reached another level with her last three novels: *The Green Road*, *Actress* and *The Wren, The Wren*. But despite being up for the Women's Prize for Fiction five times, 'you just know that's not going to happen, the magic is moving elsewhere' with 'a shift to a cooler female voice'.

'You outgrow ideas of fashionability. Writing the sort of book I write, which is interested in style and language, how the sentences fall, it used to be called literary, but things shift. Style in some mouths is a semi-insult. I'm not second-guessing the market. That is the enemy of good writing and a sure way to fail.

'There are times late at night you think you're no good at all but you learn to live with the uncertainty. Usually for me it's a structural flaw or unease, I'd break it up or smooth it out a bit. In *The Green Road* and *The Gathering*, there are tensions between the book falling apart and coming together. I sometimes wish I could write a book in one style and one voice the whole way through.'

All this made winning the $165,000 Windham-Campbell Award a huge and welcome surprise. 'I thought those days were gone.'

'You always finish a book too quickly,' she says, although she has never worked to a deadline since her debut novel, *The Wig My Father Wore* (1995), 'which I missed by two years. I was very neurotic about it in the early days. I wrote with great difficulty. I wrote every day for thirty years. I need to. I'm slightly obsessive and addicted to it.' She usually has two or three non-fiction deadlines, however, work she takes on if she believes it will bring her fiction or thinking on.

'Stylistically, *Wig* is not showing its age. Is that a very arrogant thing to say? I noticed my *New Yorker* story is doing what I do, moving from paragraph to paragraph faster than other writers. On one level, it is naturalistic, but I can sense that old energy from the first story in *The Portable Virgin* is still there. I thought I want to stop doing that now, but it still is the engine that keeps me going, that movement into surprise, the way that the paragraph ends in a way that you don't expect from its beginning, so there is a bit of a dance going on. I'm not writing modernism like Tom McCarthy but I'm not writing like William Trevor either, so there is a conversation between the two.'

She recognizes that some of her novels are couples: *The Gathering* and *The Green Road*; *Actress* and *The Wren, The Wren*. 'They are bookends, they talk to each other. You realize at the end [of writing a novel] that you haven't done at all what you meant to – if I knew that's what I was going to do, I would have started out differently – and so you do start out differently.

'Both [*Actress* and *The Wren, The Wren*] have mythological, supernormal parents. They have a glow, given them by fame, which is shorthand for how we feel about our parents anyway. In *The Wren, The Wren* I had the advantage of being able to make [Phil the poet] real by making his work real, and so it was a completely different engagement [than with *Actress*], more exciting, you could give him a go, let him have his say.

'I'm a great believer in that, which is one of the reasons why my books tend to not fragment but collate, because they have a democratic impulse behind them. You can demonize Phil, he is every kind of foolish bad man, but once you get him speaking you can also experience him. Maybe 20 per cent of my readers on a good day would be male but I've had a good male response to the Phil chapters. My work is political but not ideological.' In other words, it is polyphonic, not just one point of view.

She reminds me that during the first pandemic lockdown she surprised me by picking a collection of poetry translated from Irish as her summer read. 'Poems like 'The Yellow Bittern' and 'To a Blackbird' were moving and also key to my writing 'The Wren, The Wren'. Now the thickets of misogyny are being cleared from Irish letters I've been going back to Irish poetry, a reclamation. For decades, there was almost a hum off Irish work that was not for or about you. I became tired of having to praise it, the lie that it contains, the women's lives trapped by that sentimentality. But you can't be too cross when you sit down to write something, you have to let the feeling settle and then go back to re-access it.'

I ask to see her writing desk and she surprises me by sitting cross-legged on the sofa in a basement room, where she types on her laptop: 'slow slow, quick quick slow, it's more of a rhythm, a rush and a stop. Writing by hand feels like a voice-over; this is more in the moment.'

Dialogue, she says, shouldn't all be the same length unless you're Beckett or Pinter. There is always a power dynamic or a kind of dance going on. 'I am very interested in the pattern of interruptions. Women interrupt to be helpful; men interrupt as a territorial thing.'

She writes about Ireland but not for it, she says. 'I'm very proud of the fact I had the 46A [bus] in every single book. Now it's gone I don't know what to do. I don't think I can put the 2E [its replacement] in.'

To write precisely about the imprecise, often ambiguous nature of things is one of Enright's gifts as a writer so it is no surprise when I ask her where she grew up to learn that it was on the borders of Perrystown, Terenure and Templeogue, 'postally Dublin 12, religiously Crumlin and Terenure for the estate agents', where the Dublin bus stopped and fields began.

As to class? 'It's an evolving space for me,' she says. 'No one along the Dart line, which is so class-bound, believes this but we were, as far as I knew, indifferent to class. Possibly because we were an academic family, a lot of investment went into that.'

Her parents were both civil servants but with five children to raise, their house was very modest. 'My mother came from a falling class, middle class with no money because her father died just before she was born. She had a Catholic spiritual sense that people were people and shouldn't be judged for what they had. A lid would be put on notions.

'The English novel of a certain decade is obsessed with class and I'm not interested, those power relations are not my concern, but I am very interested in people's notions of themselves, and notions in the Irish sense.'

She always does a deep dive into her characters' backgrounds. 'I do know where people come from, how they place themselves socially, but then I lose all that and focus on something else about their lives.'

Enright was a precocious child. She won a Kodak Instamatic camera for a national essay competition when she was eleven. She preferred *Alice in Wonderland* to *The Wind in the Willows*, playful and ludic like her father but disappointing her mother. 'It was news to me that reading could be the wrong sort.' If she had been a boy, she wouldn't have been let be a writer, she has said. 'I did cause a lot of maternal anxiety. But my father said, "I don't know what she has but she has something."'

She passed her Leaving Cert at sixteen then won a scholarship to a school in Canada, whose headmaster predicted that this Irish girl would blow the world up with her writing, not the last male critic to displease her. 'I had absolutely no money and there were lots of people with lots of money, who dressed with confidence, who had travelled.' She studied English at Trinity. She tried her hand at writing monologues and acting with friends (Lynn Parker, Pauline McLynn, Declan Hughes), who would form the Rough Magic theatre company, and Martin Murphy, who she would marry. She graduated with a first.

'When I was trying to place myself as a future writer I wasn't thinking of Irish writers at all, but once you go out in the world you are obliged to talk about nothing else. I read all the Frank O'Connors as a child, just reading for pleasure what was in the house, Robert Coover, Donald Barthelme, Marguerite Duras, the modernists. I was in a state of contention with writers like John McGahern, a kind of argument, which is also a very strong connection. I felt he became a little too like his father even while rejecting him, that he was quite paternalistic. For the most part he rose above his damage with considerable grace, but I have an issue sometimes with how his language is laid on the page.'

She then started writing fragments, which Roland Barthes writes about as having the constant pleasure of beginnings, without arc or resolution. 'It works by juxtaposition, it's a scrap. *Wig* narratively relied on collage, the feeling that things are either making new meanings or breaking down.'

In 1986 she won a scholarship to the University of East Anglia in Norwich, 'the back of beyond, middle class to the max', for a master's degree in creative writing taught by Angela Carter and Malcolm Bradbury.

Carter nourished the work but was a little condescending. 'She asked why I wanted to go back to Ireland, clearly, for her, a very backward, provincial place. If you wanted to be a writer, go to London. I was a bit too Irish for them, unrepressed, a bit of an alien species. But when I fell apart they were very nice.'

What went wrong? 'Young people nowadays know staying up all night is not a good idea. I lived in an evil little room, never went for a walk, there was a lot of student depression. I worked from 8 pm to 4 am, I lost words, I had no idea what I was writing.'

It sounds a bit like Jack Nicholson in *The Shining*, I say. She laughs. 'There was a bit of *Barton Fink* going on. I was very isolated, I didn't go down to London, I had no money, £3,000 to get through the year, totally scraping by. Someone offered me a lift to London then like a nice English person turned round and asked me for petrol money, after leaving me in the wrong part of town. I was increasingly unwell. There were other difficulties. I wasn't particularly in touch with my family at the time. I do remember people thought you were funny and therefore couldn't be sad. My counsellor just laughed and laughed. A lot of my twenties were rocky, one way or another.'

In *Making Babies* (2006), her memoir of early motherhood, ten pages from the end, she quietly drops the bombshell that on Easter Monday 1986 she attempted suicide.

'The older I get the more political I am about depression, or less essentialist – it is not because of who you are, but where you are placed,' she writes. 'Ireland broke apart in the eighties, and I sometimes think that the crack happened in my own head. The constitutional row about abortion was a moral civil war that was fought out in people's homes – including my own – with unfathomable bitterness. The country was screaming at itself about contraception, abortion and divorce. It was a hideously misogynistic time. Not the best environment for a young woman establishing a sexual identity …

'My mother was very conservative, Catholic,' Enright says. 'I was very oppositional, very strong in my own opinions.' Her parents had had four compliant children and didn't know what to do with her, an overachiever in the wrong way, clever but maverick. 'My mother was … became hard to please.

That relationship didn't thrive for a number of years until reluctantly she came to an accommodation.

'Ireland was changing underneath but not on the surface. I wasn't the only person who had difficulty in that generation, the stories were legion. People had been living a false life. Denial makes people strange.'

Suicide is a sensitive topic and we leave it there but the author follows up the next day with an email that clarifies things further.

'I wasn't expecting to be asked about suicidal thoughts forty years in my past, but I suppose I have always skirted around the difficult feelings of those years. I moved in with Martin after college and my mother took very poorly to our "living in sin", so by the time I left for UEA I wasn't speaking to my family and then, for reasons that must have made sense at the time, I broke up with Martin too. I had the feeling I was embarking on my writer's life completely alone and when the writing did not come good, everything seemed to fall apart for me. That is the scoop, right there.'

I wonder how this trauma fed into her writing, the early work experimenting with fragmentation, that falling apart impulse. Her debut novel features Stephen, an angel who has died by suicide. *The Gathering*'s eponymous family reunion is triggered by the suicide of a sibling, Liam. A death wish hangs over her short story 'Night Swim'. Difficult mother–child relationships are a recurring feature in her best work. The fault line in families is often generational as much as gendered. If Enright's fiction about fraught Irish families has an extra charge, and I think it does, it must come in part from this lived experience.

'It's great to be asked after a million years of no one asking,' she says. '*The Gathering* has a suicide in it and I had written about suicide a few years prior to that. Journalists were not reading the same book I had written. The [Booker] prize skewed their idea of what they wanted to talk about. Nobody asked; that's the exercise of taboo right there. We will talk about everything else and not even notice it. It's like Poe's purloined letter, it's right there in plain view.'

That said, 'if I was writing *The Gathering* as a book about suicide, I would have done it differently. Your questions are more personal and my answers are more social: I talk about the environmental, social factors in my life at the time. In a way because the personal is too personal and also in a way not fully true, or not enough. You can become unhinged for any number of reasons. The novel, as a form, is really interested in causation. Liam's sister Veronica looks for a cause in *The Gathering* and doesn't find one, except for the fact that Liam very clearly has been abused as a child. But suicide is absolute, death is so absolute, there is no cause big enough to explain it.

'After the Booker, some of the journalistic antagonism was so extreme, I woke up twenty years later thinking that [abuse] must have happened to them. Though the book is not about the brother's abuse so much as Veronica's problem of witnessing it. All that is one of the slowest burns in Irish life. It is only two years since the Blackrock [College sex abuse] scandal surfaced.'

Stephen in *The Wig* 'owes a lot to gay Catholic iconography, Latinx gay culture, it's more a queer reading.' Again, she follows up the next day: 'Two things, though. The post-suicide angel in *The Wig* owes something to the feeling that I was in a "second", somehow magical life now.

'I am not sure if the writerly impulse towards fragmentation maps absolutely onto the psychological, though I see how you might want to make the connection. Working with fragments is not so limited as linear fiction when it comes to capturing experience – it mimics the way consciousness works, so is a lot more like life. Joyce used fragments. I am fed up saying I have a problem with authority and that is why I do not write realism. Naturalistic fiction is a lie and a dull one at that. This is me changing the narrative from your "broken" to my "honest" or even "smart".'

Miraculously, despite everything that had happened and not happened in Norwich, she came home that summer and spent six weeks in Annaghmakerrig artists' retreat, during which she wrote three stories, which were published in a Faber anthology (alongside Hugo Hamilton). Her mother sent her a clipping of an RTÉ ad: 'Producer-Director wanted'. She got an amazing reference from Malcolm Bradbury, and next thing she was a trainee director at Montrose alongside Jim Sherwin and Moya Doherty.

At a time in Ireland when most young people didn't even have a job, she was directing live TV shows such as *Nighthawks*, making great television with the likes of Kevin McAleer and Arthur Riordan, but it was eighty-five shows a year with no holidays. It was high cortisone, living on her nerves, anarchic. It ended in a breakdown, 'which I would now call a burnout'.

'How much time and young energy and talent did I throw into that effing organization,' she wrote. She quit and became a full-time writer.

What sort of creative-writing tutor is she?

'I feel we are moving towards the American consumer model of education, the idea that you're going to be doled out information that will teach you how to write. I feel that is an illusion; it makes the student satisfied with the service but not good on the page. I'm interested in reversing the polarity. I read the students' work. They will be read, not taught, and be given line edits, as well as a broader response and editorial guidance. There is nowhere else you can get all of that in one place.

'I tell them the structure of a sentence is the structure of the writer's mind. I show them what they are doing on the page and how to see what the work is requiring of them. Getting a conversation going between the page and the artist. Writing as an act of discovery. I love a fresh text, it makes me recognize the provisionality of everything you are doing on the page, because we are all in the same boat, writing badly and then making it better and finally good.'

Enright was born in Dublin in 1962. She won the Booker Prize and Irish Novel of the Year for The Gathering *(2007) and was the inaugural Laureate for Irish Fiction (2015–18). Her debut short-story collection,* The Portable Virgin *(1991), won the Rooney Prize for Irish Literature. She also won the Davy Byrne's short-story prize in 2004. Her second novel,* What Are You Like? *(2001), won the Encore Award.* The Green Road *(2015) was shortlisted for the Costa Novel Award and longlisted for the Booker Prize.* The Forgotten Waltz *(2010) and* The Wren, The Wren *(2024) were shortlisted for the Women's Prize for Fiction.* The Gathering *(2016) won the Kerry Group Irish Fiction Award. In 2025 she won the $165,000 Windham-Campbell Award.*

WENDY ERSKINE

14 June 2025, The Irish Times

Driving down the Cregagh Road in East Belfast, on passing the Museum of Orange Heritage the eye is inevitably drawn to the unbroken line of Union Jacks lining the street, which perhaps masks the shift from middle- to working-class housing. *Some things never change*, you might think, yet you'd be wrong. It's perfectly safe nowadays to park your Southern-reg car on a side street.

I am here to interview author Wendy Erskine, who has taught English in a local grammar school since 1997 (fellow author Lucy Caldwell is a former pupil) and lives nearby, and Caffè Nero is an auspicious location for the task. Michael Magee won the inaugural Nero debut fiction prize for *Close to Home*, his coruscating portrait of post-Troubles but still troubled Belfast.

Erskine's equally powerful debut novel, *The Benefactors*, similarly captures a city no longer overshadowed by political and sectarian violence, allowing light to shine instead on other social ills such as violence against women and class divisions.

The Benefactors of the title relates to several disparate groups of people, evidence of the layered nature of the work. Misty, the young working-class woman whose sexual assault by three middle-class teenagers is at the heart of this novel, has an account on an OnlyFans-style website called The Benefactors or Bennyz. Bronagh, whose son is one of the boys guilty of rape, runs a charity dependent on wealthy American do-gooders. She also colludes with the two other mothers in buying Misty's silence, dressing it up as a goodwill gesture. There are also those who do the right thing for no financial reward, such as Boogie, who takes on the responsibility of raising his daughter Misty and her half-sister Gen when their mother absconds.

If the lives portrayed are sometimes difficult, the reading experience is anything but, leavened with a dry Belfast wit and benefiting from a sharp authorial eye and ear. 'Humour is so much a dimension of life that not to include it seems like a decision,' Erskine says. 'If you don't find it funny, it's very bleak.'

Erskine's gift for authentic and entertaining dialogue is matched with one for deft and memorable characterization, honed and displayed in her two short-story collections, *Sweet Home* (2018) and *Dance Move* (2022).

Her second collection's epigraph from William Blake – 'Joy and woe are woven fine / A clothing for the soul divine' – could serve as a recipe for her fiction. She also approvingly quotes one of her literary heroes, Gordon Burn, who imagined his artist friend George Shaw 'painting the back room of the social club in Tile Hill with all the seriousness of Monet painting Rouen Cathedral'.

'There is real brutality but also a lot of fun and joy in life,' she says of her literary sensibility, influenced by Burn's fearless focus on life's sleazy, tawdry underbelly. 'There is also an attention to detail, the specifics of people's worlds. I hope I don't patronize the reader, I'm asking them to collaborate with me. You have to trust that they can cope with complex characters, a tolerance for people being contradictory. If you try to smooth it, you lose what makes them realistic. Of course, if they are just a jumble of contradictory elements, that also is not realistic.

'Specificity is not just verisimilitude,' she clarifies. 'It's not just there for surface. If it were just to provide a mimetic facsimile of reality then what's the point, why not just look at some photographs? It's about creating worlds.' She quotes Zola: '"Art is a corner of creation seen through a temperament." I'm nosy as hell, I'm always noticing, listening, paying attention. I'm really interested in people, in structure.'

The handover scene in the novel moves beyond realism and is inspired by Sergio Leone's westerns. One of the women even bursts incongruously into song.

The Benefactors is about two worlds colliding, a sexual assault bringing together a trio of middle-class mothers and the working-class victim and her family.

'It's about sexual assault but that's only part of the book because so much is about what it means to be a good parent, it's about class, money, love, charity, so many different things. And then cut into the novel we have fifty first-person monologues. I didn't want fifty different perspectives on what happened that night. I wanted a really polyphonic, kaleidoscopic, experience of a place.

'These voices are there to refract the central concerns of the novel. It's always struck me how arbitrary it is who you focus on as a writer. One writer might focus on those people sitting over there, somebody else the person serving. Often when I'm reading I'm going *OK, so I'm listening to your conversation but I wonder what that waiter is thinking*. It's to give a broad, complex consideration of a particular place.'

Erskine's creative approach is to start with ideas for a character, which she has likened to playing with coins in her pocket, wondering what to spend them on. The novel has traditionally been regarded as a bourgeois form, privileging the individual over the collective, which some left-wing authors have sought to challenge by focusing on a group of people working together. So I wonder how much her diverse, multi-voiced approach to storytelling is down to methodology and how much to ideology?

'Although I wasn't conscious of it I think there is something in what you are saying,' she responds, but her initial impetus was more practical. 'I'd written maybe thirty or forty short stories and I wanted to write a novel. I thought I would like to reside in the same world as my characters for longer than six or seven weeks, for maybe a year. Each time you write a story you have to re-establish a world, even if it is quite geographically circumscribed, it's quite tiring. I know that sounds ridiculous but it's like building a stage set then [dismantling] the set.

'I didn't want to write a novel that could have existed as a short story. I know the form is super flexible but at the same time there are limits. You can't deal with five characters' entire existences, you certainly can't put in another fifty people. I knew there would be a complexity of voices and something formally quite radical. I didn't want a wee chamber piece with a super narrow focus. I knew I wanted to do something radical.'

She was aware of the risk that readers might switch off, tiring of having to recalibrate to a new perspective in each chapter but she likes a more challenging reading experience. 'A good novel will teach you how to read it. I'm not a driver, I failed my test seven times, but I know when I get in the car if the driver knows what they're doing.'

The sexual assault at the centre of *The Benefactors* recalls the high-profile 2018 Belfast rape trial, whose defendants were acquitted.

'It would be extremely disingenuous of me to say I'd never heard of the rugby rape trial,' the author says, 'but I've lived in this city most of my life and so I'm aware of any number of different trials and experiences that aren't to do with trials, of what happens in people's lives.' She is all too aware that the North has a bad reputation for general misogyny and violence against women.

'I can't remember the statistics but this is not a good place. An extremely high number of women were killed by partners in their home. In terms of social attitudes this place is traditionally behind others, with a lot of internalised misogyny.' She highlights how prejudice is not universal and intersects with class bias, rendering working-class women more vulnerable to abuse. But the sexual assault was not the starting point. The genesis of the novel was two characters, Frankie and Boogie. 'I wanted people from different backgrounds to be brought somehow into close proximity. That became a sexual assault.'

In the initial stages, the book consisted of lots of little shards of memories just floating around in her head – 'I have a houseful of empty notebooks' – such as a YouTube video of a guy putting Mentos into a bottle of Coke. 'I liked that guy's attitude to having fun with kids. I wanted to write about someone who is an unlikely but really good parent.'

Erskine dislikes didactic storytelling. 'I don't like fiction that has huge designs on me, or where characters are used as vehicles. They have to take precedence. I know it sounds a bit Mystic Meg but you have to allow characters to push back,' rather like actors taking issue with the script. But there are times when Erskine and her creations are singing from the same hymn sheet, such as when the wonderfully potty-mouthed, born-again Christian Nan tells Misty, her great-granddaughter, that the boys who harmed her 'are not our type of people'. The divide she is reinforcing is not the North's usual tribal Catholic–Protestant one but the class divide. 'I really enjoyed that conversation,' Erskine says.

One of the fifty random, anonymous voices that insert themselves between the traditional chapters also feels like Erskine's philosophy shining through. 'Mate, let me tell you, I got to the stage of life where, if it's not about love to some degree, then I don't want to know.' She agrees, adding: 'That's on the No Alibis tote bag.' A debut novel backed with its own bookshop merch.

Time is not linear and Erskine is passionate about the ever-present nature of the past and how it influences, even dictates, her characters' thoughts and actions. She scorns the notion of a character having a backstory as some kind of optional extra. 'For what I do, it's just a word that doesn't work. To my mind everything is simultaneous. There is no such thing as past.' Instead we have flashbacks or separate timelines, where we see, for example, Frankie being groomed as a teenager in care, learning to look after herself but becoming hardened to the extent that when she in turns becomes a stepmother, the child in her care feels like an orphan.

Structuring the novel proved an interesting challenge.

'A much more traditional structure would be to have the sexual assault come in the first third. I wanted the novel to be almost like a bow tie, that well-known literary term. You've got all these people, trust me on this, it all comes together, then it all goes out again.'

The Slap by Christos Tsiolkas interested her as a model. 'In *The Slap*, there are eight different narrative points of view, constructed as a kind of relay, one coming after the other, each advancing the story. At no point do we return to the point of view of an earlier character. Whereas, in *The Benefactors* there is a rotation. We have Frankie, then Boogie, then Miriam, then Misty, then Bronagh and then we return again to their perspectives at various points.

'I also think just generally it's like *The Slap* in that a central incident is used to hold together a consideration of a range of preoccupations.'

She originally planned for the fifty anonymous voices to bunch in the middle 'like a choric interlude' but that didn't work so instead they are scattered throughout.

Miriam, another of the mothers, is grieving her late husband, complicated by the knowledge a young woman was with him in the fatal car crash. The novel she is reading is 'full of young women's non-problems'. 'Miriam had expected a kind of cool and expansive perspicacity, but this is juvenile solipsism.' What might seem a sassy diss on Erskine's part is in fact in character for Miriam, who has a grudge against young women generally.

By contrast, when Bronagh mocks Donal for a poetic turn of phrase, Erskine owns it.

'What some people think of as fine writing is very misguided. It's like the Dolly Parton thing, "it takes a lot of work to look this cheap". My dialogue is edited over and over to get it just right.'

This reminds me of Erskine's appreciation of the austere beauty of a whitewashed church wall in contrast to the baroque's excess.

'I used to get migraines all the time,' she says. 'and when I came round I felt euphoric, looking at a white wall my husband was painting and 'Lonely Sad Eyes' by Them was playing. I honestly regard that as one of the high points of my life, the simplicity of it.'

Kathryn Ferguson has directed a short film scripted by Stacy Gregg and starring Aidan Gillen based on Erskine's short story 'Nostalgie', written for *The Irish Times*. She has written an essay on Pasolini, another on fashion, a film script, several stories and 20,000 words of a new novel 'about a *Vanity Fair* Becky Sharp-style grifter in mid-Ulster in the late '70s'.

Erskine wrote an unpublished novel in her twenties but was almost fifty when her short story 'Locksmiths' won her a place on a *Stinging Fly* writing course in Dublin taught by Sean O'Reilly. 'But so much of what I understand about how to write, structure, conceptualise relationships, I learned from Chekhov.'

Contemporaries she admires include Adrian Duncan, Will Ashon, Svetlana Alexievich, fellow teacher writers Elaine Feeney and Kevin Curran, 'people who just do their own thing'.

She had studied in Glasgow then taught in England but personal circumstances meant she moved back to Belfast. Her goal had always been to return to Glasgow 'but as it turned out I love living here, it's beautiful, compact, there's a real energy here, in terms of writing, the arts, it's such an interesting place. The deep structures are obviously problematic.'

What would make it better? 'On this particular road, a bar!'

Erskine was born in Belfast in 1968, where she teaches English. She is the author of two short-story collections, Sweet Home *(2018) and* Dance Moves *(2022), and one novel,* The Benefactors *(2025). She also edited a book of essays,* well I just kind of like it: Art in the home and the home as art *(2022).* Sweet Home *was shortlisted for the Edge Hill Short Story Prize and the Republic of Consciousness Prize, longlisted for the Gordon Burn Prize and won the Butler Literary Award.* Dance Move *was shortlisted for the Edge Hill Short Story Prize.*

MARTINA EVANS

17 August 1996, The Irish Post

The notion of starving to death has carved its own niche in the Irish psyche. Now to the Famine, the hunger strikes and the ancient custom of fasting on the doorstep of the person who has wronged you can be added anorexia.

This is the subject of Martina Evans's treat of a debut novel, *Midnight Feast*, which tells of the friendship of Grace and Colette, two young girls in a convent boarding school in County Mayo. Grace is only too happy to escape the attentions of her mother – a wonderful comic creation – who has been widowed but thinks she's been martyred.

Colette is beautiful, capricious, strong-minded and very, verry thin, the introduction informs us. 'What's more, Colette has a brother, Johnny, who is even more rebellious than she is. Johnny, they say, smokes dope and rides a motorbike without a helmet. He haunts the girls' conversation and Grace's dreams.'

The two girls form a deep friendship, which offers them refuge from the ordered world of the convent, but their increasingly irrational fixation on their weight and shape threatens tragedy.

Evans, the author of this authentic and utterly enchanting book on adolescence, is a 35-year-old former radiographer from a family of ten in County Cork, who now lives in north London with her daughter Líadáin.

She attended a boarding school in Clonakilty, where she and her fellow pupils were obsessed with food and dieting. She still has chilling memories of girls making themselves sick en masse after the Rosary.

'I suppose it was wanting to be perfect,' the author says. 'We were not religious yet in an insidious way we were trying to be perfect and pure, not a bit carnal I suppose, in that sense. Body fat and body fluids were disgusting. Grace is very interested in sex but this other part of her is tearing her apart. She can't have a healthy relationship with her body, a wholeness. I read a lot of Jung, who wrote about the split between body and soul.'

Evans was working in London as a radiographer and writing poetry. Her first collection, *The Iniscarra Bar and Cycle Rest,* was published last year by Rockingham Press. But she knew she wasn't going to make a living out of poetry and radiography wasn't very enjoyable, 'quite physically hard and quite stressful, assembly-line stuff. I didn't like the job because there was no time to talk to the patients (a similar split between treating the body and soul as one).

'We talked about there being five chests waiting to be done. It came to a climax one day when I said, "I've got this brain, this ankle and this spine. I'll go and get the thumb." I went to the waiting room and said, left thumb please, then I realized and went, oh my God, I had to disappear. Someone else had to get my patients for the next hour.'

In any case, she loved literature. That's all she wanted to do. 'I was thinking about the early saints starving themselves. I didn't know in ancient Ireland if someone upset you, you would fast on their doorstep. I thought that was so close to the hunger strikes and to what the girls were doing. They were saying: "you've upset us; can you not listen to us?" There was a workhouse in Clonakilty at the time of the Famine. There are two places that have the same saying: Mayo, God help us; and Clonakilty, God help us. That's why I set the school in Mayo.'

One good thing that came out of her schooling was that because the nuns were so strict, the girls became very close and she made some very dear friends. 'When the book got loads of rejections, everything was too much so I decided to stick with the poetry, put the novel away. I would come back to it in my fifties. But an old school friend, who's a hairdresser in London, was cutting an agent's hair. She told her about my book, the agent said, "send a chapter" and within a few days she had read the book and got a two-book deal with Sinclair Stevenson.'

She believes her medical background was a help. 'It's one thing I would like to write about more. I became fascinated with anatomy, working with the insides of people's bodies all the time. That's a mystery in itself. When you look at an X-ray you see a skeleton taking a drink, like death in front of you already.'

What are her views on Catholicism post-convent schooling? 'That's a can of worms. I think Jesus was absolutely brilliant, an amazing person, but like everything else the wrong people seemed to get hold of his ideas. But not all the time. I'm reading Father Bernard Lynch's book [*A Priest on Trial*, Bloomsbury, 1993] at the moment and he was so good. But my daughter is going to a Catholic school. You know the definition of a liberal – a socialist with two children. I believe in the afterlife but it's only a feeling. I come close to it when I'm feeling inspired. I just feel there is something else there.'

Evans was press-ganged into studying science by her parents. "It's hard to get into, you're bound to get a job.' I did it because I thought it was the thing to do. I had this idea of growing up like Grace in the book, being sensible, building radios, fixing cars. Grace loses contact with her real self. As she became more scientific, she became more anorexic. I remember doing anatomy and buying all these Penguin Classics. I was doing the skull and I was reading Thomas Hardy. When we were doing the respiratory system, I was reading George Eliot.'

Being Irish in London has been a jolt to Evans's system. 'It was a shock to come over and find it mightn't be the best thing in the world to be Irish, having been used to Australians and Americans coming up and telling you that you were wonderful. Working in the Royal Northern in Casualty, and meeting people who were around in the 1950s, you hear how the black Marias would be lined up outside the Gresham ballroom. To stay or go is a constant question for us.'

There are pluses and minuses but it is the negative equity that keeps them here.

Martina Evans was born in Cork in 1961. Her first novel, Midnight Feast *(1996), won a Betty Trask Award.* Facing the Public *(2009) won the Premio Ciampi International Poetry Prize.* Burnfort, Las Vegas *(2014) and* Now We Can Talk Openly About Men *(2018) were both shortlisted for the* Irish Times *Poetry Now Award.* Now We Can Talk Openly About Men *was shortlisted for the Roehampton Poetry Prize and the Pigott Poetry Prize.* American Mules *(2021) won the Pigott Poetry Prize.* The Coming Thing *(2023) was shortlisted for the Derek Walcott Prize for Poetry and the Pen Heaney Award. Her latest book is* Drunken Driving *(Carcanet, June 2026).*

DIARMAID FERRITER

29 October 2005, The Irish Times

The old saying goes that the problem with the Irish is that they can never forget their history, and the problem with the British is they can never remember it. The probable truth is that Irish people know the details of their history about as well as they know the landscape. They know where they're from like the back of their hand and have probably visited the famous landmarks – the Cliffs of Moher and the Ring of Kerry, the Giant's Causeway and the Rock of Cashel – but they may not even be sure if they have ever passed through Laois.

So we may be familiar with the Ireland we grew up in and know our Easter Rising and War of Independence. But that still leaves a huge hinterland of which we know little. If you'd be interested in a map, then try Diarmaid Ferriter's *The Transformation of Ireland:1900–2000*. It's a century of Irish life condensed into 760 pages.

If a hundred years were not scope enough, Ferriter departs from the traditional historian's script. Religion and politics are covered in depth, of course, but so is social and cultural history – poverty; the GAA; the role of women; artistic development.

This is a history book where the tower blocks of Ballymun are as much a blot on the landscape as the Civil War atrocity of Ballyseedy. Where the immigrant boat is as significant as the boats that brought arms to Howth and Larne. Where the introduction of free secondary education by Donagh O'Malley in the 1960s was as great an emancipation as that achieved for Catholicism by Daniel O'Connell in the 1830s.

While there are occasional clunking non sequiturs in the text, when it feels like a breeze block has been added to a drystone wall as the author tries to cram in too many facts without leaving space to connect them properly, by and large, this is a highly readable book, larded with memorable quotations, fascinating facts and shocking statistics that will linger in the mind long after the last page is turned.

I'm thinking of Brian Lenihan, then the minister for education, snarling 'Get me out of this fucking place' after an official visit to Artane Industrial School in the 1960s, a political disgrace that would only emerge three decades later.

Or the *Irish Times* editorial wryly celebrating that Ireland had proportionately four times as many old-age pension claimants as England, 'a major tribute to the longevity of our race and the healthy character of our much abused climate'. Or the decline of island communities from 211 inhabited islands in 1841 to 61 in 1991, from 38,138 people to 9,700, which suggests that the periphery became more, not less, neglected when Dublin and not London was the centre of power.

Or the fact that the two bestsellers in the 1930s were a handbook on the British king's coronation and an *Irish Independent* guide to emigration to England.

In his introduction, Ferriter sets out his intention 'to assess whether Ireland by the end of the twentieth century was still aspiring to, rather than delivering on, the confident nationalistic predictions of one hundred years previously'.

His conclusion is that aspiration still outweighs achievement because poverty is still as entrenched in Celtic Tiger Ireland as it was in the decades of economic stagnation or in the dying days of empire.

'As citizens of our republic,' he says, 'the focus has been on the political aspect of that, and those of us who believe in a united Ireland are still aspiring to that. But what about the other aspects, the emphasis on equality, on liberty? That great phrase about cherishing all the children of the nation equally [from the Declaration of Independence]? That still has to be done.'

Ferriter, who is remarkably only thirty-three, studied history in Dublin, when the debate about revisionism, a critical re-examination of Irish history, in part motivated by a hostile reaction to violent modern republicanism's claim to be inheritors of 1916, 'was becoming tiresome, very narrowly focused'.

'I wanted to move away from nationalism, religion, high politics. I thought there wasn't the experience of ordinary people coming through,' he says. 'There was also a lot more new source material coming through, which shed light on what ordinary people were doing, a history from below. I wanted to have more of an emphasis on social questions, poverty, unemployment, people's memoirs of what it was like growing up in twentieth-century Ireland, the dark underbelly. It was a question of bringing all that material together, having a fresh look at it.'

Ironically, one of the most fascinating sources of new material was the release in 2003 of the statements of rank-and-file volunteers in the Irish War of Independence, which had been collected in the 1940s and 1950s by the Bureau of Military History, compelling Ferriter to take a fresh look at an aspect of history which he had considered overworked.

Another more disputed but still valuable source has been the explosion in Irish memoirs, not least Frank McCourt's *Angela's Ashes* and, significantly, the new work by John McGahern – in Ferriter's eyes, Ireland's greatest modern novelist.

'There is what I call the McGahernization of Irish history,' says Ferriter. 'His memoir is as much a sociological observation of twentieth-century Ireland. He emphasizes the distinctive things about Irish life: community, family, the language, a sense of place. But then he starts chipping away the layers. We see a lot of the dark side. People are ready to deal with that now. I think we're getting a bit more mature.'

Change and continuity run through the book. On the one hand, we witness the power of the Catholic Church's collapse from a time when Archbishop McQuaid acted like a minister without portfolio to the RTÉ news bulletin that led with three sex scandals involving Catholic priests. The sting has been taken out of nationalism post-Good Friday Agreement and the notion that farming the land is the backbone of the Irish way of life is gone for good. Emigration has also dried up.

On the other hand, the poor, it seems, are always with us. Despite economic and social progress, an underclass is always left behind. Jack Lynch described concepts of redistribution and equality as 'alien philosophies'. The strong sense emerges that Ferriter subscribes to the belief of James Connolly and Sean O'Casey that self-rule without socialism could only change the identity and not the nature of the ruling class.

Another alarming constant are the high rates of suicide, mental illness and alcohol abuse that afflict the Irish today as much as a century ago.

'The great irony is we were told we drank too much in the nineteenth century because we were poor. Now we drink too much because we are too wealthy and stressed.'

Amidst a host of mostly glowing reviews, one criticism of Ferriter's work is that there is too much what and not enough why, a glut of facts and a dearth of judgement.

'I wanted to set out a comprehensive canvas,' he says, 'not always be offering my own opinions. I think people can make up their own minds, draw their own conclusions from the huge amount of information and observations I offer.'

In fact, what strikes is the effort Ferriter makes to give both sides of the story. He lays bare the negative side to the Catholic Church, its authoritarianism, its failure to tackle the abusers in its ranks. But he also gives it credit for what it did right, not least its care for emigrants when the State turned its back.

'What struck me, particularly when I saw the government correspondence from the 1950s and '60s when they refused these emigrant groups any money, the church was the only institution to look after them. I thought those things should be recorded for posterity.'

One frustration for Ferriter was the shortage of Irish political memoirs, the 'Trappist-like custody of the tongue' of otherwise voluble politicians.

'Unfortunately, Irish politicians have burnt more papers than they have preserved,' he says. He agrees that history will almost certainly judge Garrett FitzGerald more kindly than Charles Haughey, at least in part because the former has written so prolifically, the latter so little. But he admires FitzGerald, he says, because he never retired from politics, and even in his late seventies was out campaigning in the European elections and is always engaging with the issues of Irish society, reflecting, proposing.

FitzGerald also provides Ferriter with one of his funniest and most telling vignettes of Irish life. 'George O'Brien, professor of political economy in UCD, when appointing FitzGerald as a lecturer in economics, "dismissed as irrelevant my lack of qualifications in the subject, pointing out that he himself had no degree in economics". The innocence of it all is striking.'

And what is next for the historian after so grand a project? Sex, he says. [*Occasions of Sin: Sex and Society in Modern Ireland* (2009)] 'I want to look at the whole question of sex in Irish society. Was it more repressed than other countries?' Again, the lack of Haughey's memoirs is a pity.

'For source material, I will have a lot based on people's writing about their own experience; court files which give all sorts of accounts of people being charged with "sexual immorality", infanticide, child abuse, abortion.

'There was a committee set up to check the spread of VD in the Irish army in the 1920s. Another to look into child prostitution.'

The ferreting out of Ireland's secret history looks set to continue.

Ferriter was born in Dublin in 1972. He is Professor of Modern Irish History at University College Dublin since 2008, has been a weekly Irish Times *columnist since 2014 and was elected to the Royal Irish Academy in 2019. His books include* The Transformation of Ireland: 1900–2000 *(2004);* Judging Dev: A Reassessment of the Life and Legacy of Éamon de Valera *(2007)*; Occasions of Sin: Sex and Society in Modern Ireland *(2009);* Ambiguous Republic: Ireland in the 1970s *(2012);* A Nation and not a Rabble: The Irish Revolution 1913–23 *(2015);* The Border: The Legacy of a Century of Anglo-Irish Politics *(2019);* Between Two Hells: The Irish Civil War *(2021); and* The Revelation of Ireland 1995–2020 *(2024).*

ROY FOSTER

18 November 2023, The Irish Times

'I'm technically against pantheons,' Roy Foster tells me, citing a distinguished fellow historian. 'FSL Lyons was asked where he would place Parnell in the pantheon, and he said he hated the idea of pantheons.'

Parnell was the subject of Foster's PhD and his first book, *Charles Stewart Parnell: The Man and His Family*, from 1976, of which another eminent historian, Laurence Stone, wrote approvingly: 'No heroes, then in brackets (except O'Connell).' Daniel O'Connell 'isn't as revered as I think he should be', says Foster.

We are talking of pantheons, the great and the good, because next Wednesday, at the Irish Book Awards, Foster, 'one of the most distinguished modern heirs of the great tradition of Anglo-Irish liberalism,' according to critic Terry Eagleton, 'which flows through Wolfe Tone and Charles Stewart Parnell to W.B. Yeats and on to such latter-day luminaries as the essayist Hubert Butler and the historian F.S.L. Lyons', will be conferred with the Bob Hughes Lifetime Achievement Award. He is 'surprised and delighted' to join the ranks of 'a lot of names I revere', such as Seamus Heaney, Eavan Boland, John McGahern and William Trevor.

Foster's mammoth and magisterial *Modern Ireland 1600–1972*, published in 1988, rejected 'the definition of Irishness against Britishness' and sought 'a more relaxed and inclusive definition of Irishness, and a less constricted view of Irish history'. It sold in quantities more normally associated with writers such as Maeve Binchy. Triggering the widely contested 'revisionism' debate, it succeeded in demonstrating that Irish history was more than just the story of Irish nationalism.

His two-volume biography of Yeats, from 1998 and 2003, was no less of a publishing phenomenon. His fellow public intellectual Seamus Deane had taken issue in a 1991 essay, 'Wherever Green Is Read' with Foster's treatment of the Easter Rising; a little over a decade later the same critic, reviewing Foster's *The Apprentice Mage* in *The Irish Times* in 2003, was unabashed in his admiration. Foster's *Vivid Faces: the revolutionary generation in Ireland 1890–1923*, published in 2014, seemed to represent a certain rapprochement with the men and women of 1916. Have his sympathies shifted somewhat?

'That's quite a complex question,' Foster says. 'When I wrote *Modern Ireland* a bit of tearing down idols, or at least shaking them up a bit and dusting them off, was necessary. The function of the historian at that time in the 1980s was to say things that caught people up a bit, that involved looking at the 1916 generation perhaps not as pietistically as they had been, particularly Pearse. Ruth Dudley Edwards had begun it with her very impressive biography of Pearse, but there was more to do. It was a necessary moment, and I don't take back any of it.

'By the time I came to write *Vivid Faces* that work of reassessment had been done, much had happened in politics and I had become much older. I was interested in disillusionment, in the way that youth imagines it can change the world and can't. I was very sympathetic to that. I was thinking of the 1960s, and it struck me in a way that it didn't when I was writing *Modern Ireland* that the youth of that period were like the 1960s, full of utopianism, a lack of realism, but well-intentioned in many ways. I also thought how young they were, which when I was young myself, writing *Modern Ireland*, wasn't as poignant.'

Not for the first time, trends in continental history writing influenced him, and he had become interested in the history of generational shifts. 'I began thinking of how the people who made 1916 saw themselves as different from their parents, and in some ways the enemy was their parents' generation as much as the British State; therefore I suppose there is more obvious sympathy. My wife calls that book my novel. I was trying to recreate characters as well and to write a group biography.'

Revisionism was a major debate in Foster's early career. How does he feel now about that and the prevailing consensus on our big-picture history, especially after the Decade of Centenaries?

'I think the poles have shifted. I think the way the Decade of Centenaries was approached was infinitely more interrogative than it was in 1998 for 1798.

The government took a very careful, balanced line, showed far more sensitivity to those whose stories didn't accord with the national narrative. I thought it was a maturing moment, which cheered me. My great friend Catriona Crowe hit on the phrase "complicate the narrative", and I think she was really on to something.

'The whole revisionism thing is over. I would like to say that the historians of my generation who were loosely dubbed revisionists – myself, David Fitzgerald, Marianne Elliott, Vincent Comerford – I think what we were trying to do was look at Irish history not necessarily in an anti-nationalist way but in a broader social way.' Their critics took 'too Hiberno-centric a view'. 'We were part of an international movement,' influenced by the US historian Eugene Genovese, France's Annales historians, Britain's E.P. Thompson.

The return of violence in the North must have had a bearing, too. 'It must have had. But the rhetoric got silly. We were accused of being in cahoots with the government, even with the British government. That was absolutely ridiculous, but it can't be denied that to see violent nationalism revived red in tooth and claw had to have an effect on the way we saw the history of the whole country.'

Mention of F.S.L. Lyons reminds me of his quotation that 'to understand the past is to cease to live in it'.

'I think it's one of the merits of studying history. Bertie Ahern said: we don't live in the past, we live in the future. I tend to think we live in the present myself.

'One of the reasons to study history is to interrogate the assumptions of the past. Isaiah Berlin, when asked why he had given up writing pure philosophy in favour of writing intellectual history, said "because I want to die knowing more about something than when I was born".'

Foster was inspired to study history by Eileen Webster, a Cambridge graduate who taught him history at Newtown, the Quaker school he attended in Waterford, then by Theo Moody at Trinity College Dublin.

After early biographies of Parnell, 'a Marxisant attempt to lift him out of politics and back into his social and family background' and Randolph Churchill – two half-Americans, he now realizes – he wrote important, sweeping modern Irish histories before returning to biographies, but this time on poets rather than politicians. Yet in 1993 he told *History Ireland* that he 'hated biographies'. insisting now that he meant the notion of the 'who's next' conveyor belt: 'If I did say it, I changed my mind, because I think it can be a terrifically incisive and enlightening keyhole on an age as well as a person.'

I mention the successful biographies of John Bew, which prompts Foster to recall Bew's father, Paul.

'Paul and I are exact contemporaries. We first met in the Colindale newspaper library in London, where the British Museum kept its papers. It had a better collection of local Irish newspapers than the National Library of Ireland. Paul was then a wild-haired Marxist. Now he's Lord Bew of wherever, like something from an Anthony Powell novel, but life is like that.'

While Bew became an adviser to the late unionist leader David Trimble, Foster has 'always been a kind of depressed centrist or possibly slightly left of centre. I've never believed in solutions really, just crisis management' – a believer in gradual amelioration, I suggest, and he concurs. 'I voted for Irish and British Labour with varying degrees of disillusionment.' He is fascinated by the Fianna Fáil-Fine Gael coalition, once impossible, then inevitable. 'It is often how history happens. Something is supposed to be a bouleversement, but things go on much as they did before, like Labour coming to power in 1920s Britain.'

Foster's latest book is *On Seamus Heaney*, from 2020. 'I was by no means an intimate, but I revered the work. He was such a magnetic, charismatic, generous person. You were held by the force field of that personality. I hope that inflected my view of him.' When I ask him to compare Heaney and Yeats, he tells me he is about to do just that in a lecture in his father's native Cavan, 'the way they wrote about Civil War, Yeats's *Meditations in Time of Civil War* and Heaney's very different but cognate way of writing about violence. Both were critiqued for writing from outside the cockpit, but both use language and poetry to cope with atrocity.'

The lecture may end up in a third volume of essays he is working on. He already has fourteen uncollected essays that need manners put on them, he says.

He is also editing a handwritten memoir by a relative of his wife, Aisling, a minor Catholic landlord in the late nineteenth century. A labour of love? 'I don't think you would love Great-Uncle Dermot – he was a very crusty curmudgeon – but it is a fascinating reflection on life then. He ends up living in the Hotel Terminus Nice, a perfect emblem for a class whose time has come.'

The last time I interviewed Foster was almost thirty years ago to the day; it was in his north London home, about his first essay collection, *Paddy and Mr Punch*, which addressed the complex relationship between Ireland and England through the prism of personalities whose lives, like his own, bridged the Irish Sea: Katherine O'Shea, Parnell, Yeats, Randolph Churchill, Anthony Trollope.

'Cultural diversity and cross-channel borrowings are implicit in Irish history and cannot be denied by piety or suppressed by violence.'

Today we meet in the offices of *The Irish Times*, across the road from Trinity College, two former Anglo-Irish bastions now comfortably integrated into a pluralist, modern Ireland.

'I think as you get older you get much more interested in your forebears. Now it's okay to talk about being a Protestant. It was different in the 1950s and '60s. I'm very interested in and appreciative of the Protestant background I knew as a child, a strong sense of being national but probably not nationalistic.'

When he first went to lecture in London and then Oxford, the Troubles were still raging and the relationship between Westminster and Dublin was often fraught. After five decades of being an Irishman in England, how does he feel about the two countries' relationship now?

'If you'd asked me that before June 2016 I'd have given a very upbeat answer. The late Queen's Irish visit crystallized that the past had been got over. Brexit has been one of the great shocks and horrors of my life and for many of my generation. What it did to Anglo-Irish relations has been uniformly deleterious. I cannot believe that people as mentally challenged as Theresa Villiers and other secretaries of state could have campaigned for Brexit saying it would make no difference for Northern Ireland. Anyone with a titter of wit could have seen what a disaster it was going to be. The condescension and crudeness and ignorance with which the Boris Johnson raft of politicians, such as the abysmal Lord Frost, treated Ireland over Brexit was a sobering shock. The damage will take a very long time to repair.'

Does he regret having been away for so long or has it been congenial to live in London and visit often?

'I have to bring in the B-word again. I felt very antipathetic; the worst of England seemed to have taken over; the scum had floated to the top of politics. There was a nasty anti-foreigner racism.' But he had skin in the game, children and grandchildren, and he lives in the independent republic of London, a multicultural and cosmopolitan metropolis, and he has a house in France to retreat to. His vocabulary is seasoned with French phrases.

Is Irish reunification inevitable?

'I'm tempted to refuse that altogether; as a historian I don't predict. As an Irishman with a certain interest in politics I think reunification is nearer than I would have thought it a couple of decades ago. I've a terrible fear it would come in the wrong way and with a lot of upheaval. As you know, I'm a great admirer of Hubert Butler. His idea of the Border was it would float off in the bath one day, like a sticking plaster off a wound that has healed. That would have been the logical future until Brexit. It won't be like that now, I'm afraid. There will be a lot more trauma. I'm not sure it will be in my lifetime, but then I'm seventy-four.'

Foster was born in 1949 in Waterford. He was the Carroll Professor of Irish History from 1991 until 2016 at Hertford College Oxford. His many prize-winning books include Modern Ireland 1600–1972; Paddy and Mr Punch: connections in Irish and English history *(1995);* The Irish story: telling tales and making it up in Ireland *(2001); W.B. Yeats: A Life, Vols. 1&2 (1998, 2005);* Vivid Faces: the revolutionary generation in Ireland 1890–1923 *(2014); and* On Seamus Heaney *(2020).*

CARLO GÉBLER

18 January 1992, The Irish Post

'My reactions are parochial. If the one o'clock news reports a policeman killed in Northern Ireland, I listen. But if the man has been killed in Armagh or Down, my attention drops. If Fermanagh, my concentration rises. If Enniskillen, it is acute.

'While all this is true, there is also a contrary truth I can feel nagging at me even as I write. I am seemingly untroubled by the conflict, yet there is an ancient republican part of my intelligence which is continuously reminding me of it – by asking me where I am, what newspaper the stranger I am talking to is reading ...'

This republican intelligence belongs to Carlo Gébler, an Irish author who uprooted his family from their home in London's Maida Vale and moved to Fermanagh, initially for a six-month period while he researched material for a planned travel book. But, as it turns out, they are there to stay.

The passage quoted from *The Glass Curtain: Inside an Ulster Community*, marks the point where he realizes that his time in the North has remoulded him and that he has got the measure of the place, an observation that is borne out in the rest of the book.

Gébler was born in Dublin but moved to London as a child with his parents, Edna O'Brien and Ernest Gébler, both writers. Before moving to the North, he had visited many times and recognized its potential as a possible subject for a travel book.

The author of several acclaimed novels, including most recently the excellent *Malachy and His Family* and *Life of a Drum*, he has also written a widely praised travel book, *Driving Through Cuba*, one of the few to be written on Castro's republic.

Scouting around for another travel book, briefly considering the already well-documented Sicily and North Africa, he hit upon Northern Ireland, a 'rich and untapped source of stories', with the added advantage that the natives spoke English, thus avoiding the language barrier which had hampered his getting to grips with Cuba.

'I was thinking about the market,' he says. 'No one had concentrated on a rural area of Northern Ireland. Everyone goes straight to West Belfast, hosepipes around and then leaves. People know about Fermanagh because of the Remembrance Sunday bomb.

'I knew there were lots of stories. My friends in Irvinestown said: "come and do it, you'll have a marvellous time". Indeed, Gabler had such a marvellous time that together with his Scottish wife and their three young children, he's decided to set up home there.

What has Gébler found in Fermanagh that attracts him so?

'I like it. I like those things that people would regard as the clichés of the countryside. No traffic jams, no dogshit on the pavement, space, walks, all those sorts of things.

'My friends say, why don't you live in the South where there's no tax on writers' earnings? But I don't want to live in a country that's white, male and Catholic. I want to live in a pluralist society.

'I like the temperament of the people in Fermanagh. They're not overly familiar. They're discreet. They don't gush. I like the sense of humour. It's more a place that makes you think about what you should be doing as a writer.

'I like the emptiness, the beauty. I like being quite removed from the metropolitan literary worlds of Dublin and London. I also quite like living in a place on the edge. I don't mean dangerous. But quite far away.

'There is also probably a streak of contrariness in me,' Gébler adds. 'This idea of being a writer and living in an old Irish manse in West Cork doesn't appeal to me.' In fact, Gébler lives in an old 1930s schoolhouse a few miles outside Enniskillen.

One suspects that he has a liking for incongruity. This otherwise severe, careful and watchful figure, all keen intellect, short haircut and steel-rimmed spectacles, delights in tattoos. Not for him, of course, King Billy on his white horse or a tricolour as sported by some of the individuals in *The Glass Curtain*, but rather a tiger, a unicorn, a pearl in a shell, a butterfly and a flower adorn his arms. All done in Japanese ink, which he informs me never turns black.

'The thing that I really miss about London are the black taxis, the Polish cafés, the Czech clubs, the Jews,' he says. 'Making friends in Fermanagh was a slow if rewarding process. At first it was a little difficult. We didn't think there were many muesli crunchers like us, but eventually we found that there were.'

The Glass Curtain is a year in the life of an Ulster community, stretching from July 1989 to July 1990. It is the first major attempt to explore Northern Ireland and explain it to the outside world since Dervla Murphy's *A Place Apart*. While admiring her effort, Gébler chose to adopt a different, more loosely structured approach, interweaving planned interviews with chance encounters. 'This book is a collage where everything is atomized. Dervla Murphy's book is a synthesis.'

Influenced by Graham Greene's *Lawless Roads* and *Journey Without Maps*, Gébler broke his chapters down with subheadings and introduced a diary section as a counterpoint.

'I wanted to have the freedom to bring together things that would never normally collide, like you can do in a film, cutting from one image to another. Modern forms of communication have people more ready to accept abrupt change of style, tempo, perspective and continuity.'

One of Gébler's strengths as a travel writer is his ability to recreate incidents for which he has been unprepared, like the encounter with a group of Scottish Orange men on the Larne ferry crossing. How does he manage to recapture conversations verbatim?

'Usually, what would happen is I would take notes afterwards. Then at the end of the day, when I'm dictating, I find I can go into a kind of trance and I can recall perfectly the conversation.'

Gébler also has a talent for observation, which enables him to create his own anecdotes to complement the ones he is told by others. And he has an aptitude for poignant humour.

A thread running through the book is his quixotic search for Lord Brookeborough's cook. He has heard she was a Catholic, which, if proven, would show the former Stormont leader, notorious for his call that Protestants should not employ Catholics, to have been more a hypocrite than a bigot. That particular trail runs cold, but Gébler discovers that several Catholics were in fact employed on Brookeborough's estate. In another instance, Gébler eavesdrops on two meetings of Fermanagh District Council where pettiness and politics merge into low farce.

Gébler talks with all sorts of people, laymen and politicians, Catholics and Protestants. Much good sense is spoken, but also much that is dispiriting, confirming our worst suspicions.

On hearing the reaction, for example, of the head of a Belfast branch of the Rangers Supporters Club to the signing of Mo Johnston, a Catholic, a reporter asks if dissolving the branch is not proof of old-fashioned bigotry. The Rangers supporters are unabashed. Gébler is left wondering 'if the word "bigot" has now acquired a previously unknown value and has become an appellation of the pure, of those who resist dilution'.

Consider too the insight into varying shades of unionism when Gébler asks Ben Johnston of the DUP and Raymond Ferguson of the OUP whether Catholics were discriminated against under the old Stormont regime.

'I can't see how they were discriminated against,' Johnston says. 'Many had jobs and still have them to this day. Some of the things they fought against, the business vote, I don't think they were all that unfair. Roman Catholics tend to have bigger families. The reason they're unemployed is because they get more money by not working. I don't believe they have suffered in the past. After all, their numbers have increased.'

By contrast, Ferguson admits: 'Of course, they did have grievances. Houses were on a spoils system. If there was a Protestant council, Protestants got the houses. If there was a Catholic council, Catholics got them. But the point is gerrymandering had seen to it that there weren't that many Roman Catholic councils.'

Is Gébler's book an attempt to get through to the natives of the North, who are his neighbours, whom he has described in the past as 'out of touch with the truth', or is he more concerned with lifting a veil for the outsider to see more clearly?

'One would hope to serve both constituencies, but it would be more useful to communicate to outsiders the truth of the place as I see it. The thing is, people in Northern Ireland are pissed off at being seen as troglodytes with horns who do horrible things. The place is so much more complicated than our media would have us believe.'

Gébler is convinced that crossing the Border is to move from one country to another, or from one culture to another. As with crossing from the United States into Mexico, although the climate and terrain are similar, the ambience is markedly different. Travelling over the Border, he arrives in the County Donegal town of Pettigo 'with its Victorian shop fronts, its makeshift-looking customs post made of corrugated iron and its Bord Fáilte dog snoozing in the middle of the road'.

Gébler expatiates on the otherness of the South. 'Whenever I arrive in Dublin, I get the impression that I've arrived in this benign, gentle place. I always feel that I'm a kind of cowboy arriving in a city that's ready to be taken, ready to be stormed.'

He sees the North as summed up in the signpost on the M1 for Finaghy, Dunmurry and Suffolk, which encompasses the three traditions of Gaelic, Scots and English.

'Edna Longley recently described people in Northern Ireland as having a cultural six-pack, taking sips from a different one each time. People from the South don't realize how people from the North switch between these different libations.'

Having familiarized himself with the North, does Gébler see a way out of the Troubles?

'I don't know how to solve them. I think there are things that would improve life that should be done. I wouldn't want to talk about that. It's not a prescriptive book. A writer is just someone who bears witness. Saul Bellow talks about how writers have tried to adopt a priestly significance and to write about how things should be improved as part of that.'

In his book, Gébler relates how a man in a pub describes the Protestant community in the North as a virgin bride. 'She is a bit nervous but, once she has got over the first night, she will see the light and she will be mad for it after that.'

Gébler is tempted to conclude: 'Is our national aspiration sometimes not the cover for a rape fantasy?' I suggest that it is more like one of those rural courtships which lasts for years with no seeming urgency for a wedding. Gébler smiles but withholds his agreement.

Gébler was born in Dublin in 1954, grew up in London and lives in County Fermanagh. He has written eleven novels, including his debut The Eleventh Summer *(1985);* August in July *(1986); and* Life of a Drum *(1991); a short-story collection,* W9 & Other Lives *(1996); three memoirs including* Confessions of a Catastrophist *(2015); five works of non-fiction, including* The Glass Curtain: Inside an Ulster Community *(1992);* My Father's Watch *(2008) with Patrick Maguire, one of the Maguire Seven, and* A Cold Eye *(2024); and four plays.* No One Tells You: The Final Years of Edna O'Brien *will be published in 2026. He is an assistant professor of creative writing at Trinity College Dublin.*

JOSEPHINE HART

26 December 1992, The Irish Post

The chairperson of the Ireland Fund of Great Britain is a remarkable woman. After a childhood in Mullingar, County Westmeath, marked by tragedy, Josephine Hart moved to London in the early 1960s, where she worked her way up to become a director of Haymarket Publications, a West End theatre producer and to present ITV's *Books by My Bedside* series. She has been married to millionaire adman Maurice Saatchi for the last nine years.

Now in her forties, her latest enterprise has met with equal success. *Damage* and *Sin*, two stark and searing novellas treating cardinal sins in a classical style, have become bestsellers in both Europe and America. French director Louis Malle has just completed his film version of *Damage*, starring Jeremy Irons and Juliette Binoche.

As is often the case, her talent is born of torment. Illness and accident claimed the lives of three of Hart's siblings before she left school. Her plans to go to university were abandoned as she chose to stay with her parents to help them in their grief.

For many years Hart kept her unhappy past secret, even from close friends, but now it is the stuff of interviews, an inevitable invasion in the light of her new status as feted author. Death and grief loom large in her work, but she has refrained from tapping directly into her personal store, as much out of fear of trespass as out of concern for her own equilibrium.

'I think I said I would address grief, though not necessarily in relation to my own family. Because I'm very torn about all of this, because you can use all that has happened to you in a way that is very wrong. It's a very dangerous thing in my life as well. And the deaths I write about in *Sin* and *Damage* are not the deaths that my family suffered. But I do understand the grief and I feel that until I can make something really good of this, I couldn't use it. People using events of their lives, this kind of autobiographical novel, it's a kind of robbery, predatory. There is this awful feeling that you are not harming people by using their lives. It is an outrage. I think you have to let a lot of time and other experiences filter through before the emotions can be used.'

Damage is truly a shocking book. It tells of a man drifting through life, happily married and successful, who falls fatally in love with his son's girlfriend. By eschewing sentiment, second thoughts, and moralizing, however, Hart succeeds in transmuting what might have been another banal tale of suburban adultery into a morality prose play that is all to do with meeting the perfect match at the wrong moment, the fairy tale of Mr or Mrs Right made flesh and ash.

Hart's heightened writing style adds to the fabulous quality of the subject matter. She cites as influences the 'distanced moral fables' of Balzac, Stendhal and Barthes, as well as the great French tragedian Racine and his Greek forebears.

'I was very strongly led by both of these voices, and I do look for this kind of internal rhythm, which I know drives people who hate the way I write wild, for I'm looking for a beat and I do polish every single solitary word and I think about it and I talk it out loud to see if I've got the rhythm that I'm looking for. It's very unrealistic, it lacks credibility but I want to make the novels very controlled, very stylized, and that is very unfashionable in England, where generally they elicit something close to venom. They are outside the English tradition. There is no humour, there is no irony. It is not the grand sweep.'

She says of her novels, 'I keep them short and very frightening to trap the reader into a world he can't get out of. Greek tragedies are very short and there are no laughs. And in my humble way, I am dealing with tragic themes. I read poetry, particularly Eliot. I think *The Four Quartets* is a masterpiece of this century. I don't even regard it as reading, it is so much a part of me. I draw on the rhythms more than the language.'

Hart's agent Ed Victor waxes operatic about her work. '*Damage* is an opera. If I had been an agent in the mid-nineteenth century, I would not have sold it to Louis Malle but to Giuseppe Verde.'

Hart's new novel, *Sin*, is the tale of Ruth, a beautiful, wealthy, much-loved girl who develops an obsessive envy of her orphaned cousin Elizabeth, who is adopted by Ruth's parents. Ruth feels displaced by this elder sister and, disposed as she is towards evil, secretly plots Elizabeth's ruin even beyond childhood.

Some reviewers quibble at the apparent lack of motivation in Ruth's actions, but Hart insists this was deliberate.

'To me it's a moral fable, and it does seem to me to let someone off the hook if there is a reason. To have a reason to do evil to me logically implies an excuse. The whole point about *Sin* is that Ruth has everything. I wanted to examine a character who decides to be evil deliberately, consciously, and for no reason. Because I think there are many people like that. Remember, we are very primitive, we think we are very sophisticated, but the human being fights for parental attention. There is an Auden line that says we should regard ourselves lucky to be loved at all, whereas we all want to be the only one loved.'

One of the most powerful themes in the two books is sex. No mean selling point, of course.

'I think the power of erotic obsession is completely underestimated,' declares the author, 'particularly in our very open society. And what has supplanted the reverence that people had for the power of sex and their great understanding of its dangers as well as its delights is the idea that concentrating on physical technique is the essence of sexual joy. But in my opinion, erotic obsession is actually rooted in our soul, and it's a very creative force.

'I think the difference between *Sin* and *Damage* is that the sexuality in *Sin* is lust, which comes in through the eye, is driven towards pleasure, and that's fine, the species would probably have died out without that. But in *Damage*, the man really is erotically obsessed and that is rooted in the psychology and the drive is towards unity. A unity so total that this man wants to be lost in this person, which can be very dangerous.'

Hart comes across as an intense, cerebral person, an unworldly figure in the trappings, albeit sober, of luxury. Like a don or a prelate, she is a firm believer in the daily examination of conscience, despite no longer practising her Catholicism.

'I have a moral view, but I don't think any religion has necessarily a stronger moral base than one human being understanding that there are moral imperatives and working out their own moral line. You can go back to the Greeks. Do the duty nearest to you answers 99 per cent of the problems in life. Once again, that is terribly unfashionable. The concept of duty. Anyone who's been brought up in Ireland, their parents talk to them about moral issues and I got that from my mother.

'My identity is profoundly Irish, I mean I've never changed my passport, I've never changed my name, but I love living in England. That has never been a compromise. I have enormous admiration for English society. I admire its tolerance, its very slow-burning fuse. But I have great criticisms as well.

'We have a society in Ireland that is one of the most articulate in the world, a word society whose entire artistic, indeed psychological life is built on communication. And you have this reticent, reserved society here, and yet we singularly fail in Ireland, and I'm talking about the whole of Ireland, to solve our problems through communication. But I am very proud to be Irish and I do a lot of work for the Ireland Fund of Great Britain.'

Hart is scathing of the selfishness of the me generation and believes that harsh self-criticism is a healthy thing. 'If you fall in love with yourself, it leaves very little room for loving other people,' she explains.

The author is aware, though, of a thin line between self-examination and introspection. '"Know thyself" and "the unexamined life is not worth living" can tumble over into self-obsession. I think my temperament is very obsessive. I think you have to know yourself in life for if you don't you may find that you have involved other people in your life without having any idea who you are. The line is you do it with humility rather than trying to fall in love with yourself. I do believe in the life of the mind. I mean, I love thinking. I can walk for hours, for miles. I think and think and think and I don't write anything until it is finished in my head.'

That head must come equipped with a mass of megabytes. 'I agree. I have a mad head, that is all I do. Funnily enough I can sometimes be doing other things while on another level thinking. Maybe that schizophrenia started in Carrickmacross with the Gaelic.' Hart studied through Irish at boarding school.

To have survived the tragedy of her childhood Hart developed a resilient philosophy of life, helped by the example of her parents' deep love for each other, and it seems to have served her well.

'I certainly saw with my parents that the love they shared with each other made them survive the unsurvivable. Now, I often think, *how did you live with what happened?* But that was it. They were so in love and that was an extraordinary experience, just watching that. I think the old saying about picking up your cross and walking with it is not such a bad way of getting on in life. I've known it to be a vale of tears, but you can come out of that. You're going to die anyway. Why rush it? Let's just see what happens.'

Hart was born in Mullingar, County Westmeath, in 1942 and died in London in 2011. She is best known for her novels Damage *(1991), adapted into a film directed by Louis Malle, and* Sin *(1992). Her other works are* Oblivion *(1995),* The Stillest Day *(1998),* The Reconstructionist *(2001) and* The Truth About Love *(2009). She founded The Poetry Hour at the British Library and edited the anthology* Catching Life by the Throat: Poems from Eight Great Poets *(2008). The Josephine Hart Poetry Prize is awarded by the Josephine Hart Foundation, founded by her husband Maurice Saatchi in her honour.*

DERMOT HEALY

28 May 1994, The Irish Post

Dermot Healy's new novel *A Goat's Song* is literally a tragedy. As playwright Jack Ferris explains to his future girlfriend Catherine, the word tragedy comes from the Greek – *Tragos*, meaning goat, *Oide* meaning song. The book is Jack's account of his relationship with Catherine Adams, a celebration of their love and a lament for its loss.

However, as Jack is a Southern Catholic and Catherine the daughter of a Protestant RUC man, the novel also seeks to explore the interaction of Ireland's two traditions. It is the story of two journeys: that of Sergeant Adams from Fermanagh to Mayo, that of Jack from Belmullet to Belfast. It is also a study of the landscape of these two places, the raging elements and raw beauty of the western seaboard and the different forces defining the Northern capital. *A Goat's Song* is also a meditation on the act of writing.

If this seems a lot to be getting on with, then perhaps an explanation for this rich density of substance lies in the fact that the book has taken almost ten years to write.

Healy was born in Finea, County Westmeath, in 1947. The family moved to Cavan town when he was five and he grew up there, spending a year in UCD before moving to London. More recently, he lived for a spell in Belfast as part of a relationship and he now lives near Sligo town, which suggests there is an autobiographical element to his new work.

For the first three years he worked by candlelight in his cottage, which he bought before electricity was installed. 'I preferred it. It was more intimate. Now that you have light, you're just a far-flung mercenary of urban life with the fridge humming in the corner. But the computer won't work because of the damp and the salt in the air,' he says, so he still writes longhand.

His award-winning story collection *Banished Misfortune* (1982) was followed by a novel, *Fighting with Shadows* (1984), which also took some eight years to write. Nothing if not versatile, he also has a couple of plays and a poetry collection to his name, wrote the screenplay for *Our Boys*, Cathal Black's acclaimed film on the Christian Brothers, and has edited two literary journals, *The Drumlin* and *Force 10*.

A Goat's Song is not so much a state-of-Ireland novel, offering a snapshot of a slice of contemporary life. Rather, in dwelling long over people, places and their history, Healy captures something of their essence, the climate. Patrick McCabe is quoted on the cover: 'Its description of the West of Ireland is like no other I've ever read.'

'The South was a museum. It stored quaint phrasing, soft vowels, unpunctual tradesmen, maddening longueurs, stray donkeys. Shouts at midday, cheers at midnight. And no violence. Goats strolled the village. Turf went over and back. Swans flew. And the price of goods changed every day.'

But the other, the Black North, is here too, in all its glory. 'The women were gruff and scolding and full of cheerful morbidity. The men, some thin-faced, others small and stout, sat on deckchairs reading the *Sporting Chronicle* and the *Sun*. They grew vegetables in every available plot and drank tins of Tennent's lager. Poorly clad, they shuffled to and fro on the edge of the Empire, waiting to be summoned.'

The tragedy of *A Goat's Song* is primarily the tragedy of Jack and Catherine's inability to make their love work, but Healy hopes the reader will see how their tragedy has its roots in the unreconciled traditions from which they spring, which is all of Ireland's tragedy.

'They fail as lovers, as man and woman, but there is some hint that whatever way they have been conditioned and brought up, that that is actually the failure. I don't go into that too much though; I don't project onto it.'

Recalling his memories of how Protestants and Catholics thought of each other, Healy suggested that the strain in their relationship could be compared to the sexual tension between man and woman.

'Our attitude to the North was that you could buy *Playboy* there and the dresses were shorter in Enniskillen. They had the same idea about Catholics. The tensions between the two are the same as between a man and a woman. That's a simplistic way of putting it, but she got a buzz out of his background, as he did with hers.'

A Goat's Song is unusually structured. It begins as the story of Jack Ferris, the resolution of which is his decision to tell his story, which takes in his life with Catherine, her father's life and which ends by completing the circle, at the top of the arc as it were.

'The happy ending is what the writer would wish for, even though he has put in the real story at the beginning. It's a very human thing to wish for happiness.'

This delicately structured novel also looks at the nature of fiction. Healy's musings on the meaning of fiction might appear rather self-regarding were it not for the fact that creative writing is a major influence on the lives of the characters and a significant indicator of cultural difference.

To Sergeant Adams, the unyielding Presbyterian policeman, fiction is suspect, a usurper of the Good Book, and not to be trusted: 'the language of the imagination offered licentious freedom'. His daughter Catherine, however, is struck by the truth to be found in fiction. 'It was a fright to her that a feeble story could contain a truth that assembled far from the meaning of the actual words.'

'I thought there was an interesting conflict in the Southern thing about imagination and the Northern thing about truth,' says Healy. 'The two are operating on different levels. In the South, they say now this is a true story, as if this somehow would make it a better story than a madey-uppy story. Yet sometimes they're not all truth. When you go to the North, where people don't say it's a true story, they automatically expect you to know that it is true because they don't deal in fiction. It's a trust in religious storytelling, which to them is a finer form. There is only one true story, and why waste your time projecting illusions, since you have a truth there in front of you [the Bible]?'

Healy has written a play, *The Long Swim*, about Alzheimer's disease, of which his mother was a sufferer. 'I was always interested in what was fiction, what's reality, what is memory, what is happening now.'

One of the most fascinating elements in *A Goat's Song* is an exploration of how the act of writing marks off or 'kills' an experience. As Jack the playwright contemplates making a novel of his time with Catherine, he pauses for thought. 'The minute he put a word on the page he would stop loving her. Once it became a story it was over. Some other person would materialize.'

Healy puts it like this. 'The writing act, the creative act, somehow destroys the living act. The act of fiction is a commitment of the human mind for a number of years. Therefore it can't be about reality for if it's about reality, then it's only aping reality. It's an illusion that takes you over. If you go into autobiographical fiction, you are killing the thing you love. It comes through Oscar Wilde, Yeats. It's something people don't talk about, but it's true. The creative act must spill over into the world of the imagination. Bits of reality are the props you hang the illusion on.'

Healy was born in Finea, County Westmeath, in 1947, but grew up in County Cavan. In 1989 he settled in Ballyconnell in County Sligo, where he died in 2014. His short-story collection Banished Misfortune *was published in 1982, the same year as his screenplay* Our Boys. *His novels are* Fighting with Shadows *(1984);* A Goat's Song *(1994), which won the Encore Award and was longlisted for the Booker Prize;* Sudden Times *(1999); and* Long Time, No See *(2011). He produced several poetry collections and stage plays. His* Collected Stories *were published posthumously in 2015.*

DESMOND HOGAN

3 July 1993, The Irish Post

In the same way that Desmond Hogan insists he is a traveller, not a writer, an interview with him becomes a ramble through his old west London haunts, his favourite places revealing his character as faithfully as his words. Meeting in the London Lighthouse, an AIDS hospice that also serves as a community centre in Ladbroke Grove, we move on to a couple of Portuguese coffee bars down the road.

In Hogan's fiction and in his travels a feel for the outsider, an awareness of the importance of community and an appetite for the different, the quixotic or exotic, inform and inspire.

Central to Hogan's writing, though, is Ireland, always if not only, even when he's exploring the other ends of the earth, even though he felt he didn't fit in and had to leave. Living in London is no escape, especially for someone from the West of Ireland, so almost for privacy's sake he took flight again to discover in Eastern Europe, the Deep South of the USA and South Africa intimations of Irishness and images of his hometown of Ballinasloe, County Galway, circa 1960.

The results are to be found in his collected travel writing, *The Edge of the City*.

'Outside a plantation house in Alabama, little huts near the house, miniature chrysanthemums in orange, paper-wrapped pots outside the huts; a woman had lamented to me how in her childhood the cotton fields had been a scherzo of scarlet shirts and dresses. Now the young Black people had gone to Detroit but in South Africa in September 1990 fields of neonate sorghum throbbed with coloured women in poppy-red skirts bending to pick the bad grass.'

Hogan is sensitive to colour wherever he goes. He sees faces the colour of blackened bananas, hippies with honey-coloured rat-tails and bituminous-shirted punks.

He comes into his own, however, when describing the anachronistic cultural chaos that is Russia. 'Brides with pearl-seeds on their dresses still danced in the Metropole restaurant to Buddy Holly's Peggy Sue, their mothers wrapped in shawls of green and raging fuchsine … karate and Hare Krishna magazines caused a sensation on Nevsky Prospect, drawing crowds around tables. But a woman in a dress patterned with red bell flowers cried in front of tall amber candles in the church at Kuznetsky Lane.'

On his fifth visit to St Petersburg in three years he realizes the truth. 'I came here to find Dublin and Cork and also to be away from the racist country in which I was shackled.'

Ambivalence rules Hogan's relationship with his adopted country as it does that with his native land. 'For many Irish people,' he writes, 'England, the country between Ireland and Europe, is a purgatorial world not unlike Lough Derg in *Lovers of the Lake*, "a sensation of the world's death".'

'I love Ireland obviously,' Hogan confirms,' but I'd find it very hard to live in Ireland for if you don't fit in you're out. I don't feel angry about it, it's just a fact. Everyone has a place, even outsiders. So many people choose to leave Ireland behind and they come here. It's the basis for a lot of my fiction. People who didn't fit in in Ireland and leave only to run into a sea of anti-Irish racism over here.

'I feel kind of embarrassed talking about myself yet on the other hand I realized my situation reflects that of many people who didn't fit in in Ireland and came here. The real escape is to Europe or to the States but there too there is loss and gain. What you lose finally if you cut yourself off from the British Isles is language, and that is a great loss.'

Enlarging upon his theme, Hogan produces from his briefcase a salmon-coloured hardback of Elizabeth Bowen's *A Time in Rome*, just borrowed from the London Library in St James's Square.

'The libraries are the one thing I would miss about London. After a while in Europe you're starved for language, for actually learning, extending your knowledge of things. This book is so beautiful, it's in the English language but it's almost like a different language to that which people speak or write now because it's a much more meditative language.

'I really like the way Bowen uses language but what's behind it is a great philosophical feeling. A lot of it comes from her background – Anglo-Irish, the Big House. Yeats says somewhere, "indolence breeds wisdom". I think that's really true about those people. Indolence bred in them extraordinary beauty of language, extraordinary sensitivity to language.'

Hogan is a non-conformist. Exiled by Ireland's conservative society, he finds himself alienated by a Britain where people are being ruled by computers. 'What I really fear about England is people like me who don't conform to patterns have been reduced to digits. That is not to say that life here has no benefits. I like London. At best it leaves you alone and allows you your dignity and allows you to live poorly without passing any judgement on you. That's the wonderful thing about London: I don't see myself as a writer at all. Last week in Dublin, I was a writer but here you're a brick in the wall.'

Hogan comes across with an eccentric, childlike candour rather than an adult carefulness.

'All my novels were written longhand but the problem was that I could no longer read my own handwriting so an awful lot of my last stories I actually lost because I couldn't read what I'd written. My handwriting had become so nervous – the whole thing about being in London, the stories have a nervous quality about them. They became illegible, inscrutable.'

He has now resorted to a typewriter but 'the furthest I've progressed mentally is a bicycle. I've never driven a car.'

This most private of individuals ended up then in the nightmare situation of hitchhiking in west Cork, the hapless author subjected to a barrage of questions for the length of his journey.

Abroad, Hogan is free to rediscover his roots and gather insights without being subject to such inquisitions. He quotes approvingly the Russian-born painter Marc Chagall who spent most of his life in exile: 'To preserve the earth in one's roots or to rediscover other earth, that is a true miracle.'

According to Hogan, 'that really anticipates the miracle of my going to Alabama. It's really funny, going to the American South, it's very like Ireland. People leave there and they're tracked down. Carson McCullers left the southern states very young and she lived in New York State most of her life and she said she went back to the southern states to renew her sense of horror. Well, they certainly didn't like her in the southern states because she was writing about a southern states that was of the mind, in exile. She insulted them but she needed that distance to write.'

The parallel is obvious. Hogan has had a harsh deal from Dublin critics. 'Oh sure, I've had a terrible time. Everything I've ever written was mutilated. Basically, I wasn't writing in the English language. They are very worried about the grammar of the English language in Dublin. But you create your own language. W.B. Yeats said that the Irish Catholic middle classes were into pedantry, not learning. After some production of a single play all they could speak about was how Synge got some detail about a ewe wrong.

'These guys presume you come to London and you're surrounded by Oxford and Cambridge people. They have no idea you're actually getting into a world that is closer to Galway than Dublin would ever be. The West of Ireland impinges much more in Britain than it would in Dublin.'

To travel for Hogan is to make connections, with people and between places. 'If there is any theme in the book, it's how Eastern Europe and the Southern States of America were a mirror to Galway 1959–1960.'

Talking of the most memorable places he has visited, he is typically inclusive. 'Apart from Russia, South Africa, South Africa was an amazing place. It brought everything together. Eastern Europe is very interesting, a world that's been preserved. I'd be interested to see what happens to Russian spiritual values. Travelling east you come in contact again with what is best about Ireland, that spirituality.

'As you go to Eastern Europe, you get a different sense of Ireland, much more romantic, much more hopeful. For you see that world of childhood mirrored in those images of eastern Europe. Ireland is a much bleaker place if you write about it in England. If you marooned yourself in Britain this statement would have been very tragic but moving on a bit there's something more joyous, of the moment, of the night, the aura of the party, the jazz club.'

It should be evident that Hogan's is a very personal travel writing. Although the earlier articles and essays appeared in newspapers and magazines such as the *Independent* and *New Statesman*, later ones were published in more avant-garde periodicals.

'The travel writing breaks down halfway through and becomes almost fiction. It's the art of collage more than anything, building bits and pieces from life, trying to make sense of them. The last year and a half of that book is turned inward on myself. It becomes a personal statement, a diary.'

Hogan's writing reveals an observant, sensitive man, equally blessed and burdened with a peculiar fascination for his past. In his own words: 'Part of being creative is being a bit unhappy, isn't it? I think if you get too self-satisfied, you do nothing.'

In *Edge of the City* he confesses: 'In most places where you travel you're a camera but sometimes the camera shatters and you're moved.' Likewise Hogan's writing is never less than a powerful lens and is often more.

Hogan was born in Ballinasloe, County Galway, in 1950. His debut novel, The Ikon-Maker *(1976), won the Rooney Prize for Irish Literature. His first of eight short-story collections,* Diamonds at the Bottom of the Sea *(1980), won the John Llewellyn Rhys Prize. Others include* Old Swords *(2009);* The Larks' Eggs, New and Selected Stories *(2015) and* The History of Magpies *(2017). His other novels are* The Leaves on Grey *(1980);* A Curious Street *(1984);* A New Shirt *(1986); and* A Farewell to Prague *(1995). His non-fiction includes* The Edge of the City: A Scrapbook 1976–1991 *(1993).*

PAUL HOWARD

20 December 2008, The Irish Post

The cultural clash of social classes, once the bedrock of British comedy, has never been a feature of Irish humour because Ireland is supposedly a classless society.

South Dublin, however, has always been different, a subculture of power and wealth, fee-paying schools, hockey and rugby. But now, as Celtic Tiger affluence has put money in more pockets and professionalism and success have raised the profile of rugby, suddenly snobbery and mockery have found a new home.

Paul Howard's satirical series of novels revolving around his highly comic creation, Ross O'Carroll-Kelly, a swaggering, snobbish, womanizing Leinster Senior Cup winning rugger-bugger, have sold 400,000 copies, outselling Maeve Binchy and Cecelia Ahern at home. His newspaper column of the same name is still going strong after a decade, having just migrated from the *Sunday Tribune* to its true spiritual home, *The Irish Times* on a Saturday, and a stage version, *The Last Days of the Celtic Tiger*, has just enjoyed a sell-out run at the Olympia in Dublin.

Howard was a sportswriter on the *Sunday Tribune*, cutting his teeth covering school rugby matches, when he discovered that what was happening in the crowd was far more interesting than what was happening on the pitch.

'You had the yummy mummies, who were hilarious, dressed in Pia Bang gear, 6-inch heels standing in the mud, the dads on the mobiles, but what made me laugh most were the banks and banks of junior kids, wearing shirts that don't fit them down to their knees, shouting 'you can't knock the 'Rock, you can't knock the 'Rock [Blackrock College]. It reminded me of a Hitler youth rally, indoctrination. I was fascinated. Then hundreds of girls like a flock of flamingos from Mount Anville would come in – it just reminded me a lot of American college sports, the high school football team, the jock culture. These guys were heroes, horrifically ugly, yet the girls were flocking after them. There was a huge amount of jealousy going on there as well.

'The senior games would be splashed across *The Irish Times* sports section yet it was just schools sports. These guys were like demigods. I heard a guy say to his dad, I don't care a fock how you think I played, just crack open the focking wallet. I just thought that was brilliant, how do you end up talking to your father like that? I never saw that kid again, don't know who he is, but he is the prototype for Ross.'

Howard knew he wanted to be a writer from the age of eleven, when he became a devotee of Damon Runyon, the American sportswriter who went on to capture the sporting and gambling milieu in novels and plays like *Guys and Dolls*, which Howard says he must have read fifty times.

'When I came to write Ross O'Carroll-Kelly I had *Guys and Dolls* in my mind as a template. I wanted to do what Runyon had done. He was a sports journalist who would go along to boxing matches and race tracks and gyms as a sportswriter and then he would start writing fiction about the characters he observed, the gym rats, grizzled, cigar-chomping hangers-on, like Burgess Meredith in Rocky, or the guy with the hard-luck story down at the track, like Harry the Horse and Sky Masterson.

'I also love the Harry Flashman books by George MacDonald Fraser, there's definitely a bit of that has influenced my writing.'

Howard's first bestsellers were John Hinde postcards. He was working in the office when they found out he was a budding journalist so he got the job of rewriting and updating the captions for the whole range. 'I can still recite some off by heart – Waterford is a port town in the southeast of Ireland ...'

Howard grew up from the age of eight in Ballybrack, a sprawling, working-class estate in South County Dublin beside the rich suburbs of Killiney and Dalkey that are his fictional anti-hero's spiritual home.

He was born, however, in Hackney, east London, and grew up in Luton until his father decided in 1979 that he could not live in a country run by Margaret Thatcher so the family moved back. The Troubles were at their height and an English accent was as popular in Ballybrack as Thatcherism was in the Howard home, so the move home was unromantic.

'It was a really odd thing to be brought up in England and be told you were Irish (we went to St Vincent's RC primary school in Houghton Regis, Mass every Sunday, all our parents' friends were Irish), then to come to Ireland and to discover you weren't Irish at all, you were looked on as something else. I have terrible memories of it, I remember seeing graffiti in walls saying "Brits out" and my younger brother saying to my mother, "what are they going to do to us?"

'Then there was this strange language spoken in school. I didn't know what *anseo* meant, I had no idea there was an Irish language. I remember looking at walls and seeing the Proclamation of Independence. It all looked a bit hostile to me, it felt like we had moved to a foreign country. We got bullied, I remember kids dancing round us singing, "what shall we do with the English bastards?" My first year in that school, I had a fight every week. These kids were eight or nine, and obviously just repeating what they were hearing at home. There was huge anti-English sentiment at the time, which is why when I hear people talk about anti-Irishness in England, I have another story to tell. Irish people are no different, there was pure hatred of English people, we all felt the sharp end of it.'

Howard has always been interested in more than just sport. He studied criminology at college at night and wrote a book called *The Joy* based on interviews with a drug addict dying of AIDS who had spent fourteen of his last twenty years in Mountjoy prison.

He wants to write a detective story set in Dublin but for the moment there is still a lot of life left in Ross. Howard originally planned only four books but they keep selling by the barrowload and the ideas keep coming so he has no intention of doing an Arthur Conan Doyle and sending his fictional hero to his death off Powerscourt waterfall after a tearful last cappuccino with Sorcha in the Avoca café. He insists he is not on a gilded treadmill, operating a lucrative franchise, but is happier than ever with what he is writing.

'Maybe three years ago I didn't think there was much more of this in me but then I came up with the idea of Ronan [Ross's son conceived on a cultural exchange on the Northside] and that gave me so much scope to do other things. I've had a bit of a clear-out of old characters who had come to the end of the line and am bringing in new ones, a bit like a soap opera because that essentially is what it is.

'I think the last three Ross books are better than the first four, far superior. I was going through them again looking for two particular storylines that I wanted to hark back to. If I could rewrite them I would. I'm a lot more sympathetic to Ross now and I think the books are better for it.

'There's no doubt when I started writing I did have a chip on my shoulder about class and background. When I read the early columns there's no subtlety in the humour, almost a nastiness. There was an axe being ground but I think I matured, started to like the character. I was worried with the play, would people like Ross? Without blowing smoke up my own ass it is difficult to make people sympathetic to a wholly unsympathetic character.'

Some might say he has been too successful or gone too soft, for Ross has been embraced as an icon by the very people being satirized. Has he spawned a monster?

'I think I have. When I started writing it first, it was pitched to seventeen- to twenty-year-olds, but the age profile of my readers is getting younger. It troubles me a bit when I'm signing books in shops and I see eleven- and twelve-year-olds buying it because it's not for them, they haven't developed a sense of irony yet and they're taking it literally, as a guide to life almost. I think as people get older they see he isn't real and it's to laugh at. I think Swift said satire is a glass in which everyone sees everyone but themselves. People read Ross and see their friends or their neighbours but not themselves. I'm not waging class war, it's a laugh. All it is is just mickey taking.'

Paul Howard was born in London in 1971 and grew up in Ballybrack, South County Dublin. Best known for the Ross O'Carroll-Kelly series of novels and plays, he has a record five Irish Book Awards and twenty-four nominations. Should Have Got Off at Sydney Parade *(2007),* The Oh My God Delusion *(2010),* Downturn Abbey *(2013) each won the Best Popular Fiction prize. His biography of Tara Browne,* I Read the News Today, Oh Boy *(2016), won the Non-Fiction Book of the Year and he received a Special Recognition Award for his contribution to the Irish publishing industry in 2024. He has written scripts for the TV series* Bad Sisters.

CLAIRE KEEGAN

2 September 2023, The Irish Times

When Claire Keegan began writing short stories, in the 1990s, watching the word count was an important part of the process as she entered and won competitions to build her reputation. Today, as her newest story, *So Late in the Day*, is awarded the rare accolade of being published as a stand-alone hardback, she no longer has to bother. Her writing's quality is what counts.

Keegan is one of those equally rare authors whose every work has won a major prize. Her debut collection, *Antarctica* (1999), won the Rooney Prize for Irish Literature. Her second, *Walk the Blue Fields* (2007), won the Edge Hill Short Story Prize. *Foster* (2010) won the Davy Byrnes short-story award, and *Small Things Like These* (2021) won the Orwell Prize for Political Fiction and the Irish Novel of the Year Award.

If her output has been relatively modest in size – *Small Things Like These*, her sole novel, was the shortest ever to be shortlisted for the Booker Prize – its impact has been major, especially her last two works. *An Cailín Ciúin* (The Quiet Girl), adapted from Foster and directed by Colm Bairéad, was nominated for an Oscar, while the film version of *Small Things Like These*, starring Cillian Murphy, will be released next year.

Foster, about a neglected girl who blossoms when she is farmed out for the summer to be minded by a loving childless couple, is now a staple of the Leaving Cert English curriculum, and pupils will this year study *Small Things Like These* – not bad for someone who failed English at the Leaving Cert.

Keegan grew up on a farm in deepest Wicklow, near Clonegal in County Carlow. As I drive to meet her in Tullow, where she runs creative-writing courses, I pass signposts for places familiar from her stories: Arklow, Shillelagh, Coolatin,

Parkbridge. Yet, as anyone familiar with her debut collection knows, that is only half the story, for the Deep South of the United States, particularly its scenery and its writers, has a similar hold on her imagination.

The summer before she turned seventeen Keegan spent cooking and cleaning for a wealthy American family near Gorey. She must have made a good impression, for they invited her to live with them in New Orleans – a city she found 'hot and racist' – and paid for six years' study at Loyola, a private university (a US academic friend estimates this would have cost €100,000). She cooked, cleaned, minded children and graduated with two first-class degrees, in political science and English. This sponsorship – I can't help but think of it as fostering – changed her life. Her English professor, Mary McCay, opened her mind to ideas of personal freedom and taught her how to read fiction, which in turn made her want to write.

As I wait for the author in the foyer of Teach Bhride Holistic Centre, a Brigidine Sisters convent, I dwell on the convent in New Ross, 60 km away, with its Magdalene laundry, where generations of unmarried mothers were mistreated, the dark heart of *Small Things Like These*. But Keegan sees no incongruity in the setting and feels at home in this progressive institution. 'Things have changed; times have changed. I think this is a lovely place. It's lovely to see it turning into what it could have been all the while. Nice to be part of that.'

She was never religious. 'I never really had a faith to lose. I never took it literally, even as a small child. I always thought it was a story, so I never felt broken-hearted. But I always had great respect for stories.'

She makes coffee and then, before we sit to talk, kicks off her sandals and climbs up on the sills, opening the windows to let fresh air in.

So Late in the Day is a quietly devastating character study of a man whose misogyny and meanness destroy what may be his best chance of happiness. It started as a writing exercise for Keegan's class but also has its roots in a shocking episode from her childhood.

'I was talking about how I much prefer tension to drama. For me, tension is about loss. Drama doesn't make the reader or the central character tense at all. To me it is tedious and flat and it's bad TV. Someone asked for a concrete example. I came up with this story [set significantly on the anniversary of Princess Diana's wedding]. I said, let's say we have a fella and he works in an office, he's finished work and he gets on the bus. Is there anything wrong with that [as the start to a story]? I think there's nothing wrong with that. Good singers start low is what I was taught.'

She started using the outline in workshops until a student asked whether she had written the story. 'I realized she wanted to write it, so thought *I* had better write it.'

As we follow Cathal, the protagonist, through the day, and seemingly innocuous encounters with various women (a colleague, a cleaner, women on the bus home), he reflects on his relationship with his French fiancée, Sabine, and we gradually encounter the character flaws that have led to his undoing.

Misogyny is not just a personal failing. Cathal's colleague Cynthia tells Sabine that, for some Irish men, women 'are just cunts, that she often hears Irish men referring to women in this way, and calling us whores and bitches'.

The Ireland she grew up in was steeped in misogyny, Keegan says. Contraception was banned until 1985. Marital rape was legal until 1991.

She had three brothers and two sisters. Was the family itself a misogynistic institution? 'Without doubt. I didn't know any family that wasn't. When a male came in, a female stood up.' In Keegan's story, Cathal recalls his brother pulling the chair out from under his mother as she was sitting down with her plate after serving their supper, causing her to fall to the floor. Her sons and husband laughed at her. 'I'm sorry to say that this scene is autobiographical,' the author told *The New Yorker*, which published the story last year, both in print and as a podcast of Keegan reading it. 'My own brother did this to my mother when I was a child, and it was treated so casually, as though little or nothing had happened. It stayed with me all my life.'

Little wonder that Keegan escaped as soon as she could. 'I don't come from a close family. We are not close at all,' she says.

'Women have no difficulty writing from a man's point of view. We are taught to imagine what pleases a man and what displeases him from the time our heads were lower than the table. My brothers were never taught what pleases or displeases a girl. It is of huge benefit to me as a writer, one of the few benefits of misogyny. The last two books I published are told from the male point of view.'

Children, cared for and neglected, are at the heart of both *Foster* and *Small Things Like These*. Keegan was disappointed that George Saunders and Deborah Treisman overlooked the significance of children in their *New Yorker* podcast about her latest work. 'There is a child on every page of this story.

The reason why most people of childbearing age get married is to have children, and that seemed to get overlooked in the discussion.

'Cathal's proposal is like a pounce: "We could have a child if you want." He looks for a reaction, and she didn't turn away. I think misogyny Irish-style has produced a sense that you're not really a man unless you've produced a son to carry on your name – it's that backward – and that it has to be your own flesh and blood. It produces a type of cruelty that we call a family. I like to think this story has something to say about not having children. Part of me is concerned with the child that could have been born; they escaped.'

Cathal and Sabine also have a cat, for which Keegan holds out little hope.

Keegan's writing, like her speech, is measured and precise yet rich. 'My mother was a very good housekeeper and cook. She taught me to look for meat marbled with fat that keeps it moist while it cooks. There are little marblings in my prose that may seem unnecessary but produce the feelings.'

Her opening page is a case in point, 'a brazen sun', 'a taste of cut grass', 'a gulp of swallows skirmishing' and 'beds plump with flowers' establishing the mood before a warning shot: 'so much of life carrying smoothly on, despite the tangle of human upsets and the knowledge of how everything must end'.

Cathal works for the Arts Council, but that is just for the author's amusement, as she had a friend who lived on Merrion Square in Dublin, where the organization is based, so she knows the geography – always a concern in where she sets a story. It is not a veiled #MeToo allusion, although the author, like every woman, has a story. 'I had an inappropriate encounter at the Impac awards dinner with an American gentleman who was not a gentleman. He was putting his hands in my hair at dinner, pretending I was his partner.' But she was too young and too shy to object.

'There is a problem with #MeToo, though. I think it takes the eroticism out of some of the encounters between men and women. I think part of that eroticism is a playfulness around domination. If there is an attraction between two people the risk is too great, especially for the man, to play that out.'

After university, in 1992 Keegan returned home. The first things she wrote were 300 job applications, which generated 300 rejection letters. She was living with her mother in Tullow, and found books by Dermot Healy, John McGahern and Edna O'Brien in the local library, which 'taught me I could write about rural Ireland. I found that irresistible, that here might be as good as anywhere'.

She got a job on a Fás scheme in Clondalkin in Dublin, teaching creative writing, which she loved. Every Thursday when she got paid she went to Eason in Tallaght and bought her mother a Wordsworth classic edition, such as *Madame Bovary* or a Thomas Hardy, 'and she just ate them'. Her mother, who was born in 1926 and died last year, 'was extraordinarily capable and talented. Whatever talent I have I think I got from my mother. My father would have said that anything to do with stories was just a nonsense.'

Because of the pleasure she took as a reader and because she had nothing else to do, Keegan couldn't resist giving writing a go. 'I wrote a story for a competition on Live at 3 [on RTÉ One] with Thelma Mansfield and Derek Davis, which my mother was watching.' 'Clocks in the Air' was one of ten chosen by Brendan Kennelly for the resulting anthology. 'I have never read it again. I'm sure it was dreadful and promising,' she says.

She won RTÉ's Francis McManus short story award twice; it was judged by David Marcus, who was a scout for Giles Gordon of the literary agency Curtis Brown, who secured her a book deal with Faber & Faber. Another story, *The Ginger Rogers Sermon*, won the William Trevor Prize, judged by the author. 'Word restrictions at the beginning taught me not to make a story longer than it needed to be. I think the worst writers I know have no regard for the limitations of the art form. There is nothing more dull than self-expression, and yet creative-writing classes tell people you should express yourself. I think the opposite: you should learn restraint. McGahern said all good writing is suggestion, all bad writing is statement.'

For Keegan, reading and writing are a way of life, and a way to understand life. 'I love being able to make a good living out of something I enjoy doing and am deeply interested in, but it is always the text that matters, not being a writer. It's finding out what I have to say and trying to say something fresh about what it means to be alive and what's in the human heart that matters to me.'

Keegan's devotion to the word, her thirty years of teaching creative writing, much of it carried out in this centre, makes me think of exegesis, the study of secular scripture. For her, reading means rereading.

'I don't think you've read anything properly, understood it, until you've read it twice, and closely. I think the tail of the dog feeds back into the jaws. I'd never dream of teaching anything I haven't read at least twice. Most people buy a book and read it quickly. It's the constraints of time. Most fiction readers are women, and most women have children and a great many things to do. But that's not who I write for. I don't make anything short for that reason. I write for myself. It has to pass my aesthetics in order for me to show it to anyone else, and then I write for everyone.' Her aesthetic is 'whatever pleases me as a reader, that feels original, decent prose which is clear and plausible'.

So Late in the Day is just over 6,200 words. Or 12,400 if you read them twice, as you should.

Chaucer was her first influence. 'I loved the humour and the structure.' As she was in Louisiana, she read southern writers, the 'extraordinary' Flannery O'Connor and William Faulkner, 'but I still don't understand him in the way I don't understand Joyce. The modernists escape me. Maybe I don't have enough patience.'

She likes O'Connor's notion that 'fiction is the art of making pictures'. 'We are such visual creatures: we stood up on our hind legs to see over the long grass, I think. That is how desire enters our bodies: we want something because we can see it. I like work that is not cryptic, that facilitates the reader; images that cohere, an unpretentious way of writing. It feels pleasurable to come up with a version of that with my own personality or style. I think good writing is good manners. If you are writing well, you are taking care of your readers' needs and your characters' needs. You are also abiding by the constraints of the art form and not showing off.'

Her favourite, however, is Chekhov. 'I started reading him in my thirties and I've never stopped. I keep teaching him. I find him deeply humorous. I suppose his regard for human freedom is what draws me back again. What we do with that and how we abuse that.' She feels an affinity between Irish and Russian writers: 'families, parochialism, backwardnesses, silences, superstition, the folklore, nature, just trying to survive, often in a rural place, what people do to each other, the violence towards children as well – all of that felt very much at home'.

Redrafting for her is neither cutting nor polishing but changing her approach. 'I could change the point of view, where it is set, the time it's set in. My tendency is not to go on. I try to find the kernel, what the core of the story is, something that interests me, and stay with that, and make it fatten on loss. I think of a story as it goes along as almost like a wild creature that is looking for something to eat. When it eats, it eats loss, and that's what keeps it alive. There isn't anything we care about that we cannot lose. That's what I'm looking for, not to artificially impose it on someone but to find out what they truly care about and treat it with dignity.'

Faber is issuing revised editions of her collections. 'I went in with an arrogance, thinking I might rewrite them with all the skills I have now, but I can't. I wouldn't write those stories now, but I also couldn't, because my preoccupations have shifted and I'm older, my taste has changed. I can't rewrite them any more than I can get away with wearing the clothes I wore in my twenties. They just don't suit me anymore. So really I am just editing, mostly punctuation. Neither collection was edited at all.'

The boundaries of what language is considered acceptable are always shifting. George Saunders chose not to read aloud her new story for his *New Yorker* podcast because of the cunt word, used to convey her character's misogyny. I wondered whether she might revise the rare use of pejorative terms, such as the N-word, 'tinker' and 'simpleton', in her older stories.

'I absolutely can't [be constrained], because then I can't say what I need to say,' she replies. 'I can't write about misogyny if I'm not allowed to say it. I want it to be offensive because it is offensive.' If some readers find it too triggering, 'I absolutely respect their desire not to do that and not to read my work.'

As a teenager on the farm, Keegan used to help the men felling trees to keep the lines clear by attaching a chain to the trunks and dragging them down to the road with a draught horse. She has been studying the horsemanship of an Australian, Bill Faulkner, for ten years and travelled to Queensland last April to train a wild brumby. She is retraining an ex-racehorse. 'I find it delightful and the opposite of sitting at a desk inside. It's going out and being physical.'

I ask what happened to the novel she started back in 2009, which was set on a farm on Mount Leinster, near Bunclody. 'It's still there, I just went off and wrote something else, [but] I like the language of it. Who knows, maybe that will be next.' Her next project is 'a book that is set on the farm where I was raised. You come out the front door and you look at Mount Leinster, so there may be a meeting of the two.'

She is pleased that two books have been made into films and doesn't feel protective or possessive of her texts. 'I just wish them [film-makers] luck with it but have no interest in micromanaging them in any way. I would like to write a screenplay, because I love film as much as I love books.'

She loves paragraphs, which might be a bit tricky, but more usefully she also loves writing dialogue and what it reveals. 'We are bound to reveal ourselves when we open our mouths. I think a film can be the most beautiful thing. I remember coming to Tullow to see *Snow White*, and at the end I just lay down in the foyer and cried. It wasn't a tantrum. I just was longing to go back in, as I thought it would never happen again. I've just always loved stories.'

She doesn't own a television but loves film. 'My favourite living writer is the film-maker Michael Haneke. It's astonishing what he does. He knows that nothing is ever resolved, life goes on. He writes for grown-ups.'

Keegan is happy that *Small Things Like These* may have ignited an interest in shorter texts, made them fashionable again, that books don't have to go on and on to be interesting. Story collections, however, will always struggle, she thinks.

'I think collections are too upsetting for people. Short stories are not comforting. You don't go through something and then come out of it, whereas with a novel you can give readers one huge upset, which is overcome to some extent, or there is some kind of reconciliation. I think a collection is harder on a reader.'

Keegan was born in 1968. Antarctica *(1999), her debut story collection, won the Rooney Prize for Irish Literature and the William Trevor Prize, and was followed by* Walk the Blue Fields *(2007). Her long short story* Foster *(2010) won the Davy Byrnes Short-Story Award. Colm Bairéad's Irish-language adaptation* An Cailín Ciúin *(2022) was shortlisted for the Academy Award for Best International Feature Film. Her novella* Small Things Like These *(2021) won the Orwell Prize for Political Fiction and was shortlisted for the Booker Prize and Rathbones Folio Prize. Cillian Murphy produced and starred in a film adaptation. A short story,* So Late in the Day, *was published in 2024.*

MARIAN KEYES

13 February 1997, The Irish Post

One of the most heart-warming success stories of recent times must be that of Marian Keyes, a Dublin woman based in London for the last twelve years, who has conquered alcoholism and depression and gone on to write two bestsellers, the second of which, *Lucy Sullivan Is Getting Married*, is published, appropriately enough, this Friday, 14 February, St Valentine's Day.

Petite, demure and softly-spoken, Keyes doesn't look or sound like a hell-raiser, even a reformed one. But when she went to UCD to study law at the age of eighteen, her studies took very much a back seat as she majored in parties, bar extensions and generally wild times. After graduating and finding work with the Eastern Health Board, Keyes found motivation difficult 'because I felt that nothing mattered very much and in the end nothing really mattered at all and all the while I drank as much and as often as I could afford'.

After a year and a half of this, Keyes moved to London into a squalid flat in a tower block, not quite the bright lights she had dreamed of. She found work as a waitress then graduated to working in an accounts department, Meanwhile, her drinking had become progressively worse.

'I was surprised to wake up in the morning and find I was dying for a drink and even more surprised to find I would actually have a drink in the morning. But then I stopped being surprised and it became normal. I would spend day after day being drunk. Every time I came to, I would simply reach for another drink and get plastered again. I loved it so much, so fiercely, but it got worse. I had almost no friends left. I would rather drink than do anything else or be with anyone else. I started having very strong feelings that I shouldn't go on living the hell that was my life. I was waking up with the most savage depression, the screaming horrors. I fantasized about dying, I took an overdose.'

Mercifully, she was found and booked into an addiction treatment centre by her father. After six weeks, she went home to Dublin to recover for another six weeks.

It seems too much of a fairy tale to say that that Keyes's life was transformed but that is what happened. She attends AA meetings four days a week and has been sober for three years. She had always wanted to write and in September 1993, recovering from a drinking binge, she read an award-winning story in a magazine. Spurred to write something better, she picked up a pen and started a short story.

When she returned to London after her treatment, she decided to get published. She submitted her stories to Poolbeg with a cover letter referring to a novel she was writing. They asked to see it so Keyes decided she had better get writing. The result was *Watermelon*, which topped the Irish bestseller lists and was selected for WH Smith's fresh talent promotion.

Her second novel shot to No. 1 in the Irish charts and she has signed deals with British and German publishers worth £650,000.

Was the alcohol a crutch or a tripwire? 'To be honest, I probably thought at the time it was a creative thing. You know when you're a bit locked, you think something's a great idea and you write it down. But then in the morning ... If I had continued drinking, I would never have had the time to write a novel.'

How did she lose control? 'I don't know. I've always had heavy-drinking friends and I'm the only alcoholic I know. There are millions of theories, genetic or circumstantial. I suppose I could never handle it and I hoped no one else could handle it either. We always used to have post-mortems but somewhere along the line I went too far and never found a way back. I'd love to know why but I'll never know and anyway knowing isn't going to change it.'

How does she understand it now? 'I was very emotionally immature. I didn't want to grow up. All around me people were getting married, buying flats, having kids. I just wanted to party, I didn't want to stop. I couldn't face the responsibility of having to be an adult.

'The last two years have been a process of growing up. I've come through an awful lot. I thought I'd never be able to live without alcohol. I thought my life was over and I'd never laugh again. I thought all the joy had gone out of my life and it's just been the opposite. I thought I would be jealous surrounded by people getting drunk. The only thing is beyond a certain stage it gets boring. It makes me not want to drink when I see how it makes people behave.'

When it came to writing her first novel, Keyes was determined not to fill it with a sordid, morbid story of alcoholic hell. Instead, she came up with the blackly comic tale of a woman abandoned by her husband on the day she gave birth to their child, who ends up back in the smothering bosom of her Irish family.

'I was familiar with the humiliation and rejection but also the fun and laughter. The feelings in it are universal. I think they are a really normal family in that they are really abnormal. Everyone has a veneer of well-behavedness that they present to the outside world but behind closed doors it's quite different. The number of people who've come up to me and said: "that's my family. How did you know?"'

One thing she's found terribly difficult is public exposure. 'It's one thing to say I'm an alcoholic and I'm not ashamed of it and I hope my story will help other people but it was hard to go into my day job after there had been things in the press here. I felt very raw and exposed because I'm private. I'm not a natural media personality. There were a couple of days when I didn't want to get out of bed and face the world. I suppose I thought it would be glamorous and it's not. It's been hard work. But I'm grateful for the exposure sand the chance to tell the story of my recovery.'

To sobriety and success as a writer, Keyes was soon to add the love of her life. 'He was an old friend who had always been nice to me but I always preferred meanies. But when I left the treatment centre with embryonic feelings of self-respect, he was still nice and I was able not to reject his kindness.' They married in December 1995.

After the success of *Watermelon*, Keyes's self-confidence took a knock when her editor sent back the first four chapters of her follow-up. 'I was thinking *Watermelon* was just a fluke. Anything you write is so precious and criticism is so personal. Lucy Sullivan is about a second-generation Irishwoman who suffers from depression. She has her tarot cards read and is told she will be married within the year but she doesn't even have a man.'

Now able to write full-time, Keyes is moving back to Ireland to live, but being an Irish writer in London has been good to her.

'It gives me a different perspective. I've been here for so long. I'm an outsider and I think outsiders write better because they have more of a distance. In another way it puts limits because there are things I might write which an Irish audience would immediately recognize but which wouldn't work here. I find that frustrating.'

Keyes was born in Limerick in 1963. She has written eighteen novels. Her first four – Watermelon *(1995),* Lucy Sullivan Is Getting Married *(1996),* Rachel's Holiday *(1998) and* Last Chance Saloon *(1999) – have all been adapted for television, as have* Anyone Out There *(2006) and* Grown-Ups *(2020). She won Irish Popular Fiction Book of the Year for* This Charming Man *in 2009, Popular Non-Fiction Book of the Year for* Making It up as I Go Along *in 2016 and was Author of the Year in 2021.*

CLAIRE KILROY

29 April 2023, The Irish Times

'There is no more sombre enemy of good art than the pram in the hallway,' wrote Cyril Connolly. It's a quotation that Claire Kilroy may well have reflected on over the years.

Kilroy won the Rooney Prize for her debut novel, *All Summer*, published in 2003 just before she turned thirty, and delivered her next three, all for Faber & Faber, at three-yearly intervals: *Tenderwire* (2006), shortlisted for Irish Novel of the Year; *All Names Have Been Changed* (2009); and *The Devil I Know* (2012).

The year 2012 was a momentous one for the author, who grew up and still lives in Howth. She married her partner, Alan, that May, her fourth book came out in August and she gave birth to their son Lawrence that December.

More than a decade later, and after a difficult, nine-year gestation, from conception to final draft, she has returned with *Soldier Sailor*, which weighs in at a healthy 60,000 words. Mercifully, it is a beauty and has already received a rave if premature review in the *Times*, which will not be the last to highlight an exceptional chapter of virtuoso writing about a baby's night fever that will be spoken of in the same breath as the big 'Christmas shop' in Anne Enright's *The Green Road*.

Kilroy's most personal novel to date, told in the first person, it is a mother's love letter to her newborn son that threatens early on to turn into a suicide note as, sleep-deprived and unsupported, she reaches the end of her tether. It is also a stirring J'accuse – 'Parenting is gender segregation' – addressed to a society where parenthood still all too often means motherhood.

It explores the intensity of the maternal bond – 'I would kill for you' – but also the severing of the umbilical cord connecting the mother to the wider world of work and adult society – 'Now I lived in your world. It was small' – and the fraying of a marriage as the husband puts career before family – 'I tore at my marriage rings until the knuckle cracked, but no joy. Those things were soldered onto me.'

The Sailor of the title is the baby, while Soldier is the mother, one of the 'infancy infantry' performing the thankless daily drill of raising the next generation, 'struggling to contain your screams while struggling to contain my own'. Reading *Soldier Sailor* is an intense experience, but an immensely rewarding one. It is full of heightened, hard-won emotions articulated with a rare eloquence. 'Love will sluice over you like sunlight,' Soldier tells her son.

The early years of motherhood are ironically a barren part of the fictional landscape, with precious few examples that might have opened Kilroy's eyes to what lay ahead of her. No longer. With mordant wit and acute, astute observations, she charts a world familiar to any parent yet freshly painted.

Here is Sailor in the playground: 'You tottered around like the town drunk and I tottered after you like the town drunk's mate. Little kids bolted around in all directions, their skulls narrowly missing each other. It was the Hadron Collider in there.' And in his high chair: 'You tore off your bib and cast it to the floor like a man quitting his job.' The baby blues are not blue. 'They are not any colour. They are the colour draining from the world.'

Then there is the fashion: 'My coat with the swinging pockets that was essentially a wearable bag.' And the shock to the system of becoming a mother in one's thirties. 'What struck me as the starkest contradiction of all was that, having navigated this much of life – the volatility of youth, of love and loss, the agony and the ecstasy – the closest I had come to losing my mind was during the period known as settling down.'

Kilroy may not have published a novel in a decade but she did not entirely disappear from the literary scene.

Praising Anne Enright in *The Irish Times*'s Irish Women Writers series in 2015, she wrote: 'Motherhood often signals the dissipation of a woman (writer)'s brilliant career, as it blasts down the door of the *Room of One's Own* that Virginia Woolf asserted was a necessity for a female writer. Anne, however – because she is an empathetic genius – has managed to write from within the chaos of motherhood, and to write brilliantly.'

Asked in a 2016 Q&A about her writing habits, she replied: 'I wrote the first four novels in a quiet room of my own (or a room of my parents' in the case of the second one). It all changed with motherhood. I can't answer that question yet.'

In 2016 John Banville said in an interview: 'I have not been a good father. I don't think any writer is. You take so much and suck up so much of the oxygen that it's very hard on one's loved ones.' I invited other writers to discuss being a parent and a writer. Kilroy replied: 'Motherhood meant the end of my writing life. I had written full-time for twelve years and published four novels, but I couldn't afford childcare so that was the end of that.

'I started teaching when my son was nearly two, and then I could afford childcare. But I still wasn't writing – I was now teaching. He was nearly three before I started writing part-time again. Now he's nearly four and the Arts Council recently gave me a bursary so I don't have to teach. I write in the mornings while he is in preschool. I don't yet know whether I am a better writer now that I am a mother, but I am certain that I am a better mother now that I am back writing.'

Perhaps most tellingly, though, in 2015, she contributed 'F for Phone' to *Winter Pages* while teaching creative writing in Villanova.

'It is now the summer of 2015,' she wrote. 'If I hadn't had a baby in 2012, I'd be publishing a novel this year. I published one every three years, regular as clockwork. They were my babies – Finally, after a three-and-a-half-year absence from the page (more than a novel's worth of time) I have opened a new file on my computer … I want [my son] to have a writer for a mother. This is the first step. These are my first words. Lawrence, I am back.'

It was September 2021, however, before she started her first draft, by which time there were 200,000 words of notes in that computer file, 'stuff I'd observed, things another mother said to me, all the bits and bobs of a day as a full-time mother or a freelance mother'. The final draft was done in March 2022. Did Kilroy ever doubt whether she would write another book? 'Big time,' she answers. 'It's been eleven years, I haven't been sitting here thinking, *I'm brilliant, wait till I get this finished*.'

Friend and fellow writer John Boyne described her first three books as 'an intriguing trilogy exploring different aspects of creativity – painting, music and writing – and the often unsettling and obsessive relationship that develops between the artist and the art' and her fourth, *The Devil I Know*, as 'a surreal and frequently funny analysis of Ireland's economic crash … eviscerating but utterly lacking in cliché'.

Kilroy says she made a distinct decision at the age of fourteen to pursue an artistic career, to follow her passion. Her first three novels explored this creative pursuit. 'The topic really is rapture, finding something so alluring that you chase it down, which lent itself to writing thrillers. Those books were almost quest novels of the path I was trying to track down. There is no path. You have to invent the path like Roadrunner, laying down track in front of you.'

Written during the boom, which she hated as it was all surface, *All Names Have Been Changed* was 'an archaeological novel', uncovering the bohemian Dublin she grew up in where, in the words of Declan Hughes, you could be 'glamorously unemployed'. The boom turned out to be a farce, so she wrote one (*The Devil I Know*). 'I was angry at what I saw as the ransacking of my city. By the time we got to the recession, and it became clear that a great trick had been pulled on the Irish people, I was very saddened. We had been swindled into this monstrous debt we could never repay.'

Soldier Sailor, by contrast, was an unplanned pregnancy.

'I didn't want to write this novel. I wanted to escape to my old life and write my old novels, imagining, doing my thing, but it seemed imperative I acknowledge the hugeness of this experience, use my art in any way I could to capture it. It was a challenge because nothing much happens. One of the characters can't speak, it's extremely boring or panic stations.'

She yielded on subject matter but would not compromise on form.

'It was imperative to me that something as epic as this be fashioned into a fictional narrative. A lot of writers turn to non-fiction and I didn't want to do that. The imagination is linked to freedom, the immortality of art, to quote Nabokov. Art has always been the escape hatch if you're of my vintage. I had to take risks but it did rescue me and it has rescued me again.

'A lot of women have gone this path before me, had creative lives and then that was the end of that. I wanted to convey that fear. Also, I felt if I wrote it in my own voice, it would just be a long whine that only dogs could hear.

'For a long time I couldn't imagine. I was too tired, stressed, too much was going on to get to that place I call flow. I was scared for a long time that that faculty was gone. It became a stick to beat myself with that I couldn't just sit there and create, my brain was fried, I couldn't remember sentences. Honestly, my vocabulary has shrunk. I haven't met one mother who didn't talk about failure. I'd only get going and then have to do school pick-up and feel resentful. I'm not a good organizer. Anne Enright said to me: "Before you have a baby you have to become incredibly disciplined. When you come home you do not wash up, clean the floor or pick up the pants, you go to your study and you work."'

Kilroy blames the dearth of fiction about motherhood for her being so unprepared for the reality. 'I marvel at my naivety now but I haven't seen it portrayed. The renaissance in women's writing happened after I had a child. It was a boys' club. If those novels about motherhood were written, were they published, were they publicized?'

That said, 'It's hard to write a novel about drudgery without it feeling like drudgery. Where one of the characters can't speak but is there on the page all the time.

'I knew from writing the others that they always start off as horrible failures. Can I say this? They're shit until they're not. You have to live with them being really bad and hopeless.

'For a long time the mother worked in some financial area and had to perform in that arena while going to the toilet with her breast pump. I don't know why that trickled away but it did. There was to be a nanny, and resentment of the nanny. It ended up being just this intense relationship between two people, Soldier and Sailor.'

Did they always have those names? 'No, the child was Darling for years. Then India Knight published a novel called Darling, so he became Sailor.'

I wonder if Soldier's developing relationship with the Friend, an old acquaintance who is also the primary caregiver in his family, grew out of an anxiety to offer the reader a subplot.

'I realized retrospectively the love interest is my love for the novel, the imagination. I don't remember that character, my friend, coming, and there is a whole chapter, my favourite in the book, the beach, that was just there in the notes file. I don't remember writing it. I just lifted it. It was born without the pain of birth.'

Does her husband recognize himself in the novel? 'Alan hasn't read it,' she replies. 'He says he's writing a novel, working title Motherhood: A Father's Perspective. He thinks this is hilarious, that I've written a novel about motherhood and the father does not come off well.'

A fellow school mum quoted Michelle Obama saying that for ten years she couldn't stand Barack because of the unfair distribution of labour but having put up with him for ten years she now has thirty years of happy marriage. 'I read that and I felt seen,' her friend said. That said, Kilroy is seeing great improvements. She does Pram Watch, and the percentage of men pushing them is up. Also, when the wife is the main breadwinner, the husband often does his fair share of housework.

It is not just about partners, though. It is a patriarchal society.

'That is unfortunately how society was set up in Ireland. There was no paternity leave. Alan didn't get a day off work. There is now two weeks but low take-up. I think paternity leave should be compulsory, parental leave should be shared so it becomes a joint endeavour. I asked Sebastian Barry's wife: did he help out? She said yes, 50:50. I think you can see that in his work. Someone who has devoted time to equality.

'Saying mothers need me time is like saying homeless people need homes. You need to give mothers me time. Someone has to mind the baby.' As Soldier asks: 'Who mothers the mothers?'

She never asked her mother about motherhood. 'Why did I think this was going to be easy? Why did I think the role was unimportant? That's a biggie. I now realize this is the most important thing to get right, otherwise you're going to leave a trail of wreckage with your child. We were taught to respect careers, not mothers, the breadwinner, not the bread-maker.'

And it's harder if you are in the creative arts.

'It is harder if you're a writer to establish your space. To write I have to justify in my own head the cost of childcare, to buy back my own time. The creche was €962 a month. I'm unsalaried. Could I justify this when we are trying to buy a house? No. Then I got a job teaching to justify it, but it's still not writing.'

It didn't help that by the time the family was able to buy their first house together they had had six addresses. They kept getting evicted as landlords went bust. 'It sounds very simple but you need somewhere to put the stuff you need. Vital baby supplies were always in a box somewhere. The solution is for the State to build public housing.'

Soldier is rebuked by an old man for blocking the path with her pram. 'When he declared me a stupid woman I felt not just abused but worse: disabused – that all along I had believed I was equal.' Alongside her personal run-ins with the patriarchy, the rise of Trump and Putin feels like a geopolitical climate version of the pathetic fallacy. 'I could see that to have presumed empire and patriarchy were dead was naive at best. Not only were they alive and well; they had won.'

Kilroy's novel is addressed to a baby boy. 'I presume at some point my boy will read it and have some understanding of what motherhood is, be more aware of the challenges, the importance of it.'

Now she is a veteran, she wants to acknowledge the courage of her comrades with babes in arms, women who had each other's backs. 'These women were not zombies, they were warriors.'

'As a young woman, I distinctly remember passing women pushing prams, thinking that's not going to happen to me. I thought I had better things to do, now I realize that is the best thing to do, why was I so patronizing? I put it down to ideology, the way I was raised in school. Part of the book is to confront that. This is not undemanding, it is the most demanding work.'

The novel is dedicated to her father, Jim, who was a very hands-on dad, and to her friend and fellow writer Sarah Bannan, head of literature at the Arts Council, whose son Ruairi tragically died in February.

Kilroy wants to return to her old rhythm of a novel every three years. Is there a potential trilogy on the stages of childhood? 'I don't think so, I've said my bit. I will return to pure imagination now.' She has already started her next novel, which is about a ghost.

'The job now is to reflect on middle age and mortality. We know we are going to die, it's a very unpleasant piece of information. Are we in denial? My cousin died at thirty-nine, one of the school mums died at thirty-seven, both cancer. Christine was one of the infancy infantry and we watched her slowly die, that's where the whole warrior thing comes from. She did the school run till she couldn't manage the steps, then she'd wait at the top because she didn't want to say goodbye. It was terrible. You have a human imagination and you try to shape those feelings into a story. We will die, we will lose each other. How do we accept that? I think that's what it is, you don't know what you're writing or why till later.'

Kilroy does think sometimes of the novels that might have been, but then she wouldn't have Lawrence, and she would do anything for him, do without anything. 'That is the power of being a parent. But I hope we reach a time where we don't talk about motherhood; it's parenthood.'

Kilroy was born in Dublin in 1973. Her debut, All Summer *(2003), won the Rooney Prize for Irish Literature.* Tenderwire *(2006) was shortlisted for the Irish Novel of the Year and the Kerry Group Irish Fiction Award. Her other novels are* All Names Have Been Changed *(2009),* The Devil I Know *(2012) and* Soldier Sailor *(2023), shortlisted for the Women's Prize for Fiction.*

DEIRDRE MADDEN

27 August 1994, The Irish Post

It is tempting to cite Deirdre Madden as typical of the contemporary Irish writer, as familiar with mainland Europe as with Irish society, yet her writing reflects a spirituality that suggests she is informed as much by Catholicism as by cosmopolitanism.

Madden's latest novel, *Nothing Is Black*, is set in remote Donegal, where three women's lives resolve themselves far from the crowds. Claire, a painter, while living a self-contained existence, connects with the outside world through her memories and compassion. Her wealthy cousin Nuala has come on retreat from Dublin, reeling from the death of her mother. The trio is completed by Anna, a Dutch neighbour whose life is darkened by her estrangement from her only daughter.

Madden's text is refreshingly short, just 122 pages, for this is a novel of ideas rather than action. If you care to dwell on the message of mortality, the meaning of life and the nature of art, this is the book for you.

Madden is a native of Toomebridge, County Antrim. Having studied at Trinity College Dublin and the University of East Anglia, she moved to the Continent, spending time in Germany and Italy before moving to Paris. Her third novel, *Remembering Light and Stone*, was the impressive story of an Irish girl living in an Italy on the other side of the tourist tracks, a post-Christian landscape of factories, wealth, fractious families and fractured selves.

The author agrees that by playing Irish characters off against other nationalities she is achieving a different insight into the Irish mind. 'That's probably a fair comment. I've been living abroad for quite a while now and I think you learn a lot about other countries but you also learn a lot about Ireland by having something to contrast it with.'

In *Nothing Is Black*, Donegal's key-left-in-the-door culture is strikingly contrasted with Anna's last memory of trying to see her daughter. Shut out by the security system spotlight, she pleads with her via intercom on closed-circuit TV to let her in.

Also Claire recalls how a visit to the Dachau concentration camp had left her feeling empty. She had realized then how evil can affect a place, leaving not the sense of horror one might expect but instead killing off all its spiritual energy and leaving it sterile.

The author contrasts this strongly with the atmosphere in the parts of the West of Ireland devastated by famine. 'It's completely different. Some of those places are absolutely charged with a sort of suffering, a tremendous spirit of place. Last year I was in the Doolough valley in County Mayo where lots of people died during the Famine. A tremendously bleak spot but there is a difference, to do with the landscape and the fact that life was always very difficult in those places. There are places which have [Dachau's] sterility, like certain parts of Belfast.'

Whatever about the inspiration of living abroad, it is not a good career move in terms of public recognition. 'If you're an Irish writer living away it makes it more difficult. You're not reading at festivals. Everything depends very much on your work but you do meet people [abroad] you wouldn't have a chance to meet in Ireland and get more of a sense of what's happening outside Ireland.'

Alice, a friend of Claire, is an artist who 'seemed to have freed herself from her society at a remarkably early age'. Madden does not welcome the comparison. 'That is too drastic. But by going away, whether you like it or not, you are making a statement. I'm very fond of Ireland. I love coming back and I would like to spend a bit more time here but whether you like it or not you're constantly defining yourself by what you do. It wasn't deliberate and I didn't kick over the traces.'

Another artist, Markus, touches on one of the book's key ideas. 'People in Europe now aren't interested in art because it has to do with death. It teaches you how to die and people don't want to know about that. In that way art is religious.'

Madden returns to this theme with a reference to the Swiss sculptor Alberto Giacometti, 'shocked out of domesticity forever by an early confrontation with death. In the face of certain annihilation, the clutter of domesticity was to him a monstrous lie. Why pretend life is anything other than transitory? Why pretend you are anything other than utterly alone in your existence?'

Madden warms to her novel's subject. 'This book has to do with mortality and how to live, given the life you have. Life and death are so closely linked that you have to know about one to deal with the other and that is what art is very much about.

'Death defines life. It is one of the absolutely central things. The period you have is short and you have to think about what you are doing. That makes it more precious in a way. I suppose I think security doesn't really exist. A lot of people think you can build a little empire for yourself, try and look after the money but you can't really. Big things are out of your hands.'

Madden is reticent when it comes to teasing out the religious significance of the above. 'The difficulty I would have is a lot of the definitions people have of what comes after would be quite simplistic and quite materialistic, expressed as an extension of this world, and I think whatever there is is something utterly different but I certainly would never describe myself as an atheist or agnostic.'

As Claire is an artist it is perhaps natural that two pages are given over to her philosophy of art but it is also a statement of intent on the author's part. 'I like to use the novel to explore ideas. I like to write novels that are more like real life where things happen in a very low-key way rather than in a dramatic or abrupt fashion.

'I wanted in this book to write about the creative process. Claire is a painter because a writer would have been too self-referential.' Madden sees the artist's life as perhaps free of clutter but this has to be paid for. 'I don't just think society makes it easy for you, once you get out of that nine to five. It's not so much that you struggle but how you're seen. People are a bit suspicious of you.'

'The magic of art,' Madden writes, 'is to make something charged with energy and knowledge.' Enlarging on this, she says: 'What is painting? What is art? To look at some really good paintings, that's what you get from them. Why have these things lasted hundreds of years and meant so much to people? I think there's something extraordinary and fascinating in that.'

Madden was born in 1960 in Toome, County Antrim. She won the Hennessy Literary Award in 1980, the Rooney Prize for Irish Literature for her debut novel, Hidden Symptoms *(1986), the Somerset Maugham Award for* Birds of the Innocent Wood *(1988) and was shortlisted for the Women's Prize for Fiction for* One by One in the Darkness *(1996) and* Molly Fox's Birthday *(2009). She won the $165,000 Windham-Campbell Prize in 2024. A deeply compassionate writer, she has frequently focused on the Troubles. She is married to the poet Harry Clifton.*

MICHAEL MAGEE

1 April 2023, The Irish Times

Michael Magee sat his driving theory test on the day of our interview. If his record of turning literary theory into practice is any guide – a degree, a master's and a PhD in creative writing, followed by an exceptional debut destined for Novel of the Year shortlists – he will cruise through his practical examination.

It is far from dreaming spires that the author of *Close to Home* was reared. Magee, who turns thirty-three next month, grew up in Poleglass, a working-class estate on the periphery of republican west Belfast. He sporadically attended the Christian Brothers in Andersonstown, sneaking *into* school to attend Terry Sullivan's English classes, where his eyes were opened to what literature could do by Barry Hines's *A Kestrel for a Knave*, inspiration for Ken Loach's film *Kes*.

Magee loved how it was set on a council estate like his and showed how that world functioned, how the kid in it found in a kestrel an escape route. For Magee, books were his imagination's outlet. He intended to learn a trade – his two older brothers are painters – but a few early starts on building sites made studying more attractive, so he left for John Moores University in Liverpool, where among working-class classmates he felt at home, then postgraduate courses in Queen's University Belfast, where, initially, he didn't.

Close to Home, as the title suggests, is strongly autobiographical, its protagonist Sean the author's alter ego.

'It's about a university graduate from a working-class background, the first in his family to go. He comes back to Belfast, falls back into old habits with the crowd he grew up with, gets into a barney at a house party and thumps this guy. The rest of the story is him coming to terms with what he did and navigating the things that structured his life: class, masculinity, his relationship with his past.'

Set in 2013, this is a post-Troubles, post-crash Belfast, an insider's account of the working-class West Belfast Sean is from and the middle-class university quarter his friend Mairéad introduces him to. A 'Seána the Baptist' character showing Sean a way ahead, she has made the transition from a troubled teen with 'the stickiest fingers in Belfast' to an aspiring writer with a Moleskine notebook in her bag and ambition to get on.

Sean, however, is scraping by, with hedonist friends like Ryan and Finty, always up for a session or 'a wee toot'. 'Just like that, it was party time.' Having lost apprenticeships after the crash, they are casually employed, always broke, dipping the till, bumming loans off elderly relatives, attaching magnets to electric meters, scamming the checkout machines at Tesco, drinking other people's leftover pints. This is not misery lit – it is too entertaining for that. But there is the sense of a lost generation, wracked by suicides, forced emigration and political paralysis.

'My generation was supposed to reap the spoils of peace,' Magee told *Publishers Weekly* in January, echoing the words of his contemporary Lyra McKee, who was shot dead by the New IRA in 2019. 'We were told over and over that because the conflict ended, everyone in society would benefit from peace, and in reality that hasn't happened.'

'Imagine the work she would have contributed to the world,' he says of McKee. 'The North has the most millionaires per capita outside London but the people who suffered the most, who were promised their lives would change, are still suffering terrible poverty. The Good Friday agreement was great but when you buy into neoliberal economic structures, you're going to see massive disparities of wealth. It's a very dysfunctional statelet. How many years have we had a [functioning] government in twenty-five years? Sectarianism doesn't exist the way it used to but it has been institutionalized. A lot of people are disillusioned.'

Mairéad leaves Belfast for Berlin because she can't breathe there. Anthony, Sean's wild and troubled older brother who was abused as a boy, has a panic attack in which he too struggles for breath. But Magee has made his peace with the place, negotiating a settlement between his origins and his new cultural milieu that doesn't compromise his sense of self. But it wasn't easy.

'Queen's was a different world,' he says. 'I remember feeling very lost, discomfort. That's not to say there weren't nice people.'

'Some of your best friends are middle class,' I joke. 'Too many of them, probably,' he answers, laughing.

'I was very conscious of how I talked, my voice, the social indicators that revealed my classness. In certain circumstances, I felt small. I didn't understand the rules of the game. I had no skills. I didn't know the literary world existed until I went to Queen's, people interested in books, the things I was interested in. I knew I wanted to be in that world. Your first instinct is to give up part of yourself, learning cultural indicators and references and humour. It was almost like I was learning a new language and losing my own one, like being split in half.'

An early draft of *Close to Home* was about that whole journey, but Magee wanted to focus on this very particular moment when he is on the periphery of both worlds.

He had sent a short story to *The Stinging Fly* magazine in 2013. Its then editor, the Welsh writer Tom Morris, rejected it but encouraged him to write more and the second story he submitted, 'Bottles', was published in 2014. Morris introduced him to fellow writers Sally Rooney, John Patrick McHugh and Nicole Flattery, and this informal writers' group offered each other feedback on work in progress. 'Writers teach you how to edit your own work,' he says.

Close to Home started with his PhD in 2016 but it took him time to find his voice, perhaps self-conscious of his own in a world of received pronunciation, thinking he had to operate in an elevated register to be literary.

'I had weird perceptions of what a novel was, what you could and couldn't do in a literary novel, not what I was writing about but how you told them. I had doubts about the place of my world in literature.'

Michael Pierse, editor of *A History of Irish Working-Class Writing*, helped him crystallize his thinking around class. Discovering working-class French writers Annie Ernaux and Édouard Louis was a revelation too.

He was still blocked, though, until Morris suggested writing a long letter, addressed to someone he respected, starting at any point in his life. 'Write without thinking. Say what you feel you need to say.' In the space of two months, the letter became a 60,000-word manuscript. 'Tom says, "you know what you've got here, don't you?"' Tom was his therapist, Magee says. 'I said, "there's this bit in the book that's a bit close to home". He said, "there's your title".'

It started out as almost straight memoir but with a novelistic structure, influenced by Elena Ferrante and Karl Ove Knausgård. 'I felt I needed to divulge everything but I couldn't get the right distance from the material, then I read this essay by Vivian Gornick about creating a persona. She was writing about non-fiction but I think you need it in fiction too, you need the character to be their own self. So I changed my character's name from Mick to Sean, which opened up opportunities to do what I needed to do.'

His mother had wanted to call him Sean but his father resisted such an explicitly Irish name 'because of how he was treated growing up, discriminated against with jobs and housing, slapped about and called a Fenian bastard at British army checkpoints. He thought that would carry on in my childhood.'

Magee is from a republican family and has an uncomplicated Irish identity, while respecting others' rights to identify as Northern Irish or whatever. 'My family for a long time couldn't really articulate, show their Irishness, it wasn't safe. I feel a degree of responsibility towards owning it.'

The British government, having first controlled and manipulated the narrative of the Troubles, is now seeking to suppress truth recovery. Magee grew up listening to his grandparents' and mother's experiences. 'I guess that's my responsibility as a novelist … to relate that and my community's experience.'

With rare exceptions, such as Mary Costello's *Titanic Town* and Michael McLaverty's *Call My Brother Back*, West Belfast was 'a no-go area of literature, ghettoized, refracted through the eyes of people who saw the conflict unfold on TV screens, not on their doorsteps'. What Anna Burns's *Milkman* and Paul McVeigh's *The Good Son* did for Ardoyne, Magee has done for his community.

Magee is now fiction editor of Belfast literary magazine *The Tangerine*. 'I like writers who tell stories in an interesting way, I don't care what stories they tell, I just want them told right. The one I'm proudest of is Louise Kennedy's "In Silhouette".' It secured Kennedy a place on the *Sunday Times* Short-Story Award shortlist and an agent, Eleanor Birne, who later signed him too.

Kennedy, whose debut novel, *Trespasses*, won Novel of the Year last November, says of *Close to Home*: 'Supple, rich and demotic – no one else is doing this. Like Annie Ernaux by way of Chekhov. Absolutely glorious.' Flattery, his old writing partner, concurs: 'The best debut I've read in years – a tender examination of class, masculinity and place.'

He hasn't started book two yet but he knows his turf. Next up is his childhood era, from the Belfast Agreement to the end of Operation Banner, then a novel based on his mother's experience of raising a family in the early 1980s. 'I've got my acre of land and I'll cultivate it as best I can.'

I predict a rich crop.

Magee was born in Belfast in 1990. His debut novel, Close to Home, *won the Rooney Prize for Irish Literature, the Nero Debut Fiction Award, the Waterstones Irish Book of the Year and the John McGahern Prize. He has adapted it for a Channel 4 TV series. He is a co-founder and fiction editor of the Belfast literary magazine* The Tangerine.

BERNARD MACLAVERTY

31 July 2021, The Irish Times

Many short-story collections by established authors remind me of albums, several of whose tracks have already been hit singles. The first thing that struck me about *Blank Pages*, Bernard MacLaverty's brilliant short-story collection, his sixth but his first in fifteen years, is that not a single story had been published elsewhere.

'I don't send them away anywhere now,' the affable Belfast writer tells me over the phone from his Glasgow home. They just sit on his desk until the pile is sufficiently high to send to his editor at Cape, fellow author Robin Robertson, to turn into a book.

'I would use him as a kind of touchstone in a way. He was pleased with this one. I don't know magazines in the same way. What's the one with the spider in the title in Ireland? [*The Stinging Fly*.] In the beginning I used to keep a big chart of every story I sent away. In one column there'd be "no reply" or "never heard from again". Maybe I'm afraid of that happening again.'

There is surely little risk of that fate befalling this master of short fiction, 'simply the best that has come out of Ireland in the last fifty years along with that by the late William Trevor and the late John McGahern', according to critic Richard Rankin Russell.

He is no slouch at the longer form either. His first two novels, *Lamb* (1980) and *Cal* (1983), were adapted by him for film, starring Liam Neeson, and Helen Mirren and John Lynch respectively. *Grace Notes* (1997) was shortlisted for the Booker Prize and his late masterpiece, *Midwinter Break* (2017), won Irish Novel of the Year.

I grew up with MacLaverty's fiction so it was a pleasure to say a few words when he was given a Hennessy New Irish Writing Hall of Fame award in 2018, recalling how I had gone with a Protestant girlfriend to see the film version of *Cal*, about a Catholic's affair with the widow of an RUC man who he had helped murder: 'a great novel, a fine film but a terrible date movie'.

Despite having left Belfast for Scotland with his wife and young family when the Troubles were at or near their worst in 1975, early memories are still the main source of his inspiration – 'I tend if I sit down at the desk to have thoughts and pictures from the North of Ireland' – and even his writing style is identifiably Northern: Tom Adair praised its combination of lavishness and restraint as 'the ultimate Northern Irish prose style, all Catholic curlicues and Calvinistic sparseness'.

In 'Blackthorns: County Derry 1942' (his birth year), the final story in the collection and one of its finest, set in the North during the Second World War, a doctor's wife hosts a US officer to dinner: 'Myrtle took no account of Brad's unfamiliarity with local Irish words or constructions or expressions.' MacLaverty similarly delights in Northern words such as midden and glory hole and turns of phrase – 'You're some pup!'

'I think it's OK, in the same way Flannery O'Connor writes with such a Deep South drawl and words. The responsibility is on the reader, the duty to go away and see what's indicated here.'

He is, however, unsentimental about the North. The doctor in 'Blackthorns' and his US army counterpart together save the life of a Catholic man with the help of a new wonder drug, an antibiotic made by Pfizer (a nod to the present pandemic), but the scientific breakthrough stands in contrast to their unenlightened sectarian and segregationist beliefs, a cure for which is still to be found.

Similarly, in 'Sounds and Sweet Airs', Lisa, a young harpist on a ferry from Belfast to Scotland, asked what she misses about home, replies: 'I miss the hatred. And the bigotry. Oh and all the flags.'

'That's where I come from,' MacLaverty says simply. 'That's where you come from too. What was your piece, *Dirty Linen*? That was full of it. It is a bigoted place. The thirty years of the Troubles were awful. There was a fear on the hundredth anniversary of the State people might want to celebrate it but I don't think it was a good thing, yet another wrong turn of the British empire, the desire to rule the roost, the gentry who lived off the everyday Orangemen who think that they rule the place.' He scoffs at the BBC's attempts to appear even-handed. 'They would compare Ian Paisley and Bernadette Devlin – one was a bigot and the other was a working-class intellectual. Coming to Scotland, it was a joy to be away from it. Working-class, left-wing people – that would be my territory, so much better than conservative, unionist.'

He went on some of the smaller civil rights marches, including one in Belfast after Bloody Sunday, but he wasn't a great activist, he says. He was very fond of John Hume, 'a huge politician'. 'You must want to write but anger spurs you on, you know it's not going to change anything but you might communicate something, help someone else with empathy.'

MacLaverty has always been a writer. He remembers a teacher, Gerry Treacy, at his primary school in Belfast giving him a sixpence for his essay 'A Rainy Day' and reading it out to the class. 'That tanner was my first literary money, the only thing I think my mother was ever proud of. She used to say, "I pray every night, son, that you'll not write anything dirty."'

He went on to St Malachy's but didn't shine, even failing his English A level. 'I enjoyed school but I wasn't a really smart kid.' He is proud of its literary heritage, however. 'I think there are four novels which feature St Malachy's: *The Feast of Lupercal* by Brian Moore; *Call My Brother Back* by Michael McLaverty; *Ripley Bogle* by Robert McLiam Wilson; and my own *The Anatomy School.* I don't know how many schools can claim that.'

He went to Queen's University, not as a student but as a laboratory technician. However, he began writing for student magazines and Philip Hobsbaum invited him to join his writing group along with Seamus Heaney, Michael Longley, Derek Mahon and Stewart Parker. His near namesake Michael McLaverty was another influence. His handwritten tribute to Heaney, displayed in the Laurel Villa guesthouse near the HomePlace in Bellaghy, is worth seeking out. 'He had a certain rooted loftiness – a down-to-earth brilliance.'

Born three years after Heaney, he escaped Belfast three years after him too, in 1975, having qualified as a teacher. 'I was married and had children. Belfast became so dangerous and unacceptable and filled with hate, I thought, *I don't want to live here anymore*. I wanted to remain somewhere Celtic, and the only place I had ever been out of Ireland was Edinburgh, to learn about chromosomes.'

His first job was in a big Catholic comprehensive, St Augustine's 'or, as we nicknamed it, St Disgusting's'. Then it was on to the Isle of Islay (the y is silent, he explains), from where on clear days you can see Ireland. 'When I first went there, the only TV signal you could get was from Northern Ireland, so we were bombarded with [ads for] George Best and Donnelly's sausages, a reminder of home. On rueful days, you felt like Columba.'

Eventually he settled in Glasgow, where he still lives, sharing a postcode with all his children and grandchildren. Gregarious and good-humoured, he found like-minded friends in Tom Leonard, Jim Kelman and Alasdair Gray, several of them also Hobsbaum protégés. He also delights in his adopted city's rich classical-music tradition, a love which inspired *Grace Notes* as well as several short libretti.

He reckons, though, if he had not become a writer, he might have been a painter. His father was a commercial artist and he has illustrated a book of bedtime stories, which he wrote for his own children.

MacLaverty has been a full-time writer for forty years now, having quit teaching in 1981. 'I said to myself if I earned as much as a teacher then that would be OK, I could put cornflakes on the table for the family.' Adapting his work for radio, television and film helped, starting with 'My Dear Palestrina', a long story which won a Jacobs award as a TV play. 'At the awards ceremony in Dublin Madeline [his wife] felt an impostor till she met a man at our table who bought the figs for the fig rolls.'

The finest story in *Blank Pages* is the truly superb 'The End of Days: Vienna 1918', about the deaths from Spanish flu of the artist Egon Schiele and his wife. It is also the last story written for the collection. 'I felt when the pandemic came, the world might not be interested in pre-pandemic stories. I had great affection for the work of Egon Schiele. I had seen that drawing he did of his wife the night before she died. I had written an earlier story ['Life Drawing' from *A Time to Dance* (1982)] about an artist who comes home and draws his father on his deathbed. I revisited that emotional material. I felt it was in a way ushering in the pandemic, paying attention to the suffering it's inspired.'

Schiele the artist is ruthless, drawing his wife Edi dead even as he grieves for her, before having second thoughts and burning the work. (There is a devastating moment when he realizes the sound he hears, 'the beat of trains over tracks', is his unborn child's fading pulse; Edi's 'body being both cradle and coffin within a minute'). MacLaverty's description of Schiele, looking repeatedly up at his subject then down at the page 'like a bird drinking', could be his own manifesto. 'Sometimes the line is like the human voice. It sings. Variations and complexities … Accuracy is what he was after. Accuracy and an intensity of awareness. Paying attention with his eyes.'

How ruthless an artist is he? Is everything fair game? 'I would say you can use stuff that you know provided it is sufficiently distorted. When I was teaching, we were trying to establish what fiction was. A girl in third class said, "sir, sir, it's made-up truth". I thought that was a wonderful definition.'

It is striking how autobiographical the inspiration for these stories is. Some are inspired by a news item, a historical fact or a work of art, but many spring straight from memory. 'The Dust Gatherer' stems from teenage memories of the mortal danger of an overhanging slate and an aunt with varicose veins who cut her leg on the jagged edge of a bucket.

Like MacLaverty, whose father died when he was only twelve, a harsh and lifelong lesson in the fundamental unfairness of being, the boy in 'The Dust Gatherer' lost his father young. 'It was traumatic,' he says. 'I didn't know it was happening. If anyone ever spoke about it for years after it would make you want to cry. You gradually get over it and realize we are all going there. He was a well-loved and well-liked person.'

'You're a writer … You're supposed to notice,' the protagonist in 'Blank Pages', the titular story, is told. And MacLaverty is all-seeing, observing for example the 'cold sandpaper roughness' of frost, 'which had covered the inside of the glass with feathers'. 'A Love Picture: Belfast 1940' is ostensibly about a woman grieving for her son – 'Great gulps of air inflating her' – who is missing at sea, who someone thinks they might have seen on a Capitol cinema newsreel disembarking in Galway. But MacLaverty's parents met at the Capitol. His father drew the posters, oblivious to the danger of lead and cadmium in paints, and died of cancer at forty-five. Perhaps if you lose a parent young, even if you later lose your faith, you never quite lose hope in resurrections and miracle cures.

MacLaverty's well of memories is old and deep but has still not run dry. The home invaded by the British army in 'Searching, Belfast 1971' was his family home. The cricket ball found by the officer belonged to his brother. Catholics don't play cricket, the soldier says. 'That shows you how little you know,' the mother replies.

The alcoholic in 'The Fairly Good Samaritan' is reminiscent of Gerry in *Midwinter Break*, his late masterpiece, which became a huge word-of-mouth success, a relatively quiet story about an ageing couple's estrangement which slowly builds, like a night of steady snowfall, into something sensational. This new character is based on an old neighbour from Islay, a very witty, ex-public-school down-and-out, who had lovely phrases, but was led astray by drink. 'We were very good friends, we would occasionally go drinking together, always a dangerous thing.'

MacLaverty is comfortable writing female characters, be it Catherine in *Grace Notes* or Stella in *Midwinter Break*. 'There was a story I wrote called 'At the Beach' in *Walking the Dog*, about a couple on holiday, much like 'Midwinter Break'. It began in the man's voice then I decided I'd switch, that she leaves him in apartment and wanders around at siesta time. I felt her voice sounded right. It was the last story in that collection and I then went on to write *Grace Notes* to keep that female twang of the voice. I've tried the female voice or empathy on the page whenever I feel like it now.'

You write whatever comes along, MacLaverty explains. 'You think of a sentence and write it down and it might please you, then you write another one beside it. It builds up like a wall, you make a house of it then you go into the house and look out the window. It leads you, you don't know where you're going, you follow the words, then you begin to shape it forward and backwards, intensify it and subtract, all that. With a dozen stories, you have different nuances, some are more intense, some slightly funny, a kind of range, I hope.'

MacLaverty was born in Belfast in 1942 and moved to Scotland in 1975. He has written five novels and seven short-story collections. Secrets and Other Stories *(1977) was followed by novels* Lamb *(1980) and* Cal *(1983), made into films starring Liam Neeson, and John Lynch and Helen Mirren respectively.* Grace Notes *(1997) was shortlisted for the Booker Prize. His other novels are* The Anatomy School *(2001) and* Midwinter Break *(2017), which won Irish Novel of the Year and was shortlisted for the International Dublin Literary Award. He was inducted into the Hennessy Literary Hall of Fame in 2018.*

EIMEAR McBRIDE

8 February 2025, The Irish Times

There is a moment very late on in *The Lesser Bohemians*, Eimear McBride's marvellous modern love story, when her two protagonists first call each other by their name, an act so poignant that those names remain engraved on a reader's heart.

So even though her publisher, Faber & Faber, is not marketing her new novel, *The City Changes Its Face*, as a sequel, the back cover's very mention of Eily and Stephen tells me we are back in their world of Camden, north London in the mid-1990s, two years on from the tumultuous days of first love, with the couple gingerly navigating the wash of an undisclosed crisis in their relationship.

Eily is a twenty-year-old Irish drama student, Stephen a successful English actor two decades her senior, both recovering from abusive upbringings, the significant age gap in their relationship complicated by the reappearance in his life of his long-lost teenage daughter Grace. While Stephen is putting the finishing touches to an autobiographical film, Eily seems isolated in their new flat, retracing mis-steps in their relationship in her mind and on paper. So this is a novel about a couple attempting to adapt their past into art.

It's standard to ask a writer about the embryonic idea that quickened into the finished work. Here, however, the question is: when did McBride realize she wanted to write a second novel about Eily and Stephen? *The Lesser Bohemians* was published in 2016, won the James Tait Black Memorial Prize and was shortlisted for the Goldsmiths Prize, the RSL Encore Award and Irish Novel of the Year but it had taken nine years to write and McBride had known for a long time that her story was too big for one book.

'I knew from 2010 I wanted there to be another book, set two years later,' she says. 'I wasn't done with them.' Her intention had been to leave it to gestate for a while to give her a bit of distance from the original but other projects kept presenting themselves. She is happy with the result, however. 'There are things you will understand in greater depth.'

This obviously begs the question: is she done with them now? 'Twenty years ago, I'd have been a bit snobby about a trilogy but there will be a third one, I've thought that for a long time. I think there will be three and that's the end.'

What happens next? 'Wait for another nine years,' she laughs. She doesn't have a narrative arc for the three books. 'That's beyond me, I can just about go from book to book. I know my own process more, which is that I don't know anything and I have to find my way whereas before, I was always trying to make a plan and then everything would just die because it was too much in position and it wasn't interesting to write something when you already know what happens.'

We are conversing over coffee in a Dublin hotel. The author has just flown in from London, where she lives in Forest Gate with her husband, William Galinsky, a theatre and arts festival director, and their daughter Eadaoin. She cuts a dash in her dark trouser suit, patterned shirt and loose black tie.

Although very much Irish, she is at home in London in a way that she never was growing up in rural Sligo. She moved there as a toddler from Liverpool, where she was born in 1976, just after the papal visit in July 1979. 'My parents told me the flags were all out for us coming to Ireland.' In truth, 'we were always blow-ins'.

John and Gerardine, both psychiatric nurses, were from the North but moved to England soon after the Troubles broke out after Catholic colleagues received bullets in the post. The North, always a cold house for Catholics, had now an added chill factor of sectarian murders. Her mother is from Belfast and now lives there again. Her father was a farmer's son from Ballycastle, County Antrim. 'Mum said it was like Victorian poverty, she'd never met anyone as poor as my father's family, like they didn't have any running water. They used to get sent black bread from Canada.'

Her father's parents had died young so his sister, a nurse, brought him as a teenager to England with her. Having left school at fourteen, he instilled in his children early a love of reading. Eimear's brother Cillian lectures in political theory at Queen's University Belfast and another brother trains film technicians and plays music. But Eimear's father died of cancer aged forty, when she was only eight, the first of two devastating blows in her young life.

The family moved to Castlebar, 'like Paris' with a cinema and an arts centre, run by Sally Rooney's mother, where she first saw a Harold Pinter play. McBride took part in feiseanna and attended drama classes in Sligo's Hawk's Well Theatre. At seventeen, having watched a BBC documentary about London's Drama Centre, she was accepted for a place there to study acting, there being at that time no such third-level course in Ireland.

It was a radical place, influenced by Stanislavski's method acting school and Joan Littlewood, with graduates such as Pierce Brosnan, Tara Fitzgerald, Geraldine James, Helen McCrory, Tom Hardie and Michael Fassbender (two years her junior).

'It was terrible but also amazing, the kind of thing you love when you're a teenager but you wouldn't love it if you were forty-five. They asked a lot and made you ask a lot of yourself and didn't let you take it easy. Most of it would be illegal nowadays. It was eleven hours a day, incredibly intense but very inspiring. You took what you did seriously; culture was something that deserved to be taken seriously. And yeah, they could be very brutal, didn't sugar-coat criticism at all. But there was also a tremendous sense of closeness. Nearly thirty years later, we have a WhatsApp group.'

There she met her future husband, William, who was doing a director's course. In 2007 he was appointed director of the Cork Midsummer Festival so after ten years' living in Tottenham and soul-destroying temping, she began work on what would become *The Lesser Bohemians*. Absence made the heart grow fonder, however; exile from the English capital turning the book into a sort of love letter to London.

But she had already written her first novel, *A Girl Is a Half-formed Thing*, over six months in 2004, a disturbing portrayal of a young girl's abusive upbringing in rural Ireland written inversely at a remove in London. 'I suppose, distance gives a fresh perspective and maybe makes you aware of the differences.'

McBride had abandoned acting within a year of graduation because her 28-year-old brother Donagh died of a brain tumour when she was only twenty-two. Slowly the idea evolved that she wanted to be a creator, not an interpreter. Random misfortune had changed her.

'I felt changed by that experience and realized temperamentally I didn't want to be around people all the time, which is not great if you want to be an actor. I don't think you can ever be the same after, the guilt that for no good reason this happened to someone else not you, the unfair, random cruelty of that.

'I think because I lost my father as a child, I had created some fantasy idea that that was the bad thing and there would never be any other bad things. And then when my brother died that exploded that so it was not only losing him but losing all the illusions that I had built up in my teen years that you were going to be safe and feel safe in the world.'

Did that make becoming a mother a very vulnerable experience? 'I was very frightened. I am a terrible hypochondriac. When my daughter was quite young, she was unwell and that was very difficult. I just couldn't bear the thought of having to deal with it again. And fortunately, she is fine but I think for a long time I resisted becoming a parent for exactly that reason.'

Perhaps like the author, Eily in her new novel is having a crisis of direction.

'Eily's being dishonest with herself about what her intentions are and that she sort of lets her body get her in trouble because it's easier to deal with than having to confront the fact that she maybe doesn't want to do what she was doing with her life anymore and she's already put a lot of investment into that and it's difficult to change sometimes, especially when you're young.

'I remember my cat getting sick and it just went into the bottom of the wardrobe for three days and it wouldn't eat or drink anything. I thought he's going to die and I left him alone. After three days he came out. And I feel like this is Eily. She just needs to go away from the world and have this time by herself to rediscover where she is.'

McBride's mother turned to religion to cope with her loss. McBride put her faith in fiction, a way perhaps to explore and deal with the cruel hand fate had dealt her. 'I don't find comfort in communal belief. I hope for the best but I don't expect it.'

I imagine her mother is not her ideal reader. 'It was certainly tricky. They're not parent-friendly novels. No one wants their mother to be reading their sex writing. But, you know, she's taking it in her stride. She has read them all. I think she finds it a comfort her daughter being a writer.'

Girl's traumatic subject matter and fractured, modernist prose found no takers in British publishing until Norwich's tiny Galley Beggar Press published it in 2013, winning a host of awards.

Back in 2007, however, McBride's thinking was: 'If I'm going to be a writer, I've got to write something different, get it published and then *Girl* will get published on the back of this.' Except *The Lesser Bohemians* took nine years to write. It began as Eily's story, before Stephen's character emerged in later drafts and took equal billing. An early draft was 800 pages, which it took her a long time to distil. Once she knew what the book was about, it was relatively easy to cut the extraneous details, the bits she didn't remember when she went away and thought about the story.

McBride has also written a screenplay of *The Lesser Bohemians*. The rights were bought by Michael Fassbender's company and are now with Rose Garnett, former head of BBC Film, who invited her to direct it too. She means no criticism of Annie Ryan, who adapted *Girl* very successfully for the stage in a production starring Aoife Duffin, but McBride now knows that creative control of her work matters hugely to her. 'It's not my favourite thing because it's not my book. I don't like other people touching my work but I didn't know that then. *The Lesser Bohemians* is my heart's blood. I just couldn't let anyone else touch the stuff.'

Garnett advised her to make a short film first to gain experience. The result was *A Very Short Film about Longing* (2023), about a love triangle, starring Joe Alwyn. 'Now I just need to find some maverick millionaires.' As for her directing style: 'Panic-stricken at first but no, I found it fascinating, very stressful but I really loved it.

'Rose Garnett said to me, a novel can be about a lot of things but a film can only be about one thing. Of course, it had to be Eily and Stephen so everything had to go around that.'

Ironically, despite her success as a writer, she now finds herself back in a world where she is creating work that is not getting produced.

'This is exactly my life. Everything is kind of stuck in slow development hell.' At least now it's not her artistic vision being rejected, it's just the nature of the industry. 'Yeah. And I can also do other things. When it was *Girl* that no one was buying, there was nothing else you could do.'

The age-gap relationship appealed because it meant Eily 'didn't have ready access to him the way she would have if it was someone from her own year. But also, I always felt that they were like distorted carnival mirrors of each other – one is tall, one is small – given that they have these similar backgrounds at work in two different parts of life. He's living with it all his adult life and the choices that he's made as a result of not dealing with it. Whereas she's at the beginning of her adult life.

'There is also the sexual element. Sex is a huge part of the storytelling process. I asked myself why it kept recurring then I realized it was to do with character development. There is that part of Stephen that has been thwarted that would really like to take care of someone. They've got a sexual intimacy before they've got a shared emotional language to describe it, the thing that actually allows them to become emotionally a couple, which is kind of back to front.'

But then he falls in love, reveals his deepest secret and that makes him vulnerable. 'She can break him in a way that he can't break her. Because he's her first love and she'll get over it and he won't get over her. *In The City Changes Its Face*, they've moved beyond the fatherless daughter / daughterless father element and are on a more level playing field, but then *his* daughter arrives. That's very complicated for him because they are so close in age and for her because there is another girl in his life that he really loves.'

Both books shift from focusing on Eily's story to Stephen's in the latter half. In the first, it takes the form of a confessional monologue, inspired by Stavrogin's confession in *The Devils* by Dostoevsky. 'I was intrigued by this – you think a character is one type of person and then you find something else inside them, which changes everything that you think about them. I like that with Stephen's story.'

In her new novel, Stephen, Eily and Grace watch and discuss his film. 'Ekphrasis is the description of a visual work of art as part of a literary work. I had never seen it done in a novel about a film before, where you have access to the character's internal life. It also helps Stephen separate Eily and Grace as Eily and he share a creative relationship.

'This passage devotes sixty pages to what was told in a paragraph in the first novel, and the story Stephen tells is different. I was interested in how things transform from actual life into art. Do you have the right to change it? And how can you not change it?'

What are her favourite love stories? 'It brings out the teenager in me. Cathy and Heathcliff: a relationship can be very troubled but also true. The Transylvanian trilogy by Miklos Banffy is a great set of books, on one level fiddling while Rome burns but also the most beautiful love story, with an understanding of women's suffering very unusual in a male author, particularly of that era.'

Reading Edna O'Brien's *The Country Girls* at fourteen introduced her to the world of the body. 'It was so close to my own experience even though there were forty years between us. Her childhood and mine were not so different in the way that my daughter's and my childhood are radically, completely, different. It did feel like reading myself in a way, permission for all the shocking things that she says in it, which still seems exciting, forbidden. And wonderful.'

McBride was working on a BBC adaptation of the *Country Girls* trilogy when Covid hit and it was abandoned because of a backlog of productions. She had shown the first script to Edna who had given notes in return. Its cancellation was a big disappointment for them both. 'I have very happy memories sitting in her kitchen and drinking champagne, eating bread.'

Joyce is her other great influence. 'The monster?' she says. '*Ulysses* changed everything, I was twenty-five and it just opened the doors. I just thought anything is possible, which is why when I wrote *Girl* I was so surprised people seemed so shocked by the way it was written. It's like they've forgotten modernism existed. I didn't realize you could just decide a whole movement was over.'

But perhaps what is most interesting is the way McBride's works are in conversation with themselves.

'I feel as though both *A Girl Is a Half-Formed Thing* and *Strange Hotel* exist as little islands of their own, whereas maybe because of all the years of writing *The Lesser Bohemians* and *The City Changes Its Face*, that's the continent.

'I didn't mean to write *Strange Hotel*, it just sort of came about and interrupted writing this, it was a bit of a rebellion maybe. There's a sense in *Strange Hotel* of wanting to step back from emotion. It's a book about someone who's trying not to feel anything and protecting herself and won't let anyone in.'

Eily is kind of locked into the flat. So is that a read across?

'I think if you wanted, maybe that's Eily in twenty years' time in *Strange Hotel*. There's certainly some crossover in the story, yeah. All of the books, they do feel very connected to me. You know in *Lesser Bohemians* Eily dreams about the girl from *A Girl Is a Half-formed Thing*?'

Obviously, Girl and Eily are not the same person, but are they from the same universe, or community?

'I think so, which is why I've never written a lot about Eily's childhood and background. You only get what she tells Stephen. I felt as though I had already written that story. And it isn't the same character, obviously it can't be because of the way *Girl* ends but I think they come from the same root. That's why the language is different in *The Lesser Bohemians*. It's very broken at the start but by the end because the character is growing and healing, Eily is the person who will survive. The girl can't, so language breaks down.'

McBride was born in Liverpool in 1976 and grew up in Sligo and Mayo. Her debut novel, A Girl Is a Half-formed Thing *(2013), won the Goldsmiths Prize, the Women's Prize for Fiction, the Kerry Group Irish Fiction Award and the Geoffrey Faber Memorial Prize.* The Lesser Bohemians *won the James Tait Black Memorial Prize. As well as novels* Strange Hotel *(2020) and* The City Changes Its Face *(2025), works include* Mouthpieces, *three performance texts, and* Something Out of Place: Women and Disgust *(both 2021).*

EUGENE McCABE

18 June 2005, The Irish Post

With mud on his boots and ink on his fingers, writer and farmer Eugene McCabe has been getting under Ireland's skin with pen and plough for more than forty years.

His collected short stories, *Heaven Lies About Us*, published in this, his seventy-fifth year, have been greeted with universal acclaim by critics and fellow authors as one of the essential texts of modern Irish literature. John Banville said: 'These superb, sorrowing tales are not old-fashioned, only timeless.' Alan Warner, hailing him as the greatest Irish living prose writer, said: 'One day, great twentieth-century prose in the English language will be acknowledged to include Eugene McCabe's breathtaking facility and the deep necessary anguish of his fictional universe.'

The stories can be broken down into three sections. *The Orphan*, *The Master* plus *The Landlord* and *The Mother* were initially a series of monologues filmed for TG4, an interlocking series of stories about a family's destruction by poverty in Famine times and one girl's determination to survive.

Then there is a Troubles trilogy (*Cancer*, *Heritage* and *Siege*), which was filmed by RTÉ in the mid-1970s and caused controversy with its depiction of deep-rooted prejudice on both sides of the community divide during the worst years of the conflict.

'While fiction rarely escapes from the fictional ghetto,' Dermot Bolger wrote, 'television enters every living room and a whole generation grew up informed by McCabe's portrayal of the hatred, suspicion and misunderstanding in both communities along the Border.'

The author knows the subject well, living as he does four hundred yards on the Monaghan side of the Border with Fermanagh, a place where many still view

Protestants as colonials who grabbed the good land, leaving the native Catholics the stony higher ground.

For McCabe, the 1641 uprising is a more seminal moment in Irish history than 1690, sowing the seeds for centuries of fear, suspicion and hatred.

In four of the other five stories, a common thread is the unruly and destructive power of sexuality, aggravated by church-inspired shame and confusion.

And then there is 'Music at Annahullion', an exquisite gem of a tale in which a spinster sister, living with two bachelor brothers on a boggy Border farm, dreams of getting a piano to add a little beauty to their lives. Her wish is answered but the piano will not fit into the room and ends up abandoned in the yard and finally destroyed.

It is a classic McCabe tale of lives that may not appear to amount to much but which the author imbues with all the majesty and misery of the human condition. This is no easy read but if you want fiction that tugs at your heart rather than tickling you under the chin then look no further. The overriding vision may be bleak but it is incisive and insightful. The language may be unadorned but it rings clear and true.

An English friend once balked at the prospect of borrowing another Irish novel, having been thoroughly depressed by the last batch I had lent her, but in McCabe she recognized the mother lode of Irish misery. It's a tough read but it makes you more sensitive to others' suffering, both today and in the past.

McCabe was born in Glasgow and brought up there until the age of ten – a world away from the drumlins and dunghills of Monaghan. McCabe's grandfather John McMahon was one of the richest men in Scotland, owner of the biggest greyhound racing stadium outside London and chairman of Clyde football club.

'He was an extraordinary entrepreneur,' the author recalls. 'He was born in a little cottage down the road where my son now lives and when he was nine he went to live with an aunt who had a shop in the Gorbals. He was one of the founders of telephone rentals but he had the Midas touch. He was into so many things: cinemas, hotels. My mother was the only child so quite a lot of money came into the family. It left us all independent.'

The family had a holiday home in Clones and when the Second World War broke out decided to stay in Ireland, changing the course of McCabe's life. But his Scottish birth did give him an invaluable starter's kit for a writer – the outsider's perspective.

'I think it gave me a very objective, dispassionate view of the country,' he says. 'I came here then went to prep school in Kildare, Castleknock in Dublin and then university in Cork, so until the age of twenty-one I was away out of the whole small-town Irish thing. Then when I began to farm and meet people, read more, I approached things with a much colder eye than if I was brought up here.'

His father thought he should be a journalist rather than a farmer and although he bought him a 169-acre farm, he expected him to last no more than three years. Instead, McCabe farmed until he was seventy. 'I really loved it,' he says. 'I just wished I was better at it. It's now rented out to two Catholics and two Protestants.'

His life as a farmer accounts for the deliberately small literary output – the short stories, a few plays and *Death and Nightingales*, a novel described by Colm Tóibín as 'a masterpiece'.

'I was a working farmer,' McCabe says. 'I milked thirty cows, had up to three hundred sheep at one time. To me farming was as important as writing. I wasn't a good farmer but I felt it was an important thing, contributing to the well-being of the land and humanity. I was also never a commercial writer. The only way I made money was writing for Irish TV.'

He had said to his wife after watching some rubbish on television that he could do better so she challenged him to try. He did and by return of post it was accepted. The work was *A Matter of Conscience*, featuring a Traveller and a priest. He then wrote *King of the Castle* about an old farmer who hires a young stud to squire his wife because he himself can't father a child. 'They had the League of Decency outside the Gaiety [Theatre] and letters in the papers for ages,' he recalls. 'I was regarded as "the dirty playwright" but it was a morality play – if you do that sort of thing you're going to lose your wife. It was like a sermon really.

'When we read *Madame Bovary* now we can't understand why all France was up in arms. This is just a terribly well-written novel about a doctor's wife who has an affair and kills herself when she gets into debt but the truth of that frightened people. I think the truth makes people uncomfortable. They shy away from it. We are all awful blockers.'

The success of his plays saw RTÉ commission him to write the scripts for their star soap, *The Riordans.* The only way he could have matched that money as a farmer would have been to go down the intensive farming route with battery hens but he could not countenance it.

McCabe's writing and his outlook on life are informed by his faith in life and not in God.

'Where did all those Hail Marys lead but down the darkest road of all?' says Roisin in *The Orphan*. He is not hostile to the Church, he says, just deeply sceptical. He believes religion is dangerous but cannot be suppressed.

'It's an instinct that man is not satisfied with this world. There must be something. They can't adapt to the idea that what we have here is OK and let's just enjoy it. It's partly denial. People are afraid of death. They want something more. What they want is peace and beauty and that can be found by looking around. Walk down the road, walk into a field. Despite the horrors that go on, the world is a beautiful place.'

McCabe was born in Glasgow in 1930 and died in Cavan in 2020. He wrote several plays, most notably King of the Castle *(1964), an award-winning trilogy for television,* Cancer, Heritage *and* Siege *(1973), about the Troubles, and several short-story collections including* Heritage and Other Stories *(1978),* Tales from the Poor House *(1999) and* Heaven Lies about Us *(2005). His only novel,* Death and Nightingales *(1992), was adapted for a TV series in 2018.*

PATRICK McCABE

4 July 1992, The Irish Post

Clones in County Monaghan is the occasional home of the Ulster football final; the birthplace of that prodigal featherweight Barry McGuigan; and home also to Eugene McCabe, a considerable playwright.

It would be fair to say, however, that it is a typical example of small-town Ireland. But one of its citizens, Patrick McCabe, has written a powerful novel set in one such town, a 'comedy of terrors', which goes to prove that madness and shocking violence are not the preserve of urban nightmare and terrorist outrage.

The Butcher Boy is the story of Francie Brady, seen through his eyes and told in his words. Nothing special in that, you might think, until you realize that Francie, the often funny child of a problem family and loveless marriage, is also frighteningly prey to furious violence and prone to obsessive interest in another, model family, the Nugents.

The novel is the inner monologue of Francie's bewildering spiral into delinquency, social rejection and ultimately murderous violence. Yet such is the skill of the author that the reader does not lose sympathy for the boy but follows his unreason, never condoning but slowly understanding, gripped by a perspective that is pathetic and perverse and yet acute and perceptive.

The author took a real-life murder as the basis for his story. 'In 1904 in Clones there was a murder, a really celebrated case at the time. This young fellow slaughtered his best friend like a pig and buried him under a pile of manure. That was just the germ of the story. I just moved it forward to 1961, the time of the Cuban Missile Crisis, which was a strange, anxious, weird time, and the external world is meant to mirror Francie's internal anxieties.

'The idea is that the great events of history, all right, they happen, but what really affects people is what happens in their own lives, not these earth-shattering events. It's not a new idea – look at *The Unbearable Lightness of Being* – but it's a constant and I think it's still valid.'

It must have been hard enough for Flaubert carrying the temperamental Emma Bovary about in his head for a year. What was it like gestating the psychotic Francie Brady?

'Very intense, for it's not like any other book I've written, very dispassionate and considered. This book, if it was to burn it all, had to be white-hot. So I was glad to finish it, put it that way.'

The story is related from the haven of an asylum by the main protagonist. Is there a parallel with the terrible Oskar in Günter Grass's *The Tin Drum*?

'There is a resemblance there that is almost subliminal but definitely Oskar with that primal scream he had – I think the book's about damaged innocence, a person not allowed to flower and turned in on itself. You're the first person that has mentioned that and I didn't bring it up because I didn't think people would clue into that but definitely I would say that Oskar is a valid comparison, more so than others that have been mentioned.'

The Butcher Boy, like John Banville's first book, *Long Lankin*, takes its name from a ballad.

'The reason I used that ballad was because I love it. I remember hearing it at a field day outside Clones sung for a feis cheoil. It was really plaintive and the sun was shining. The final verse of it is very melancholy and bleak where death is almost wished for and if you juxtapose that against the beauty of the world that seemed to be on the earth that day … Francie constantly refers to the beauty of the world.

'The book is almost written like a ballad. It starts off nice and easy then gets intense, fades again, then dovetails into a kind of sadness.'

Having written with such insight about a deranged child, does the author have any particular viewpoint on madness?

'If you think of bombers flying out of Northolt to strafe Iraq, and bodies melting, is that mad or is that normal? If something happens in your own life or if someone gets sick then what was once normal can then veer seriously towards something anything but normal. I don't have very strong views on the subject but obviously I feel very strongly *about* it.'

In the wake of Shane Connaughton's *The Playboys*, which pokes fun and points the finger at the narrowness of small-town Ireland, and thinking back to Brinsley McNamara's *The Valley of the Squinting Windows*, is McCabe's book another coffin nail in the reputation of small-town Ireland or indeed is there nothing good to be said for it?

'There's loads of good things to say about small-town Ireland that will be the subject of future books. I mean, I love small-town Ireland, the sense of community and generally the peaceful ease with which children can grow up. In the book I'm not saying those things, Francie is saying them. It's time that a book was written to emphasize just how life-enhancing and expansive small towns can actually be. I think narrow minds belong to the fifties and early sixties.'

Does McCabe identify with the much-vaunted 'new' generation of Irish writers?

'Everyone ploughs their own furrow ultimately. I belong to the literature of small towns and I would see myself as having as much in common with writers like Benedict Kiely and Bryan McMahon as with the Coen brothers, who made *Barton Fink*, or Günter Grass.'

McCabe has also involved himself in a local literary magazine, *The Frontier Post*, on sale both in Britain and in the Border counties. He sees it as a useful platform for aspiring talented writers without a publisher.

'There are a lot of writers who lack a platform. The papers haven't given the space that was once there. New Irish Writing is limited now. As well as that there was the desire to develop a consciousness about the small town. Dermot Healy has done it with *The Drumlin*. He interviewed people but he didn't render their speech in dialect, which so often tends to trivialize the content of their story.'

Do Border writers have a different outlook or voice?

'I think as you move further out there is a sharper style of writing, a sharper speech. Southern writers tend to gild the lily a bit. Eugene McCabe is a good example of this, a very flinty kind of dialogue rather than this baroque speech. Both of course have their place.'

Although *The Butcher Boy* is McCabe's first novel with a mainstream British publisher, he has two previous novels, *Music on Clinton Street* and *Carn*. It will be published in paperback later this year by Picador. The author also won the Hennessy award in 1979 for a short story, 'The Call', and has a string of radio plays broadcast on RTÉ and BBC Radio to his credit.

McCabe's next project is a play for London's oldest Irish theatre company, the Bridge Theatre, which he is hoping will be staged early next year. *Psychobilly* is about country and western music in small towns. 'It takes the songs that everybody knows like "Bunch of Violets" and "Gentle Mother" and a lot of Big Tom stuff. It seems to me to be as part and parcel of Irish culture as anything else. From the time I was going to dances there's been Philomena Begley and Ray Lynam. I think it's in the blood as much as pure traditional music and I don't think it's been explored enough to see what it actually means. I think it's unwise to sneer at it.

'Many small towns in Ireland now have as much in common with the Deep South of William Faulkner, guys driving tractors with a Charley Pride eight-track stuck on the deck, things like that. All those kinds of images are certainly stronger in my imagination than all those Anglo-Irish relationships. I would swing more towards the American influence. All the kids that I was teaching back home, they were all dressed in American clothes.'

If this sounds like genuine devotion then that's because it is. In a previous incarnation McCabe played organ after a fashion with Paddy Hanrahan and the Oklahoma showband, who had a hit single with 'A Tombstone Every Mile' back in the 1970s when the band were fixtures in London's Gresham, Galtymore and the Forum.

The writer fondly recalls how 'Paddy insisted we play no more than two chords so as not to confuse the dancers.'

The American influence seems destined to be to the fore in McCabe's next novel [*The Dead School*] as well for he has described his work in progress as 'a cross between Hunter S. Thompson and Percy French'.

'Of course, in six months' time there might be neither of them in it but I like the whimsy of Percy French and the fire and power of Thompson. I'm trying to bring the two influences together, the older-type Ireland and the so-called progressive or at any rate modern Ireland.

'My father and mother's generation is as important to me as the possibly ephemeral world we're living in now. It is a different world but it's nevertheless a fascinating one.'

McCabe teaches in a special needs school in Kingsbury, north London and though he loves the work he finds it draining. 'You come home and you're tired, the wheels don't turn as smoothly as they should and it takes you a lot longer to write a book than it should. *The Butcher Boy* took me three years, maybe more, but then there's always the danger that you can write books too quickly.'

McCabe is blessed, 'insanely so', with a firm sense of belonging. He feels 'not in a sentimental way but in a very positive way' that he has never really left home. He moved with his wife and young family to London about five years ago as his wife had won a place at art college there.

'I love Kilburn. It's fine if you embrace it. There's a danger if you don't throw yourself into some extent into whatever life has to offer. What I'd really like to do is get a writership-in-residence somewhere in Ireland. That could happen but the world is so small. I mean, you're home three times a year.'

Small-town Ireland has a likely champion in Patrick McCabe as the quality of his writing seems destined to win for it, as well as for him, a place in the sun.

McCabe was born in Clones, County Monaghan, in 1955. The author of a dozen novels, he is best known for The Butcher Boy *(1992) and* Breakfast on Pluto *(1998), both shortlisted for the Booker Prize and made into films by Neil Jordan.* The Butcher Boy *was also adapted for the stage as* Frank Pig Says Hello. *Other notable novels include* Winterwood *(2006), which won the Irish Novel of the Year award, and* Poguemahone *(2022).*

COLUM McCANN

1 March 2025, The Irish Times

Last August Colum McCann sat in New York's Cathedral of St John the Divine watching Philippe Petit, almost seventy-five years old, traverse its nave on a high wire while Sting sang songs from a musical he and McCann are writing about the tightrope artist.

Later that month, the Irish author took part in a conversation at the Vatican with Pope Francis and Rami Elhanan and Bassam Aramin, two fathers bereaved by the Israeli–Palestinian conflict.

He is currently collaborating with Senator George Mitchell on a speech that the architect of the Good Friday Agreement is to give in Belfast next month.

What these three things have in common is that they are all fruits of McCann's fiction. *Let the Great World Spin* (2009), a 9/11 allegory which won the US National Book Award and the International Dublin Literary Award, recounted Petit's 1974 tightrope walk between the World Trade Centre's Twin Towers. The Booker Prize-longlisted *Apeirogon* (2020) explored the Middle East's most enduring conflict through the lives and deaths of two daughters, one Israeli, one Palestinian. *TransAtlantic* (2013), also Booker-longlisted, linked Frederick Douglass's visit to Ireland in 1845, Alcock & Brown's first transatlantic flight in 1919 and George Mitchell's chairing of the Belfast peace talks in 1998.

Inspired by real events and people, they are now in turn inspiring real people and events. 'I'm sitting there thinking, *is this really my life now?*' the writer says. 'Am I this lucky that that this sort of stuff happens?'

He is home from the US to visit his 97-year-old mother Sally, still living independently in Dublin, and sitting in a seaside pub to discuss his eighth novel, *Twist*, which is published next week, days after his sixtieth birthday.

It comes five years after *Apeirogon*, but its writing was interrupted by last year's *American Mother*, the deeply moving non-fiction book he wrote with Diane Foley about the kidnap and murder by Isis of her journalist son James ten years earlier. McCann had written to her when he came across a photo of James reading a copy of *Let the Great World Spin*.

Its tangled roots date back to the pandemic, when he was locked down in New York City with his wife and three children, yet able to stay connected with his mother by that miracle of modern communication, the smartphone, which paradoxically is blamed for our current epidemic of loneliness.

'We had that moment where it's like time was crushed and we were so dependent on these little machines and it was a real mystery to me how I could call Sally in Clonkeen Road from New York. It's a wonder of science and it is also a wonder of connection.'

This enigma of connection and disconnect started him thinking of a world in need of repair and specifically about the ocean-crossing fibre-optic cables that link our continents and cities, and the people whose job it is to mend them when they are damaged by accident or design.

'Everybody thinks that the cloud lives in the air,' McCann says. 'The cloud is really right at the very bottom of the ocean.'

Twist is the story of two Irishmen: Conway, a free diver who helms an internet-cable-repair vessel based in Cape Town, and Fennell, a writer commissioned by a magazine to describe a salvage operation at sea. McCann himself wrote a 10,000-word essay, 'No Rest for the Wired', on the subject for Alexander, an audio app.

As Fennell writes to his son: 'It was no great surprise that the world felt as if it were in chains since they actually trawled the ocean floor and tied us up in easy knots.'

At one level a thriller examining the powerful, fragile network that connects the modern world, *Twist* also seeks to plumb its characters' souls, an equally delicate operation, as Conway disappears off grid and Fennell searches for him.

The vulnerability of underwater cables to sabotage is big news now with allegations of Russian and Chinese trawlers dragging their anchors on the seabed to wreak havoc. But five years ago, McCann had little to go on.

'You could take down the world's internet or certainly damage it very significantly with a fleet of twenty ships,' he says. You don't even have to go out to sea as the landing stations are easily accessible. 'It's incredible to me that we have such access to something that's fundamental. I've been in landing stations in Long Island and New Jersey. All I had to do was climb over a little gate. There was no surveillance that I could see. All you'd need is a crowbar to prop open the manhole.'

'It's probably impossible to write about things you don't know,' reflects McCann on the inspiration for *Twist*, 'but if you write towards what it is you want to know, sometimes you discover things that you knew but weren't entirely aware of.'

Knowledge is important, then, but curiosity is perhaps the essential ingredient in firing the imagination.

'I knew almost nothing about Israel/Palestine before I embarked on *Apeirogon*. The same with this book. I'd never been at sea, I don't know why I wanted to write about cable repairs except I knew we are living in broken times. Initially it was all going to be about repair, how do we repair ourselves; in the end the book ends up flipping itself on me because it becomes about sabotage.

'It's a deceptively simple book for me, I'm still trying to fathom it, it's about two characters, it's chronological, it goes in a straight line, it's not multiple voices, not really outside my realm of experience like I did with *Apeirogon* or *American Mother* or *Let the Great World Spin*.

'I feel almost embarrassed at how seemingly simple it is. My narrator doesn't go wild with language, or off on crazy tangents. My own instinct is to go wild but in certain ways I felt it was Fennell who wrote the book, it had to belong to him, not me. I don't feel like characters are my galley slaves, I feel beholden because I have imagined him. With *Apeirogon*, I felt I could go absolutely anywhere, the structure allowed me to do it, it felt right. With this book, I knew it was going to be interior, realist, but I wanted the aftertaste to have echoes of Prufrockian loneliness.'

McCann had to fight for the title of his previous novel, *Apeirogon*, because his US publishers were understandably concerned that very few readers would know what the word meant – a polygon with a countably infinite number of sides.

Twist, the title of his new novel, met no such resistance. It economically captures the sense of something going awry, with the secondary sense of an unexpected change of direction in the plot.

One of the beauties of fiction is that a novel can start off as one thing and evolve during the creative process into something very different. It is also very often in conversation with previous works of fiction. *Twist* begins in the vein of *The Great Gatsby* before veering off in the direction of *Heart of Darkness*, with a flick of the film it helped inspire, *Apocalypse Now*.

Stylistically, it is very different from *Apeirogon*, which had 1001 very short chapters, exploding the novel form into shards of stories.

'Beckett said the job of the artist now is to find a form that accommodates the mess. So that is what I set out to do with *Apeirogon*, to capture the mess and some of the mystery and madness.' As if in reaction to that, he set himself next the challenge of writing a simple love story. 'I like to surprise myself and the reader. I generally never write the same sort of book.' He wanted to write something straightforward and almost confessional, through a character like Nick Carraway, *The Great Gatsby*'s narrator, looking back on his younger, more vulnerable years.

But as his research led him to realize that the world's internet cables followed the old colonial shipping routes, he conceived of a rupture of an Atlantic cable caused by a flood from the Congo River, a nod to the plot of Joseph Conrad's *Heart of Darkness* – as is Conway working for a Belgian company, like Marlow in the original. His favourite scene in *Twist* is set in a dump on the outskirts of Accra where the narrator is shown that locals are selling as scrap metal once mined as ore in Africa, a continent's riches reduced to what will feed a family for just a week.

There is also an awareness of the developing world bearing the brunt of climate change, an environmental concern signalled with an epigraph from Rachel Carson. Conway's partner, an actor, is interpreting Beckett's *Waiting for Godot* as a climate play.

McCann made a deliberate decision not to treat this story in what might be seen as his trademark fashion, juxtaposing the contemporary story with that of the first sea cables laid from Valentia Island to New York in the nineteenth century. (There are photographs of this in Conway's cabin, an allusion to what might have been.) This was his model for both *TransAtlantic* and *This Side of Brightness*. But having done that already, he wanted to do something different, focus on the contemporary, see if he could tell a story straight from A to Z, with one narrator and a straight timeline, and say something about who we are and where we are now.

McCann feels that the fiction writer faces an uphill battle for relevance today, compared to the era of Roth and Mailer and Toni Morrison, who had more influence in the public sphere. Fennell says: 'I was unsure what fiction and drama could do anymore.'

'You want to write a novel that breaks people's hearts and maybe wakes people up to some of the things that are going on. I need to engage with what is current. You could end up being pretentious, believing that you have something to say and that's always a scary thing. You could be like Claire Keegan and go small and beautiful and gorgeous and the tiny becomes epic. But can the epic become tiny?'

He is evangelical about the essential nature of storytelling, however. 'We might eventually be able to live without books, without opera, without drama. The one thing that we will never, ever, be able to live without is stories. They can take away all the apparatus of printing but essentially the world is held together with stories.'

McCann is not just concerned with story but is very focused on the sentence too. 'I think the music of a sentence is as important, if not more important than the words. The meaning gets parsed out in the music. I would like every sentence to sing.'

Twist is studded with lapidary lines and a couple of virtuoso passages capturing the cornucopia that these internet cables contain. There are what he calls echoes from the garden of literature, small homages to writers such as Gerard Manley Hopkins, Herman Melville, Philip Larkin and T.S. Eliot, whose Prufrock for a time influenced his description of Fennell. 'We get our voice from the voices of others,' he says.

Donald Trump is referred to in *Twist* as 'a damp white loaf'. McCann's response to the election of the US's most successful seller of sinister fictions since Stephen King was to lick his wounds. 'But then I got this wonderful email from a friend. She said, "we'll spend a day trying to figure all this out. But then tomorrow we ride at dawn."'

As a dual passport holder, he could stick or twist, but his roots in New York are deep now. That said, he recalls a phrase of his friend, the late writer John Berger, who told him once after a good few drinks apiece that he considered himself 'a patriot of elsewhere'. 'I'd like to be able to appropriate that phrase because I like the idea of being elsewhere.'

In 2012 McCann co-founded Narrative 4, a global educational organization that promotes the exchange of stories to connect students to each other, to build a culture of inclusivity and connectedness.

He offers as an example bringing together schoolchildren from the South Bronx and eastern Kentucky, one group Black and or immigrant, urban, the other white or Cherokee and rural. By exchanging personal stories, not ideas or beliefs, connections are made.

'Often I use the prompt of repair [*Twist*'s theme, again]. Now it could be a story about the repair of a bicycle, or of a relationship or a neighbourhood. And they begin to understand things about one another, that they aren't quite as distant as they thought. What we have in common breaks down the borders, the stereotypes.'

It is now in forty-two countries, in 40 per cent of Irish schools, with an annual $8 million budget, funded by donations including $25 million over five years from Jeff Bezos's parents, Mike and Jackie. The ambition is to build a platform for children globally to share their stories. 'I believe stories lead to action lead to change.' The real heroes, he says, are the teachers who run the courses.

In January he was back in Rome for a Narrative 4 event with two hundred faith-based journalists and to give a Jubilee speech for Pope Francis. 'I thought he was one of the greatest listeners that I had ever come across. He felt like a spectacularly empathetic human being.'

Next month, Narrative 4 will bring young people from secondary schools North and South together. George Mitchell will address them. 'He is keen to pass the torch to the next generation. We have had peace without reconciliation, it's not as strong as it could or should be.

'I have a powerful fondness for the North; my mum is from there. She grew up on a dairy farm near Garvagh. She came up to the Seamus Heaney HomePlace with me, it was a sort of homecoming.'

Despite being a Dubliner born and bred, he once said he felt more like a Northerner. Why was that?

'I'm not really sure, that's my new answer to everything: I don't know. I think that is an honest answer these days. I like to say we are diseased with certainty. I didn't grow up there but I did a lot of my growing up there, seeing the tensions, ideas of the land.'

Perhaps with age come an acceptance that not everything is knowable or solvable. The omniscient narrator is dead. The complexities of Conway's motivation are not explained. Some US editors wanted more clarity but McCann didn't want to produce a simple puzzle. He quotes Cesar Vallejo: 'Mystery joins things together.'

McCann is worried that readers will conflate him and his narrator as Fennell is a journalist and a writer, middle-aged and Irish. 'However, I found him more difficult to write than characters out of my immediate experience. There is a lot of talk about cultural appropriation. I wanted to pay a nod to it and stretch it. When [these critics] first emerged they were laughed at, but essentially what they were saying was entirely right. For centuries writers and corporations have condescended, stereotyped. On the same hand, there is a way to go in with head bowed and a degree of wonder and curiosity, it's a form of cultural celebration.

'I probably wouldn't be allowed to write about a 38-year-old hooker in the south Bronx now, from a first-person point of view [as he did in *Let the Great World Spin*]. But we are coming out of it, we will look back on that time and say we were handcuffed, we came indoors, we put a GPS co-ordinate on our imaginations and said you can't go north or south of that.

'When I was meeting poor Black families in Mississippi, then wealthy white people in Aspen, I didn't know how lucky I was. My first [unpublished] books were bad because they were based on my own experience. I've spent most of my career trying to operate outside this space. I am more honest. I don't want to look in the mirror that way. Everything you write is autobiographical to some extent by nature of putting your words down on the page, it has elements of the self.'

Print is part of McCann's DNA. His father, Sean, was a writer as well as features editor of the *Irish Press*. 'The music of my childhood was my dad on his typewriter, writing kids' soccer books about Georgie Goode [obviously a nod to Georgie Best], a Traveller from an Irish family in England. He wrote on big rolls of paper (very Kerouac) with a carbon underneath, which he gave to me to do edits. My teacher in St Brigid's, Foxrock, would read my dad's book aloud to the class. I remember a boy in front of me jumping up and punching the air when a goal was scored in the book. The imaginary had become real. This moment had been dreamed up by my father.'

As a boy, McCann cycled round Sallynoggin, Dún Laoghaire and Bray, picking up football results and match reports. He studied journalism in Rathmines in 1982 and worked for the *Connacht Telegraph*, the *Evening Herald* and the *Irish Independent* before joining his father on the *Press*. He won young journalist of the year in 1993 for a feature on the physical abuse of inner-city children, 'The Bashed Street Kids', and wrote a 'terrible' column called 'The

Bottom Line'. He fondly remembers interviewing the journalist Con Houlihan in his home in Portobello, struggling to make out a word, what with the strong Kerry accent and the way he covered his mouth when he spoke, until he rang his bookmaker and in the clearest voice imaginable placed a bet.

Benedict Kiely was literary editor of the *Press* and a friend of his father's. 'He is probably the most significant Irish writer for me, perhaps because of the Northern connection. Absolutely the best books about the North for me are his *Proxopera*, then *Nothing Happens in Carmincross*. 'He took me under his wing, took me to Long's in Donnybrook, telling stories, poems, songs.

'I also remember Mr [John] Banville in the newsroom, always wrapped in big, heavy scarves.' Did that inspire McCann's famous taste in scarves? He laughs. 'No, that was inspired by being on the road and wearing a bandana.'

He'd been reading a lot of Beat writers such as Kerouac and felt that he had to get away, so left for the States to write a novel. He rented an apartment in Cape Cod with other Irish on J1 visas, bought a typewriter but realized he had nothing to write about so he crossed the States on a bicycle, from Boston to Florida, New Orleans, Texas, New Mexico, Colorado, looking for experience, five or fifty miles a day, meeting interesting people. 'Now I can look back and see I was listening for stories.'

He wrote two unpublished books: *Uncle Saccharine*, 'terrible title, terrible book', about cycling across the US, and a non-fiction book, *The Wilderness Llamas*, about working with juvenile delinquents in Texas. His brother Sean bought the manuscripts, which kept him going, and he got £2,000 from the Arts Council, 'pretty forward-looking for them'.

He had won Hennessy New Writer of the Year in 1990, chosen by Clare Boylan and Desmond Hogan, but had wallpapered his bathroom with publishers' rejection slips by the time his short story 'Sisters' was published in *Analecta*, the University of Texas's student magazine. When Hennessy Awards founder David Marcus asked his father, Sean, how Colum was getting on, he gave him the magazine, which Marcus sent to a literary agent. 'Sisters' became the first story in *Fishing the Sloe-Black River*, which won the Rooney Prize in 1994.

McCann has written that art can outlast buildings. Which of his works is most likely to be read in fifty years' time? 'It is not really for me to say,' he responds, but he concedes that he is particularly proud of his short story about a young girl and the Troubles, 'Everything in This Country Must', which was made into an Oscar-nominated short film. He also hopes that *Apeirogon* will be read, perhaps *Let the Great World* 'and maybe *Dancer* [his 2003 novel based on the life of Rudolf Nureyev] was my best book'.

Apeirogon has captured the public's imagination. 'People come to me all the time and ask, are Rami and Bassam still friends? And I say yes, of course they are.' He admires the risks they have taken and still take, stepping out from their tribe, being friends, talking about things that matter. He is in contact with them every week. 'So I'm actually thinking that I might embark on another book about them, which would be the first time I would ever do something along those lines.' He expresses bafflement that both men are barred from visiting the US. Bassam has a conviction but Rami does not, so his exclusion must be political. 'They're anti-occupation but they are talking about peace. Peace threatens people who are making an awful lot of money out of what's happening in the West Bank, in Gaza and in Israel.'

McCann is also contemplating what he calls 'a big Irish novel'. 'That's definitely on the horizon and it's shaping up in my head right now and will take a couple of years for me to think of, something that traverses time and not just small amounts of time, something that goes back to St Kevin in the cave in Glendalough. I keep thinking about it.

'I do think it's time to come home within the next few years in terms of the Irish novel. I can feel it assembling in my head, I do have these ideas, and they build for a long, long time. I'm reading some quite interesting stuff about ancient warfare and I'm also interested in how we Irish were involved in some of those American slaughters.'

McCann was born in Dublin in 1965 and lives in New York. His debut short-story collection, Fishing the Sloe-Black River, *won the Rooney Prize.* Let the Great World Spin *(2009) won the National Book Award for Fiction and the International Dublin Literary Award. His short-story collection* Thirteen Ways of Looking *(2015) won a Pushcart Prize.* TransAtlantic *(2013) and* Apeirogon *(2020) made the Booker Prize longlist and the latter won the Prix du Meilleur Livre Étranger. Other works include the non-fiction book* American Mother *(2024), the trio of stories* Everything in This Country Must *(2000) and the novels* This Side of Brightness *(1998),* Dancer *(2003) and* Twist *(2025).*

MIKE McCORMACK

14 October 2023, The Irish Times

It is little wonder that Mike McCormack's fiction is haunted by death and fascinated with fathers and their families' fates.

The father of Nealon, the protagonist of his new novel, *This Plague of Souls*, had a few pints after a funeral, came home, went to bed and never woke up, four months before his son's Leaving Cert. This was also the fate, almost word for word, of McCormack's father.

The author became a father at forty-eight, about the same age his own father was when he died. A few hours before his son, Saul, was born, McCormack had finished his third novel, *Solar Bones*, and sent it to his agent. The author had been dropped by his prestigious London publisher, Jonathan Cape, after his second novel, *Notes from a Coma*, failed to sell, and his new one was roundly rejected at first by publishers perhaps more focused on the till than on the experimental.

Tramp Press believed in it, however, and the book went on to win the Goldsmiths Prize and the Dublin Literary Award. A superb stage adaptation by Michael West won *The Irish Times* Irish Theatre Awards for the actor Stanley Townsend and the director Lynne Parker.

Solar Bones is the story of Marcus Conway, a recently deceased Mayo engineer who roams his empty house reflecting on his life. Told in a single sentence, it is a beautifully constructed novel, profound yet accessible.

This Plague of Souls is the story of Nealon, a Mayo artist possibly turned scam artist who returns home after his trial collapses following a long period on remand. His wife and child have gone and a mysterious stranger keeps ringing, offering information about his family in exchange for details of Nealon's activities. All this against the backdrop of a national emergency, an inchoate sense of threat, possibly payback for Ireland's ambiguous role as a staging post in the war on terror.

As the parallels suggest, the new novel is set in the same world as *Solar Bones* and is the second part of what will be a trilogy, but this is a metaphysical thriller, a mystery that prompts the deeper question 'what's it all about?', not just the usual 'what's it about?' Readers seeking the satisfaction of a whodunit may be disappointed. A Francis Bacon quotation springs to mind: 'The job of the artist is always to deepen the mystery.'

'There is no good time to lose your father,' McCormack says, 'but there is a special difficulty in losing him at eighteen when you are just finding your way in the world. In some sense that is the incident that made me. It has inflected my depictions of fathers in my books. They are generally decent men trying to do their best for wife and family, frequently floundering, uncomprehending, not sullen, oppressive figures. I think that is partly wishful thinking on my part.'

Becoming a father himself has been 'a continual source of wonderment' but also a great responsibility to look after his health and the planet's. 'Having a family is an incredible adventure, but I come from a line of men who get heart attacks. I want to be around for Saul. I don't want his eighteenth year to be like mine. I also buy books now thinking I'm going to hand them on to Saul. I was in Bell, Book and Candle in Galway and bought him a gorgeous box edition of *The Chronicles of Thomas Covenant* by Stephen Donaldson.'

McCormack has a grá for genre fiction, and his writing has long paid homage to the works that inspired him as a reader. He studied English and philosophy at NUI Galway, where he 'was the dullest student ever but a great reader'. J.G. Ballard and Philip K Dick's science fiction inspired *Notes from a Coma*. 'When I was eighteen, at home in Louisburgh, nothing outside but green fields and cows, my head was with Isaac Asimov in the stars. I thought that was a powerful, magical achievement, a continual enchantment. It doesn't have to be a place; it can bring you into the mind of someone else,' McCormack says, citing Claire Kilroy's *Soldier Sailor*. 'It's why we read fiction in the first place: to have our heads and our minds and our worlds expanded.'

As McCormack's trademark cowboy hat – a fortieth-birthday present – suggests, cowboy books are another love. He uses the first page of Jack Schafer's *Shane* as a masterclass in how to start a novel. He is also enamoured of Louis L'Amour, his first encounter with landscape as nurturing or adversarial. The peat bogs of Ballycroy are McCormack's Mojave Desert. He wanted his own Flann

O'Brien story so wrote one as the opening tale in *Forensic Songs*. *This Plague of Souls* is his homage to the suddenness, the sharp rhythms of noir authors such as Pascal Garnier, Frédéric Dard and Georges Simenon.

'Would it be possible to write a book of which it would be impossible to speak, where I don't know what happens, and how to make that artistically credible and skilful without it coming across as clueless, as an authorial failure?

'I wanted it to be a metaphysical noir, by which I mean reality and the world itself would be at stake; it has all the dark shading and tough-guy rhythms, but not in the sense of revenge or an orthodox prize, or reward.'

The idea of a man on trial for a mysterious offence struck me as Kafkaesque.

'It's not something that crossed my mind, but Kafka's *In the Penal Colony* would have been a touchstone text for years.' *Notes from a Coma* features a penal experiment in which prisoners agree to be put in a coma on a ship in Killary Harbour.

Covid-19 changed the focus of *This Plague of Souls*. 'I started this book a long time ago, and it really shifted shape during the pandemic. It started out as how did the world fall apart, but it morphed into how we put it back together. I see it now as a post-pandemic novel: this will pass; what sort of world are we going to make? Is it going to be hedge-fund managers and financiers? The heroes of Covid for me were artists, who kept our spirit alive, people who worked in shops, who took our bins away, healthcare workers.

'I loved the first lockdown. We spent three months in our little garden with our child. But it got progressively more wearisome after that – creeping mental exhaustion, like your soul had a slow puncture; you didn't realize you were becoming deflated. I also became very aware of living in a world where my rights of assembly and travel were seriously curtailed, although it was the right thing to do.

'This book shares a thematic kinship with *Solar Bones*, in that it is about men trying to make the world: how do they go about it? To what extent do they succeed or are self-defeating? The world coming apart is synonymous with families coming apart.

'When I finished *Solar Bones* I knew I was going to do this. It's not a thematic or linear development, more three meditations on a theme. I conceive of it as an altarpiece of three panels, where the two side panels, including *Solar Bones*, are landscapes. This is the dark centrepiece in portrait. Is it a purgatory? I don't know.'

McCormack believes his writing has changed not because of parenthood but because of the wisdom of age. His 1996 debut collection, *Getting It in the Head*, is full of explosions, fires and guns, 'big swinging amplitudes'. There is a knife in *Solar Bones*, but it is a kitchen knife, worn smooth with age, symbolic of domesticity. 'I'm glad my characters have grown up with me. There is more of a focus on family.'

Even the soundtracks he writes to have mellowed, from Scandi death metal to Hank Williams, George Jones, Tony McMahon's *An Buachaillín Bán* and Burial's second album, *Untrue*. 'I was thinking, *How can that be made into a novel? Is there a dubstep novel?*

This book was so long in gestation that McCormack had forgotten one of its influences, 'the stars under which it is written', until his former creative-writing student Brenda Romero, the award-winning video-game designer, heard him read the opening pages and pointed out its similarities to the architecture and storytelling of a video game, something McCormack's fellow Mayo author Colin Barrett also recognized in his blurb. 'I'm not even a good game player. *Eco* is the only game I played to the end, but I found it compelling, the world-building, the way it pushes and pulls the character along.'

McCormack was born in London to emigrant parents from Mayo, but at the age of three, having spent the summer with his grandparents on their farm in Doohoma, he announced he was staying, and he did. 'Isn't that crazy? I lived with my grandparents and aunts on a farm in north Mayo. The older I get the more vivid and valuable it becomes to me. My grandfather was a big hero. I followed him around like a lamb. He seemed to me to be a giant. I drew on it heavily in *Crowe's Requiem*. My brother said he was only a small fella, but I can remember him clear as day walking out into a field of oats with a scythe.'

Connacht, Mayo specifically, is subconsciously core to McCormack's writing. 'My pen seems to think that that is where my mother lode is. I never made any conscious decision, but this obsession with place is more than just landscape, even though landscape is a huge part of it. It's an imaginative standpoint, the light, the interactions. The first transatlantic flight and cable came in and out of the west. Mayo is full of penitential shrines and pilgrim paths. The whole Mayo, God help us thing. I lived under Croagh Patrick, and there used to be a night pilgrimage, lads getting into cars after dance halls to climb the Reek, a continuous stream of light up Croagh Patrick, till the bishops knocked it on the head, for there was too much blackguarding.

'I worked on a project on emigration in the Linen Hall in Castlebar. Our imagination stretched from Kilburn and over to Boston and New York; that's where our families were. Lads in the midlands working for Bord na Móna: what were their horizons? Our conception of the world was actually very big.'

If he rejected London for Mayo aged three, it feels as if the metropolis was never on his wavelength either.

'Do you know, it's funny: I've never worked with an English editor. Robin [Robertson at Cape] and Francis [Bickmore at Canongate] are Scottish. I don't think English editors get what I do. When I did my fourth book with Lilliput, I found it really striking, the amount of things I didn't have to explain or nuance. I realized before I'd been translating myself, continually in explanatory mode. It reminded me of an essay by Desmond Fennell: there is no such thing as Irish literature as long as we are trying to win the ear of Oxbridge graduates. He overstates the argument for effect, but he has a point. It was a smoother process again bringing *Solar Bones* to Lisa [Coen of Tramp], who is from Cross, outside Ballinrobe. In retrospect it was obvious that it had to have an Irish publisher.'

McCormack was born in 1965 in London. His short-story collection, Getting It in the Head *(1996) won the Rooney Prize for Irish Literature. As well as a second collection,* Forensic Songs *(2012), he is the author of four novels:* Crowe's Requiem *(1998),* Notes from a Coma *(2005),* Solar Bones *(2016) and* This Plague of Souls *(2023).* Solar Bones *won Irish Novel and Book of the Year, the Goldsmiths Prize and the Dublin Literary Award.*

MARTIN McDONAGH

14 December 1996, The Irish Post

Already dubbed the Tarantino of the theatre, Martin McDonagh might equally be described as the Shane MacGowan of the stage. The analogy is not that far-fetched, for the two London Irishmen share the same literary agent and both fire their imagination with fuel cut from Irish soil, with language and stories as dark as turf and as pungent and illicit as peat-smoked poitín.

December sees McDonagh, still only twenty-six, establish himself as a major player in British theatre with *The Beauty Queen of Leenane* opening at the Royal Court and *The Cripple of Inishmaan* premiering at the National Theatre. When you consider that both are the opening chapters of commissioned trilogies, one set in Connemara, the other on the Aran Islands, it becomes clear that by the end of the decade his name will be up there with Brian Friel and Frank McGuinness in the first rank of Irish playwrights. Except by then he plans to be in Hollywood.

It came as something of a surprise to Garry Hynes, one of Ireland's leading directors, to discover that the local talent she thought she had discovered in Galway after reading McDonagh's *Beauty Queen* was in fact born and bred in south London. McDonagh's mother is from Sligo and his father is from Lettermullen in Connemara, where they have since retired, but his experience of Ireland has until now been restricted to summer holidays.

He still lives in his parents' home in Camberwell with his elder brother John, also a writer. And yet he demonstrates an intimate knowledge of the speech patterns and social details of the West of Ireland. It was a subconscious process of absorption, he insists, unlike Synge eavesdropping on servants.

McDonagh explains the attraction of Irish subject matter as the strangeness and theatricality of a language at once familiar and slightly foreign. He also likes the distance it offers him, writing at a remove.

Beauty Queen is set in a cottage in Connemara where the only action to be seen out the window is falling rain. But what might have been a conventional melodrama – a forty-year-old spinster tied to her mean and slightly senile mother – turns out to be a claustrophobic comic thriller, closer to the cesspit than the kitchen sink. At its centre is the power struggle between Maureen and her hag of a mother, Mag, which comes to a head when Maureen looks like escaping with the returned Pato.

Around the edges, though, McDonagh weaves a brilliant pattern made up of the unlikeliest threads – Complan and Kimberly Biscuits, returned Yanks, confiscated swing balls and daytime television. Highly amusing and utterly appalling, *Beauty Queen* is an unforgettable pageant of pain.

The Cripple of Inishmaan is set on the Aran Islands in 1934 as Robert Flaherty is filming *Man of Aran* on neighbouring Inis Mor, which leads to much excitement among the locals, especially eighteen-year-old Billy, who sees fame and fortune as a film star beckoning. Already the McDonagh hallmarks are becoming evident, etched in acid. Virtue and viciousness vie for the upper hand in key characters. Dialogue is not so much conversation as a giving vent to frustration, and the plot has more twists and turns than a viper trying to scratch an itch on its back.

The characterization is a joy. Billy is an orphan who survived his parents' drowning in suspicious circumstances. His fondness for staring at cows has saddled him with the reputation of a simpleton. Johnnypateenmike is a local gossip who barters news for a tin of peas at the local shop and tries to kill off his alcoholic mother with drink. Then there's Helen, a Trojan beauty with a terrible tongue in her head.

It is film, however, that fascinates McDonagh. He became a playwright through a process of elimination, or rather, rejection. 'I just exhausted all the other options.' After leaving school at sixteen, he cut his teeth writing film scripts then shorter screenplays but, meeting with no success, he tried his hand at radio plays, at which he was ... really unsuccessful.

'Stage plays were just the next thing I hadn't tried, where people didn't know my backlog of rejections. For a play, all you need is a good story, a good dialogue style. Some good characters. It's the easiest form of writing, whereas with the other artistic media you need a much bigger bag of tricks. I don't think I could ever do a novel. I know my strengths: dialogue, stage or film, images and stories. I don't have a good enough prose style or big enough vocabulary.' That last admission might seem out of character for McDonagh, who has enough self-confidence to take over at Manchester City. But it reinforces his claim that he is not arrogant, simply secure in his self-belief. He was always turned off, he says, by playwrights who presented their work as a poor thing but mine own. 'I wouldn't read a script presented to me like that.'

McDonagh also has no time for the cliché of the scruffy writer. He borrowed one of his brother's suits for his first big interview and has since gone out and bought one. One convention he has allowed himself, though, is to fall for an Irish actress.

There is a fascination with film and television in McDonagh's work. He set *Beauty Queen* in Leenane, he says, probably because Jim Sheridan's film of John B. Keane's *The Field* was shot there. 'In my head, it's more set in Lettermullen. 'He's not a fan of Irish cinema, though. 'I love the play of *The Field*, but I felt the film mangled the whole thing. I think it went for the middle ground, which too many Irish films do, making an Irish film but keeping an eye out for what America wants or what the English would like, whereas I think you should make films exactly for yourself. To get world respect, ignore the world.' This ties in with one of the things he doesn't like about Ireland, which he satirizes in his second play. 'I don't like this need to be congratulated, to be approved of by outsiders. It suggests a lack of self-worth.' In *The Cripple*, one of his character's refrains is 'Ireland mustn't be such a bad place if German fellas, American film-makers etcetera, wanted to come to Ireland.'

If the Irish need inoculating against an inferiority complex, McDonagh has got enough antibodies in his system to eradicate it in the same way as Noel Browne did for TB.

It takes a certain amount of chutzpah also to start work on a play about the INLA, when that organization has just endured another bout of murderous infighting.

By his own admission, McDonagh doesn't know too much about the North. 'But even as a little kid, with all the troubles going on, I saw the stupidity on both sides.' He's unlikely to be silenced either. I asked him if he believed we all have the capacity in our hearts for murder and his affirmative sounded theoretical. But when I asked him if he had a quick temper, he recalled the blazing row with a Muslim woman taxi driver who told him Salman Rushdie must die.

McDonagh lives in a curious limbo land. It must be odd that when you grow up, it's your parents who move out and leave you the key of the door at twenty-one. He sees himself as neither English nor Irish, not proud but happy to have the influence of both cultures.

'I don't feel you have to pick and choose between them, especially in a playwriting sense. It's good to be both and to be neither.'

Still, you can't help feeling … Ireland must be a great place if Martin McDonagh is writing about it.

McDonagh was born in London in 1970. He has won an Academy Award, six Baftas, two Golden Globes, three Olivier Awards and five Tony Award nominations. His plays include the Leenane trilogy of The Beauty Queen of Leenane *(1996),* A Skull in Connemara *and* The Lonesome West *(both 1997),* The Cripple of Inishmaan *(1997),* The Lieutenant of Inishmore *(2001),* The Pillowman *(2003),* A Behanding in Spokane *(2010), and* Hangmen *(2015). His screenplays are* In Bruges *(2008),* Seven Psychopaths *(2011),* Three Billboards Outside Ebbing, Missouri *(2017) and* The Banshees of Inisheerin *(2020).*

PATRICK McGINLEY

12 November 1994, The Irish Post

Patrick McGinley will get some people's goat with his gripping and moving new novel, *The Lost Soldier's Song*, for its universal anti-war message has a very specific setting of the Irish War of Independence.

The writer's view is summed up by Ganley, a disillusioned republican: 'We're fighting high-handed imperialism with high-minded barbarism.'

This is 57-year-old Donegal-born McGinley's eighth novel. *Bogmail*, his first, was screened by the BBC as *Murder in Eden*. *Goosefoot* was filmed as *The Fantasist*. Yet his profile at home is low. He puts this down to exile and perhaps exasperation with his style. He has lived in England since 1962, a refugee from the conservative 1950s at home, and is now managing director of a publishing firm.

The Lost Soldier's Song marks a change in direction after a string of outlandish, black comic thrillers. It follows the fortunes of an IRA flying column, whose members become brutalized by war. Neither he nor I can think of another novel covering this terrain but he did research the numerous memoirs written by republican veterans.

'The best writing done about the period is by Ernie O'Malley – *On Another Man's Wound*. I read it when I was very young, and I remembered it very distinctly. He's the only writer who interests me in a literary way. Some of the rest is very tedious. There is too much rhetoric, too much nationalistic excess. The difference is Ernie O'Malley has a reflective cast of mind. The rest are just recounting one damn thing after another. I wasn't writing history. I see it purely as an anti-war novel in the tradition of Remarque and Barbusse, in a small way, obviously.'

An Irish historical novel will inevitably be interrogated to uncover revisionist or republican nits to be picked over. McGinley doesn't hide his sources.

'I was aware of the historiographical work of Roy Foster. I wouldn't have written it if I hadn't read that.'

Ganley declares: 'All national history is no more than a tribal dummy. This war has weaned me.'

Whether the War of Independence should ever have been fought is still fought over today. 'I felt it was a subject which elicited ingrained responses on both sides of the Irish Sea. I tried to destabilize that by introducing a vein of comedy or wit, something that must be taken with a pinch of salt. There are cynical characters who should make the reader question what's going on. One of the difficulties was how to be objective. Even the four Evangelists writing in unison simultaneously couldn't please everyone on these islands on this subject.'

McGinley did not slavishly confect each character to represent the various strands of Irish opinion from Sinn Féiner to West Briton. 'I was trying to see it from a more human perspective, my truth rather than a historical truth. The purpose of the novel isn't didactic. I didn't have a brief for either side. My concern was to show the utter ruthlessness on either side.'

This is done by incidents such as the summary execution of a possibly innocent man by the flying column. 'A life would end and with it an unrepeatable way of looking at things.'

But the whole thrust of the book is a call away from arms. Declan's farmer father greets his decision to join up by declaring that their family had always made their own independence, rejecting soup and insurrection alike. Declan himself comes to quarrel with the bestial means used to a just end. The column's leader McColl is unfavourably compared to Finn McCool, the shortened vowel sound signalling a narrower, less heroic Ireland. A country doctor, treating Declan's wound, tells him there is no need for a scalpel: let nature take its course.

The suggestion is that the war was not worth fighting. 'There is a strong case to be made for that. It certainly hasn't done much for Ireland in terms of political life. Soldiers became ministers and made a fat living out of the war. Are those the men who should have been running the country?'

The war is described as the result of 'the vexed and degrading relationship between two neighbouring countries that in a rationally ordered world would have been set poles apart'. This led, McGinley suggests, 'to a lack of respect on one side for the other, which meant anything goes'.

Living in England, McGinley has not suffered because of his race and his relationship with home is tempered by distance. 'I don't wake up in the morning tearing my hair out at the latest Irish political absurdity as I might do if I were living in Donegal.' However, he believes his son's upbringing in Kent, though more privileged than his own, is also more impoverished, deprived of the quirkiness of Irish country life.

McGinley prefers to set his novels in the country despite half a lifetime working in London. 'I see urban life as lacking in resonance. I think there's more significance in a man being killed by a falling tree than there is in falling under a bus in Oxford Street. Dickens wouldn't worry about that. The country sets my imagination alight.'

A reflective cast of mind is what makes a writer, McGinley suggests, 'thinking of things no one else thinks about. There is pleasure in putting one word in front of the other, getting the rhythm right,' and in structure, one event following another, with or without logic.

'I suppose there's also the pleasure of making some form of statement, and the pleasure of covering your tracks. Having made that statement and having covered your tracks, you don't want to be interviewed afterwards and be invited to uncover them. You haven't got that thing still on, have you?' he ends on a note of caution, nodding at my tape recorder.

Readers should overcome their caution, should they have any, and listen to the words of *The Lost Soldier's Song.*

McGinley was born in Glencolmcille, County Donegal in 1937 and has lived in England since 1962. The Donegal Democrat *called his debut novel* Bogmail *(1978) 'a horrific concoction of filth – a picture of life in Donegal that is revolting in the extreme. Virtual pornography veneered with the assumption of literary value. A shocking libel.' Other novels are* Fox Prints *(1983);* Foggage *(1984);* The Trick of The Ga Bolga *(1985);* The Red Men *(1987);* The Lost Soldier's Song *(1994);* The Devil's Diary *(2012); and* Cold Spring *(2013). He wrote a memoir,* That Unearthly Valley: A Donegal Childhood *(2011).*

FRANK McGUINNESS

2 March 1996, The Irish Post

For Irish nationalists 1916 was the year of the Easter Rising, whereas for unionists it is remembered as the date of the Battle of the Somme. Only four months separated the two events, which still evoke powerful images of sacrifice for their respective traditions, yet they seemed to belong to two completely separate worlds.

Frank McGuinness, from Donegal, where Ireland's two traditions overlap, has attempted through his writing to bring the two together. He has just completed *Rebellion*, a film script for producer Noel Pearson on the Easter Rising, and his stage play *Observe The Sons of Ulster Marching Towards the Somme*, 'the finest Irish play of the 1980s' according to *The Sunday Times*, has been revived by the Abbey Theatre for a British tour.

Observe follows eight Ulster Protestants from being raw recruits to war veterans to cannon fodder, shedding light on their loyalties, prejudices, differences and bonds. As the grim reality of the impending Battle of the Somme replaces the grandiose rhetoric of the Battle of the Boyne, we are made witness to one of the events that still shapes the loyalist consciousness today.

At once an elegy for the fallen, a lament for spilt blood and an examination of the legacy of suspicion and bloodlust, McGuinness's play manages to combine tragedy and comedy. History repeats itself as farce when the men, to keep their spirits up, stage a mock piggyback battle between King James and King William of Orange, only for King Billy to take an unscripted tumble.

McGuinness's writing is lyrical and large-hearted, full of resonance, rhetoric and references. This new staging is spartan, accompanied by a continuous, ominous drumbeat and a slowly bleeding backcloth. The play is steeped in bloody imagery. One act opens with a character accidentally pricking his thumb (something evil his way comes) and closes with him deliberately cutting his hand, the red hand of Ulster, striving like Cúchulainn for some desperate glory.

McGuinness is from Inishowen, a town cut off from Derry, its natural hinterland, by the Border. He has a natural sensibility to the North. 'You grow up very much with partition on your soul. Not so much a historical fact as an imaginative reality, political truth. The other is very close to you, at times so close that there seems to be no difference between you and the other.'

There is, of course, a great difference, but it has long been denied. Which made the staging of McGuinness's play at the Abbey such a poignant event. 'For the Irish national theatre, it was an act of recognition that here was another culture on the island, apart from the Catholic, nationalist tradition. If we are going to move forward, there has to be recognition of and respect for diversity of cultures.

'This play is a recognition of a force to be reckoned with in the country. I had learned nothing about it in my schooling and I had lived beside this cultural force and this religious power, trained to think of it as the other and the enemy, so it is no shock there will be civic hatred.'

McGuinness wrote *Observe* after reading two novels dealing with the First World War, Jennifer Johnston's *How Many Miles to Babylon?* and Susan Hill's *Strange Meeting*. The main inspiration, though, was the Bible.

'When I was working on the play, I read the whole Bible because that was very much the big text in the Protestant mind. They have a very passionate belief in the Old Testament God, who is a god of darkness.'

Indeed, the Protestant protagonist in Dermot Healy's *A Goat's Song* says the Bible is the only book, all fiction being suspect. 'And it *is* the greatest fiction ever propagated by the Western mind,' adds McGuinness, who lectures in English at Maynooth University. He's comfortable there. 'Stupidity in intellectual terms has never been a mark of the Catholic Church.'

The playwright went to teach at the University of Ulster in Coleraine in 1977 and began to learn of the immense Ulster Protestant sacrifice at the Somme.

'I just thought this was an incredibly tragic, terrible story and I wanted to write about it. I thought it linked in with the great terrible stories of Irish mythology, the ironies of someone like Cúchulainn, who said "I die fighting the men of Ireland." It was making Protestant Ulster culture part of a much bigger pattern of what was Ireland than anything I had been trying to think of. It was a big challenge to my own imagination.'

The Somme, as well as being a counterpoint to the Easter Rising four months previously, stands in contrast to the Battle of the Boyne in Protestant tradition, which also, under the old calendar, took place on the 1st of July.

'The Boyne marked the triumphalism of loyalist community. The Somme was this extraordinary disaster, massacre, that gave a desperate resonance to counteract it. Coping with defeat made as much impact as coping with triumph.'

What was the impact of the slaughter at the Somme on Protestant culture? 'I can't speak for Protestant culture. That's been one of the downfalls of the national ethos, the attempt to give them an appropriate language, but I think it left them with a very strong determination never to trust anyone beyond their own community, the British establishment as much as the Irish.'

There is a small scene in the play where two characters fall out when one says something about the other's grandmother, which though true still hurts. It speaks volumes for the power of the tribe. How free, then, is McGuinness of his Irish Catholic, nationalist background?

'I would hope I interrogate it very much, but I recognize the enormous power and influence it has.'

Does he still aspire, though, to a united Ireland like fellow playwright and neighbour Brian Friel?

'We come from different generations, have had different experiences, traumas. The terror of the last twenty-five years has changed our vocabulary. Even the word unification itself is something we've learned the dangers of. Or we should have. I think we're looking now for a new language of managing to live beside each other. We need a more varied debate than the sloganeering that's gone on.'

The tragedy of the North over the last quarter of a century is in part down to the legacy of a generation's blood sacrifice over eighty years ago. How can you compromise on a creed written in blood? There is a striking similarity between the philosophies of Pyper in the play and that of Padraig Pearse, one of the key figures in McGuinness's latest screenplay. McGuinness agrees.

'They shared a common worldview. There were local differences, but at the time there was this preaching of blood all through Europe. It was seen as a cleansing force, the reclamation of manhood, freedom achieved through blood or empire maintained through blood.

'I think it came from a very heightened, literal understanding of what being a nation was. It was such a changing time in terms of art, religion, this big revolution in imaginative, intellectual thought accompanied by a very fundamental conservatism in terms of national identity as defined by national boundaries.

'As in all human activity, there was the pull and the stasis tearing each other apart. The positive creative achievements were being seriously undermined by the negative achievements of political conservatism.'

Ironic then that this great work of art, restaged to mark the ceasefire, opens next week amid renewed political violence and political stalemate.

McGuinness was born in 1953 in Buncrana, County Donegal. Best known as a playwright, he has published eight poetry collections and screenplays including adaptations of Brian Friel's Dancing at Lughnasa *and Kate O'Brien's* Mary Lavelle (*as* Talk of Angels). *Awards for his play* Observe the Sons of Ulster Marching Towards the Somme *include the Rooney Prize for Irish Literature and the Ewart-Biggs Prize.* Someone Who'll Watch over Me *was nominated for Tony and Olivier Awards. He was professor of creative writing at UCD from 2007 to 2018. He won an Irish PEN Award and UCD Ulysses Medal.*

LISA McINERNEY

9 May 2021, The Irish Times

Lisa McInerney's debut *The Glorious Heresies* won two major prizes and her follow-up, *The Blood Miracles*, another, so you might think her biggest concern ahead of the publication of *The Rules of Revelation*, the third and last of the set, would be making space on the mantelpiece. But no – she might live near Lady Gregory's estate but she is not the Queen of Coole.

'The nerves are at me big time,' she says, 'I'm a real hoor for attention. It has to be good attention, though. You're not supposed to read your bad reviews but I got one and it gutted me, and that was four years ago and I haven't recovered. I'm supposed to be a cool writer – I want to be like Mr Banville who just doesn't care. I still feel like an emerging writer, three books in, still struggling out of the hedge.'

The Women's Prize for Fiction, the Desmond Elliott Prize and the RSL Encore Award were a huge boost, of course, but a burden too, even if only in her own head.

The plan was to write three novels and gradually become good. Success ahead of schedule has made her put pressure on herself, the fear of letting readers down. 'You've gained these readers and there's this expectation you've got to keep them happy and that's a bad space to be in when you're writing. You should never be thinking about the book as a product that has to eventually go on a shelf. When you start doing that [the writing] ceases to be real.'

Her anxiety is unfounded. If Roddy Doyle captured working-class Dublin in his Barrytown trilogy, McInerney's set is as Cork as Barry's Tea and just as strong. 'I've always wondered why there wasn't more fiction set in Cork,' she says. 'It's this playground for language, for slang and vernacular. It doesn't seem to get the love it deserves.'

Though she is now back in her native Coole, County Galway, McInerney studied English and geography in Cork, taking a year out to have her child, then didn't go back – 'I'm holding out for an honorary degree.' She was more into geography, fascinated by how cities were built, and wanted to be an urban planner. Now, in a sense, she has created her own city.

Heresies, a wild, hugely entertaining tale, introduced readers to her cast of characters, most memorably Ryan, the bright, charismatic but wayward son of a feckless father, his girlfriend Karine and Maureen, a local gangster's mother on a revenge mission to cause mayhem.

Blood Miracles was more portrait than landscape, a taut thriller tightly focused on Ryan as he becomes enmeshed in drugs and the criminal underworld. *The Rules of Revelation* is another landscape – looser, funnier and less frenetic, completing the 'sex, drugs and rock'n'roll' narrative arc as Ryan returns home to both face the music and make it, recording an album with his band on Inishbofin then performing it in Cork, reuniting with Karine and trying to make peace with his past or at least keep one step ahead of it.

'I've written this sprawling thing so it's very hard to sum up,' the author says. 'It's a polyphonic novel with five voices, about art and homecomings, finding yourself. I wanted to give my characters a good ending, wanted it to feel satisfactory but real. They are reimagining their place in Ireland, there's a lot of looking inward, so the pace is softer, but still a lot of fun in there, I hope, especially with Maureen going round trying to rattle the city's cage.'

Some Irish fiction could be set anywhere, but McInerney's novels are not only rooted by the Lee, they also document the state of the nation, just as she did with her name-making *Arse End of Ireland* blog.

'*Heresies* starts in 2010, this finishes in 2019; over that decade, Jesus, has Ireland changed,' McInerney says, citing the crash and recovery, the legalizing of same-sex marriage and abortion and the reshaping of the political landscape. 'Why would you not want to capture that?

'How do these characters exist in this changing Ireland? *Glorious Heresies*' Ireland is very cold and judgmental, just post-crash. I can't write that Ireland anymore because it doesn't exist. Those referendums gave people a sense of ownership of and hope for their country – shit, we can change things! – that I don't think they had up to that point.

'We have some ways to go yet but we are starting to get more confident in ourselves and in our capabilities. We do go abroad and bring home the best of what we've learned. We can be very hard on ourselves for slang and our accents. That comes from the D4 RTÉ thing. We need to cop on and let ourselves just be Irish. We are not English, we are not British, we never will be and that's fine.'

Her mother-in-law, Geraldine McInerney, was RTÉ's first female newsreader, who also ran a glamorous PR agency in New York. 'I married into RTÉ royalty. My sister-in-law sent me a photo of Geraldine with Peter O'Toole's arm round her, a far cry from my life, let me tell you. I sent her *The Stinging Fly*'s Maeve Brennan book for Christmas about another Irishwoman who went off to New York.'

The Rules of Revelation dwells on characters' struggle to define themselves by their own lights, not their roots. The author, like most of her characters, is a council-house kid, so she relates to their struggle to get on without abandoning where they come from. 'It's the old crab in the bucket thing – the one who climbs out gets pulled back.'

Another character, Mel, was a peripheral figure in the first novel, known then as Linda, the daughter of Ryan's nightmare neighbour and nemesis Tara. While living in Glasgow, they realized their true gender identity. Writing a trans character 'didn't feel like a thorny issue at the time', the author says. 'When I was writing this there was a sense of hope, especially for young people to be able to move into whatever identity they are most comfortable with, moving beyond gender as this ridiculous social construct, free themselves up.

'My son, Aodh, is a trans boy, we've been having all these discussions about gender and making people feel comfortable. He is nineteen, going on twenty, and a lot of his friends are experimenting, questioning identity, society and norms. If we never did that, what sort of society would we be in now? We'd still be under the thumb of Archbishop McQuaid.'

McInerney is scathing about women who used to insist feminism was all-inclusive and working-class women like her should show solidarity with actors like Reese Witherspoon getting paid less than their male co-stars, 'but suddenly it doesn't include trans women next door, who I would have way more in common with, so where is the intersection there? Meanwhile, female to male is a total blind spot to these people.'

Does the new novel also reflect her evolution as a writer? 'I hope so, there is less of a reliance on nuts-and-bolts plot. I gave myself space to do more of a deep dive on characters, allowed them to have a moment to themselves, to explore and to think. It allowed me to write with more of a contemplative, even shrewd, eye, which led, I think, to some nice passages.'

Rereading the book doesn't make her groan.

'But I hope every book I write shows me I am progressing till you get to the point where you write something that might last forever, that's what you always want.

'Not having to follow the same plot and rhythm and atmosphere all the way through three books was quite freeing. The difficulty is if you write three very different books but have them in the same expanded universe, like Marvel, you're going to have readers missing the black comedy or wanting another thriller. Why isn't Ryan cavorting around Europe being a drug dealer? Well, the reality is you don't last long in that job, they'll either kill him or it will kill your love for him – it's not a healthy thing to keep doing.'

The interview is conducted via FaceTime, which allows me to have a good gawk at McInerney's enviably tidy study, spotting photos of the River Lee and Inishbofin and the handwritten lyrics to the song 'Napoleon' by Canadian singer-songwriter Sarah Slean, which she adores and dreams one day of incorporating into a screenplay.

'I've always had a great grá for music but never been musically gifted. My mother sent me off with a second-hand accordion once – disaster! We can't all be rock stars – musicians need fans just like writers need readers.'

She is looking fit. Coole Park is within her 5km so she has been running a lot in lockdown, though she is jealous of those writers who can plot as they run, while she has to concentrate on keeping her legs moving. She misses friends a lot. Her best friend's son is an adorable three and her nana, who raised her, is eighty-eight. She would love to go and sit in her kitchen and have a chat but is trying to be the sensible one. Of course, she appreciates others have had it much worse.

Kevin Barry, a mentor who published her first story in 2013 in the Faber anthology he edited – 'a Cork city blow-in like me and a great supporter' – launches her book online on 13 May. 'I never thought I would miss the terrible book launch wine, I'd give anything to shuffle from foot to foot while someone goes on too long about a book while drinking red wine that tastes of socks.'

'Saturday, Boring', her Faber story, is 'a rudimentary, primitive version of Ryan and Karine', although they are not named. 'When I go back and read the start of it now, I go, Jesus, someone could have said, this is overwriting, Lisa. But we must progress.'

She has lived with her characters for decades, though, dreaming what their story might be. The end is not goodbye, however. 'They are not going anywhere, I can check in and see how they're getting on. Never say never. When I finished *Rules of Revelation* I said that's it now, I'm done, but recently I slipped a bit. You know Roddy went back, checked in on the lads thirty years after *The Commitments* with *The Guts*.'

There is also, of course, ITV Studios' TV adaptation, which was ready to go when Covid happened. A big star was attached, but she can't say who. She has discovered a talent for screenwriting, which helps pay the bills, although adapting *Heresies* was challenging. 'Everyone says it would make such great TV but there are a lot of difficulties. You have Ryan who grows from fifteen to twenty in the space of that book – try to get an actor who can do that.'

McInerney was born in Gort, County Galway in 1981, where she still lives. Her debut novel, The Glorious Heresies, *won the Women's Prize for Fiction and the Desmond Elliott Prize. Its French translation won the 2018 Ireland Francophonie Ambassadors' Literary Award. Its sequel,* The Blood Miracles *(2018), won the Encore Award and the trilogy was completed by* The Rules of Revelation *(2021). She has written the screenplays for a TV adaptation, which is in development. She is editor of* The Stinging Fly *magazine.*

DANIELLE McLAUGHLIN

30 January 2022, The Irish Times

Such was the brilliance of Danielle McLaughlin's 2015 debut short-story collection, *Dinosaurs on Other Planets*, that expectation levels for her first novel were extremely high. Its long gestation – conception dating to a writing workshop with Nuala O'Connor in 2012 – must have added to the anxiety.

We need not have feared. *The Art of Falling* is exceptional, and critics are already falling over themselves to praise it. The text has such depth, it could have been sent to a 3D printer.

The novel is firmly anchored in the author's native county. Her protagonist Nessa's description of the light by the sea in West Cork as not soft but 'glorious, razor-sharp and unsparing' is a perfect description of McLaughlin's own writing.

Nessa is in her forties and facing a perfect storm of problems in her personal and professional life. Already dealing with financial, marital and parental difficulties, she is confronted with her history in the shape of a dead friend's son. Her curation of a sculptor's collection is similarly complicated by an intrusion from his past.

'My main concern was to tell a story,' says McLaughlin. 'I wasn't setting out to showcase any particular concerns, though looking back over it now, I can see themes emerging. We are drawn to tell the stories that interest us. Among the territory covered by the novel is feminism; structural discrimination; the need to challenge accepted narratives; the gap between how we pretend things are and how they actually are; the mystery of why people put up with bad relationships; art and how we talk about it; how guilt can follow a person through life; is the past ever really past?'

Nine years before the author could hold her published novel in her hand, it began with her rubbing a chalky piece of broken crockery as a writing prompt. The novel took a long time to come right, and she found it hard to write. Switching from the first to the third person at her agent's suggestion helped unlock something.

'I have a number of short stories among my drafts called "The Chalk Sculpture". They are all quite different and, at the same time, they also have things in common. It became a novel about two years after it started out. A previous setting and some characters from a novel in progress merged to form a new entity. I think that switching to third person gave me a better perspective on Nessa – after all, she's not me, and I think I was fairer to her when I wrote about her from close third. There was less self-indulgence, and also less self-hatred, creeping in.'

Writing may be rewriting but McLaughlin is known for her multiple drafts. Is this a normal polishing process or an obsessive pursuit of elusive perfection? 'Not an obsessive pursuit of perfection, but very possibly just plain obsessive! In one sense, that has always been part of my personality or psychology, that tendency towards obsession, or to frame it more positively, a very intense focus on whatever has captured my interest.

'As a small child, I had obsessive-compulsive tendencies. As an adult I've been diagnosed as on the autism spectrum. I think being very particular and doing lots of drafts is part of the way I'm wired, and so it follows that it's how I write.

'It also has to do, I think, with the fact that I work things out on paper, rather than in my head, so I maybe have a physical record of more drafts than other writers might. I'm also comfortable with that repetitive process of doing something over and over.'

Redrafting is also a clarifying process, helping her discover the way ahead.

'The story, the different layers of it, the depth of it, definitely builds over the course of the various drafts. The drafting builds the fabric of a piece. The great thing about human exchanges in fiction is that we can keep revisiting them until the underlying meaning reveals itself to us, the motivations and misunderstandings or connections that lie behind the characters' interactions. So much of real life could be improved if we were allowed redraft it.'

Writing in notebooks at the early stage, 'the freedom of paper', is a vital part of her non-linear creative process. 'I have to write longhand at the start of any project. It's a more direct connection to whatever soup of ideas might be sloshing around in my brain. Often when those ideas start making their way out on to a page, it will be a tangle, and sometimes that tangle will split off into different stories that might end up being in conversation with one another.

'Writing on paper, I like the sense of being "unplugged". The page and a pen or pencil has a more direct route to my brain than trying to write via a computer.'

The title has changed over the years from 'The Chalk Sculpture' to 'Retrospective' to 'The Art of Falling'. Why?

'It was "The Chalk Sculpture" for years and years, named after the best-known piece of art made by Robert Locke. I liked the idea of something standing as a piece of sculpture but at the same time crumbling and vulnerable from its inception – the idea that perhaps its vulnerability was the most true thing about it, the contradiction between shape and essence. But there were many books with similar titles.

'I then came up with "Retrospective". I liked the way it tied in with the plot, as well as the way, whether by choice or because we are forced to, we come to reassess the story we tell ourselves about our own lives, and also others' lives. "The Art of Falling" speaks to the novel on a number of levels, and the fact that there are various different kinds of "fallings" in the book.'

To what degree is the switch from short story to novel a natural progression or a publishing industry expectation? 'I can only say that personally I didn't feel any sense of expectation. I wanted to write this novel, to tell this particular story. And Nessa's story, and the story of the characters who journey with her, wouldn't have suited a short story.'

Does she feel the novel is held in greater esteem? 'I don't know about esteem, but it definitely has a higher commercial value placed on it.'

The author has spoken of the short story's power as not just something you read but that happens or is done to you. What is the novel's singular power?

'Perhaps the greater length of time we spend with characters in a novel allows a friendship of sorts to develop, a sort of companionship. Short stories are more akin to an experience of solidarity. The short story can be compared to someone we meet briefly, but who we subsequently find ourselves thinking about. The novel perhaps provides the opportunity to see how a character develops over a longer period, even a life or, in the case of a family, several generations, with room too for insights into what might have made them who they are, or their reasons for making the choices that they do.'

How did McLaughlin's time as a lawyer – a serious illness forced her to quit a decade ago – serve as an apprenticeship to becoming a writer in terms of the use of language and as a fund of human stories?

'Law gave me the opportunity of writing very precisely to deadline where the stakes, should one get a word or a paragraph wrong, were open to far more worrying consequences than somebody complaining about clunky prose. Deadlines were more strictly enforced in law and I was better at meeting them back then.

'I loved to read the Law Reports. You get valuable insights into a person's character when you are reading how they acted under pressure, when they are obliged to tell you things because they are under oath, things that they might otherwise never breathe to another living soul. And the detail, the requirement for evidence that law insists upon, is so enriching – no gliding over the surface allowed. There's no need for anyone to ever be short of ideas if they have access to Law Reports.'

The Art of Falling steadily strips away (self-)deceptions to get at the truth of a character's nature and motivations, the debunking of the sculptor's self-mythologising mirrored in the cleaning of his statue and the gradual discovery of its true origin story and meaning. The novelist as restorer or revisionist historian?

'Or perhaps novelist as challenger,' says McLaughlin. 'I like the ability that fiction has to challenge existing narratives. Fiction can fill gaps left by other parts of society. I'm interested in why we blithely accept some things, simply because we're told them. And conversely, why we refuse to accept other things, even though we are repeatedly told them. So much of what we tell ourselves about our lives, or the lives of others, might be described as fake news.'

Nessa is horrified when her daughter is given a diary. The sculptor Locke, echoing Nessa's friend Amy, says 'there's nothing I wouldn't use in my art'. Nessa mentions digging up a rabbit once, an incident from McLaughlin's own childhood. Are there things she wouldn't dare dig up?

'There's subject matter that I think I'd want to be in a very good place before exploring, especially since I'm a slow writer, because it means I'd be visiting dark places for a protracted period. I also think, when dealing with material that's very disturbing, that a writer needs to have a good reason for bringing more ugliness into the world, always allowing that perhaps a story may manage to make something disturbing into something beautiful.'

McLaughlin has spoken of a bleak world view and described herself as anxious. How would she describe her personality and outlook? How does that feed into her fiction? 'I'd say, yes, I'm anxious and an introvert. That can be helpful when making fiction, all that catastrophizing can be put to good use, and I never feel that writing has robbed me of time I could have spent partying.'

McLaughlin is much loved. Marie Gethins, in a 2016 article for *The Irish Times* about being in a writing group with Danielle, wrote: 'It is rare that great talent is combined with genuine good in a person.'

How intentional is the strong feminist current in the work, from the domestic to the artistic? Locke took the glory for the work of women in his life. Nessa multitasks while her husband fraternizes. Ireland has not treated its female citizens well or equally. Female artists have been neglected. Is that a legacy or ongoing issue?

'I didn't set out to tackle any theme as such. But I'm conscious always of how the world treats women, being one – and also, given the history of how Ireland treated women through the twentieth century, how could I not be very much aware of it? So it's there in what I write, because I write about life as I've come to know it. Definitely very much an ongoing issue.'

Discussing influences, McLaughlin cites: 'Anne Enright, for the fierce honesty of her writing, how she manages to close the gap between reader and character; William Trevor, for the grace of his writing; Alice Munro, how she can conjure whole worlds with just the right amount of detail, and can cover great swathes of time and make it look effortless; Kevin Barry, for the lyricism and music and humour of his writing, the way his stories ring so true; George Saunders for the way he writes his characters with both compassion and humour.'

A second novel is underway, but she doesn't want to talk about it too much, because she hasn't shown it to anyone yet. 'The first chunk of it, which is at a slightly more polished stage, is going to my writing group this week as I continue to redraft the rest.' She has written a dozen stories since her debut, and more are at various stages of construction, so a second collection can't be far off.

McLaughlin's art tells us we may have fallen and may be damaged but we are salvageable, still worthy of not just notice but admiration and love. The future is another country. We can do things better there.

Her star too is in the ascendant. But did she begin to doubt herself as a writer at any stage? How important were the two big prizes she won in 2019 (the *Sunday Times* Short-Story Award and the Windham-Campbell Award)?

'The affirmations of the prizes arrived at an important point because I had been thinking about what I was doing with my life and if I should return to practising law,' McLaughlin says. 'Doubt is the default position, and I can't say that there's any stage at which it stops.'

McLaughlin was born in Cork in 1969. In 2019 she won a $165,000 Windham-Campbell Literature Prize and the £30,000 Sunday Times *Short Story Award. Her short-story collection* Dinosaurs on Other Planets *(2015) was followed by her novel* The Art of Falling *(2021), shortlisted for the International Dublin Literary Award. She edited the anthology* Counterparts *(2018), a synergy of law and literature.*

ROBERT McLIAM WILSON

25 July 1992, The Irish Post

Robert McLiam Wilson – the name is a bit of a mouthful, and the man behind it has got a mean mouth too, and he's not afraid to use it. A novelist, a term which he invests with all its late nineteenth-century grandeur, he collected so many awards for his debut, *Ripley Bogle*, that he would put the average Irish dancer's trophy cabinet to shame.

With his third book, *Manfred's Pain*, he has served notice that here is no flash in the pan. Here, rather, is a trailblazer.

Manfred's Pain is the story of a dying English Jew, whose life is as ruined as his health. Through a series of his recollections, we encounter some of the worst excesses and horrors of the twentieth century, the Second World War and particularly the Holocaust, an evil that still needs to be exorcised.

When I put it to the author that his book's true centre seems to be an exploration of the Holocaust, he replied: 'No, I wouldn't agree with that at all. If you extended that into an examination of violence in general, I'd agree more. Not just the Holocaust but the Second World War itself, the military war as opposed to the civilian war. Also the violence between men and women.'

It is an obvious question to ask someone who grew up in Turf Lodge, one of West Belfast's districts most affected by poverty and the Troubles, but how big an influence is the author's background on his treatment of the theme of violence?

'My background definitely has a lot to do with it,' Wilson says. 'You know, when I was about seven or eight, I would be watching cowboy films on television, where these cowboys who wore white hats and went around shooting Indians were great. But I stepped out of my front door and the guys who wore hoods weren't great people. I found that very confusing.

'I had a problem with the adult world where children were expected to be orderly and yet my versions of adult authority continually let themselves down and were disgracing themselves.'

The Holocaust clearly exerts a fascination on Wilson as it has done on many others.

'The hatred of European Jews is fascinating. If someone hates someone because they are coloured, you can see some kind of difference there. But for European Gentiles to hate European Jews at that time was spectacular because European Jews distinguished themselves by how well they had coalesced into a meritocratic society of achievers. For Europeans to have done what they did, when their own culture was basically Judaeo-Christian – if you're Christian, you're half Jewish – I can't really get a handle on it at all.

'You see that in Northern Ireland. Both communities hate each other because they fear each other. The fear is based on some fantastic notion, but it's completely spurious. And that's what happened in Europe. It was politically convenient as well to find someone to hate. I think it sucks. That's why it's important that Gentiles or a 28-year-old Catholic Irishman should write about the Holocaust because if it is allowed to be owned by Jews the point is lost. We have to learn what we are capable of.'

Manfred speaks of feeling Jewish only when Jewishness is impugned or when he is racially abused. Is that how Wilson understands his own identity?

'Yes, substantially,' the author agrees. 'Manfred reminds me very much of myself at times when he talks about his religion, his culture, his background. I have problems understanding the word "Irish". I'm not sure what that means. But certainly there are things that you see on television and you're back into that and you feel like a Mick.'

There is a fluency to Wilson's writing, which on occasion veers towards an intoxication with language reminiscent perhaps of Martin Amis's style. Coincidentally, Amis's last novel, *Time's Arrow*, also dealt with the Holocaust. Cue outrage. 'The notion of Amis's book is disgraceful, for he ripped it off from Kurt Vonnegut in *Slaughterhouse 5*.'

This prompts some musing on the American novel. 'Norman Mailer, Joseph Heller, Kurt Vonnegut and Gore Vidal all wrote brilliant books about the Second World War and never really did that again.'

Are American writers happiest when dealing with large subjects? 'That's probably fairly true. I think what happens is when they are writing a novel that doesn't have an overwhelming subject matter, they become very self-conscious. There is a great desire to write the Great American Novel because American culture is so extraordinary, so impossible to describe.

'The other problem for them is that the American cultural mafia doesn't honour what is great about American literature. I mean, Vonnegut and Heller are ignored – well, not ignored exactly, but if they had been European, those guys would have been saints.'

Manfred's Pain contains a pricelessly prejudiced comment on the English working class, 'the great mindless underclass of England, the most witless and depressing proletariat in Europe'. Understandably enough, Wilson, retreating into defensive humour, is not prepared to admit that this is his own view. 'The author,' he recites, 'cannot be held responsible for any views expressed on the premises.'

Wilson, however, recently gave an interview to *Time Out*, which was either incredibly indiscreet or wildly inaccurate. Wilson pleads the latter, denying that he told the interviewer that fellow author Ronan Bennett's writing was incredibly bad and that, when told he had been in prison, he replied: 'Not for long enough.' Another thing he claims he was misquoted as saying was that Northern poet Damian Gorman, who refuses to publish his own verse, 'will not publish because no one will publish him'.

Time Out's Suzi Feay responded that she had recorded the interview and stood over the quotations, adding that Wilson had described OTG, later published as *Eureka Street*, as 'the Belfast *Ulysses*'. During the interview over lunch in Covent Garden, he had abruptly left the table to be sick. He signed her copy of *Manfred's Pain:* 'For Suzi, Sorry for throwing up. Nothing personal, Robert'.

Wilson is no stranger to controversy, of course, having hit the front pages of the *Sunday Express* and other tabloids a couple of years back when he received the Betty Trask Award and a cheque for £16,000 from Prince Charles 'in my shirt sleeves and braces', having taken off his dinner jacket because of the heat. It wasn't primarily this that had riled the yellow press, but rather the fact that this scribbler from the Falls Road was taking money from the heir to the throne as reward for a book, *Ripley Bogle*, whose protagonist had described the nobility as the sons of thieves.

Ripley Bogle is a superb book, if flawed. Wilson is not a writer to play it safe; he prefers it fast and loose. One marvels at the ambitious risks he takes, even when they only half come off. His next novel, after the controlled discipline of

Manfred's Pain, promises to be another tour de force and this time the setting will be Belfast.

'There is a novel I've always wanted to write. It's what I've started now, about Belfast. *Ripley Bogle* helped me in some ways towards that. It's going to be a long novel full of jokes called OTG. Everything that happens in Belfast eventually gets written up on the wall. So this OTG starts getting written on walls and none of my characters knows what means. It's revealed at the end of the book.'

Wilson is a busy man. As well as his magnum opus, he is currently writer in residence at Coleraine University and is in the process of making a television series based on his factual book on poverty in Belfast, London and Glasgow, *The Dispossessed.*

He was so affected by his experience of interviewing people suffering from poverty in London's East End that he abandoned his research in Glasgow after a couple of days, leaving his collaborator, Belfast photographer Donovan Wiley, to record poverty there in words as well as images.

The Dispossessed was Wilson's personal response to poverty and urban misery rather than an exercise in giving a voice to the silent poor themselves. He felt this was the most effective approach as his book was aimed at the unconverted, those who might have read his first novel but still held that the poor were not really impoverished or simply brought misery down on their own heads.

Despite the TV documentary he has no notion of writing for TV. 'I don't mind doing TV work in front of the camera, but I wouldn't want to write for it,' he says with an engaging preciousness. 'I'm a novelist and I have an old-fashioned, sacramental notion about writing."

Recalling his two years at Cambridge University, Wilson candidly admits having 'played the Paddy role a bit' but insists he really queered the pitch for students from middle-class Protestant schools like Methody and Campbell College, who had been indulging their English audiences for years.

A favourite college moment was when he played a police interrogator in Martin Lynch's *The Interrogation of Ambrose Fogarty*, while the two IRA suspects were played by students from Inst, another bastion of Protestant privilege.

Whatever of the implications of this jolly Saturnalia, the realities of Belfast life are not lost on Wilson. Thrown out of home at the age of sixteen by parents who would not brook the idea of him consorting with a Protestant girl, he ended up marrying another Protestant, whose parents promptly disowned her, he claims.

With such bitter experience under his belt, and equipped as he is with such undisputed talent, [Eureka Street] promises to hit home hard and true.

McLiam Wilson was born in Belfast in 1964 and lives in Paris, where he writes for Charlie Hebdo *and* Liberation. Ripley Bogle *(1989) won the Rooney Prize for Irish Literature, a Betty Trask Award and the Irish Book Award. His other novels are* Manfred's Pain *(1992) and* Eureka Street *(1996), which was made into a BBC TV drama series in 1999. He also wrote a non-fiction book,* The Dispossessed *(1992). A fourth novel,* Extremists, *was due to be published in 2006 but has yet to appear. An extract, 'The Dreamed', was published in* Granta *magazine.*

EOIN McNAMEE

19 February 2011, The Irish Post

Eoin McNamee might have been predestined to write a novel about the murder of nineteen-year-old Pearl Gamble after a dance at an Orange hall in Newry, County Down in 1961, for which Robert McGladdery became the last man to be hanged in the North after a trial controversially presided over by Judge Lance Curran, whose own nineteen-year-old daughter Patricia had been murdered only nine years previously.

Patricia Curran's murder, and the wrongful conviction of Iain Hay Gordon for the crime, was the subject of McNamee's brilliant and darkly compelling 2001 novel, the Booker-longlisted *The Blue Tango*, which dwelt at length on the suspicious behaviour of Lance Curran on the night of the murder, so when he discovered that Curran was the hanging judge in a similar case, the idea for another novel slowly began to germinate.

There was another, personal connection. 'I was born about one hundred yards from the Orange hall about three weeks before McGladdery was hanged,' the author reveals. 'There was a psychic connection there which I never realized I had.'

McNamee has made his name as an author of psychologically penetrating and stylized literary reimaginings of real-life crimes and suspected conspiracies, from the Shankill Butchers (*Resurrection Man*) to the dubious activities and murder of undercover British intelligence officer Robert Nairac (*The Ultras*) to the death of Princess Diana (*12.23*).

Fellow author Liam McIlvanney sets the bar rightly high when he makes comparisons: 'Like James Ellroy and David Peace, Eoin McNamee makes visceral fictions from the hidden history of his native place. McNamee's prose has the cadenced majesty of McCarthy or DeLillo, but the vision it enacts is all his own.'

Eddie McCrink, the fictional detective returned from London who is tasked with the case, is put under pressure from the establishment, the real-life unionist leaders Harry West ('rule by fear, reward by favour' sums up an RUC man) and Brian Faulkner, to pin the murder to McGladdery so that society could be avenged and the law upheld while justice could go hang.

McCrink, a damaged figure nursing a broken marriage and with no stake in this society, is more concerned with the truth, and is inexorably drawn to the Curran murder, revisiting the scene of that crime, seeing a bloodstain on a bedroom floor although the body was found outside, and interviewing the judge's wife in the mental hospital to which she has been committed, coming to the conclusion that the McGladdery trial would result in 'a guilty man hanging an innocent man'.

Despite the tantalizing theorizing of both his novels on the subject, McNamee insists that his finger does not point but merely holds the pen. 'I've always said when people ask me what I think happened that it was speculation that got Iain Hay Gordon convicted of the crime in the first place. I don't want to add my speculation to that. I suppose in a way I have as much insight as anyone else. There is no certainty to the case at all.'

Are his fictions not speculative attempts at the truth? 'No, I don't think so. I think with *Blue Tango* I became as much interested in who Patricia Curran was, almost a proto-feminist character, a very independent young woman. Her character assassination after her death, all the affairs and so on – that interested me. What the books do is recount the story and build fiction around that. It's speculative in the sense you develop characters and put words in their mouths but the skeleton of fact remains.

'I often feel if you get the art right, the truth tends to follow. Someone said the job of the artist is to deepen the mystery, there aren't any easy solutions and I'm not trying to offer any. I would like people to come away with an appreciation of the depth of humanity and the mysteries of life, not offer glib solutions. This is where my books differ from the crime genre where things are tied up neatly at the end.'

It is understandable, commendable even, that McNamee does not wish to assign guilt to a real-life character, but is he prepared to say he is convinced of McGladdery's innocence?

'No, I wouldn't say that, but I would say from a forensic point of view – I did a law degree a long time ago – a man whose nineteen-year-old daughter had been murdered nine years previously should not have been put in charge of a case where a man is charged with murdering a nineteen-year-old girl in similar circumstances.

'The judge was not legitimate, then the court was not legitimate and McGladdery should not have hanged. I don't think he should have been hanged on the evidence put before the court anyway. The police picked McGladdery as a suspect and didn't investigate anyone else. McGladdery's own character didn't help his case one bit. But this was a society where Faulkner writes "let the law take its course" on a document turning down the appeal. Faulkner thought the law was one thing, justice another. So there has to be doubts but I'm not saying McGladdery didn't do it.'

There is a principle that justice must not only be done but be seen to be done. McNamee sets out to show how under a corrupt Stormont regime, justice was not done and that the law, far from being blind, was blinkered, and sought vengeance, not the truth.

'I suppose I was always interested in the character of Curran. He epitomized for me a corrupt authority, which was the government of the North over fifty years of Stormont. In a deeper sense I was interested in how people become corrupted.

'There's always a moment when something clicks and you find your way into a subject,' says McNamee. 'I didn't actually realize [about Curran's connection to the McGladdery case]. I went to the newspaper archive and read Lance Curran's charge to the jury. I remember sitting on this warm summer's night in the Central Library in Belfast and a chill went down my back when I read the last page of his charge to the jury. It more or less undermined the two planks of McGladdery's defence, which should have been left to the jury to decide.'

Did he feel that Curran had acted like judge, jury and executioner? 'It very much read like that. I mean the case was very complex, all the evidence was circumstantial and there was six days of evidence, but the jury came back within forty-five minutes, they barely had time to sit down.'

McNamee has come in for more than his share of grief for having the temerity to make fiction out of notorious murders. The Belfast UDA even tried to sue the makers of the film version of *Resurrection Man*, which was almost funny, he says. 'There was an underlying nasty note of what's this Catholic doing writing about this,' but he makes no apology for pursuing a subject that he feels was staring in his face growing up.

'People used to say to me, why do you write about the Troubles in general or the Butchers in particular? I always thought, *why would I not write about it, these things happened on my doorstep*. I remember a painter at art college in Belfast in the seventies teaching about the radicalism of German Expressionism while bombs were going off outside. Look outside the window! A lot of people didn't look out the window, but a lot of writers from my generation tried to take responsibility for what was going on with the tools at our disposal.

'Crimes are stories with inherent drama in them. Why would you not write about them? For example, I had no interest in Diana or any of her pomp or doings, until I opened *Death of a Princess* in a second-hand bookshop and felt this atmosphere of Graham Greene, Eastern European intrigue. Her story, till I got into it, seemed to belong to a lurid kind of journalism, like the Kennedy assassination, what Don De Lillo called the sinister buzz of implication, the ripples spreading out from it.

'When you write fiction you write within certain structures that work. Factual stories offer different structures, they only work because they actually happened, otherwise they would be too far-fetched.'

If McNamee's subject matter is dark and ugly – violent death, cover-ups, conspiracies and corruption – his writing style is in stark contrast lyrical and heightened, full of finely wrought passages and memorable turns of phrase – for example, McGladdery and his friend finding a hiding place to smoke becomes 'an apprenticeship in the clandestine' – punctuated too by staccato sentences, a masterpiece of small-town Gothic and the 'dark grammar' of murder.

McNamee was born in Kilkeel, County Down in 1961. He is professor of creative writing at Trinity College Dublin and has written nineteen novels, six Young Adult novels, three thrillers as John Creed (winning the CWA Ian Fleming Steel Dagger award for The Sirius Crossing*) and screenplays.* The Last of Deeds *(1989) was shortlisted for the* Irish Times/*Aer Lingus Award for Irish Literature.* Blue Is the Night *(2014), part of his Blue trilogy with* The Blue Tango *(2001) and* Orchid Blue *(2010), won the Kerry Group Irish Novel of the Year.* The Vogue *(2019) was longlisted for the Gordon Burn Prize. He adapted his novel* Resurrection Man *(1994) into a 1998 film starring Stuart Townsend.*

BRIAN MOORE

20 March 1993, The Irish Post

Catholics believe that this life is the prelude to eternal life or damnation. For Brian Moore, there is no other life, only the different kinds of lives one might lead on this earth. If faith is a gift from God then it's a gift this Belfast-born writer claims he never got.

Other lives he has had in plenty – born into a middle-class Catholic Belfast family; non-combatant soldier in Europe in the Second World War; journalist in Canada; writer in New York; novelist and screenwriter in California.

Despite his agnosticism, Moore has an apparent fascination for lives informed by a religious belief. He insists, however, that this faith is just a metaphor for any conviction, be it political, social or even in one's own abilities.

In any event his characters' faith is frequently faltering. The title character in Moore's debut novel, *The Lonely Passion of Judith Hearne*, feels abandoned by God, having been left on the shelf. In a harrowing passage, Moore describes her scrabbling at the tabernacle, professing her anger and despair.

In his latest novel, God is equally absent for the narrator's mother. On her deathbed she confides in her priest son that 'there is no other life', a phrase that gives the work its title. The tone has changed from rage to resignation, just as the author's early anticlericalism has been submerged in a tolerant humanism.

Moore agrees. 'I was anti-clerical in my early books, very much so. That's because I was working my way out of that. I don't believe in religion or priests but I am no longer hostile to them. I see them like the rest of us, victims of their choice.'

No Other Life, though, is primarily a study of the messianic Jeannot, a boy who rises from poverty via the priesthood to political power on the Caribbean island of Ganae. It is loosely based on the recent history of Haiti where a Catholic priest, Fr Aristide, became prime minister before being deposed.

Moore's publicists persist in trumpeting the fact that he is 'Graham Greene's favourite living writer' even after that crooked disciple's death, a citation whose repetition might well get on one's nerves. So I wouldn't have mentioned it except that Greene did write a novel set in Haiti and had a celebrated run-in with its dictator, Papa Doc Duvalier, himself.

Moore takes it in good spirit. 'This book is the first time there would have been a connection for he wrote a book about Haiti many years ago, *The Comedians*. When I started to write this book, that suddenly flashed in my mind: *Oh my God, I'm going to get that Graham Greene thing again*. So I went and got it off the shelf and of course it was very different. My book *is* based on Haiti, on Fr Aristide, but I was always attracted to messianic leaders and here was a Catholic priest becoming leader of a country where no Catholic priest is allowed to hold any position in politics. Interestingly enough, they didn't dismiss him and the reason, I think, is they would have risked losing the faithful in that country.

'I discovered when I was writing novels that I was very interested in people who believe in something. All of us, when we're young, want to believe in something, be it political or religious. We want to have some ideal in life which we think makes it worth doing what we're doing.

'For most of us, we're disappointed, disillusioned at a fairly early age but I find that, if you write about a political loss of belief in 1960, by 1990 no one will remember what it was all about. Whereas if I write about a loss of religious belief, people will identify with that and that's probably the main reason I do it.

'I've always been interested in the idea that someone could influence other people's lives to the point that when they spoke or exhorted them to do things, they would do them. So much of the trouble in the world has come from that, from Jesus on. They all seem to me to be Jesus figures, whether they're Lenin or the Ayatollah, and they all seem to have that charismatic thing of being able when they speak to move other people. For the rest of us, we can only ask: are they saintly or are they not?'

The author made the decision not to write the novel from the perspective of the messianic figure but through the eyes of an intermediate figure, a French-Canadian priest.

'My idea is that if you're inside the head of a possessed person in your book, the readers will not follow you. It is hard to identify with a mad person. But if you're looking at them from outside you sometimes get a picture.'

Moore placed his early faith in socialism but he spent his first two post-war years in Poland where as well as Auschwitz he witnessed the rise of Stalinism.

'That changed me,' says the author. 'It didn't make me right wing, though. I'm still left wing and liberal by nature. I just don't believe in any system. That leaves me back where I started. I never joined the Communist Party. I suppose that's because, not having bought Catholicism, I wasn't going to buy anything else.'

Perhaps, though, it is this left-wing, liberal agenda that is coming to his rescue as he moves from the played-out territory of an individual's personal relationships to the relationship between the individual and an often turbulent wider society, as evidenced by such latter works as *Black Robe*, *The Colour of Blood* and *Lies of Silence*.

'I think it happened with *Black Robe*,' Moore explains, 'for I suddenly found I could write about another period or people quite different from me. At some point, your own life and the lives of your friends, their adulteries and their different things … you've written those books and you don't have any more to say about that.'

In *No Other Life*, Jeannot is an educated member of an oppressed and impoverished community, who engages politically on their behalf. Does or did Moore identify with the Catholic community in Northern Ireland in a similar way?

'No, I don't really. It's so different from what it was in my childhood when Catholics were heavily discriminated against. In fact, they still are but not to the same extent as then and the lines are broken down now. Everyone was religious and ghettoized completely. The only people who are ghettoized now are the very poor, the urban poor, who are made to hate the other side. The difference between my youth in Northern Ireland and now is that in the middle classes Catholics marry Protestants all the time. People are not religious the way they used to be. They still retain their animosity but I feel in some ways it's not so strong as it was. I feel if you remove the violence then it'll wither away. I thought it would wither away after the war.'

Surprisingly, despite having seventeen novels to his credit, many of which have been made into films, Moore has had to write screenplays to supplement his income.

'Screenplays are not fun to write. People who say that my writing is cinematic have never written a screenplay for a screenplay is boring to write – shifting angles, points of view et cetera. You can't get your own writing into it.'

So even at seventy-one Moore has no plans to retire. 'You have to keep going.' Teasing, I suggest if he were a priest, he could retire. 'If I was a doctor, I could retire,' he rejoins. 'That's one of the good things about it. It keeps you young.'

How does he handle the prospect of death? 'People used to tell me when I was younger I was always saying I was old and now they tell me that since I've become old I've stopped saying that. I think I've had a good life and would just like to go out happily.'

For Moore, love is what gives life its value, while writing is at best a source of pleasure, at worst a papering over of the abyss.

'What makes life worthwhile? Love between a man and a woman seems to me to be one thing I couldn't lose my belief in. I don't like to make these pontifical statements but that really for most people is the most important relationship in their lives. Whether they're happy or not, an awful lot of it depends on that relationship. That's why so many novels are written about it.

'There is an excitement to me in writing a novel when it's working that I don't get with anything else. There's a despair when it's not working out, when you're not going to finish it. For instance, with this book, I was worried about the ending and then it just came into my head at the very last moment and the feeling of pleasure was incredible.

'Writing is like making yourself deformed, for you're deliberately cutting yourself off from other people, deliberately choosing this thing, which is a solitary occupation. A lot of people can't take it. They write novels and then go on to write screenplays and go back into the world again.'

Moore, of course, is married and lives in Malibu, not in a monastery, but there is surely something monkish about this withdrawal, this detachment from the world. When he spoke of his disillusionment with organized socialism coming on top of his rejection of Catholicism, I asked him where that left him.

'It leaves me in a bad position, one that most of us are in. Writing novels is a way to dodge thinking about that. Sometimes, I think that's all it is.'

Moore was born in Belfast in 1921 and died in Malibu, California in 1999. The Lonely Passion of Judith Hearne *(1956) won the Authors' Club First Novel Award, one of several of his novels to be made into films. He wrote numerous screenplays including* Torn Curtain *for Alfred Hitchcock.* The Luck of Ginger Coffey *(1960) won the Governor General's Award for Fiction.* The Great Victorian Collection *(1975) won the James Tait Black Memorial Prize.* The Colour of Blood *(1987) won the* Sunday Express *Book of the Year and was shortlisted for the Booker Prize, as were* The Doctor's Wife *(1976) and* Lies of Silence *(1990).*

DERVLA MURPHY

4 December 1993, The Irish Post

Travel broadens the mind; cycling broadens the behind. To cycle from Kenya to Zimbabwe is a rare feat of stamina for a woman in her sixties. To gaze upon and ponder that continent's terrible problems of poverty, famine, political turmoil and, overshadowing everything else, the AIDS epidemic, demands an equal store of spiritual strength.

Dervla Murphy was born in Lismore, County Waterford, in 1931, where she still lives. When not travelling, her youth was spent caring for her chronically ill mother. After her mother's death in 1962, Murphy fulfilled her lifelong ambition of cycling from Ireland to India, which resulted in two travel books. *The Ukimwi Road: From Kenya to Zimbabwe* is Murphy's eleventh travel book. A love affair with travel has become a career.

The Irish author is no joyrider or sightseer, however. She travels light, sleeps rough and talks to whoever crosses her path, more often than not over a pint or three of the local brew. The travel writer with a Tusker in her tank. Her last trip, to Romania, and book, *Transylvania and Beyond*, were dogged by misfortune. Serious accidents resulted in a broken coccyx and foot, as well as concussion. Murphy also got embroiled in the problems of individuals she met. The book she quite candidly dismisses as a best-forgotten failure. Things went better on *The Ukimwi Road.* Despite close scrapes with U-turning lorries, debilitating exhaustion miles from anywhere and the almost inevitable malaria, Murphy has managed to bring the beauty and suffering of Africa and its people much closer to her readers.

Murphy's journey is made more demanding by the parlous state of many of Africa's roads, a point put in poignant perspective by this quotation from

Ugandan historian Ali Mazrui, which introduces her book: 'It was Julius Nyerere, founder president of Tanzania, who once said: "While the great powers are trying to get to the moon, we are trying to get to the village." Well, the great powers have been to the moon and back and are now even communicating with the stars. In Africa, however, we are still trying to reach the village.'

As the infrastructure crumbles, so too has society in many African states, reeling from an AIDS epidemic which, unlike any other disease, attacks not the very young or old, but the most able, leading only helpless dependents behind. Meanwhile, the West is asleep or is involved only for its own gain. Murphy reserves much of her spleen for the Third World worriers roaming the stricken countryside in brand-new white Land Rovers, aloof from the misery that surrounds them.

The beauty of cycling for Murphy is that it allows time both to absorb the beauty of the slowly-passing scenery and to soak in the feel of a place, rubbing shoulders with one's fellow man. Murphy has no time for the travel writer as shrewd, removed observer. 'You can't just regard fellow human beings as raw material to be observed and described.'

This is not to say that she doesn't do her homework. An impressive bibliography lists fifty-five books on Africa and her observations and arguments are usually backed up by passages from them. 'I read a lot of historical and sociological stuff,' Murphy agrees, 'not without a grain of salt. Your own reactions might contradict what they have written.'

Murphy makes every attempt to travel light, both in terms of physical luggage and ideological baggage. She strikes me as someone willing to learn, not straining to teach. However, her brand of feminism leads her astray even when drinking in friendly company with Jill, who runs a bar in a small Ugandan town.

The author, with thoughts of women's liberation and individual freedom, declares that the dowry is the first thing African women should get rid of, only for the sisters to 'quite rightly' put her in her place, explaining that it was one of the few ways in which their value was recognized.

According to Murphy, travel doesn't always broaden the mind. 'I think it depends on how you do it. I've met some people and travel narrowed their mind, gave them new prejudices. They would come in with their own prejudices and allow them to be reinforced. Not look for anything that might contradict.'

As for her own prejudices, she has the grace and self-knowledge to acknowledge a few: 'I suppose I find it quite hard to come to terms with the sort of day-to-day corruption. You've got to understand why people behave in that way. Jobs for the boys. We've got enough of that in Ireland to be going on with. I've never given a bribe in my life and mostly haven't found it necessary.'

En route from Nairobi airport to her bed for the night, Murphy winces at the plethora of advertising hoardings advertising 'The African Experience', a dispiriting and utterly unappealing sight for someone setting out to traverse half the continent in search of their own African experience. I already knew the answer when I asked her what she thought of Ireland's forays into interpretive centres.

'Don't talk to me. They've got one in Lismore now, in my little village. You can walk from one side to the other in seven minutes. So why do we have an interpretive centre that costs £26,000 in European money? You can't package a country. It's a hideous idea. If you want one of my prejudices, I imagine it came from America.'

This, of course, is only a side observation. Tourism is low down on the list of Africa's problems and hence Murphy's concerns. Within days of arriving in Kenya she is caught up in the tumult of anti-government demonstrations and after witnessing a riot, the Irishwoman declares, 'I do not, and never will, understand the role of violence in modern Africa.' Does she mean by that the curious air of pretence, of fun and games, that she detects in the broadly grinning faces of fleeing rioters, this whiff of lightheaded anarchy?

'I think I understand it a bit more now after spending six months in South Africa, but that's another story. What threw me was the light-heartedness. There is no doubt there is a different reaction to killing. The death rate has always been higher than in Europe simply because of the climate. Perhaps we were more fatalistic in the last century when women died in childbirth.'

It is heartening to read in *The Ukimwi Road* that Irish aid workers in Africa are not regarded in the same negative light as so many other Western, particularly UN, field workers. One African described them as 'missionaries, not experts', implying that they were in Africa because of their conscience, not just because of their competence. However, religion has in the past been the cutting edge of colonialism, so isn't such a description perhaps necessarily double-edged?

Not so in Malawi, where an Irishman, Bishop Roche, was the toast of the populace for his outspoken criticism of the Hastings Banda regime, which had led to his expulsion. Murphy bathed in the reflected glow of her fellow national's reputation. High esteem but official hostility at the sight of the harp on her passport was the inevitable price paid.

It was also in Malawi where she was forced to wear a skirt for decency's sake. This was not the first time when her dress had caused distress, though. Earlier on her journey she had been advised that the combat trousers which she had thought so practical when she bought them in Belfast marked her out to a wary people as a CIA spy or worse.

Again and again, however, the spectre of AIDS overshadows Murphy's journey. The route she takes is known in Swahili as the *Ukimwi* [AIDS] Road, giving her book its name. A multitude of beliefs and attitudes have sprung up around this catastrophe. AIDS has lost its stigma, having become like malaria; the West has a cure, which it is keeping to itself; it is a plague like any other except the West is suffering too, hence the interest; the West is making an industry out of Africa's tragedy.

One man suggests that the US needs a new enemy following the collapse of communism. Why not AIDS? No, says Murphy, aid to the developing world is a multinational business, not a crusade.

The United Nations bears the brunt of Murphy's ire. 'I think the UN has to be abolished and replaced with some organization that doesn't shell out these enormous salaries, perks and hardship allowances that obviously attract the least desirable sort of person for that work.'

On the plus side, Murphy cites the increasing practice of Western-trained doctors working alongside medicine men, the former diagnosing and the latter prescribing an African remedy. On the negative side, she cites family-planning clinics where advice is only given when both partners are present. 'What a misapprehension about the way things work in Africa. A woman has to do it on her own or not at all.'

Twenty-five years ago, Murphy visited the source of the White Nile. She remembers wondering if she would ever visit the source of the Blue Nile. On this trip, she does. Are there any other circles to be completed? 'No, I'd like to go to the Caucasus. I love mountains, there's something that grabs me.'

India she hopes to revisit; other places, no. 'I wouldn't want to go back to Nepal. Because mass tourism has made it unrecognizable and war has devastated Afghanistan and Ethiopia. I just prefer to keep my memories, though that's unrealistic as well.'

In *Tales from Two Cities*, she studied racism in Bradford and Birmingham. 'The Irish were some of the worst – three ha'pence looking down on a ha'penny.' How then does she see Ireland herself, having seen such beauty and misery all around the world – as a relatively wealthy, privileged country?

'Oh, definitely. You get very impatient with the Northern Irish. They all need their bottom smacked. There's no problem here except what they are in a sense artificially creating at the end of the twentieth century. They have no drought, starvation or epidemics. The South is virtually as corrupt as any Black African country. It's unforgivable really. But maybe we're at fault for electing this crowd of gangsters.'

And with a last puff on her cigarette, after downing her brandy-fortified coffee, she was off.

Murphy was born in Lismore, County Waterford in 1931 and died there in 2022. The author of more than twenty travel books, she made her name with her debut Full Tilt: Ireland to India with a Bicycle *(1965). Her final book was* Between River and Sea: Encounters in Israel and Palestine *(2015). She often travelled with her daughter Rachel, trips documented in* On a Shoestring to Coorg, Where the Indus Is Young, Eight Feet in the Andes, Muddling through in Madagascar *and* Cameroon with Egbert. A Place Apart, *about her travels in Northern Ireland, won the 1979 Christopher Ewart-Biggs Memorial Prize.*

PAUL MURRAY

13 November 2010, The Irish Post

It took Paul Murray seven years to write *Skippy Dies*, his A-star tragicomic novel set in a Dublin boarding school – longer than it takes to get a secondary education – and six months to chop it down from 1000 pages to 660. So however long it takes you to read it, that's the easy part, and it won't feel like homework but rather like some of the best days of your reading life.

I liked it so much I immediately started his debut novel, *An Evening of Long Goodbyes*, which was shortlisted for the Whitbread Prize in 2003, and just in case you think I'm turning into an author's pet, I found it rather disappointing, half the length but twice as hard to finish.

Skippy Dies was longlisted for the Booker and is to be adapted for the screen by Neil Jordan, which should boost sales. Murray, while pleased that the film rights have been bought by a fellow Dublin author, whose films he admires, still admits to the concern that when books are adapted for the screen they can become 'the film's stepchild'.

Skippy is fourteen-year-old Daniel Juster, a boarder at Seabrook College in Dublin, a school with striking similarities to the author's elite alma mater, Blackrock. His nickname comes from his prominent teeth, like the kangaroo, one of many examples of teenage cruelty that give the book its dark comic heart.

His best friend is Ruprecht van Doren, a tubby genius with a passion for maths and music and the search for parallel universes. The novel itself is a bit like a planetary system for there is not one main character but several, supported by a vast cast of fascinating satellites. Among these is Lori, the Frisbee-playing girl of Skippy's dreams from the school next door, and Carl, the school psychopath and drug dealer who, unfortunately for Skippy, is also in love with Lori.

Then there is Howard the Coward, Skippy's history teacher, who has returned to his old school with more than one blot in his copybook, and is torn between his American girlfriend and the hot new geography teacher, 'not to be taken Aurelie'. Also on the teaching staff is French teacher Fr Green, whose name appropriately translates as Père Vert, and acting principal Greg 'the Automator' Costigan, impatiently waiting for his ailing clerical superior to die so he can make Seabrook a model modern finishing school for the upper middle class.

This is a state-of-the-nation novel, full of ideas and lessons, with a packed curriculum that includes history, maths, physics, music and the school of hard knocks that is the playground.

For Murray, a secondary school is fertile territory for storytelling, packed with adolescents and their raging hormones, outrageous behaviour and dramatic set pieces like school discos, concerts and playground fights.

'When you're fourteen you're really vulnerable, even if you're from a wealthy background at a posh school,' says Murray. 'You're still exposed to psychopaths, whoever's walking down the street could just give you a punch. There is so much going in the teenage years, it's very dramatic, operatic, a time of high emotions.

'It is very liberating to have young characters, they're unconstrained, teenagers haven't absorbed social conventions and will say almost anything. They can be very cruel, say to a friend you're a spa or gay, whereas as you get older you learn to mask extreme feelings.

'In terms of the comedy of the book, I wanted it to be funny but realistic, you can have them saying crazy, funny things without it distorting into comedy. In the first book, [because he is so much older] Charles saying funny things turns it into a comic novel, which reduces the ability to say serious things.

'At school you're chucked in with very disparate characters from different backgrounds, you're never that close again. That allowed me to write this type of book. I wanted many different voices.

'Today we are encouraged to live in a narcissistic, self-absorbed way, to think of yourself and consume, whereas maybe twenty years ago it wasn't regarded as laudable for a grown man to pursue his fancies in the way people do now. Each character has a dream he pursues – Skippy falls in love, Ruprecht has his M theory, Howard lusts after Aurelie, all selfish pursuits that end up isolating them from other people around them in a destructive way. One point of the book is you're not an island, everybody's connected. It's a school and there's lessons in it. One lesson is you have to take care of each other.'

Is falling in love bad then?

'I don't think it's bad,' says Murray, 'but infamously it only lasts for six to eighteen months and then it has to grow into something more open, integrated into rest of your life. Everyone has had friends who fall in love and become insufferable; they don't return calls, or if they do only talk about themselves and their lover, it's a bubble that disconnects you from reality. It's an escape; some become addicted to the pursuit of the next romance.

'We are encouraged to see ourselves as the centre of the world and look for interesting dramas to insert ourselves in but that removes us from paying attention to what is around us, the relationships we're already in.'

Murray is very strong on relationships, how they can be built on preconceptions and misconceptions, literally romantic notions, but if they are to survive must penetrate beyond the facade to the heart of the person. 'Love is the area where people have to face up to reality, they are flawed, you are flawed, they are really complicated and you're never going to fully understand them.'

Skippy Dies's success has meant Murray's last six months have been spent promoting the book, which is not conducive to writing the follow-up [*The Mark and the Void*] that he promises will be a short comic novel, '300 pages max', which he intends to complete in three years. Now Skippy is such a cult hit, however, might he consider restoring all his deletions and releasing a mammoth director's cut?

The short answer is no. 'It's got good reviews,' he says, 'but quite a few say this is a long book. I don't think anyone is saying, give us more. There were problematic chapters that I'd ask myself, where will this go? When that's happening there's no room for that chapter even if it's the best you ever wrote.

'I worked really hard to get it tight, it's all set in the present tense, which technically is very challenging. People say there's too many characters but I like books that are sprawling with lots of characters, Roberto Bolano's *2666*, *Gravity's Rainbow*. The length is part of the appeal. The author has given himself leeway to develop ideas as far as he could take them.'

How much of a moral education did he have at Blackrock, run as it is by the Holy Ghost Fathers? 'I feel bad criticizing Blackrock, there were good people there. That said, it's a place of privilege. One priest was very involved in St Vincent de Paul. That aside, there was always a sense that it must be shit in Africa but never a sense that to have rich people you have to have people being shafted, never a sense that when you went out into world you could be an agency to change that. I found it very disappointing in that regard. The school motto is "Be caring, be there", but it just wasn't; there was a sense of entitlement.'

Skippy Dies may have so many characters with competing perspectives as a reaction to the straitjacket he put himself in by writing his first novel in the first person. 'I realized midway through the first book that everything had to come through Charles, which was really limiting. There were so many things you couldn't say because this character wasn't capable of feeling certain emotions or seeing certain things around him.'

While Murray is trying to communicate some deeper truths about life through his fiction, this book is also about lying, from betrayals in relationships to the elite school peddling myths about history and the present. The author documents a string of recent deceptions on an anti-heroic scale, from the Iraq war, 'such a fucking distortion of democracy', to the internet bubble, the end of history, the property bubble, the financial crash. 'We live in a world where we proceed from one enormous lie to another.'

Murray is a storyteller with a deep suspicion of narratives that claim to explain the world. 'Notions of honour and patriotism sent nine million men to be butchered for no reason [in the First World War]. It seems to me that the desire for a narrative is a really destructive thing. Life is unknowable. After the last century, one thing you'd be wary of is a guy who's got this great system and all you've got to do is go along with it. Life is arbitrary, it unceasingly amazes me how people are so drawn to the idea reality can be mastered despite things happening again and again like credit bubbles.'

A character quotes Rupert Graves approvingly saying that the secret of survival is to keep a strong sense of humour. Murray manages to juggle big ideas with big laughs.

'As a person I would be quite drawn to making jokes. Faced with the terrifying unknowability of reality, make jokes about it! Thomas Beecham refers to metaphor as a thrust at truth and a lie. A joke is sort of the same thing, a way of engaging with the world without trying to impose a false construction on it. This is a way of surviving, a way of connecting to other people in a very honest way. Connecting to other people is a way of staving off the coldness of life. What I don't like is literature that is serious in a didactic way.'

Murray was born in Dublin in 1975. His debut, An Evening of Long Goodbyes *(2003) was shortlisted for the Whitbread First Novel Award and the Kerry Group Irish Fiction Award.* Skippy Dies *(2010) was shortlisted for the Costa Novel Award, longlisted for the Booker Prize and was a finalist for the National Book Critics Circle Award.* The Mark and the Void *(2016) was joint winner of the Bollinger Everyman Wodehouse Prize.* The Bee Sting *(2023) won the Nero Book Award and Irish Novel and overall Book of the Year and was shortlisted for the Booker Prize.*

ÉILÍS NÍ DHUIBHNE

20 July 2025, The Irish Times

It is typical of Éilís Ní Dhuibhne's modesty that she was delighted even to be shortlisted for the €50,000-a-year role of Laureate of Irish Fiction. This week's news of her appointment, succeeding Colm Tóibín, Sebastian Barry and Anne Enright, has left her 'overwhelmed'.

It feels like 'even more of an honour', she says, than her PEN award for an outstanding contribution to literature, the Hennessy Irish Writing Hall of Fame award or her appointment as Burns Professor at Boston College.

More pragmatically, she observes that another difference is that it involves 'a fair amount of responsibilities and duties. It's a very public role. You don't just grab the medal and walk off.'

This laureate will not be resting on her laurels. While she is still discussing with the Arts Council the details of her three-year programme, one idea that appeals to her is visiting every county to celebrate its distinctive literary heritage.

As a bilingual writer, the daughter of an Irish-speaking father from the Donegal Gaeltacht who grew up speaking Irish in Dublin, she will also be promoting literature in Irish, 'which I've already been doing thanks to *The Irish Times*', a reference to her reviewing work, which she thinks helped raise her profile for the laureateship.

'People believe they can't read a book in Irish, that it's too difficult, but it just takes a bit of effort. Even when I'm reading, I would come across words every couple of pages that I'd need to look up, but it's a lot easier now with the internet. I've been learning Bulgarian for ten years [she has a Bulgarian daughter-in-law] and have to look up a word on every line. I know that sounds a bit schoolmarmy.'

Ní Dhuibhne has already done her bit to popularize reading in Irish by writing a bestselling series of crime novels as Gaeilge, beginning with *Dúnmharú sa Daingean* (Murder in Dingle). 'People told me they'd never read a book in Irish before and were surprised that they could.'

She is also interested in exploring European literature and Ireland as part of Europe; new Irish from other parts of the world; and exploring what makes a good story.

Ní Dhuibhne is a most versatile author, having written more than thirty books, in both Irish and English, for children, adolescents and adults, spanning novels, short stories, plays, memoirs and literary criticism. Although her best-known work is probably *The Dancers Dancing*, which was shortlisted for the Women's Prize for Fiction (then the Orange Prize) in 2000, her preferred form is the short story.

In her introduction to the author's *Selected Stories* (Blackstaff Press, 2023), Prof Margaret Kelleher of UCD praised 'their incisiveness and wry humour, and her keen eye for the incongruous and the familiar made strange'.

'When I'm writing at my most serious and deepest, it's the short story,' Ní Dhuibhne says. 'When I'm writing for younger people, it's made up completely, although the stories do end up with something of you in them. My short stories are closer to my true personality.

'The short story is a focus on a moment of truth, when the veil of reality is lifted for a moment to reveal a deeper truth. Because it is short, it has a connection to time which is more controllable. Shelley described inspiration as like a spark to a coal, which begins to fade as soon as you start writing. With a novel it fades on day one and you have to keep rekindling it. With a short story it doesn't have time to fade. You can grab the energy of inspiration and get it drafted before it's gone. That's why short stories can achieve a sort of perfection it's almost impossible for a novel to achieve.

'The only guideline I like about short stories is that something has to happen to someone on the surface, a dramatic incident of some kind, and something has to happen underneath, an excavation, what the meaning of the story is.'

And yet the short story is, for many readers, the poor relation to the novel. 'Readers like to get lost in a story, immersed,' Ní Dhuibhne says. 'They don't like dipping in and out, just getting to know a setting and the characters and then it's on to the next one.' That's why she feels long short stories are the most successful, more like short novels.

The Dancers Dancing, a coming-of-age novel set in an Irish college in the Donegal Gaeltacht, that uniquely Irish rite of passage, grew out of a short story, 'Blood and Water', after Dolores Walsh, a fellow member of her writers' group, told her she could get a novel out of it.

'It's about a group of girls who go from Dublin to Irish college and it explores the relationship of the English- and Irish-speaking worlds, the urban–rural divide. My main character Orla is in a slightly challenging position. She is not a complete outsider as her mother's family is from that area, she has lots of relatives there and is ashamed of them.

'Orla doesn't yet accept the wholeness of her personality. This teenager is trying to navigate a way through middle-class Dublin life and this other side of her, poor Irish-speaking people in Donegal. That arose from my experience as a child and teenager. I aspired to be more upper-class than we were. Quite a lot of my fiction explores the connection between past and present, our ancestry.'

She is not sure she can describe her voice as a writer. 'Maybe I'd aspire to make it intimate, very gripping. I have quite a comic voice, I'm at home with irony.'

Ní Dhuibhne has also spent many years teaching creative writing, at UCD, Trinity, Boston College and the Irish Writers Centre. Her pupils included Colin Barrett, Henrietta McKervey, Andrea Carter, Jamie O'Connell and Jessica Traynor.

The new laureate has a rich literary social life, with a lot of writer friends. She has been in the same writing group for forty years now with authors Catherine Dunne, Lia Mills and Liz McManus, among others. It started as a national Irish women writers' workshop set up in 1985 by Eavan Boland to address the under-representation of women's voices in Irish literature.

Ní Dhuibhne studied folklore at university alongside English and is now president of the Folklore of Ireland society. The old stories are a big influence on her own writing.

'That is one of my characteristics. I often counterpoint contemporary, modern stories with a folk legend or tale. It gives a different dimension, a deepening.'

The first time she did it was with 'Midwife to the Fairies', the story of a secret birth, in which a midwife goes to a fairy hill and assists with the birth of a child. (The other inspiration was newspaper reports about the 1984 Kerry babies case.)

'Perhaps it was a way the community had of telling reality in a coded way. I am a folklorist, I do it to offer an interpretation of the old story. On the other hand it gives depth and lustre to what might be a thin little story without it. Old stories have a luminosity and beauty, a wildness of imagination that can be lacking in contemporary life. These stories have survived for centuries because they have some attractive quality.'

Ní Dhuibhne's Irish-language memoir, *Fáinne Geal an Lae* [*The Dawning of the Day*] (Clo Iar Chonnacht, 2023), tracks her childhood until the age of twelve in 1966. 'It ends on a very optimistic note with the fiftieth-anniversary commemoration of the Rising. My sister and I were lucky with the time of our birth, just in time for free secondary education and grants for university. I wrote it during Covid when everyone was writing memoirs. My life was so different to my children's, I wanted to document it.'

Her other memoir, *Ten Thousand Days*, addresses the death of her husband, Bo, and their lives together. Was its purpose to process or record? 'In the first instance, the former, to process my feelings of devastation and grief at the loss of my husband, but also to record the story of our relationship.

'Bo's death was very difficult, traumatic and horrible. It does take some years, but gradually one gets back to being myself. I think of Bo and I miss him in various ways but I feel healed. Writing the book certainly helped me get through the first three or four years but the real healer is time.'

Her grief was also channelled into two superb short stories, 'The Coast of Wales' and 'New Zealand Flax', commissioned by Sinéad Gleeson and Belinda McKeon respectively for their anthologies. 'I couldn't write about anything else. That was the only thing I was thinking about. They are example of stories I would not have written if I hadn't been invited to.'

Ní Dhuibhne has had two great influences in her writing life, Alice Munro and Ailbhe Smyth.

Back in the 1980s, soon after she had married and had two children, she joined a women's studies forum that Smyth had set up in UCD. 'She opened my eyes to cultural feminism, the facts of literary history, that there weren't as many women writers as there should be. I had been blind to the facts. I did English at UCD without realizing we only read three women (Emily Dickinson, Emily Brontë and Jane Austen) in three years. It was consciousness-raising.

'I could have let writing go but it became more than a matter of self-expression or personal ambition. It seemed I was now part of a movement of women writers of Ireland. It took off and now we have gender equality in fiction. Women are no longer ignored. There is no way you could have a syllabus these days that excluded women.'

Alice Munro, the late Canadian author, 'showed me a way of writing about the past and connecting it to the present' through her stories about her ancestors. 'It definitely influenced "Blood and Water". Before that, my stories were really corny, probably because I wasn't linking past and present, just taking my father's anecdotes and trying to transform them into literary stories.'

Munro's mesmerizing, intimate style pulled her right into the story and her protagonists' unpretentious lives. 'It seemed artless though obviously was not at all. I loved her luminosity, the way she handles time, the way her stories spread out and are not tight little stories focused on one thing. I learned a lot about composition from her.'

A wry, dry humour is another of the laureate's trademarks. 'The Literary Lunch', a satire on self-serving members of an arts organization dining for Ireland, is her most popular story. The Arts Council must have a sense of humour, too.

'Perhaps they haven't read it,' she laughs. 'I know everyone thinks it is based on the Arts Council but it's not at all. It was inspired by another committee.'

As well as the late English comic writer David Lodge and Samuel Beckett's bleakly comic novels, she was weaned on an Inter Cert anthology featuring Somerset Maugham and Saki.

Finally, why should people read fiction?

'It's hard to answer that without sounding trite,' she says, 'but it is the best way of getting inside the head and heart and personality of other people, total empathy. I think that is its trump card in art. It's so entertaining, you're entering into the lives of other people. In fiction there is an intimacy of contact with humanity, it's psychologically insightful, it teaches you something.'

Ní Dhuibhne was born in Dublin in 1954 and named Laureate of Irish Fiction in 2025. She is the author of five novels in English and six in Irish, including Aisling nó Iníon A *(2015), as well as seven short-story collections, seven books for children, three plays and a memoir,* Twelve Thousand Days: A Memoir of Love and Loss *(2018). She was shortlisted for the Women's Prize for Fiction for* The Dancers Dancing. *A member of Aosdána, she won the Hennessy Literature Award in 2014 and the 2015 Irish PEN Award.*

CONOR O'CALLAGHAN

13 February 2021, The Irish Times

In *We Are Not in the World*, Conor O'Callaghan's compelling and profoundly moving second novel, a middle-aged Irishman journeys in a borrowed HGV from the North of England to the South of France with his damaged daughter as a stowaway in his cab and a lorry-load of regrets trailing behind him.

Together with his 2016 debut, *Nothing on Earth*, about a family disappearing from a ghost estate, which the late Eileen Battersby praised as an 'extraordinary, low-key and pitch-perfect novel … one of the most impressive pieces of Irish fiction writing' in more than twenty years, the new novel establishes O'Callaghan as one of the most talented contemporary Irish writers.

The author teaches at Sheffield Hallam University and first made his name as a poet; he has five collections with Gallery Press, the first in 1993, the latest in 2017. Fellow poet and critic John McAuliffe says: 'Iconoclastic about the more traditional subject matters of Irish poetry, Conor's poems travel freely between American, Italian and English locations, although often returning to the unglamorous joys of his home town Dundalk. His poems are often driven by a relish for ingenious and distinctive sound effects and he likes experimenting with poetic forms, from the sonnet and villanelle to a long sequence which began as a Twitter feed with each section using a tweet's 140 characters …'

O'Callaghan admits he first approached novel writing with 'a poet's superiority complex. I thought it would be easy.' He soon learned 'the skill of the thing is the choreography of characters, getting them upright, moving forward through three-dimensional space, doing stuff, talking to people, in a way that is credible, original and recognizable. Poetry doesn't do any of that stuff.'

He is also in awe of the novelist's command of time and pace. '*Brokeback Mountain* by Annie Proulx is amazing. Her timing is like a set of foxtrots, *slow slow, quick quick, slow*. In one passage she moved five years forward in two paragraphs, without saying the stupid stuff.'

His method is to write a first draft – not a short story; more a blueprint or a treatment – of 5000 words, then rewrite it as 10,000 words and keep doubling. 'A novel is a big beast of a thing; it's like having a dragon by the tail. What I was doing is amplifying space, pushing out the walls, a gradual accretion. To sit down and write 70,000 words from scratch, it would be a runaway train, with no idea where it is going.'

'A friend says words in relation to a novel have the same relationship as bricks to architecture. The words are the last thing you pay attention to. Coming from the world of poetry, that is anathema. But I never wanted to write that weird hybrid called "a poet's novel". They were always this lyrical handful of fog, literary dry ice, and no narrative momentum.

'I discovered that writing nicely, elegantly, has almost nothing to do with it. Any twit can write a lyrical sentence. A novel is a feat of imaginative engineering. It's an architectural structure. Up to a point, the words are the least important bit.'

O'Callaghan and his protagonist have much in common – both Irish emigrants who have lived in the US and England; a marriage break-up; a HGV licence; and a fascination with the myth of Oisín. So the fiction is underpinned by a solid foundation of personal truths.

'The best books are the ones you shouldn't write,' he says. The novel as confessional. *Are you really going to write about this?* you ask yourself.

'All fiction starts in fact,' he goes on. 'Over the process of realization, a story migrates from fact into fiction. You describe something that really happened, and inevitably you come to the crossroads where you recognize that inserting something that didn't really happen makes for a better story. You do that once and forgive yourself for doing so. Then you do it again and again, until the story has shed its factual basis like an old husk.

'In the end, you have a story that feels true but is not remotely factual. Novels start years before they get written or published. They geminate. This one? Maybe as long ago as the mid-seventies, when I first heard the story of Oisín and Tír na nÓg.

'An elderly priest would get wheeled in once a week to tell us stories. Biblical parables and Irish myths. Fr Collins told us about Oisín: going home after three years that turn out to be 300 years, to a home changed beyond recognition and everyone gone. I was only a kid, but I remember finding the story mind-blowing. The original dystopia.'

In 1993 O'Callaghan did a FÁS scheme in Dundalk. Obliged to do a training course, he picked truck driving 'as a gesture of youthful ironic arrogance'. He drove a rigid fixed-axle truck around an industrial estate and passed with flying colours. 'Ever since then I had this idea of a story about driving a truck.'

After his marriage ended in 2008, he was living alone in Manchester and seriously considered going on the road. 'But I didn't go on the road, nor even close. Instead, I developed in my head a story about an Irishman based in England who goes on the road to escape his life. That's what writers do: we write stories in lieu of experience.

'When I came back to Ireland in the late noughties, after the financial crash, I always felt like Oisín. All the shops closed down, and nobody around. So the story of the man in a truck and Oisín on his horse got sort of superimposed in my head.'

In fact, if the protagonist shares some DNA with his author, it's because he is partly based on O'Callaghan's father, previously the subject of an extended prose collage in his 2017 collection, *Live Streaming*.

'I come from a family of insurance brokers. My father's family. I think on some level loss is a natural theme for me as a result, since that whole industry is predicated around the risk of loss and the assessment of loss. This character, this exile with the stage-Irish moniker of Paddy, has lost everything: his family, his home and his sense of belonging. He is adrift on the road with his broken daughter, in the wake of the banking crash and in the midst of a refugee crisis. He talks to her, and he remembers lots about his past, particularly his relationship with his mother, after whom his daughter was named.'

O'Callaghan's father trained at Lloyds in the City and was in digs with the comedian Dave Allen. 'My father was a drinker and ultimately his younger brother took over the family business. My father ended his professional life driving a truck for Fyffes, delivering bananas around the North. Their mother lived alone out on the coast, and after he left the family home my father lived with her.

'If I wanted to do anything in this book, I wanted to anatomize that side of Ireland which rarely gets into books: the moderately affluent lower-middle classes, who play golf and bridge. And I wanted to add to the landscape of Irish fiction the littoral north-east. From Baltray up to Carlingford Lough; the part of the world that means more to me imaginatively than anywhere.'

Born in Newry and reared in Dundalk, O'Callaghan has a Border sensibility. As entertaining as he is erudite, he laughingly recalls a job interview at Queen's University. All was going swimmingly until he sank himself at the end, shooting himself in the foot. O'Callaghan was asked the softball question had he any family connections to Belfast? He said no, then remembered that, actually yes, his grandfather had served eighteen months in Crumlin Road jail after a raid on Clones police station.

The past has an uncanny habit of catching up with you. O'Callaghan didn't get the job.

Another inspiration was the work of artist Eithne Jordan. For a long time O'Callaghan's kitchen was decorated with postcards of her beautiful marginal landscapes of the south of France, car parks, a billboard on waste ground, a flyover and underpass.

'I wanted to write about liminal spaces, car parks and supermarkets after hours. I wanted to get text messages into it as it's so much a part of the way we live now. The single biggest challenge facing writers now is how to get virtual experience into a novel, so much of our lives are screen time. Part of the job of the novelist is to embody what it is like to be alive at a certain time, a commitment to realism.'

As the text messages that bubble through the story are a form of disembodied speech, so is much of our lives spent in our heads, processing events. For the bereaved, the present is a pale imitation and the past is more precious and real, the land where they long to dwell. But for all that you can fiddle with a lorry's tachometer, turning back the hands of time is another Sisyphean struggle.

O'Callaghan believes his two novels are very different tonally, yet both have a susceptibility to the Gothic, the otherworldly.

'Characters are there and then are not. I never understood why that was considered unrealistic or fantastical. It happens all the time. Our loved ones just disappear. They were in the same room as us yesterday, and now they're gone, and we have to circumnavigate their ever-diminishing absences. We try to rationalize it with biology. We construct a grammar around it. We call it death. But truth is we have no idea what just happened, where they went to and if we'll ever see them again.'

While *Nothing on Earth* was completed with an ambiguity that was intentional and remains absolute throughout, the new one has a resolution. 'I set myself a challenge to insert a little light at the end. Hope is really hard to do well, in a way that isn't clichéd.'

Dialogue that is often caustic and always realistic is a particular strength of his.

'My father was a sort of gentleman barfly. I spent so many hours of my childhood eavesdropping on the phatic exchanges of him and his cronies. Meaningless blather I loved and found so funny. Freud supposedly once said that the Irish was the only nationality impervious to psychoanalysis. We use language to conceal rather than reveal. Saying all these gorgeous hollow phrases to one another, we're hiding behind language.

'The exchanges between the father and the daughter in most of the chapters of this novel are like that. They speak to each other as if blowing bubbles: lovely shiny, floating bubbles that just disappear.'

We Are Not in the World is also remarkable for his frank treatment of sex. 'I have many faults,' O'Callaghan says. 'Cowardice is not one of them. It is quite explicit. *Nothing on Earth* has a couple of sex scenes that went completely unnoticed, maybe because they're too subtle. Be hard to miss them in this novel!

'There is this received wisdom that we shouldn't write about sex. Most sex scenes are terrible. And now we have the tyranny of the Bad Sex Prize, which is just small-minded, reactionary prudery dreamed up by Auberon Waugh.

'It has to be possible to write about physical love in a way that isn't nasty or sexist. We can't just relinquish that to public-school satire. We can't pretend desire and sex don't exist, for fear of being ridiculed. If a Martian came down to earth and read a fair cross-section of literary fiction to get a handle on human life, they'd have no idea how our species procreated.

'I love Eimear McBride's fearlessness in the face of sex. Sally Rooney too. I thought the representations of sex in the TV adaptation of *Normal People* were great. It was so refreshing to see it thought through and made original, rather than just the usual pimply bottom between a pair of legs while the orchestra hammers away in the background!'

We Are Not in the World is also an emigrant novel. Accepting as an exile that you cannot go home is to reconcile yourself to the myth of return. The Ireland that you think of as home is in fact your childhood. It is not so much a place as a place in time. So you stay away and reconcile yourself to the dislocations of the emigrant life or go back and absorb the shock of the returnee, to discover your friends are dead and gone or turning grey, or to make a half-life on a ghost estate as O'Callaghan once did, captured memorably in *Nothing on Earth*.

'I've long been obsessed with the stage-Irish trope. The thing about being Irish in England is they assume this is you – the feckless, garrulous drinker – and it's hard not to slip into that role. There's a gravitational pull towards that cliché that's almost impossible to resist.'

'The plight of Paddy in Blighty,' his protagonist calls it, 'they hear the accent and guess salt of the earth … You realize how expedient it might be to let them go on thinking that.'

Last summer O'Callaghan did a one-man protest over deafening demolition work at Sheffield University near his house. 'It was on the BBC: daft Irish bloke brings building site to a standstill and sings "You'll Never Walk Alone" for the cameras. The point is, I couldn't have done that in Ireland. I wouldn't have had the nerve. Being Irish in England gives you liberties, based upon supercilious prejudice on their part, but you take advantage all the same.

'Exile has changed me massively. When I moved to America in 2004 I was a fairly regular lad by Irish standards. I became this character overnight. I could see Yanks nudging one another and whispering "This guy's hilarious!" I suddenly became Billy Connolly. Then I'd go home to Ireland in the summer and realize that the character routine simply doesn't wash at home.

'Once you leave, there's no going back and you never really arrive on the other shore. You're stuck indefinitely in between. You have to make your peace with that. There is a fork in the road, where you go home or you make your peace with the fact you will never live in Ireland again. I love Ireland, love the crack, the fact people speak to each other, which doesn't happen anywhere else. Returned emigrants are among the saddest of folks. Lost souls.'

The year 2020 was a tough one. O'Callaghan was in Ireland promoting this novel the week before lockdown. Slow learners, we bumped elbows when we met and thoughtlessly shook hands when we parted. A week later the book was bumped to 2021. He has tested positive twice for Covid and been quite sick.

'A bloody awful year, all told. Culminating with the fireworks for Brexit all over Sheffield at 11pm on 31 December. Every once in a while history throws its cards up in the air – wars, financial crashes, pandemics – and we're left to see how the cards fall.

'Just to come back to the Oisín myth: we've all been in exile from our lives for most of the past year, in this weird timeless exile from the old normal. Like home, do we really imagine that those lives will be there intact when we are allowed to go back? I don't think so. At least not exactly. The old normal isn't there waiting for us, any more than home or the past are there awaiting our return.'

Still, O'Callaghan was relieved that his book got pulled. 'But it was printed and sat on my shelf all year, which was weird. [His editor] Fiona Murphy sent me a bottle of Redbreast whiskey, which was rather classy. All 2020 I couldn't stop thinking about Flann O'Brien's *At Swim-Two-Birds*: it was published in 1939, they sold a hundred copies and then war was declared. The book was stored in boxes in Longmans and then their offices got bombed and the book was lost until the mid-sixties. Happily, that didn't happen here and mine now appears.'

When we spoke last year, he had no intention of starting a new novel immediately, citing approvingly the example of Richard Ford taking two years to think and makes notes before creating *The Sportswriter*. Then Covid intervened.

'I've spent all last year working on a novel. I usually work very slowly. I had no intention of starting a new big thing, but had an idea and I just blasted into it to keep the head above water. I wanted to write about the lockdown experience, but these things take processing and writing about it while it's happening seems impossible to me.

'It's set in Ireland in the Second World War. A time of weird stagnation, when bodies from this distant conflict occasionally washed ashore. I realize that it's about, indirectly, what we're going through now. Sounds grim, but it's actually very jolly. I'm writing about the Border up in Cooley, and the Emergency, and bodies washing ashore.'

O'Callaghan was born in Newry, County Down, in 1968 but grew up in Dundalk, County Louth. He lives in Sheffield and teaches creative writing at Lancaster University. He published six poetry collections: The History of Rain *(1993);*

Seatown *(1999)*; *Fiction (2005);* The Server Room *(2013);* The Sun King *(2013); and* Live Streaming *(2017). His debut novel,* Nothing on Earth *(2016), was shortlisted for the Kerry Group Irish Novel of the Year. His second,* We Are Not in the World *(2021) was also well received. He also wrote* Red Mist: Roy Keane and the Football Civil War *(2004).*

BRIDGET O'CONNOR

23 June 2007, The Irish Times

The ticking of life's clock has always been prominent in the stories of London-Irish writer Bridget O'Connor. But five years ago when she was forty, and pregnant with her first child, the alarm went off. She found out she had breast cancer.

It's a subject she is naturally sensitive about, but her reluctance to dwell on it has less to do with protecting her privacy than the fear of being pigeonholed and how she will be perceived.

'I don't want to be a breast-cancer writer – and also I won't get any work, no one will employ me,' she adds, tweaking tragedy by the tail, the hallmark of her temperament and her writing.

Today, Connie-Rose is in her second year at primary school and O'Connor has had a very good prognosis – 'I've just got my five-year legs' – so she can afford to dwell on a welcome side-effect of confronting the ultimate deadline: increased productivity.

Having got to her mid-thirties with just two fast-paced and blackly funny short-story collections to her name, *Here Comes John* and *Tell Her You Love Her*, she hit writer's block as she attempted the transition to a novel. But now, with one leap sideways, she finds herself free and rattling off scripts for stage and big screen, both solo and with her partner, Peter Straughan.

Sixty Six, their screenplay about the neglected younger son of a London Jewish family whose bar mitzvah clashes with the World Cup final at Wembley, is just out on DVD.

Mrs Ratcliffe's Revolution, their film about a family of English communists who swap Marks & Spencer for Marx and Engels by emigrating to East Germany in

1968, is due out this summer, starring Catherine Tate. And they've just handed over their version of *A Christmas Carol* to their production company, Working Title – it's 'another black comedy, keeping to the spirit of the Alistair Sim one, which we loved, but more frenetic, with a nastier, lonelier Scrooge, and we have more fun with the ghosts'.

She has also just finished adapting for the screen her play *The Lovers*, about a blind gigolo passing on the secrets of the trade to a young apprentice. Because the location has shifted from Newcastle to the US, the material is a little racier, edgier. 'It's now getting to the stage of thinking, *God, I hope Connie doesn't read this*, or will she think I'm really like this or just pretending to be like this.'

O'Connor believes her harrowing experience galvanized her writing. 'It was a double whammy,' she says. 'Having a daughter as well, everything changed anyway. The same switch went on – oh, I haven't got all day suddenly. God, I'd better do some work, not sit round watching breakfast television any more. I felt a kind of electricity – the day is not as long as I thought it was. Also, being a mother for the first time, I definitely want to be around. I don't know if you would feel that anyway though, if you had a child: suddenly a bit more cautious.'

With survival comes a sense of duty, however. 'It's a difficult thing to talk about. It's almost as if you're supposed to write better stuff if there's a slight stain on the horizon – and that's not necessarily true. You keep on reading the same rubbish books and watching rubbish television.'

As part of her recuperation, Bridget, Connie and Peter moved to Cork for a year (Bridget's parents are from Cork and Limerick) armed with a few commissions. 'It was a bit of an odd thing to do in a way because we didn't know anybody,' she says. 'We ended up in quite a nice little house opposite an industrial park on South Douglas Road, There was a huge dip in the road that filled up with water so we could hardly cross it. Because I'd had Connie and I'd been a bit ill we thought we'd start again somewhere else. It was an excuse to clear out of Hackney.

"We wrote loads, that was the good thing. We were holed up on the top floor. But it rained so much we came back. It poured and poured. It was a very quiet, recovering time.'

The couple wrote *Mrs Ratcliffe's Revolution* there, based on the real-life experience of Maggie Norris, a producer and actor. 'She was Mike Baldwin's florist girlfriend in *Coronation Street*,' says O'Connor.

Mr Ratcliffe is an idealistic communist, who shifts his family behind the Iron Curtain, where his wife, inadvertently at first, helps people to escape to the West.

'That's why it's her revolution. It's a black comedy with a twist. It was originally supposed to be quite a dark tale about a woman being quite lonely and isolated. It's about political idealism and the corruption of that, about how you should live your life, finding out about the shabbiness of the DDR, of the secrets. We went to the museums, saw the files; you could see a family pitted against each other in a schoolgirl's notebook.'

It took five years and countless rewrites to make the film, as each new director and investor wanted a new draft. Now O'Connor is worried it will be overshadowed by *The Lives of Others*, the brilliant dissection of East Germany's petty tyranny, and the earlier *Goodbye Lenin!*.

The couple also wrote a site-specific play, *News From the Seventh Floor*, which was staged as a promenade play in Clements, the old-fashioned, patriarchal Watford department store on which *Are You Being Served?* was based. 'We even met the funny woman who Mrs Slocombe was based on.'

O'Connor also wrote a play, *The Flags*, a black comedy reminiscent of Martin McDonagh's works, about two unreliable lifeguards on a deserted Irish beach plotting their promotion to lovely Banna Strand. It was staged in Manchester and Dublin and is to return to the Royal Exchange in Manchester in September.

'It went down well in Manchester but got a few mean reviews in Dublin,' O'Connor says. 'Part of the gag of the play is the Oirishness of it. It's got this slightly Father Ted-ish thing, but really it's a black comedy. I planned it more as a tragic tale, a follow-on from my short-story writing, where I'm interested in friends and relationships, almost psychological, I hope. I was trying to play with the idea of people being slightly monstrous, stuck together in their own world on the edge of the Atlantic.'

Whether deliberately or subconsciously, cancer has always cropped up in her writing. 'Oddly enough, it always has. My two collections of short stories are riddled with it,' she says. 'I always wrote about it even before I had it. I suppose I've always been conscious that my family has a history of cancer.

'In *The Flags*, which I wrote when I was in Ireland recovering and having bad hair, one of the characters is a cancer survivor. But then every single family seems to have somebody with it – maybe that's why I don't like to go on about it.'

The rattle of new life was O'Connor's second wake-up call.

'Actually, I found having Connie very energizing,' she says. 'I was bone idle before. Now I've written more than I ever have, especially in the first couple of years because of where we lived. Before, because I didn't have a commission, I wrote when I felt like it. When I was single my day was my own. Now, with a child, you've got to organize your time. Suddenly the day is very short. Also you need to make money in a way you didn't have to before.'

How did she make the transition from short-story writer stuck on a first novel to successful screenwriter?

'I was writing a third collection, which I still go back to every now and again, but I had to write a novel to sell my stories – that's just the way it was,' she says. 'I tried to flog a novel, but really I wasn't very good at it. I still would like to write one, but I think I'm really a short-story writer. I have a ten-page span and then I collapse under the weight of it. I couldn't maintain the interest in the whole thing myself. I suppose I could have been a different kind of novelist, I could have had multiple narratives, but I never really wanted to do that. I was really interested at the time in fast-talking characters, where the story's over in the blink of an eye and done and dusted. I was also interested in lots of monologues, so that's why I started moving into playwriting. Because I had this long hiatus and I had a child, and because I was with Peter, we started writing films. It was a kind of natural progression.'

Their creative partnership is 'fairly amicable', she says. It grew out of writing side by side in a tiny flat in Hackney, sharing one computer, taking it in turns to write. 'Now we try to do a slightly more sophisticated version of that, where we're not in the same room. One of us will do the first draft, the other will then take it on, have different ideas. We come together to discuss it, but we also wake up talking about it.

'We had disagreements when we were in Ireland because we were in a learning curve, lot of spats and slamming doors, but Peter was slightly more experienced than me. The thing about screenwriting is that if you have a good idea then it doesn't go away, you can reinvent it and slot it in somewhere else. Nothing is set in stone. I didn't know that at the start, so you'd fight for something you didn't have to fight for. Film-making is very collaborative. It's not really your work, everyone has a say, and most of the film gets done in the cutting room anyway. It's an odd relationship – you disown it almost instantly, or you don't own it in the first place.'

The team behind *Sixty Six* were a little worried about it missing its moment, as it was released after the World Cup last year, but it did well.

'The football in it was fantastic,' says O'Connor. 'There was unseen footage. I think the film worked on quite a few levels: it's not threatening, it's quite warm, family-centred.'

There are quite a few films about the Jewish experience in Britain but almost nothing about the Irish in Britain. 'That's true,' says O'Connor, who once wrote a funny column about an Irish dancer for me at *The Irish Post*. 'I don't know why that is. I have a half-baked idea about doing something called "The Medals" about an Irish dancer. I remember in the 1970s going round in coaches doing Irish dancing, part of a troupe almost, at a time when it was not the greatest thing to be Irish.

'I did a radio play ages ago called *Becoming the Rose*, a stupid comedy about somebody who was desperate to win the Rose of Tralee, a kind of Irish overload where she was force-fed the singing and dancing but really loved it, was really competitive and wanted to win at all costs, including wiping out the opposition. We went to Tralee with a Kodak camera and a microphone and had a great time interviewing beauty queens until they got wise and told us to clear off.'

O'Connor was born in London to Irish parents in 1961. She died in Hove in 2010. Harp *won the 1991 Time Out Short-Story Prize. Her story collections are* Here Comes John *(1993);* Tell Her You Love Her *(1997); and* After a Dance: Selected Stories *(2024). Her work features in* The New Picador Book of Contemporary Irish Fiction. *Plays include* Becoming the Rose, *which won an Arts Council England award in 2000, and* The Flags. *She and her husband, Peter Straughan, won a Bafta Award for Best Adapted Screenplay for* Tinker Tailor Soldier Spy *and were nominated for an Academy Award.*

JOSEPH O'CONNOR

25 May 2019, The Irish Times

On the morning of my interview with Joseph O'Connor to discuss his new novel, I posted on social media our two previous interviews – one from 2010, when *Ghost Light* was published; another from 1991, with the author looking raffish in a leather jacket and thick-framed Elvis Costello glasses.

The spectacle triggered a domestic tsunami of slagging, he says, for the writer has long since swapped black leather for linen, and now looks more like a cultured cleric, a literary canon.

His writing style and philosophy have also evolved. 'That interview you sent me from '91, this young fella saying "the purpose of the novel isn't to entertain, it's to change the world" – there's moments as a 56-year-old you don't feel that anymore!'

He began his career with the coming-of-age novel *Cowboys & Indians* but came of age as a novelist with *Star of the Sea*, a Famine epic that became a number one bestseller thanks to its endorsement on the first Richard & Judy Book Club by Bob Geldof – 'a childhood hero' – and Bonnie Greer, 'whose critical writing I love'.

O'Connor has always been an entertaining writer – from his much-loved columns collected as *The Secret World of the Irish Male* to his RTÉ Radio Drivetime essays – but setting a book in the 1840s had allowed an author raised on the spare style of John McGahern and Raymond Carver to play with the traditions and flourishes of the Victorian novel.

'Dennis Potter said every author should look back on their early works with affectionate contempt. I think with my first few books I was learning how to write – in public. I did my MA in creative writing by publishing novels. *Star of the Sea* gave me the confidence and security to approach my writing in a different way, publish less often, make every book as good as it could be.'

O'Connor has found his forte in historical fiction, often with a literary theme. The 'belligerently literary' *Redemption Falls* was followed by the superb *Ghost Light*, the love story of J.M. Synge and the actor Molly Allgood, brought vividly to life by a generous act of the author's imagination.

Shadowplay sees O'Connor return to the stage and a more complicated love affair, a ménage à trois featuring two of the greatest actors of the Victorian era, Henry Irving and Ellen Terry, and, in their shadow and in their thrall, Bram Stoker, whose success would sadly be posthumous, 'one of the delicious and delightful ironies for the novelist'.

Stoker, like O'Connor more than a century later, would leave Dublin for London to pursue his dreams, lured by Irving to manage his Lyceum Theatre. The real drama, of course, takes place off-stage, as the enterprise teeters on the brink of financial collapse, Irving's reckless genius barely restrained by level-headed Stoker. The Dubliner's own creative ambitions are disparaged by Irving and he is also the most distant point of the love triangle. Waiting in the wings is his long-suffering wife, once betrothed to Oscar Wilde – his parting gift to her, Dracula fans, was a crucifix – and suspects that lightning may have struck twice.

This is also the London of Jack the Ripper, pea-soupers and the swirl of suspicion that surrounds Wilde. Out of this ferment we witness the first stirrings of what will become Stoker's masterpiece, *Dracula*.

The story is told through diary entries, letters and the odd newspaper clipping, so *Shadowplay* carries thematic and structural echoes of both *Star of the Sea* and *Ghost Light*.

'There are actually very specific references to those books, which not everyone will spot. Henry Irving is interviewed by American journalist Grantley Dixon. Nerds will spot that he is the central narrator of *Star of the Sea*. Later, Stoker is living in a nursing home on Bricksfield Terrace, the same building that Molly Allgood lives in in *Ghost Light*.'

Bram and Joe go way back. 'Bram Stoker has been with me from [when] I was six or seven. He is the first Irish author I ever heard of, the first Irish author I loved. My maternal grandmother was a great teller of ghost stories, she loved telling us about Marsh's Library being haunted and if you walked three times round the Pepper Canister church the Devil would appear.'

His favourite story was of a relative who was a lamplighter, who met Stoker near St Michan's Church then read that Stoker had died in London the previous day. 'It's the tallest of stories but it made me feel connected. The first fiction I tried to write was influenced by Stoker, very Gothic.'

Stoker was intensely private, says O'Connor, and less celebrated as he was not identified with cultural nationalism. 'What he wanted to do, a bit like Eddie Virago in *Cowboys & Indians*, was to get on the boat to London and be in showbiz. He was a genuine outsider, a genuine rebel.'

How good is *Dracula*?

'I love *Dracula*, it has its moments of clunking self-parody but one of the really striking things about it is its modernity. *Dracula* includes telephones, sound recordings, blood transfusions, women's magazines, you can see Stoker trying to make it as up to date as possible. It's so brilliant that he sets the vampire in the world of the reader. We often think mistakenly that it is set in Transylvania but most of it is set in England, the vampire is living in an abandoned townhouse in Piccadilly, he could be walking past you. That's where it is tempting to think the story of Jack the Ripper could come in.'

Then there is the novel's epistolary style, which O'Connor has explored since *The Salesman*. 'It's marvellous how Stoker teaches you to vary the texture. It doesn't have to be one authorial voice, you can have newspaper articles, ballads, songs, diaries. There's a narrator in this book who's a ghost and whose grammar is very far away from Bram's meticulous diary keeping. Stoker taught me that the music of a novel is as important as the plot. It should be like a concert, some moments are guitar solos, some are silence, some should be a symphony but use them all.'

Shadowplay grew out of a BBC radio play O'Connor wrote about Stoker and Irving called *The Vampire Man*. 'It was grand but when it came to write the novel, when Ellen arrived I felt the crackle of electricity, of possibility. All the blokeish stuff could be undercut. It wouldn't be the book it is without Ellen Terry.

'The three of them had this ardent, passionate friendship for which there is only the word love. I thought this story might say something about the nature of love and sexuality and magic and what happens backstage. Stoker wrote an unforgivably long memoir of Irving, like a snowstorm of facts that Stoker hides in. He never tells anything about himself. All of those silences create a space that is very inviting for the storyteller.'

While O'Connor has fun exploring the possible threads from which Stoker might have woven his masterpiece, the tyrannical Irving and the Ripper's bloodlust, he is as keen to subvert as to suggest. 'I don't think it is as simple as you see someone and they become the blueprint for one of your characters, it's more a process of osmosis and transference.' For instance, to help him with a scene involving Terry, he asked himself how Patti Smith, his heroine, would have handled it.

O'Connor is a witty, stylish writer who has a lot of fun gently sending up Gothic tropes, as did Paraic O'Donnell's *The House on Vesper Sands*. 'There is something preposterous and ponderous about the Gothic. The characters almost know how ridiculous the situation is. I wanted Ellen to be funny, to take the piss out of Irving's pomposity. Actors are witty, performative in how they talk, camp and mischievous.'

Stoker's sexuality is ambiguous – his relationship with Terry and Irving intense but complex.

'My sense of their view is that sexuality is an omnipresent current, a bit like radio waves,' says O'Connor. 'I was going to suggest it is a bit like broadband except that would suggest that sexuality in parts of rural Ireland is only intermittently available. A current of sexuality runs between people all the time, a smile could be sexual. There's a moment where Bram says that love is a lot more than who puts what where and that is my notion of the three. Hence the title, it's more about what's happening in the shadows, not the limelight.'

O'Connor does his research, puts it in a drawer and gives his imagination free rein. Twelve years after Stoker's death a German company filmed Dracula as *Nosferatu*, only for Stoker's widow to pursue them successfully for royalties.

At that time, only plays could be copyrighted so a key scene is the Lyceum's staging, unrehearsed, minus scenery, for one morning only, of *Dracula, or The Un-Dead* – 'The Un-read', scoffs Irving.

'I would love to have been in the Lyceum that morning,' O'Connor says, 'so that was a real-life thing to discover and play with.'

Shadowplay's epigraph, by Ellen Terry's son, begins: 'In every being who lives, there is a second self very little known to anyone.'

'I think it is the key to the book,' says the author. 'What Bram is doing is discovering a second self. It is a great trope of Victorian literature – *Dr Jekyll and Mr Hyde* and *The Picture of Dorian Gray* – and people had great unease about it. The reason we have storytelling is we know we contain other selves. Through fiction you get to have that very radical adventure of seeing the world through someone else.'

His new project is a novel *My Father's House* based on Hugh O'Flaherty, the Kerry priest who saved more than 6000 lives from the Nazis in Rome. 'Being a priest would not have saved him – the Gestapo murdered two priests who had been assisting the partisans – so he was a man of immense courage. I just have his voice in my head, right at this moment he's telling me to shut up. He's now telling me he can't wait to read *Shadowplay*.'

Sound advice.

O'Connor was born in Dublin in 1963. He is the author of twelve novels, two story collections, four plays and several works of non-fiction. Since 2014 he has been the inaugural Frank McCourt Chair in Creative Writing at the University of Limerick. His debut, Cowboys & Indians *(1991), was shortlisted for a Whitbread Award.* Star of the Sea *(2002) was shortlisted for Irish Novel of the Year.* Ghost Light *(2011) was shortlisted for the Walter Scott Prize and* LA Times *Book Prize.* Shadowplay *(2019) won Irish Novel of the Year and was shortlisted for the Costa Novel Award and the Walter Scott Prize.* My Father's House *(2023) was also shortlisted for the Walter Scott Prize.* Ghosts of Rome *(2025) won Irish Book of the Year.*

CATHERINE O'FLYNN

18 September 2010, The Irish Post

If Catherine O'Flynn were a stick of rock, the sort her father might once have sold in his sweet shop, running through the middle would be the words Birmingham Irish, for while England's second city, her birthplace, is as much a character in her first two novels as a setting, there is something quintessentially Irish about her sensibilities.

It may seem an incongruous comparison, but having recently read Glasgow Irish comedian Frankie Boyle's autobiography, *My Shit Life So Far*, full of black humour and loathing, it strikes me that O'Flynn is his antithesis, her books life-affirming and uplifting, inspecting her characters and her city but with affection, her wry, sardonic humour avoiding sentimentality.

'This is a real concern of mine,' laughs the author. 'One interviewer described me as hugely likeable and now my husband always refers to me as the hugely likeable Catherine O'Flynn.'

O'Flynn's own story is appropriately heart-warming. Her first novel, *What Was Lost*, was rejected by nineteen publishers before it was published by Tindal Street, a small local publisher, in 2007, winning the Costa First Novel Award and Galaxy British Book Newcomer of the Year Award among others and being longlisted for the Booker and Orange prizes.

What Was Lost is a wonderful read, poignant yet funny, a mystery in two parts about a girl who goes missing in a shopping centre in 1984 and the people who try to discover what happened to her twenty years later. It is also a portrait of a changing city and a society's obsession with consumerism.

The News Where You Are, O'Flynn's 2010 novel, begins not with a disappearance but a death, that of a TV presenter in a mysterious hit-and-run, and a former colleague's attempt to get to the bottom of it. Beneath an awkwardly corny screen persona, Frank is a decent family man tormented by an all-pervading sense of loss – the mysterious death of his predecessor Phil; the demolition of his architect father's brutally ugly buildings; the constant drip of stories of elderly people dying alone and unnoticed for weeks in the city; and his relentlessly miserable mother in a nursing home.

If that all sounds depressing, it isn't, because O'Flynn imbues her writing with observational humour and amusingly perceptive ruminations on the vagaries of modern life.

O'Flynn was born in Birmingham in 1970. Her mother, from Oylegate, County Wexford, was a teacher, while her father, from Hillstreet, County Roscommon, ran a sweet shop in Nechells, 'a bit like Arkwright in *Open All Hours*'. There was a nine-year gap between Catherine, 'the mistake', and her next-youngest sibling.

'The character Maureen [Frank's mother] is to some extent based on my mum, a very intelligent, well-read woman who was also almost comically melancholy. She could find something sad in the most innocent thing. You realize it's not normal for your parents to be always reading the obituaries in a newspaper first. I don't know how much that was to do with leaving Ireland when she was young, the dislocation. As I get older I sometimes find myself thinking like her, being wistful and melancholy. She'd always say how she cried the day she found out she was pregnant with me. She was very lovely to me growing up, I think it's fine she was honest that I wasn't actually planned.'

O'Flynn grew up in 'a weird Irish bubble'. 'My parents were Irish, the primary school I went to, St Joseph's, all the teachers were Irish, 90 per cent of my classmates were Irish, the priest was Irish and the parish was very Irish too. We were living in inner-city Birmingham but it was a very densely concentrated Irish immigrant area. By the time I went to secondary school in a different area it was a bit of a culture shock for me because people there thought I had an Irish accent.

'I never felt the need to be over the top about it, like some people do if they feel a bit insecure about their identity. I always just felt very comfortable that that was my background and who I was.'

O'Flynn was only four at the time of the Birmingham pub bombings in 1974 but she remembers the after-effects. 'It had a personal resonance for us because one of the pubs that was bombed, the Mulberry Bush, my sister went there every week with a friend and for whatever reason at the last minute they didn't go there, so it felt very close to home for my parents and my family. At the same time my dad ran a sweet shop, he had always had good relations in the area but a short time after the bombings he had one or two phone calls threatening him, which upset him quite a lot. I was reminded of it recently by the 9/11 situation, which led to suspicion of all Muslims. Then there were suspicions against every Irish person.'

Might a future book address that Irish heritage? 'I tend to write about contemporary things,' she says. 'I think it comes out in more generalized ways. In *What Was Lost*, I didn't make a big thing about it but all the names were Irish because clearly that was the background she was coming from. There is a lot about loss in my books. I think that for anyone who moves from one country to another, like my parents, there is a lot of loss, of melancholy, of nostalgia. That affected my writing.'

O'Flynn was also deeply affected by the early deaths of her parents. Her father died of a stroke at the age of sixty-four when she was only sixteen and her mother died just after she graduated.

'My parents worked really hard all their lives. My mum had almost three jobs, teaching, helping out in the shop and bringing up six children. Both died before they got a chance to enjoy retirement. It turned me off the idea of a career, giving over your life to work, that kind of deferring of happiness. In some ways that ties in with my generation being seen as a bit slackerish, a bit lazy.'

So despite her degree in sociology and anthropology, she adopted a philosophy of working to live, not living to work, 'not in any grand hippyish way, just doing low-level jobs that didn't make me unhappy like admin or working in a shop'.

She worked briefly as a music journalist, then for HMV in a shopping mall, where she became fascinated by the difference between the daytime buzz and the eerie silence after it shut. She began making notes, observing the customers she was serving. She and her husband sold their house and moved to Barcelona for a year after realizing they didn't have to win the lottery to live their dreams. While there, she began writing *What Was Lost*.

Barcelona is one of Europe's hippest cities. Birmingham … isn't. Yet O'Flynn likes it.

'I'm very fond of Birmingham, partly because it's always been undervalued a little bit, always looked on as a bit of an embarrassment. Unlike other cities like Liverpool and Manchester I think Birmingham is a lot more self-deprecating.

The thing I love about [Birmingham] is it's always had this huge mix of ambition and insecurity, to be the city of the future but always changing its mind about what that future should be and erasing past mistakes. I find it quite moving to come across fragments of former dreams - their 1960s plan, their 1970s plan. Things get demolished very quickly.'

Nechells was an industrial wasteland of concrete and canals that doubled as a vast playground for her growing up. Today the blanks have all been filled in but she misses the gaps. 'I grew up at a time in between things, when the factories were closing down and being demolished but before the shopping centres, it was just a big blank. To go back where I grew up is utterly changed, quite disorienting really. Loss is probably too strong but it makes you feel cut adrift.'

O'Flynn was working as a postwoman when she got the inspiration for her second book, making notes about buildings she passed that were due for demolition. Her research led her to the Rubble Club, a group of architects whose buildings have been demolished in their lifetime, the ultimate dashing of dreams of a legacy when even concrete turns to dust.

Her TV presenter Phil cannot face growing old – he is 'all for facelifts and when that stops working then I'm afraid it's time for demolition'. There is a parallel with one of Frank's father's buildings, which has had its own facelift, 'a cheap eighties fascia on a Seventies building', and now awaits the wrecking ball. Frank, like O'Flynn, believes that the past should be preserved, not erased, and opposes this architectural euthanasia. 'Birmingham was trying to change its reputation for the way it treated its architectural heritage: the famous lack of sentimentality that bordered on self-harm.'

Likewise, he cannot bear the thought that someone might die and not be mourned or even missed. 'What remains is our absence, that's what I feel really, a gap,' says O'Flynn. 'When a building goes, you're aware of this gap in the landscape.'

Serving a local TV presenter with a cheesy reputation in HMV also got her thinking. 'What must it be like going through life knowing people think you're an idiot. I've got a real fondness for books like Kurt Vonnegut's about characters who are really underestimated by everybody.'

The News Where You Are has been well received, but one reviewer suggested the plot could have been stronger. O'Flynn is unapologetic. 'When I start thinking what I want to write about it's often themes and atmospheres I'm keen to get across. I quite like books that don't have much of a plot. In some ways for me as a reader the less plot the better, but that's because the writers I like have a strong enough style to carry that off. I'm not sure if I have. I'm just starting out.'

O'Flynn was born in Birmingham in 1970. What Was Lost *(2007) won the Costa First Novel Award and Newcomer of the Year at the British Book Awards, was shortlisted for the* Guardian *First Book Award and longlisted for the Booker Prize and Women's Prize for Fiction. Her other novels are* The News Where You Are *(2010) and* Mr. Lynch's Holiday *(2013) and the children's novels* Lori and Max *(2019) and* Lori and Max and the Book Thieves *(2020).*

DEIRDRE PURCELL

7 June 1991, Irish in Britain News

Deirdre Purcell is a most accomplished woman. From modest beginnings in the civil service she has graced the stage and the media and now is making her mark as a novelist. Her first effort, *A Place of Stones*, has gone straight into the Irish bestseller list at number one.

Junior civil servant; Aer Lingus clerk; starlet of the Aer Lingus musical and dramatic society; actor at the Abbey Theatre; European theatre artist at Chicago's Loyola University; RTÉ newscaster; award-winning journalist and now bestselling author, Purcell may have had a chequered career but she has zig-zagged her way to the top.

A Place of Stones is by no means Purcell's first sortie into writing. She has also contributed to many nonfiction books, including *Ethiopia: The Dark Hunger* about famine in Ethiopia; *The RTÉ Book*, a behind-the-scenes look at the Irish State broadcaster; and ghost-wrote *The Time of My Life* (1989), Gay Byrne's autobiography.

Ghost-writing is a brilliant test of stamina, she says. 'I always thought I had a very low boredom threshold, and I wanted to know if I could finish a long project, so when I was asked to do this novel, I no longer had to fear that I would leave the thing half-finished. Gay's brain operates in a revolving way. He retains very little about himself. Gay is an exceptionally modest person, lives a modest life. He is quite a simple man. I think he's the best general broadcaster in the English-speaking world. I am very loyal to him. Ghost-writing is a very thankless job, but Gay has amply paid me back. He gave me a 24-minute interview on *The Late Late Show*.'

Did she always intend to write a novel?

'My friends claim now that I said all along I was going to write a novel but I never thought I had it in me, to be perfectly honest. I think perhaps being asked to do it concentrated my mind, like hanging, you know.' It was commissioned by the Irish publisher Townhouse but Pan Macmillan is publishing it in the UK. 'It's wonderful, a complete change of direction at my age. This is my thirteenth career. I am a really lucky person. All the changes in my life have been down to outside sources. Apart from my jobs in the civil service and with Aer Lingus, from then on, everything has been offered to me, first the Abbey, then the chance to go to the States. When I came back, I applied for literally everything, for jobs in banks and building societies, but the one I got was as an RTÉ radio announcer.'

She had decided to give up acting. 'My ex-husband was an actor, but the two of us couldn't be actors and bring up a family. Anyway, I'd had enough. I'm a thin-skinned person. I find it very difficult to take rejection. When I was at the Abbey, it was like the civil service of theatre, a job for life with a pension. I don't think I'd have made it as a freelance.'

Soon tiring of her work as a continuity announcer, Purcell became a TV reporter and then Ireland's first woman newsreader. From there it was on to the *Sunday Tribune*, where she did a series of interviews with actors, then to the Irish Press, and finally to the revamped *Tribune* under Vincent Browne.

'*The Sunday Tribune* asked me to join them, I know this for a fact, though they deny it to this day, because they didn't have a single high-profile woman writing for them, and they thought my name would look good on the masthead. For a year they didn't know what to do with me, and then I went back to my natural medium of the long interview pieces and features.'

Whatever about the reason for her hiring, the decision was sound, for she won two prestigious journalism awards in the next four years. What was her best interview?

'By far them was memorable was the Gary Hart saga [a US Democratic presidential contender who withdrew amid revelations of extramarital affairs]. He dropped out of sight in March. No one could find him. I heard a rumour from the aunt of one of the *Sunday Tribune* photographers that Oliver North was in Connemara. When I got down there, I suddenly realized it couldn't be Oliver North as he was on TV in the States, so I knew it must be Gary Hart. I tracked him down in a private house. I started a gavotte with him, asking him for an interview in a letter. He wrote back refusing. I wrote again, and eventually I got an interview with him, a world exclusive. I had a lovely, long interview with him, and then went out to dinner with him at Sweeney's Hotel in Oughterard and ended up killing a bottle of whiskey with him. I gave him my word, though, not to mention anything about Donna Rice, though he talked about her off the record. I almost lost my job. I was under a fierce amount of pressure from the *Tribune* to publish the interview before anyone else got hold of one, but I had promised Hart that I wouldn't publish it until he had left Ireland.'

Maeve Binchy described Purcell's *A Place of Stones* as 'an unputdownable story of Irish life and love'. Set in Chicago's wealthy suburbs, the Aran Islands and London's theatreland, the story begins with a tragic plane crash in the mid-1950s. The novel follows the complex relationship between the affluent Chicagoan Smiths and the impecunious O'Briains of Inisheer. The heroine, Molly O'Briain, suffers as she battles her way to stage success, and then is forced to face the truths which begin to emerge about her real family.

A lot of personal experience obviously went into the writing. Did she not fear she would use up a lifetime's experience in one novel?

'I've heard that's a danger, but I hope in my case since I have done so much that there's plenty left. When I used to interview authors, they told me the most unexpected things come out when you're writing, things you didn't know you knew anything about suddenly spring to mind. I suppose it's your subconscious rescuing you. I am now halfway through my second novel. It's about a pair of twins from Monaghan, who emigrate to Prince Edward Island in pre-Famine times. A particular local priest went there, discovered that there was cheap farming land to be had, and brought a lot of parishioners out there.

'My favourite Irish author is Jennifer Johnston, but everything I've ever read from the back of a Bisto packet to Enid Blyton has influenced me.'

Determined to make it as a full-time writer, Purcell can only be heartened by the success of her first attempt at literature. Not only popular success either, for it has also gone down well with the critics. 'Certainly, it would have been thought of as a woman's book,' said Purcell, 'but the best reviews so far have been from men.'

Deirdre Purcell was born in Dublin in 1943. She wrote a dozen bestselling novels, including A Place of Stones *(1991);* That Childhood Country *(1992) and* Grace in Winter *(2019).* Love Like Hate Adore *(1998) was shortlisted for the Orange Prize, now the Women's Prize for Fiction.* Falling for a Dancer *(1993) was adapted for a BBC TV series in 1998. Her non-fiction books include* Aengus Finucane: In the Heart of Concern *(2014) and her memoir* Diamonds and Holes in My Shoes *(2006). She died in 2023.*

FRANK RONAN

16 January 1993, The Irish Post

Like Voltaire, Frank Ronan has retired from the hurly-burly of the metropolis to cultivate his garden. The New Ross, County Wexford-born writer, who won the *Irish Times* Literature Prize with his first novel, *The Men Who Loved Evelyn Cotton*, spends the best part of every year tending the plants in the grounds of his Normandy home, only returning to Dublin every summer to knock out a new novel in a rented room in Ranelagh.

The Irish author has also cultivated a rather striking personality for himself. In person, he ties up his long locks at the back with a chopstick and he speaks in a languorous drawl. His writing led one French reviewer to speculate that doubtless he makes love naked except for his monocle. This is not to detract from his writing, which is most impressive. *A Picnic in Eden* is a deeply moving study in male friendship, falling out of love, problem parents, unhappy childhoods and the shadows they cast over otherwise successful adult lives.

Dougie Miller's father died by suicide after being rejected by Dougie's mother, a woman who went on to torment her illegitimate child for his father's perceived shortcomings. Adam Parnell's childhood subsided into shame and disgust as his father's alcoholism gradually disrupted the family's lives. When the two come together their shared experience of a blighted childhood draws them to each other, inevitably at the expense of their wives.

Chasing up autobiographical tie-ins is a fruitless pursuit, but Ronan is happy to volunteer, when asked what his father did for a living, that the answer was 'a bit of this and a bit of that'. 'He always had about three or four things in various stages of decline,' the author remembers. He accepts, though, that this was no bad thing necessarily. 'It may be better to have a picaresque kind of childhood, I don't know. When the Irish decide to be middle class, they lead a fairly stultifying life.'

Ronan himself has led a rather maverick existence. He trained horses in England and worked his way around Australia before settling down in London with his wife, Penny, an architectural journalist. The money was good but 'it was all going to support a lifestyle which we didn't want in the first place' so they moved to Normandy.

Flowers are a passion for Ronan, not a passing affectation. 'They're always moving. The garden changes every day. There's a formal terraced bit, and there's a herbaceous bit and then at the bottom there's a wild bit and across the river there's a water meadow, which is a bit of a fiasco as it's quite hard to get to.'

A Freudian friend suggested that the three parts of the garden respectively are his superego, ego and id, a fancy he lapped up with a laugh.

Asked to sum up for a stranger to his work what he writes about, Ronan volunteers: 'an analysis of feeling, of emotion, the switching of narrative to show what people see in life and what people feel in life. *The Better Angel*, *Evelyn Cotton* and *Picnic in Eden* are about relationships. They create a pattern – before you came; now that you're here; and after you've gone.'

For Ronan, writing is all about 'communication – I don't think there's any other object in publishing a novel. To write is to make the unfamiliar relevant.'

The author's specialist subject is love, and the different ways men and women experience it. 'You have to look at men and try to find out what brutalizes them. The way society works, men don't express emotion. So if you are a child expected to grow up and be a man, it isn't that easy to try and work out how you should do it. We are still feeding off the back of a tribal society, that thing about women being breeding machines and men being hunter-gatherers.'

Despite the feminist thinking that evidently influences him, Ronan has avoided the straitjacket of political correctness, finding a new unity behind gender differences, albeit a negative one.

'Women have a skill for inflicting emotional damage that men can't deal with because they haven't developed the same emotional footwork. There was a theory that men liked pornography because they were so messed up and that women weren't into that kind of thing but now you've got the Chippendales and male strippers at hen parties and it's becoming more and more evident that whatever a man is capable of, a woman is too.'

Ronan sees himself carrying on the good work of Flaubert and Joyce when he writes about women, taking care to make the female real. 'What Flaubert almost did with *Madame Bovary*, what James Joyce did with Molly Bloom, almost by accident, was to make women human.'

Despite the dark depths that *A Picnic in Eden* exposes in the psyches of its seemingly well integrated characters and the gulf that emerges between husband and wife in what had been an affectionate marriage, Ronan's view of love is buoyant, not bleak.

'I don't think love is a lost cause at all. I think probably if you didn't fall in love from time to time you'd go mad or grow hard. It is something that takes you outside yourself. It is like dreaming. If you deprive people of their dreams, they go mad. Dreams seem to be rubbish but they help you make sense of the other things that are going on and I think love has a function rather like that.'

Ronan was born in New Ross, County Wexford in 1963. He wrote a monthly column for Gardens Illustrated *magazine from 2005 until 2018. His debut novel,* The Men Who Loved Evelyn Cotton *(1989) won the* Irish Times/*Aer Lingus prize. His other novels are* A Picnic in Eden *(1991),* The Better Angel *(1993),* Dixie Chicken *(1994),* Lovely *(1995) and* Home *(2002). He has also published one short-story collection,* Handsome Men Are Slightly Sunburnt *(1996).*

SALLY ROONEY

14 September 2024, The Irish Times

Two years ago, when Sally Rooney returned to her old campus, Trinity College Dublin, to discuss her novels in a public interview, her publisher asked event organizers to provide not one but two escape routes for the Irish novelist, should she require them. Such is the price of fame.

With six million sales of Faber editions alone, Rooney's novels *Conversations with Friends*, *Normal People* and *Beautiful World, Where Are You* have become literary touchstones for a new generation of readers, and BBC adaptations of her first two books have only served to magnify interest. Named one of the hundred most influential people in global culture by *Time* magazine in 2022, Rooney has attained a level of celebrity rarely encountered by literary novelists. But she herself is no fan of the spotlight, preferring the study and reading light.

In a matter of days, Rooney will publish her new novel, *Intermezzo*. It's a big literary event, yet Rooney has done a bare handful of interviews to publicize the book. In truth, there have been times when she has regretted putting her name to her novels at all, perhaps looking to the example of Elena Ferrante, the Italian novelist who publishes her wildly successful novels of love and female friendship under a pseudonym.

'I often think it would have been better if I had published my work under an assumed name and stayed out of the public eye,' says Rooney. 'It's not where I belong. I feel a lot of anxiety about my privacy and the privacy of my family and loved ones. But if I refused to speak to journalists or do any public events in connection with a new book, I think it would look as if I didn't have faith in the book, and that would feel wrong. So I feel a bit trapped by that. On a personal level I'm just not cut out for life in the public eye. I'm a very private person and I like to go unnoticed. That has become harder in recent years, and I struggle with that.'

Rooney, still just thirty-three, has long seemed destined for the spotlight. Even before the publication of *Conversations with Friends*, I had an early heads-up about Ireland's most promising new literary talent: Rooney's fans included the writer Thomas Morris, who first introduced me to her at the launch of Kevin Barry's novel *Beatlebone* in the Workman's Club in Dublin in 2015, two years before her debut was published.

Attired in a long, striped dress and low-heeled court shoes, Rooney meets me this time in the grander surroundings of the United Arts Club in the heart of Dublin's Georgian quarter. The venue seems like a good idea in part because of the new novel's themes: the Dublin Chess Club meets here and *Intermezzo* focuses on Ivan, a 22-year-old chess prodigy.

In the beginning, the reader finds Margaret observing Ivan beating all-comers in a set of exhibition matches in the arts centre Margaret runs in Leitrim. They have a mutual attraction, which is complicated by a fourteen-year age gap. Ivan has a brother, Peter, who is involved with two women: Sylvia, his college lover now reduced to close friend because an accident has left her incapable of physical intimacy; and Naomi, nine years younger, a connection that develops into something more serious.

Age gaps have surfaced in Rooney's fiction before, but 'I have no conscious thematic interest in that,' she says when I mention the affair in her debut novel. 'I'm interested in relationships that aren't simple because if they're simple, it's hard to get a whole novel out of them.' Fiction needs friction.

At least part of Rooney's success is built on her consummate gift for writing literary novels about friendships and intimate relationships. A lover's bare skin is 'like pared fruit'. 'Who can explain such a thing, and why even try to explain: an understanding shared between two people. Her breath warm on his lips when she sighs, and when he kisses her again, a muted sound from her throat.'

Come for the romance; stay for the meaning of life, of which, of course, love is a fundamental part.

Ivan and Peter are grieving the recent death of their father. Their mother, never that maternal, has remarried. Ivan is finding solace with Margaret but Peter is 'frighteningly unhappy', struggling to square his love triangle with his respectable status as a barrister. Already an outsider as the son of an Eastern

European – 'what they were born to, he has to work for' – he cannot bear becoming an outcast were it to become known he is effectively in a throuple.

The novel's heart is Peter's dark night of the soul, as his efforts to resolve his relationships only seem to make things worse. Reminiscent stylistically of James Joyce, there are questions of faith in the novel that trace their influence to the great Russian novelists. Rooney loved Dostoevsky's *The Idiot* but his last novel made the deepest impression.

'I don't think I could have written this exact novel if I hadn't read *The Brothers Karamazov*,' says Rooney. Ivan's dog is called Alexei in ludic homage. 'This book has its fingerprints all over it. Everything I read becomes part of a mental library, it's almost like building vocabulary in another language. When you sit down to write a novel, the only tools you have are all the books that you've ever read.

'Dostoevsky's works are so immersed in hand-to-hand combat with these difficult questions about faith, beliefs, the figure of Christ, philosophical and ethical questions about life, how is it possible to live by a Christian ethic and abide by our sense of community with other people, the big supernatural questions about whether there is order, a structuring principle, in this universe. I find the world of Dostoyevsky's novels so incredibly immersive and compelling, and they're beautifully plotted and paced. It's intricate like clockwork. As a reader, you enjoy how smoothly it runs. But as a writer, you want to get in there and start taking the little gears apart and thinking, how is that done?'

Religion has a place in Rooney's previous work – Frances in *Conversations with Friends* finds comfort in the Gospels, and Simon in *Beautiful World, Where Are You* is a practising Catholic. But *Intermezzo* takes it to another level. Rooney, the famously Marxist writer, is also a cultural Catholic, intellectually too, who finds meaning and beauty in Scripture, ethical inspiration in Simone Weil and solace in the poetry of the Jesuit Gerard Manley Hopkins.

'I find his poetry really comforting, and I like to memorize it. That is almost like a little therapeutic practice for me. Memorizing poetry is something that I do for my nerves.'

Decades after Kate O'Brien, Brian Moore and John McGahern, faith is making a bit of a comeback in Irish fiction, with Mike McCormack's *This Plague of Souls*, Niamh Mulvey's *The Amendments* and now *Intermezzo*.

I had perhaps lazily assumed that Rooney's home environment – the Trinity graduate was raised in Castlebar in County Mayo – was lapsed Catholic as well as liberal, left-wing and feminist but it was more traditional, typical of the times. The family went to Sunday Mass and she attended convent school.

'Questions of faith and Christianity are important in my work from my first novel up till this one, for sure.' This is more than just the vestigial tail of Catholicism in Irish culture. 'I think it is more.' As a teenager, influenced by her parents' strong political convictions and values, she rebelled against what she saw as the authoritarian power of the Church and its teachings on abortion and gay relationships. That was the first stirring of her political conscience, long before she read Marx and became more interested in economic inequality, geopolitics and imperialism.

Years later, however, while writing her first novel, she wondered whether she had been wrong to throw the baby Jesus out with the bathwater of the Church's more controversial teachings.

'I suppose I felt that brushing religion aside had been very easy because I was hearing things I didn't agree with and still don't agree with, I want to emphasize. Ergo, I don't believe in any of this. I don't believe in Jesus, don't believe in God and I don't care what any of those old books have to say. But later on I became more interested in rethinking religion as a source of ethics. If I've rejected all these things, where then am I drawing the moral lessons that are so important to me? I think it was just a process of becoming honest with myself and saying they do actually come from Christian teaching; that is the world in which I was raised.

'And I think it is a really beautiful, rich and worthwhile spiritual and intellectual tradition of thinking about ethics, about our relations with other people. I forgot to acknowledge its centrality to my ethical life. Not to claim that it's a uniquely useful or beautiful tradition for thinking about ethics, but it was the one that I was raised in and that had formed so much of my thought, and I'd failed to come to terms with that. So I think part of what I'm doing in my fiction is trying to come to terms with that.

'I have gone from being a dogmatic atheist to being very interested in the intellectual and spiritual traditions of Christianity. That's a heritage that it would be dishonest of me to say isn't central to who I am as a thinker and as a writer. There is something Christian about my work, even if I would not describe myself as straightforwardly religious. Like, I still struggle with the more supernatural aspect of religious belief.'

Another key inspiration for *Intermezzo* was Joyce's *Ulysses*. Rooney had reached an impasse in Ivan and Margaret's story. 'I'm always down on the level of the sentence just creeping ahead, then reversing and then going again.' She doesn't plan ahead but, like Zadie Smith, builds and decorates and furnishes the hallway as she goes, with no idea what might lie in the rooms off it.

She had to go to London for the launch of *Beautiful World, Where Are You* and travelled by sail and rail. What in other circumstances might have been an unwelcome distraction from the creative process turned out to be just what she needed. On the ferry home, 'it was like a bolt-of-lightning moment. I remember sitting up straight and thinking, [Ivan] *has an older brother*. I actually opened my laptop and wrote what's now very close to the first page of the book. It was [Peter], his life, the two women in his life and the voice. And that then opened up the whole novel.'

She talks of *encountering* Peter for the first time. 'I know that may sound affected, that I'm trying to pretend that there isn't a process of intentional creation, but there really isn't. I actually have to wait for the idea to come to me.'

Later she reveals what she was reading on the long return trip to London. To escape the travails of the present she had immersed herself in the world of Dublin in 1904 – 16 June, to be precise – and it unlocked a door for her. As Stephen Dedalus says in Joyce's *Portrait of the Artist as a Young Man*, 'the shortest way to Tara was via Holyhead'.

There is much in *Intermezzo* reminiscent of *Ulysses*: the clipped, elliptical sentences of interior monologue; the richness of the cultural references; the intertextuality; the brothers with their eastern European surname, Koubek; grieving over a close male relative. Rooney wasn't conscious of any of that but realized at some point that Bloom, Dedalus and Molly were the same age as Peter, Ivan and Margaret. Peter is, like her, someone who sees the world through a cultural gauze, constantly reminded of lines from a poem or novel. It's a natural symbiosis of creator and character. At another level, she loved what Joyce did with *Ulysses* and wanted to play with his toys.

'I am self-conscious when I talk about that because *Ulysses* is this gigantic work of genius that defined the modernist novel and broke the structure of the novel in a fascinating way. So I'm really anxious about trying to place my work in that lineage. I want to acknowledge the enormous influence that this beloved book has had on my work without in any way trying to make any special claims for my work. I feel like I've learned so much from Joyce and I'm still learning.'

A love of Joyce is something that connects Rooney and another famous Faber author, Edna O'Brien, whose *Country Girls* trilogy successfully explored female friendship and burgeoning sexuality. O'Brien, who died the weekend before this interview took place, was a huge inspiration for Rooney, if not a direct influence.

'I wish that I could speak more knowledgeably about Edna O'Brien's work, particularly her novels, but her role in the culture was obviously so important. A couple of years ago I went to see her play *Joyce's Women* at the Abbey, and I left so invigorated by its searching intellectual brilliance and feeling so in love with Joyce again.' She met O'Brien once through Faber and again in Listowel. 'I was just completely in awe. It would have been early in my publishing career, and she was this towering cultural figure. So I was a bit petrified. What a great gift to be able to say that I did meet her and get to experience that incredible personality and charisma, however briefly.'

Dublin is a real presence in *Intermezzo*, more than just a backdrop, another Joycean parallel. Some of her early readers have said it's her most Dublin book yet, an interesting observation given Rooney has put the city behind her, moving with her husband, John, back to Castlebar, where he teaches maths. The couple met at Trinity, where they debated together, and married in 2020. In *Intermezzo*'s acknowledgments, she writes, 'John, what a joy and a blessing it is for me to share my life with you.'

'It's funny that I didn't live in Dublin for any of the period that I was writing it,' says Rooney. 'I almost think that I've preserved some of the romance of Dublin for myself by not living there. When I moved here first as a teenager, I felt very transfixed and captivated by the romance of Dublin. I felt like this was the beginning of my life.' We look out the window at the Georgian streetscape, the ornate lamp posts and fanlights. 'Peter lives not too far from here in the book, so this is kind of his neighbourhood. I did spend ten years living in Dublin and I do really love it as a city, even though of course it has many problems too.'

The move home has enabled her to root down and concentrate on her work in a rewarding way. 'It was a really enjoyable book to write, even though it goes to dark places. There's a lot of grief, a lot of sadness. Maybe what I needed was the quiet and space to get to those places.'

Beautiful World by contrast was the hardest book to write as she was moving around and travelling a lot for work. 'That was still the era where I was doing book tours. I don't do those anymore.'

Whereas as a child she loved fiction for its escapist quality, its invention of magical worlds, since her teens she has loved realist novels, 'that sense of being able to inhabit our world through the lens of fiction that allows us to access the interiority of other people, which we can't do in real life'.

Growth through dialogue could be a slogan for her work. In these fractious times, it would make a good party political slogan. 'I love repartee, in real life and in fiction,' she says, but she would never use an overheard phrase, 'because it doesn't emerge organically from the world of the work. It would feel sacrilegious to real life and to the fictitious life of my characters.'

She writes on the level of the sentence and the scene: there is no big picture. Only at the end does she have to step back and think: what is this book about? To pronounce upon that feels a bit fraudulent. It also makes the resolution hard.

'Every book that I've written, I began to feel like I had written myself into a corner and I couldn't finish the book in a way commensurate with the stakes that I'd set up for myself. I just didn't know how to stick the landing. For some reason I ended up reading Wittgenstein's *Philosophical Investigations*, which I felt allowed me to finish writing *Intermezzo*.

'I'm really invested in the characters and the project of getting to know them, placing them in relationship to one another, following them through an important phase in their life that changes them, which is almost a way of saying what it is to write a novel. I've never written anything strictly autobiographical, and I don't think I could, but my characters certainly become so real to me that they must be on some level a facet of my own dilemmas, something submerged.

'Both Ivan and Peter realize they are driven by this desire for perfection. Ivan wants to play perfect chess, Peter wants to make the perfect argument, and I think that's there for me, too, which probably sits uncomfortably alongside creative work. You can never write the perfect novel. It's not even a legitimate artistic pursuit. My favourite novels [such as *Ulysses*] are gloriously imperfect, full of contradictions and ambiguities, things that don't quite work or make sense.'

If she weren't a writer, she thinks she could have gone, like Peter, from debating to being a barrister. 'I love reading judgments.' 'I wonder if in a sense he's living like an alternate version of my life. When I was writing his sections, as I often feel with my characters, I felt myself getting into character.'

Rooney acknowledges her good fortune as a writer. 'I am an extraordinarily privileged creature. But I'm a little bit hesitant to use the word because so many of the things that I'm trying to describe when I use the word "privilege" are things that I wish were rights. I would love to live in a society where people have the right to do the work that is meaningful to them, and not have to feel anxious about having a roof over their head.'

Christianity may have been rehabilitated but capitalism is beyond redemption. 'I do not think that the capitalist system is compatible with an inhabitable planet in terms of the absolute chaos that the capitalist growth imperative has wreaked on our planetary ecosystems.'

Can she genuinely envisage a transition from late capitalism to a better system? 'You could reorient that question and say, can you envisage a way that capitalism can become compatible with an inhabitable planet? Every scientist who models carbon emissions, soil degradation, biodiversity loss, is telling us this economic system is simply not compatible with the continuation of human civilization as we know it.'

She recommends Andreas Malm's *How to Blow Up a Pipeline*, which visualizes what the next phase of climate protest might look like, and *Slow Down: How Degrowth Communism Can Save the Earth* by Japanese Marxist academic Kohei Saito.

Rooney has written critical opinion pieces for the *London Review of Books* on abortion and for *The Irish Times* on the government's housing policy and its failure to challenge the US over its military support for Israel's invasion of Gaza. How does she conceive of herself as a public figure?

'I feel a little bit conflicted. I am an expert in nothing. I rarely feel that I have anything original and interesting to say about the real world. As a novelist, I invent fictitious people and write about their lives in a way that I hope might be original and interesting. But even if it is, why should that qualify me to pontificate about politics or culture in real life?

'On the other hand, I feel very strongly about certain political and cultural issues, as many people do; and because of my prominence as a writer, I have a platform that most people lack. So I sometimes feel a kind of moral pressure to make use of my privileged position and speak about certain things.

'I am very far from an expert on the Israeli occupation of Palestine. I don't feel I have any new or original analysis of the problem to contribute personally. But I also don't want to stay silent in the face of genocide. The horrors unfolding in Gaza feel to me like a turning point in history. How are we allowing this to happen? How is it possible that we have collectively failed to stop such a flagrant and unconcealed campaign of mass murder? These are extremely serious questions, maybe more serious than we have realized yet. In the meantime, I just hope and pray for peace.'

In respect of Palestine, Rooney has learned much from reading the work of writers such as Isabella Hammad, Mohammed el-Kurd, Rabea Eghbariah, Raz Segal, Nathan Thrall.. As for fiction: 'Some of my all-time favourite writers are alive and working today – Sheila Heti, for instance, whom I admire and love with all my heart. And I feel lucky to be writing at the same time as Isabella Hammad, Colin Barrett, Zadie Smith, Thomas Morris, Miranda July and many others.

'On the other hand, I often feel discouraged by the publishing industry. I often see new novels marketed as "for fans of Sally Rooney". I find that so dispiriting – the invention of a certain type of person for the purposes of book marketing. And it makes me feel complicit in the commodification and cheapening of literary culture.'

Rooney edited *The Stinging Fly* literary magazine but for just two issues. Was it too time-consuming? 'I really enjoyed my time at *The Stinging Fly* and I learned a lot there. But yes, ultimately I wasn't able to manage the hefty workload as well as other editors have! I think Lisa McInerney is doing wonderful work there now.'

How important is it to share work in progress with fellow writers? 'When I was writing my first novel, I was reluctant to share sections with anyone before I had completed a first draft. These days, I have to restrain myself from sharing too much of a project too early. My friend John Patrick McHugh has been a particularly important presence in my working life from *Normal People* onwards. We exchange drafts from the early stages of a new project, and more than once his feedback has helped me to find a new pathway through a problem in my work. And as a reader, I cherish the opportunity to read his writing.'

Reviewing the French translation of her work – '*Superbe! Cinq étoiles*', I joke – she was struck by how often things were described as '*compliqué*'. ('Complications with Friends' could be an alternative title.) 'Things are complicated and don't get simpler. That, to me is life. Death is extremely simple and pure. And life is, in all its richness, full of complexity. The will to live itself is the love of that complexity.

'Some of the project of a novel is coming to understand your characters and through that process, allowing them to understand themselves, but it's also allowing them to make peace with not understanding themselves. And that's something that I think is part of the complexity of life itself, and certainly of writing a novel.. Things can't always be made sense of in that very clear kind of argumentative way that a debater or lawyer or chess player might want to make sense of them. And realizing that is the essence of life. There's something really beautiful in that if you can accept it.'

Rooney was born in 1991 in Castlebar, County Mayo. Conversations with Friends *(2017) won the* Sunday Times*/Peters Fraser & Dunlop Young Writer of the Year Award;* Normal People *(2018) won Irish Novel of the Year, Waterstones' Book of the Year and the Costa Novel Award;* Intermezzo *(2024) won the 2025 Sky Arts Award for Literature.* Normal People *(2020) and* Conversations with Friends *(2022) were adapted for television. In 2022,* Time *named her among the 100 most influential people in the world. She was briefly editor of* The Stinging Fly *magazine.*

DONAL RYAN

15 August 2020, The Irish Times

With its beautifully observed Tipperary setting and tenderly created characters telling a story of loss and redemption, *Strange Flowers* is immediately recognizable as a Donal Ryan novel. Less so the author himself, as he looms into view on Zoom, his new lockdown beard giving him the air of a continental football manager.

'It gets wild very quickly, a proper caveman job,' Ryan says, but otherwise he feels he has got off lightly during the pandemic.

'No one close to me has contracted the virus, thankfully. I've been very lucky to have been able to continue working from home. We switched over to online teaching at UL with no major trauma and I finished a draft of a novel so I've been pretty busy all through it. I'm gutted for the small businesses that have been flattened by it, though, and all the people whose livelihoods have been affected by the halted economy.'

Ryan, however, is all too familiar with grief. It kicked down his door when his father died suddenly three years ago.

The motif that runs through *Strange Flowers* is the separation of parents and their children and the anguish this causes. The idyllic life of Paddy and Kit Gladney is shattered in 1973 when their twenty-year-old daughter Moll disappears. The prodigal's return five years later brings joy but also repercussions that will transform their lives. A generation later, history will repeat itself when Moll's son Josh vanishes too.

The novel is also remarkable for its portrayal of a Black man making his home in rural 1970s Ireland.

'I wrote the first draft in 2017 after my father's sudden death in a haze of shock and extreme grief,' Ryan says. 'I think I used it as a way of deflecting reality for a while, of holding it at arm's length. It's a very personal book, the most personal I've written, a kind of oblique confrontation of loss and a celebration of familial love. I'm really happy with it. I owe this book. I was falling hard and it softened my landing.

'I heard the great Mike McCormack once say he had no memory of writing *Solar Bones* and I couldn't see how that could be possible, but I see it now. My only clear memory of writing the first draft of *Strange Flowers* is of being in my office in UL writing the closing scene and of feeling my father's presence very strongly and feeling his approval, almost physically hearing him say "Good man, Do. That's exactly right."'

We think of writing a book as a solo effort, but Ryan acknowledges two people for 'saving this book with your cool heads and unerring eye'. Did the novel undergo radical changes?

'Part of the book went off on a fairly wild tangent. It was kind of untypical of me, an oblique, abstract expression of grief, but it was like I was writing just for me and might alienate readers. Josh had a wild adventure in England that moved into this phantasmagorical territory. Lemmy from Motorhead was there, stuff like that. It was so enjoyable to write but I was being indulgent. I was a metal fan myself. Josh is very close to me the way I saw the world when I was that age. That's why the book is set then as Josh is the same age as me.'

This also explains an unusual, not to say unlikely, aspect to Josh's appearance, which gives the novel its title: 'the perfect, unblemished whiteness of this strange flower'.

'I always give Anne-Marie [his wife] the credit for pushing me to be a "proper" writer – whatever that is! – and for saving me from my own hubris. She usually reads as I write, and I judge from her reaction whether it's up to scratch or not. She loved the first draft, which was, in part, radically different to the published book. But my editor, Brian Langan, and my publisher, Fiona Murphy, weren't as enthusiastic, and they very gently and tactfully suggested a rethink. Which I did, and I redrafted, and it's a far better book for their interventions.

'This happens all the time. Writers think they have a finished product on their hands, but good editors see a flawed early draft.'

Ryan's *From a Low and Quiet Sea* featured Farouk, a Syrian refugee, and he foregrounded Travellers in *All We Shall Know*. *Strange Flowers* features another outsider who faces discrimination, Alex, a Black Englishman. Ryan avoids the N-word but other hurtful terms of abuse are included. Was it a dilemma how to portray racism both realistically and sensitively?

'You have to be careful and respect other people's feelings,' says Ryan, 'but I don't think we should shy away from portraying racist people. I think it is important for us to recognize it, just as Hans Fallada depicted Nazis in *Alone in Berlin*.'

His publisher commissioned a sensitivity reader, and certain changes were made as a result. Alex is undoubtedly an attractive character, whose career as a landscape gardener is surely symbolic, an immigrant literally reimagining, improving and embellishing our native land.

'I tried very hard to imagine what it might have been like for a Black Englishman to come and live in a cottage on a hillside in north Tipperary in the 1970s and, because this novel's milieu comprises for the most part the kinds of people that I know and love, I'm happy that I've got it as right as I can get it.

'I know from years of meeting and speaking to people from different backgrounds, and from my own life experience and that of friends and acquaintances, how "casual" racism would have been present in the life of a man like Alex, and how he might have confronted it, or not. There's a scene in the local bar and shop when he's buying bread that's based closely on a scene from real life.

'The village I base my fictional village on is the place I was born and reared, and a place I love: the people in it are for the most part composed of kindness and generosity and Alexander would definitely have been talked about, wondered about, joked about, but ultimately accepted and loved for the man that he was.'

Ryan's work is very grounded in realism – he is a disciple of John McGahern – but there are powerful flights of characters' imaginations too: Paddy dreaming of driving the car to Galway and on into the ocean; also of Christ on the cross talking to him; Kit imagining Moll's homecoming. Were these a particular pleasure? A way of illuminating characters' inner lives?

'This book was a pleasure to write. Even though those months spent writing the first draft are a blur, my impression is of being comforted daily by the unfolding story and the people in it. Paddy and Alexander and Barney are composites of my own father; Kit and Moll and Ellen definitely contain parts of people I love.'

Ryan has enjoyed a remarkable rise since his debut, *The Spinning Heart*, was plucked from the slush pile after countless rejections and won the Irish

Book of the Year and *Guardian* First Book awards. Each subsequent book has featured on numerous prize lists, his most recent longlisted for the Booker and shortlisted for the Costa. *The Spinning Heart* and *The Thing About December* were successfully adapted for the stage, a sure sign that work is becoming canonical. December has now been adapted as an Irish-language film, *Foscadh* (Shelter), which is due for release later this year.

Writers who apparently have it all, literary acclaim and commercial success, are not universally appreciated. Ryan has been hurt by what he feels is uncalled-for criticism, while emphasizing that other Irish writers' support has boosted his career enormously.

'I mind my own writing business like all writers should. I never, ever throw shade at anyone else's efforts. Life's too short, the world's too small. I've got one or two sneering reviews from fellow writers where it was obvious that they'd barely skimmed the books but were bitter about what they saw as my "success". If only they knew. But what can you do? I try my best to get from one bit of life to the next without harming anyone. I know how blessed I am and it'd be a betrayal of my blessings if I was to go about denigrating anyone else's work.'

There is a strong emotional streak in Ryan's writing, similar to that of Sebastian Barry and Niall Williams. Anne Enright, praising his 'unnoticeably beautiful' paragraphs and devastating social accuracy, says 'his heart is always on show'. His character Alex lived his childhood 'suffused in love'. Love permeates Ryan's work too.

'It was very nice of Anne to say that,' says the author. 'I am emotional, yes. I'm usually good at keeping a rein on my emotions, though things spill over sometimes. I find myself getting upset now and then out of the blue, always when I'm alone, and usually while travelling. I had a bit of a cry in O'Hare airport in Chicago once, at the end of a book tour. I was really shocked at myself – I'm not a crier at all.

'I ducked into a Krispy Kreme or Donut Shack and this lady behind the counter said, "You okay, honey?" And I said I was fine, I had hay fever. She looked at me and smiled and said, "You don't got no hay fever, honey. Why don't you sit down and I'll bring you some breakfast?" And she brought me over coffee and doughnuts and said nothing except, "You'll be okay." She was like an angel.'

Religion plays a big role in *Strange Flowers*, whose chapters are named after books in the Bible. Moll's parents and Alex's are both very religious. Josh takes a Bible story and makes it his own. Moll is the prodigal daughter and it is also acutely observed that Jesus was Mary's prodigal Son of God. Ryan's late father was a daily communicant and the author calls himself a semi-observant Catholic, who rejects the 'mumbo-jumbo' but believes that the core of it is kindness.

'Organized religion has caused too much suffering and devastation to be allowed to offer anyone templates for living,' says Ryan. 'But I consider myself a Christian in that I was raised in a Christian tradition and was told early on that the core tenet of Christianity was kindness. Love your neighbour and forgive, and you need do nothing else in order to call yourself a Christian. Jesus Christ had nothing to say about any of the things that the people who wield power and wealth in his name have obsessed about for two millennia.

'I'm all for secularism. Politics should never be informed by religious beliefs. I've never received anything but kindness from the Church but I know the terrible damage that has been inflicted on people.'

Strange Flowers is like looking through a stained-glass window at our puritanical past. 'Moll Gladney was either pregnant or dead and it was hard to know which one of those was worse.' Paddy imagines his daughter at the altar on her wedding day 'fat with sin'. There is also a powerful depiction of class distinctions in rural Ireland where Paddy is spoken down to by the son of the farmer he works for, treated like a herded, cowed animal. Ryan says that Ireland is belatedly waking up to what it means to be a proper republic.

'I often think of the Ireland we might have had if men like James Connolly had survived to lead us. Greed for power and wealth and control mightn't have proliferated so readily and choked the potential for true greatness from our young country.

'I love the way Roddy Doyle confronted this in *The Last Roundup* trilogy: the Church and the landowners closing ranks on the poor and sliding comfortably into the seat vacated by the empire. Henry Smart, the young rebel, is thanked for his service by a member of the new elite and told to basically fuck off back to the slum. We're getting out from under that stratified system now, at last, but slowly.'

Ryan likens himself to the character in Michel Houellebecq's *Submission* who says he is as political as a bath towel. If so, he uses it as a scourge to lash the rampant neoliberalism that he feels is destroying the country and society.

Creative fiction is an unnatural act, Ryan says, an attempt to impose narrative on senseless things. Is there an obvious parallel to organized religions and their origin stories and another in the notion of fiction's point being an extension of empathy?

'I think a lot about the obvious syntheses between religion and storytelling,' Ryan says, 'how religion is in its essence narrative, all the major belief systems being rooted in epic stories of creation and destruction, sin and redemption. But the attempt in fiction to feel what others feel, to describe the experience of another person, sets it above and apart from didactic tracts, prescriptive and proscriptive lists of how to behave and what to believe.

'Being told what to believe hobbles and ultimately kills the imagination. Fiction has wonder as its propellant and sustenance; religion has strict, unyielding belief. Art can be anything its creator and its witness want it to be, but dogma narrows its adherents' focus down to a singularity of blind obedience with the ultimate aim of having a happy afterlife. Live, live, while you can.'

Ryan's next novel, based on a conversation in Crete with 'an extremely unreliable source', features the return of Mickey Briars from *The Spinning Heart* as a modern-day pirate in the Aegean Sea, ramming the boats of 'the undeservedly wealthy' to rob them. Its title is taken from Anne-Marie's affectionate nickname for Donal, *The Nearly Man*, on account of him having nearly won so many awards and being nearly six foot tall.

Ryan may not get any taller, but his reputation keeps growing.

Ryan was born in 1976 in Tipperary. A former civil servant, he is the author of seven novels and a short-story collection and lectures in creative writing at the University of Limerick. The Spinning Heart *(2012) won Newcomer and Book of the Year at the Irish Book Awards and the* Guardian *First Book Award, was shortlisted for the International Dublin Literary Award and longlisted for the Booker Prize.* Heart Be at Peace *(2024), a sequel to his debut, won the Orwell Prize for Political Fiction, Irish Novel and Book of the Year, and was shortlisted for a Nero Award.* Strange Flowers *(2020) won Irish Novel of the Year.*

PATRICIA SCANLAN

29 February 1992, The Irish Post

Patricia Scanlan, in case any reader is unaware, has become something of a phenomenon in the Irish book trade, outselling everyone from Wilbur Smith to Barbara Taylor Bradford in the hardest market to crack and the most lucrative, that of mass-market fiction.

Tom Owen, book marketing manager of Eason's Wholesale, describes her as 'a genuine phenomenon, and I'm a cynic'. According to him, Scanlan 'has sold faster in the first two weeks after publication than Maeve Binchy. I'm delighted for her and for her publishers Poolbeg. It's good to see an Irish publisher beating the British at their own game.'

Her novel *City Girl*, launched on the British market the other day in London, is set firmly in modern-day Dublin and follows three women, whose enduring friendship survives all the changes in their lives. The title inevitably recalls Edna O'Brien's *The Country Girls*, but Scanlan is deliberately aiming to capture the mood of modern Ireland and, more specifically, Dublin.

While adopting the tried and tested device of a novel structured around the contrasting characters and fortunes of three female contemporaries, Scanlan feels she is breaking new ground in exploring the realities of women in Dublin today, a way of life has changed more than somewhat since Molly Bloom last said yes.

'I think that the novel will appeal to women and men who are contemporary in outlook and are interested in a really good story with an international setting,' she says. 'The object in writing the book was to show independent women in a modern urban setting, who have the ability to shape their own lives.

'I think Irish women are very glamorous, very cosmopolitan. I wanted to write about modern Irish women for a change and I think I was very lucky in that respect in that I was the first to spot and hit that market.'

Scanlan has certainly hit a nerve with the Irish reading population. In an island of five million people, her first two books, *City Girl* and *Apartment 3B*, have sold over 100,000 copies in less than two years.

The launch of *City Girl* in Britain is another big step for her on the road to international success. It also represents an ambitious change of policy for her publishers, Poolbeg, who for the very first time will be marketing and distributing their own fiction title in Britain rather than selling the rights to a British publisher.

Poolbeg has, of course, scored a major success in the non-fiction market in Britain with Chris Mullin's bestseller *Error of Judgement*, which was crucial in the vindication of the Birmingham Six. But debutante novelist Scanlon had only a few years' experience behind her as a Dublin city librarian (a profession she once shared, incidentally, with author and publisher Dermot Bolger) when she had her first book published in April 1990.

Scanlan's was a frustrating apprenticeship, twice having manuscripts rejected by Mills & Boon and missing out in a *Cosmopolitan* short-story competition. But ambition and self-belief kept the librarian up half the night, tapping away at her typewriter – although initially the only reward for her efforts was a bout of arthritis – as she searched for the story that would lift her out of the daily grind of making do into the comfortable and glamorous world of her fiction.

Financial considerations were a very real stimulus to her ambitions as a novelist. Making ends meet as a single woman with a mortgage to pay and a car to keep on the road was not easy and she saw her salvation quite clearly in a successful novel.

'I'd just treated myself to a mortgage and I was driving my Toyota down to Enniscorthy one day and something just flew past the window and I said to myself, *my God, what was that?* And it was the wing of the car, so I knew once the car was gone I wouldn't be able to get another.'

With her job as a librarian, Scanlan was ideally placed to know exactly what people wanted to read, and her voluntary work with a Citizen's Advice Centre gave her an acute insight into the problems and lifestyle of a whole variety of people.

'The library was a great grounding,' she says. 'You had to know what the market was and the market is mass-market, popular fiction, no matter what people say. You know a lot of people are very snobby about it but there's no point in writing a great literary Irish novel if no one will buy it.

'*City Girl* is mass-market fiction and there is a snobbery about that. For example, one journalist said it left her intellectually comatose. Another said it was written in a style that was accessible to the mentally handicapped. But I mean, why take it so seriously?'

She quotes the controversial American biographer Kitty Kelly with approval. 'My favourite line, in any event, is Kitty Kelly's, who said to her critics: "Excuse me, I can't stop, I'm on my way to the bank."'

Scanlon grew up immersed in books. Her mother was an avid reader, and her father went so far as to ban television from their home so that Patricia, her sister and four brothers would have less to distract them.

'I used to listen to the radio a lot. And for that, you had to use your imagination. I used to love writing essays at school and I used to read everything,' she recalls. Years later, working in her library, Scanlan quickly latched on to the fact that while Maeve Binchy had struck a rich seam with her popular novels set the 1960s no one was holding up a mirror to today's Irish women and society.

The germ of an idea that was to become *City Girl* was developing apace. Aided by advice from Binchy and Gemma O'Connor, herself a writer and agent, Scanlan wrote to Philip McDermott of Poolbeg Press asking him if he wanted to become a millionaire – because *she* did. Two weeks later, the contract was signed.

Although her advance of £150 was hardly enough to drive her into tax exile, this would be just the start. Last July, New York publishers Dell placed a trans-Atlantic seal of approval on Scanlan's talent and selling power by offering her a three-book deal and a six-figure contract, which allowed her to take a five-year sabbatical from the library to concentrate on her new career.

City Girl is to be released in the States this summer as a 'super-lead title', which means 600,000 copies will be printed, accompanied by a high-profile publicity campaign.

In the midst of all, Scanlan remains calm, engaging, unaffected. She is keen to stress that she is learning all the time. 'When I submitted the first version of *City Girl*, the editor wanted me to put much more of Dublin in it. Verisimilitude was the word she used. Did I pronounce that right? I didn't know what it meant and I couldn't spell it. She wanted me to develop the characters more, to develop where they lived. Her advice was really good. I learned a lot.'

The pressures of being a feted writer are considerable, however, affecting not only her own reading for pleasure but also her writing. Her recent publicity tour of Britain, for instance, interrupted completion of her novel *Finishing Touches*.

Could she one day write about Irish men in the same way she has written about women?

'I know this is an awful thing to say, but I think women are much more interesting. I think women have to work much harder than men to get somewhere.'

But surely Ireland hasn't done too badly by its women writers from Edna O'Brien to Maeve Binchy and from Alice Taylor to Deirdre Purcell? Or is it the case that only Irishwomen buy the books and are thus supporting their own?

'It's very interesting, but after doing *The Late Late Show* last year there were a lot of men coming up to me afterwards asking me to sign the book. I thought they'd be looking for it signed for their girlfriend or whatever, but no, it was for themselves. This friend of mine came up to me and said "thank you, you've given me a great insight into the female mind; I'd never realized it was so hard to bring up children".'

So Scanlan, whatever the critics say, is getting through to her readers. And if her success spreads to Britain and the States, as her publishers expect, she'll be laughing all the way to the bank.

Scanlan was born in Dublin in 1956 and was a librarian for many years before her first novel, City Girl *(1990) became a bestseller.* City Girls Forever, *the fourth in the series, was published in 2025. It brings Devlin, Caroline and Maggie into their midlife prime dealing with complex issues but sustained by their deep friendship. Her books, all number-one bestsellers, have sold worldwide and been translated into many languages. She created the Open Door adult literacy series. She is currently co-writing a novel about the Goddess Macha – Armagh was named after her – with Deborah Sheehy.*

ALICE TAYLOR

24 May 1991, The Irish in Britain News; 10 December 1994, The Irish Post

The author of *To School through the Fields*, Ireland's bestselling book of all time, is a pleasant, unassuming woman in her fifties who has chronicled the passing of a way of life in rural Ireland and, in so doing, struck a chord with generations, both young and old.

Alice Taylor lives in Innishannon, 'fifteen miles from Cork City, on the road to West Cork on the River Bandon, surrounded by woods in a lovely part of the country, ten miles from the sea, twelve miles from the airport, in the country but near everything.'

As we speak, she is looking out over the village from the converted attic where she writes. Appropriately for someone who values the past, the money she has made from her reminiscences has been invested in restoring her family home and antique furniture, practical oaken dressers and the like, not fancy mahogany that only gathers dust.

Taylor is a charming conversationalist, needing no prompting. Thoughtful without being solemn, full of good sense and philosophy, she laughs easily and quotes comfortably from Shakespeare and Scripture.

Her first book was published at fifty but 'I've always been writing. As a child I wrote always, mostly for my own entertainment, mostly poetry. I never had publishing in mind. The farm where I grew up, so many generations of my family had lived there and so many had moved away, for emigration was a part of life. I wrote for my children so they would know how people had lived then.

'I think my generation was the crucial one, for we stepped from the old methods to the new. When we were young, there was no telephone, no running water, no electricity. But in my lifetime all that changed. So I thought it should be recorded, otherwise it would be lost. A hundred years later, it might be researched, but that could never capture the essence of what it was like then.'

Her book had an obvious appeal to Irish readers, but did she think its appeal would cross the Irish Sea? 'Although it has only just been published in Britain, some copies of the book have already found their way to England. I got a letter from a Sligo lad, only twenty-one or twenty-two. He told me he kept the book under his pillow and read it at the end of the evening and it made him feel he was back at home.

'I was signing copies at the Irish Centre in Camden last year and it was lovely meeting all these people over here thirty or forty years and some who had only recently come over. There have been books written about rural Ireland before. Patrick MacGill has written about the grinding poverty and William Trevor and Molly Keane about the landed gentry but in between there were a lot of ordinary people who were never written about.

She never originally intended to be published. 'I was just going to copy it and get my children one each but people move around so much these days, they lose things and don't tend to accumulate things in the same way as if you live your life always in the one house. So I was at a bookstore and picked up a copy of John B. Keane's *The Bodhran Makers*, noted the name of the publisher, Brandon, sent it off and they accepted it straight away. I never realized what a miracle this was until later I met other writers, who asked me how many I had written to, and when I told them "only the one" they didn't believe me.'

To School through the Fields went on to sell over 250,000 copies, making it Ireland's most successful book. The sequel, *Quench the Lamp*, sold another 120,000 copies.

'I think what happened me was the book came out at the right time, written in a style that appealed to people. You've got to write about what you know and do it your way. I remember Steve McDonagh from Brandon saying to me, you've got your own distinctive style. I think people should write the history of their own family, the every day to day. People coming after them would be absolutely fascinated by them. I think another thing is if you enjoy something, it's very important.

'I took up painting classes a couple of years ago and the people who stayed with it were the people who enjoyed it. Others went home and put away their paints, only painting for the class, but myself and two or three others painted all the time. If you enjoy doing a thing, you're halfway there.'

The books are not just a nostalgic trip down memory lane for the older generation. 'Schoolchildren took a great shine to it, especially the animals. It was like a fairy story to them, it was so far removed from them, the hens and pigs. Farming has changed totally. You never get a farmyard teeming with life anymore. It's a pity if the small farmers go and only the big farmers survive. You'll lose the quality of life.

'I first came to the village of Innishannon in 1961 and I noticed that when old people died they took with them the old history of the village. If you wanted to know something, people would say so-and-so would have known that but he's dead now. So to preserve the local history, I started a magazine called *Candlelight* and everyone writes in it. We produce 750 copies each year at Christmas and the emigrants love it. There had been factual histories before but what wasn't documented was the memories of people, what people thought and felt at the time.'

She doesn't have a writing routine. 'I mightn't write for weeks and then get a mad notion and write for two days. I live attached to the shop and so I write when the humour is on me. I love writing poetry. My poems follow the road of my life and I still write them as I go along: poetry about simple things, no lofty thoughts.'

Has success changed her? 'I'm not a celebrity. I was always getting people to write for *Candlelight* and writing myself, so they already had me in that pigeonhole. These promotional tours are the only changes really. People think you're an authority on things you know nothing about. I never did anything in public, indeed was always a very private person but then when this thing took off, I was put into situations I could never have imagined myself in. My first radio programme was *The Gay Byrne Show*, the most listened-to show in Ireland. Talk about starting at the top. A lot of ordinary people can do a lot more than they think they can.'

Taylor claims no prodigious gift for memory. It is more a question of taking the time out to think. 'You go back mentally and it's extraordinary what you remember. One memory triggers off another and gradually it all comes together.' Having five sisters to bounce memories off also helps but why don't we all recall so well? 'We live in a very fast-moving world. It takes time to go back. Maybe people don't give it the time.

'People say you must have a wonderful memory, but I don't think I do. People have a lot of subconscious memory. I think that's what happened when they read my book. It awoke their memories and then they discussed it with friends and family. It made people feel good after reading it and that's great.'

Remembering is important to the author. 'We are a bit like a tree. A tree depends on its roots and we are the product of our past, it's a part of us. A nurse in a geriatric hospital rang me up and told me they were using *To School through the Fields* as reminiscence material. Stories about their childhood bring old people out of withdrawal. The strange thing was I had a letter from a primary school teacher the same day and she was reading it to six- to eight-year-olds.'

Understandably, Taylor doesn't buy the notion that nostalgia is an unhealthy pursuit, a fugue from the present. 'The reverse is true, actually. The more comfortable you are with yourself and the present, the more the past is no threat to you. I wouldn't see it as escaping back into the past. I love the now. With the old way of life there was a lot of hard work, very few comforts. But at the same time there was great respect for people. We have a lot we hadn't then in the material sense but we were a little indiscriminate in what we threw away.'

What's been lost is time. 'Time to talk to people, time to yourself, time to just sit and do nothing, just be at one with yourself. That was built into the old way of life because people walked a lot of necessity. That gave people time to think and work things out, gave them a serenity.'

Taylor takes up the comparison with reading. 'Reading is soothing. I've always read in bed. It relaxes the mind, unhinges you from the day.'

How has Ireland changed?

'There isn't the same communication between houses that there was before the advent of TV and cars, which is like a contradiction in terms. The small community was like an extended family, but now people stay at home, watch TV and drive to town in cars.

'It is important that this should be discussed. The hard work has gone but the companionship between people has dwindled. If a conscious effort was made not to let that happen … Often when a thing is happening, people sit back and let it happen, thinking someone else should do something about it instead of doing something ourselves.'

It has been said of one well-known Irish journalist that he never has a thought without writing it down. Does Taylor still have a memory untapped? 'When I finish a book, I think that's it now, but then the dust settles and I'm off again. As it says in the Bible, sufficient unto the day is the evil thereof. There's a season for everything. Things unfold in their own time. As you grow older, you get more philosophical, more tolerant.'

Taylor has done us all a service, pre-empting tomorrow's researchers with works of soulful remembrance. It's been a pleasure and it shows.

Taylor was born in Lisdangan, County Cork, in 1938, and lives in Innishannon. She made her name with a series of phenomenally successful memoirs starting with To School through the Fields *(1988), which became the biggest-selling book ever published in Ireland,* An Irish Country Diary *(1988) and* Quench the Lamp *(1990). She turned to fiction with the novel* The Woman of the House *(1997) and has now written more than thirty books. Her latest are* A Place Called Home *(2024) and* Weathering Storms *(2025).*

COLM TÓIBÍN

6 September 2025, The Irish Times

'What is a novella?' Colm Tóibín asks rhetorically in an essay, 'In Brief', from his tremendous new collection of writings, *Ship in Full Sail*, covering his three years as Laureate of Irish Fiction. 'First of all, a novella is something no one wants. Publishers live in dread of them because no one much will buy them.'

Why then, one might wonder, is he also publishing this week one such outcast, *A Long Winter*, which furthermore was already published twenty years ago at the end of his short-story collection *Mothers and Sons*?

The answer perhaps lies in the fate of John McGahern's novella *The Country Funeral*, which Tóibín cites in the above essay as one of the finest examples of the form, alongside *The Dead* by James Joyce, *Heritage* by Eugene McCabe, *Heart of Darkness* by Joseph Conrad and *The Turn of the Screw* by Henry James. McGahern gave Tóibín a manuscript copy of *The Country Funeral*, which he mistakenly thought had never been published.

McGahern's novella, 'which may be his best piece of fiction', was rejected by several magazines before finally being published at the end of his *Collected Stories*. 'Very few readers noticed it,' Tóibín declares. 'In France, however, he published it as a single volume and it was recognized as the masterpiece it was.'

A Long Winter may not be his masterpiece – his novels *The Heather Blazing*, *The Master*, *Nora Webster*, *Brooklyn* and *The Magician* have all won prestigious prizes – but it holds a special place in his heart and, like a cherished album track that should have been a single, it at last gets its place in the sun.

In a sense, Tóibín literally bought the plot for *A Long Winter*. In the early 1990s he and a friend had bought and converted a barn in Farrera, a remote Catalan village 4000ft up in the Pyrenees. In 2004 he had bought an adjoining plot and discovered that a ruin on it had once been home to a woman who had perished in a snowstorm trying to make her way back there from the other side of the mountain after falling out with her husband. Her body was not found till the spring, when the ice thawed.

In his version, the woman leaves after a row with her boorish husband over her secret drinking, only to be lost in a blizzard. The story is told from the perspective of a son, whose brother has also recently left to do his military service. As the desperate communal search becomes a long waiting game for spring, grief's frozen season plays out.

As Tóibín wrote *A Long Winter* in February and March 2005, the snow in the story was swirling outside his window.

He is speaking to me, aptly, from his home in the Pyrenees, where he spends every August, with nothing to distract him from work. He has been coming here since 1976, with a group of friends who had moved there from Barcelona. He first met them through Bernard Loughlin, a fellow teacher in the Dublin School of English in Barcelona, who with his wife Mary went on to run the Tyrone Guthrie Centre artists' retreat in Annaghmakerrig, County Monaghan, from 1981 to 1999, after which they returned to Farrera for good.

'In the period around the death of Franco, people wanted different lives to their parents. I was much more an urban cat at that time; looking at the mountains day in day out wasn't my thing. As I got older I would come for longer. It's the end of the known world, there are no shops in the two nearest villages. It is really good for work, long days.'

In 'Losing the Plot', another essay from his new collection, Tóibín reflects on two different literary traditions: fiction that is plot-driven, where actions have consequences, and fiction that succeeds primarily by creating an atmosphere through rhythms and textures of language. He is usually in the second camp, along with writers he hugely admires such as Mike McCormack and Eimear McBride, but twice, a plot has fallen into his lap. The first time was *A Long Winter*, the second *Long Island*, his sequel to Brooklyn. Edward Mendelson, a colleague at Columbia University, had unpicked author and *The New Yorker* editor William Maxwell's misguided contempt for plot. 'I found it fascinating, I don't think I could have written *Long Island* without that, thinking about consequences.'

Maxwell thought 'plot belonged to genre fiction, full of cheap coincidences such as you find in Thomas Hardy and Maeve Binchy. I have a poem in *Vinegar Hill* called "Variations on a Theme in Maeve Binchy".' She could pull off a joyous reunion of long-lost Sicilian relatives in *Evening Class*, whereas he could not. 'Becoming a high priest of disappointment is a bit wretched.'

In fact, I have heard it said that if Binchy had written *Brooklyn* or *Long Island*, it would not have got the same praise. 'There is one novelist, I can't remember her name,' says Tóibín, 'but every time she has a book coming out she says that about me, "if it was by Eileen or Mary Tóibín, nobody would pay any attention to it".'

It is famously a duff question to ask writers where they get their ideas from, yet Tóibín can usually pinpoint the moment of inspiration, such as seeing the judge Declan Costello in full regalia in the Four Courts, which led to *The Heather Blazing*. But often the magic happens subliminally, when the surface subject chimes with some struggle in the writer's subconscious. The shape and substance of the story evolve, as bad ideas are rejected and the true essence emerges like a sculpture from a block of stone.

'Sometimes you think you know what the origin of something is but that's often because you don't, in other words you have a surface alibi,' Tóibín says. 'Someone told me half a story and I thought it was interesting and I pursued it. I got some preposterous versions of it along the way, which I hope I refined out. The initial story was to be someone like me arriving in a place like this, trying to convert a barn without knowing what had happened, but that would require ghosts and I didn't want ghosts.

'I brought it back down to the story of the son and kept foreigners out. It was a particular period after my own mother had died, and my own brother. I didn't know where the story was going to take me when I started it. I knew the general shape but I didn't know its length or the amount of intensity would go into it, the sense of mournfulness, the sense of ritual going out every day to see if he could find her, the other brother completely missing, the deep melancholy sense of it. I'm so good at deluding myself that I thought it was maybe even coming from the Schubert song. It was a good while later that I realized that it was all this emotion I was suppressing or concealing that I didn't know what to do with, which was grief, that's probably what the story is. If I'd done it deliberately it would have been awful, the metaphors would have been too clunky and easy. I had a vehicle but it was really unconscious.'

He started work on what would become *Nora Webster* around the same time but that was more deliberate, he says. 'This comes first, it's almost stages of grief.'

Tóibín was a friend and patient of eminent psychiatrist Ivor Browne for forty years. There is a story, 'Sleep', in his forthcoming collection, already published in *The New Yorker*, based on him being formally hypnotized by Browne. 'He said to me once, there's something wrong with you, you've fully repressed a tremendous amount of pain, I can see it in you, and the more you make jokes, the more you deflect, the more you will have to deal with it at some point. We'd all shout at him to stop looking at me at the dinner table. He'd say, tell me again what age were you when your father died? I did a workshop with him that lasted a weekend, very intense, which included ketamine injections. I've never been a druggie but I loved the ketamine. A lot of it was just opening yourself up to extraordinary levels of unconscious feeling and knowledge.'

Tóibín likens the perfect simplicity of the novella's plot to the clean lines of a ballad or folk tale.

'At a certain point with *A Long Winter* I realized I won't get anything as pure as this again, the way the story was working, the sense of ritual, going out every day, the weather, his solitude, his father, his brother's absence, the neighbours, the arrival of a servant boy, all of this had some element of almost pre-fiction, as if set in medieval Europe. You need a shape for it, the shape of a ballad. I'm thinking of 'The Croppy Boy' and a version that predates it called 'The Holland Handkerchief'. It has some very short four-line stanzas that manage to do a huge amount of work, convey an extraordinary amount of action.'

The family's isolation is intensified as the father has fallen out with his neighbours. In an early version, the disputes were about the Spanish Civil War, but Tóibín came to realize that while the war had been fought bitterly locally, the village itself was not divided, as Franco's forces were all outsiders. However, there were often huge disputes over water rights and fences.

A piece of music also influenced his story, he believes, Bryn Terfel singing Schubert's Litany for the Feat of All Souls, a prayer for the dead. 'It seemed to be right, I kept putting it on, the melody interested me. Every so often so often there is a song that really gets in on your ear. There is an extraordinary song ['Killeagh'] by a group called Kingfishr, about a hurling team.'

At a certain point, Tóibín decided that *A Long Winter* would be part of his story collection, *Mothers and Sons*, so that focused his mind on tailoring it to fit that theme, making it the story of Miquel and his mother, favouring the son's perspective – 'slow, immersive, third-person intimate' – rather than the mother's or father's or multiple points of view. 'If I concentrate on that configuration it will give me a purer drama than if I try a number of perspectives. Once I got that in my head I was away.'

He wishes something like that would happen to him now with his work in progress. 'I can't work out, is it first person, third person, is there an author who is seeing all this from above? What is the point of view? That can become an intractable problem.'

Does he have a style or sometimes does the work require a deviation?

'I don't see it normally as a style, I see it as a non-style or anti-style, trying not to have loads of side-clauses and flourishes, but you can overdo that and become a sort of parody of yourself. Thinking too much about your own style is like Narcissus, it ends badly,' he says, 'but even when I was working as a journalist there was a lot of laughter about my little sentences. It's always been a problem. A few times I realized I couldn't go on with the short sentences.' *The Master* and *The Testament of Mary* were both written in 'first-person staccato'.

The vital thing, however, is 'if you don't feel it, you can't write it. If you do it without feeling it, it will show. No one is looking for it. A friend would say, I have to go and write this book. I said, is someone waiting for this book? No, is the answer.'

Whereas a short story can reach an audience in literary journals, 'the novella is a lonelier and sadder thing because it won't fit into a magazine.' Tóibín regrets not really pushing for *A Long Winter*'s stand-alone publication twenty years ago. He did suggest it but his publishers demurred.

As well as being published as a novella in Dutch, Swedish and Catalan, *A Long Winter* came out in an expensive limited edition of twenty-five copies for bibliophiles by Tuskar Rock, an imprint Tóibín set up with his agent Peter Straus to publish books and authors who they felt were being ignored by British publishers, and limited editions of writers such as Alan Hollinghurst.

'It was a scandal that László Krasznahorkai was not being published at all, beyond belief, so we simply sought to rectify this. In Ireland we publish Adrian Duncan. We did very well with *The Slap*. Christos Tsiolkas's book was not being published in the UK. He wrote to me and asked what's going on, I read it and thought, *this is a disgrace*.'

Did the success of Claire Keegan's *Foster* enlarge the space for novellas? 'Very much so. I suppose the reason why *Foster* did so well is it's so good. You realize, stop moaning about the novella, just make it good.'

Did *Foster* hit home not just as a fine piece of writing but more personally, given he was fostered out for a time as a child when his father was gravely ill? 'Yes, in a good number of ways, one being her description of Gorey, it is so accurate, and when she goes to the coast the particularity. There were things in *Foster* that I recognize but I think that is true of any story where there is a parent missing. I would get it in McGahern as well.'

Miquel [the protagonist] is guardedly gay. This emerges through where his gaze falls but does not lead to action, only disappointment. Tóibín's story is being published in the US with Annie Proulx's novella *Brokeback Mountain*. 'Mine is like hers except all mountain and hardly any brokeback,' he jokes.

'I suppose the big issue was how self-conscious to make him, in other words, when he is alone, does he think about his sexuality? And no, he doesn't. It's all what he sees, notices, remembers, wants. When you talk about points of view, include that one: how self-conscious is he? And he is not at all.'

The limited edition helped him identify passages to remove from later editions. What were they? 'Oh, a horrible bit where Miquel starts to muse about the meaning of the universe and think about time. They are very banal, these thoughts, but they are mine, the idea of things being inhospitable, areas of the globe from oceans to mountains to the tundra, complete rubbish. A writer trying to give his character opinions. You must give the character full autonomy, not mix them up with you.'

This reminds me of Tóibín's wince-inducing revelation that he had cut 55,000 words from his novel *The Magician* on his editor's suggestion. 'Editors are very important for some books and not others. With *A Long Winter*, I don't think there was any editing. With those big books, *The Master* and *The Magician*, the problem is how much information do you need to give the reader? When does it become tedious? What is the drama? What are you trying to do? Is it possible that twenty pages are beyond belief in their banality and badness and dullness?'

His editor Mary Mount made him realize that his fascination with an intellectual argument involving Adorno, Schoenberg and Thomas Mann was choking the emotional heart of the novel, which was about Mann's relationship with his son, who kills himself.

Tóibín spends most of the year in Pasadena, Los Angeles, in the home of his partner. 'You can live in LA without Hollywood impinging even slightly. I don't drive ever, which calms life down a lot. Your backyard becomes your realm, it's very good for work. He teaches one fourteen-week semester at Columbia in New York, where he stays in university accommodation, and divides the rest of his time between his Georgian townhouse in Dublin and his beachfront retreat in Ballyconnigar, where he spent whole summers – 'My father was a teacher and you could rent huts there very cheaply' – until his father died when he was twelve.

It's a peripatetic lifestyle. If he hadn't been a writer, 'I think I would have gone with the circus.' He is working on a long piece about the Beatles. 'John Lennon has this marvellous thing where he says, "I'm a cross between a monk and a performing flea." I thought that was great. I wrote it out in longhand.

'Every time I leave Wexford, I'm sorry,' he says, 'I wish I could spend more time there. It's very familiar.' Tóibín spent many years in Dublin as a student, then a high-profile journalist and was very sociable but those days are gone, he says. Unlike fellow Wexford-born writer John Banville, the capital has never inspired his fiction.

'I've never really written about Dublin, it's not my place. I am much less sociable now as I don't drink any more. The great thing for me about not drinking is not that you don't waste time or have hangovers but you don't get the exuberance. I'm pretty solitary these days. I work every day. I've left all that behind really.'

Having just celebrated his seventieth birthday, is Tóibín conscious of the clock ticking more loudly? 'What should writers do at the dying of the light?' he asks in *Ship in Full Sail*. 'What about one big final statement about life and death?' Or, like Thomas Mann at eighty, a comedy. He has written a comic libretto.

'You realize that a decade hence you will be eighty,' he says. 'It's not as if there is any great tradition of writers producing much work after a certain age. The problem is you get less sleep and for work, you need to have slept properly, otherwise something won't come. I think that makes a big difference.'

He has a new collection of short stories out in 2026 [*The News from Dublin*], his third and probably his last. It has no particular theme. One of the stories he has worked on for twenty years. He usually feels, however, that work is abandoned in a drawer for good reason. He has written a few poems and is trying to start a novel. He has been writing its beginning for a while but it's not working. His method is to write the first chapter and then leave it for a year.

'That's intentional, so you can keep ruminating on how to proceed. The process is you write it and probably don't even look at it again even, then leave yourself free to see if it is going to continue to ferment and to bubble, if you're going to get new ideas, new ways of seeing it. That must happen in the ordinary random business of getting on a train or driving somewhere. If you force it or make it deliberate, then the whole idea of it fails you, you get the most preposterous ways forward.

'Just write something down that has a point of view. How much is going to be known? Who is it going to be known by? It doesn't matter if it sings, it just has to be clear to me so I can proceed. Once I had the first line of *Blackwater Lightship* I had the book. I had an espresso at 6pm, went to see a film, walked past pubs with everyone drinking, went home and wrote that sentence.'

He has spent a lot of time researching Irish military archives, pension applications and censuses but unlike Roddy Doyle, some of whose family like his were active in the revolutionary period, he has no plans to fictionalize it.

'I don't know why. I lived with its legacy but the events themselves seem to belong to ballads or historians. I can't imagine setting a novel in that period, but you can never tell.' Nor, having written about Henry James in *The Master* and Thomas Mann in *The Magician*, is there a third writer he might fictionalize to create a trilogy.

In a marvellous essay 'A Toast in the Dark', which ends with a virtuoso celebration of the light Irish artists shone in a dark time for the nation, Tóibín recalls Anthony Cronin telling a group of Irish artists that they probably lacked the courage to thank Charles Haughey in public for what he had done for the arts so they should go home and raise a glass to him in the dark.

There will be no toasts in the Tóibín household to Patrick O'Donovan, the minister for culture. 'There is no artist I know who thinks the current minister is the best thing that ever happened to the country,' he says. Josepha Madigan, one of his predecessors, gets short shrift too for her failure to secure for the nation 15 Usher's Island, where Joyce's *The Dead* is set, despite the lobbying of Tóibín and many others.

'I got thousands to sign, including Salman Rushdie. Imagine if Don Quixote's house was still in Madrid. The house of *The Dead* is intact but is being allowed to rot. It could have been a national monument. Why don't we put cows or a data centre in Newgrange? If Michael D had been minister, if Haughey had been taoiseach, if Cronin had been an adviser …'

He shares Brendan Gleeson's frustration at the low priority RTÉ gives to reporting on the arts, in contrast to its saturation coverage of business news, literally a turn-off for Tóibín every morning. He cites such newsworthy items as Mark O'Connell's [*Mars*, with composer Jennifer Walshe] which is set to tour the world, Garry Hynes's *Macbeth*, the production of Conor McPherson's *The Weir*.

'Why isn't that being mentioned as news? I have it in for this business news, which seems to be on four times a day. I mean, really, it has to stop.'

If he were minister, what's the first thing he would do? In reference to the controversial departure of the head of the Arts Council, he says: 'I would apologize to Maureen Kennelly.'

Tóibín was born in Enniscorthy, County Wexford in 1955. His first novel, The South, *was published in 1990. His non-fiction books include* Bad Blood: A Walk Along the Irish Border *(1987). He won the Encore Award for* The Heather Blazing *(1993).* The Master *(2004) won the International Dublin Literary Award.* Nora Webster *(2014) won the Hawthornden Prize.* Brooklyn *(2009) won the Costa Novel Award. Saoirse Ronan starred in the film adaptation.* The Blackwater Lightship *(1999),* The Master *and* The Testament of Mary *(2012) were shortlisted for the Booker Prize.* The Magician *(2021) won the Folio Prize. He was Laureate for Irish Fiction 2021–25.*